PLACES OF WONDERMENT AND DELIGHT...

*One of Washington, D.C.'s best-kept secrets—The National Aquarium is intimate, friendly, and not crowded . . . and lets kids watch shark and piranha feedings while offering a Crab Cove discovery room for kids to see sea creatures up close.

*Electronic magic in New York City—the AT&T Infoquest Center is a kid's computer paradise: make your own video music, play photo guessing games, and manipulate mazes by voice commands—great fun!

*Kids will think they're "California dreaming"—at the San Francisco International Toy Museum . . . a heavenly place where children can touch and play with fabulous toys, as well as gaze at antiques from bygone days.

*The Old West comes alive in L.A.—Gene Autry's Western Heritage Museum shows us the real-life cowboy and the movie version, too, with authentic six-shooters, chaps, John Wayne's gun, and a full-size stagecoach.

*More than burgers at a Chicago McDonalds—the Golden Arches on N. Clark Street is the place for rock 'n' roll buffs, with a free jukebox, a vintage Chevy, and 60s music memorabilia.

KEN AND MARILYN WILSON—WHO KID-TESTED EVERY CITY WITH THEIR THREE-YEAR-OLD DAUGHTER MOLLY—ARE YOUR INFORMED, FRANK, AND FASCINATING GUIDES TO AMERICA'S DON'T-MISS CITY SIGHTS AND UNIQUE, FUN ACTIVITIES ALL AGES WILL ENJOY IN . . .

KIDS ON
BOARD

KIDS ON
BOARD

A 10-City Guide to Great American Family Vacations

KEN and MARILYN WILSON

WARNER BOOKS

A Warner Communications Company

Warner Books, Inc., 666 Fifth Avenue, New York, NY 10103

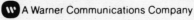 A Warner Communications Company

Printed in the United States of America
First printing : June 1989
10 9 8 7 6 5 4 3 2

Library of Congress Cataloging-in-Publication Data

Wilson, Ken, 1951-
    Kids on board : a 10-city guide to great American family vacations
/ Ken and Marilyn Wilson.
        p.   cm.
    ISBN 0-446-38767-3 (pbk.) (U.S.A.)
        1. United States — Description and travel — 1981-   — Guide-books.
2. Cities and towns — United States — Guide-books.   3. Family
recreation — United States — Guide-books.   I. Wilson, Marilyn.
II. Title.
E158.W76   1989   89-30599
917.'304927 — dc19   CIP
    ISBN 0-446-38768-1 (pbk.) (Can.)
            Book designed by Giorgetta Bell McRee
                Cover art by Heather Taylor
                Cover design by Harold Nolan

To our parents,
Bill and Lorraine Boies,
Charlie and Marion Wilson
and
to our daughter, Molly . . .
"she who must be obeyed."

Acknowledgments

It would have been impossible to put together all the information contained in *Kids on Board* without the help of a great many people. Some are longtime friends, others have become friends thanks to this book.

Special thanks to our agents, Joan and Lydia Wilen, for their help, advice and friendship. Without their guidance, this book would never have been written.

Thanks to Warner Books Vice President Ling Lucas for going to bat for us. Thanks to our editors Jamie Raab, for her patience, and Terry (the Terminator) Fischer, for whipping our manuscript into shape.

We deeply appreciate all the help and encouragement we received along the way from the likes of Janey and Tom Abbott, Walter Anderson, Tracy Baskerville, Aviva Bergman, Jack Bierman, Julie Boies, Michael and Nina Boies, Michael Bush, Rosie Casey, Fred Corrigan, Andi Coyle, Dave Cruz, Joyce Davis, M. J. Gapp, Beverly Gianna, Jay (Isn't the Book Done Yet?) Gordon, Sandy Goroff-Mailly, Heidi (Luggage Rack) Halverson, Craig Hudson, Mary Hughes, Cindy Westbrook Hu, Marlene Iglitzen, Charlie Inlander, Sharon Keech, Candy Lampeze, John MacBean, Bruce Riley McDaniel, Nancy Magnus-Irwin, Rick Mailly, John Molloy, Daysi Montesinos, Annie Moore, Tom Murphy, D'Arcy O'Connor, Zulema Perez, Scooter Pietsch, Elvira Quarin, David Sayre, Frances Schultschik, Kate Shore, Bruce Sterten, Marie Levin Tabor, Micheline Tremblay, Gene (Snapshot) Valet, Homer Wells, Jane White, Gail Wilson, Jennifer (Gotta Study) Wilson, and Dorothy Woolfolk. You're all great.

Contents

INTRODUCTION

"There are two classes of travel—first class and with children."
                                    —Humorist ROBERT BENCHLEY

If parents of a generation ago agreed with Robert Benchley, they kept it to themselves. Back in the 1950s and 1960s, traveling with children was a breeze. The highways were America's vacation shipping lanes, and we kids were the cargo. Cars were large and built for long-distance cruising. Gasoline was cheap and plentiful. We were a society of families in which Dad worked and Mom stayed at home with their 2.4 children. And, like clockwork, there was that two-week vacation trip once a year.

The face of travel with children has changed a lot in the past thirty years—and many of those changes are not for the better.

Car travel is no longer the preferred mode for a long trip. Automobiles are smaller, gas is more expensive, and, in every state of the union, young children must be strapped into car seats, a law that saves lives but takes its toll in parental nervous stomach disorders. If the kids sleep at all while strapped in, you're lucky. And you still have to stop at least every 2 hours, usually just to break the monotony of the visually boring Interstate highways. Despite changes in some areas, speed limits in many states remain at 55 MPH, 10 to 20 MPH slower than in years gone by.

Today's families also have less time available for traveling together. These days, the average American has less than two weeks of vacation per year. That's further compounded when you consider that most two-parent homes are also two-career homes. After meshing Mom's schedule with Dad's (never mind the kids' activity schedules), you aren't left with very much.

While all this makes air travel a much more viable alternative, the airways are fraught with their own pitfalls. In terms of amenities, planes these days are little more than buses with wings. The food is bad, and flight attendants can be indifferent. Luggage handlers magically make suitcases disappear into thin air. Delays for bad weather are becoming regular occurrences even when the sun is shining and it's 75 degrees.

Nevertheless, traveling with your kids can actually be just as rewarding

1

for the family today as it was in the "good old days." To make your vacation work, all you need is careful planning.

What we offer in this book are tips on how best to devise that plan, transportation options, and what to expect when you arrive. For destinations, we've chosen ten of the top vacation cities in the United States. We picked them for a reason. Considering time constraints and accessibility, urban areas have become extremely popular. Because many parents now travel for business, big-city vacations are attractive, and the business/pleasure vacation is often the only kind for which there is time or money. Large metropolitan areas offer many of the exciting and educational attractions kids have heard about and want to see. Further, children are curious about what Mom and Dad do for a living. Often just being included on a business trip is enough to put a child on Cloud Nine for months.

THE PLAN

It may sound corny, but family meetings to discuss vacation plans work. A family summit lets parents lay out their ideas (an educational trip to Philadelphia or Boston) and also lets the kids put in their two cents ("Disney World!" "Disneyland!"). If you're dead set on Philadelphia, you can sweeten the pot with a day at Sesame Place in nearby Langhorne, Pennsylvania. Such collective decision making may not completely take the sting out of not spending a week riding Disney's Space Mountain, but you've let the kids feel like participants in the planning.

Start thinking about your trip a few months ahead of time. That will give you enough time to read the pertinent material in this book, and to do some other important fact-finding.

Visitors and Convention Bureaus. Contact the bureaus in the cities you plan to visit (for phone numbers and addresses, see the introduction to each city). The people there will answer specific questions and send you up-to-date materials on upcoming events, attractions, lodging, and restaurants—some even include discount coupons. If you have a specific need, such as a list of facilities with access for the handicapped, ask the Visitors Bureau, which often will also provide information about special events.

Travel Agents. Take advantage of professional guidance, especially if you're flying or taking a train (see "Transportation"). Travel agents can make all the arrangements and are better equipped to get you the best fares. Use of a travel agent is free: They receive commissions from airlines, hotels, and car rental firms. Agents usually provide two copies of your itinerary, so you have one to leave at home with the neighbors or to send along to friends in your destination city.

Hotel Reservations. Reserving ahead of time—as far in advance as you can—is very important, especially if you plan to travel during school vacation periods or festivals.

Money. We recommend travelers checks in denominations of $20 and $50. Fifty-dollar checks are good for expenditures like dinners and amusement park tickets. Twenties are great for smaller purchases.

Many banks are hooked up to a computerized automatic teller machine (ATM) network, which means that the same ATM card that works at your own bank will access cash in an affiliated bank's ATM in other states. Most ATM systems provide lists of affiliated institutions nationwide.

A credit card is essential, especially if you carry the right one. Gold cards (American Express, Visa, MasterCard) are more expensive and tougher to obtain but can pay off in a number of important ways. First, gold cards access more emergency cash. Second, gold bank cards and green and gold American Express cards pay collision insurance liability when you rent a car, a saving of $8 to $12 a day.

PACKING

Whether you're a seasoned traveler or just a novice, there's no getting around the drudgery of packing. It gets a little easier if you follow two cardinal rules: First, make lists, make them often, and compare them. Second, keep your child's and your own clothing and accessories in separate bags. In the harried last minutes before leaving for the airport, a parent's ability to judge the sizes and colors of sweaters, socks, and underwear is greatly impaired—whether they're green, blue, or white, all you see is red.

THE LISTS

Each child should have two lists: one for the suitcase that's placed out of reach in the plane's cargo hold or the car's luggage rack, the other for the carry-on bag that can be easily accessed during the trip.

The Suitcase List. This basic inventory shouldn't be made haphazardly. We think of the child from bottom to top, starting with footwear and working up to socks, underpants, bathing suits, pajamas, pants, under-shirts, shirts, sweaters, mittens, jackets, coats, scarves, and hats. If your child has a special pillow and a stuffed animal, add them to the list.

The Carry-on List. Items for easy access should include everything your child will need to get through the travel day. That can mean toys, puzzles, books, crayons, special surprises, eyeglasses (including sun-glasses), snacks, bibs, security blanket, wet wipes, powder, ointments, diapers, bottles and pacifiers, and a sweater or jacket. If your child is under age 5, include a change of clothing. Put a child's toilet kit (tooth-brush, toothpaste, and medicines) in the carry-on bag: You may need these items during the day, and you'll definitely need them at night if your luggage is lost.

The Snacks List. A stash of edibles and drinkables is also recommended. If you're traveling by car, you have the luxury of a large cooler. Include ample liquids (juices and water, but try to minimize sodas, which make kids hyper) and snacks (we like trail mix, nuts, crackers, and peanut butter). If you don't want to stop for fast food, add sandwich fixings for tailgate lunches at roadside rest areas. And don't forget a generous supply of plastic sandwich bags and kitchen-size garbage bags.

Include the kids in the packing process—but only after you have the bulk of your luggage filled. Being included in the packing makes kids over age 3 really feel involved.

TRANSPORTATION

AIR TRAVEL

Making Reservations. This part of the planning is a relatively easy proposition, especially if you use the services of a qualified travel agency. Travel agents are empowered by the airlines to book reservations. For this they get a commission from the airline; there is no cost to the pas-senger. We use travel agents when we are going to book a series of flights on different airlines. Agents can usually get travelers the lowest possible fares because they're in daily phone contact with the airlines and are connected with airline computers.

You can do it yourself, but you'll have to make some phone calls. Call the airline, give them the particulars, have them quote a price, and book the flight. Then call back and ask for another booking. Chances are that they'll quote you the same price, but sometimes they don't. If the second price is less (and this has happened to us three times in the last year), take the new rate and have them cancel your original reservation.

Fares. To get the best price, make reservations at least a couple of weeks in advance. This will entitle you to rates that are often hundreds of dollars less than the regular coach fare, the amount that you'd pay if you bought your ticket on the day of the flight. The restrictions placed on those low super-saver fares are heavy and in constant flux. If you cancel your reservation, you may forfeit part or all of your money. Childhood illnesses and injuries may make this a gamble, but, if you can produce a doctor's letter when illness strikes, the airlines may refund your money or re-schedule your flight.

Children's Fares. The airlines offer discount fares for children between the ages of 2 and 17. However, they are available only on regular, full coach tickets. While the savings on these tickets is usually 25 to 50 percent, the discount rarely equals the savings on an adult super-saver ticket. There are no discounts for children offered on super-saver fares.

Children under age 2 ride free, providing they sit on Mom's or Dad's lap. This may sound daunting, but since there are often vacant seats, parents and kids seldom have to share. Once the seat belt light is turned off, you're free to lay claim to any empty seat in your section of the plane. You may want to book around an empty seat when making res-ervations. Often middle seats, like those between the window and aisle locations, go begging and make a perfect ''free'' seat for a small child.

The Plane. The bulkhead seats are perhaps the biggest boon to flying with small children. While these much-sought-after locations at the very front of the coach section offer different amounts of leg room on different planes, they're always more spacious than other coach seats, and wide-body planes have several bulkheads. The extra room allows fidgety chil-dren space to stand up and tired kids a place to stretch out and sleep. Some of the more ample bulkhead locations have enough room for a child to sit cross-legged on the floor.

Unlike regular seats, however, the armrests in bulkhead seats don't retract, and you can't fashion a bed from two empty seats. Another major bulkhead drawback is lack of access to carry-on luggage. Since there's no front seat to store it under, flight attendants spirit it away and stow it out of reach for the duration of the flight. If the bag holds important stuffed animals, spare diapers, bottles, and special snacks, you'd better take them out and put them in your overhead compartment shortly after you're seated.

One of the great misconceptions about carrying a young child onto a plane is that your small, everyday equipment will work. The tiny, boxy infant carrier that doubles as a car seat is welcome aboard, but it's too large to fit on a coach seat. Usually, the flight attendant will replace it with a much narrower cardboard bassinet. While full-size Aprica ''cruiser'' strollers are too wide, an umbrella stroller makes it down the aisles with loads of room to spare.

As far as encountering compassionate airline personnel who accede to your every wish, you won't find them in coach. Flight attendants are nearly always pleasant and more than willing to give you the whole can of soda while passing out drinks, but that's usually the most you should expect.

Essential Airline Carry-ons. Snacks are important, even if you're going to be served a meal. For small children, take crunchy things like nuts and trail mix (nuts and dried fruits) that are nutritious and have interesting textures. Buy the unsalted kind and the kids won't get overly thirsty. Another winner is crackers. Flight attendants can provide crackers and bags of nuts; however, most of those are heavily salted, which means more liquids and more trips to the bathroom. For liquid refreshment, take boxes of juice: They're self-contained, have their own straw, and, if tipped over hardly leak at all.

For babies' palates, there's nothing quite like bagels. Bagels are made without shortening (unlike crackers) and are healthier than most bread. They're also chewier, and that hole in the middle makes them easy to grasp. When packing for babies, it's wise to take extra formula and at least two plastic, disposable bottles, one for water and the other for formula.

For kids and adults alike, the increased ear pressure at takeoffs and landings can be excruciatingly painful. Most adults know to yawn or swallow to alleviate that pressure, but children don't. That's why gum, mints, and, for babies, pacifiers and bottles are so important. If you don't trust your younger kids with gum or small pieces of candy, give them a box of juice. Sucking on that tiny straw really does the trick.

To alleviate in-flight boredom, take small, inexpensive toys (such as dolls, puzzles, Silly Putty) and wrap them like Christmas or birthday gifts. Let your child open one at a time and play with it until his or her interest is completely exhausted. Only then should you bring out the next package.

Flight attendants can help in this area, too. Most airliners stock an ample supply of playing cards that make a great auxiliary toy. Most also have a large reserve of plastic pilot's wings. If flight attendants fail to offer them, don't hesitate to ask.

AUTOMOBILE TRAVEL

Traveling by car is a viable choice for short distances or trips during which the family wants to stop and smell the roses (or whatever else they find on the side of the road).

Planning Ahead. Car seats are required by law in every state: Most stipulate that children under age 4 and weighing less than 40 pounds be restrained. Car seats come in different sizes and varieties (from self-contained seats with their own straps to those that incorporate the car's seat belts), and they all save lives.

If you're a member, stop at the nearest American Automobile Association (AAA) office for free maps, travel books, and a Triptik customized to your order. The AAA is usually aware of the latest highway developments, like major repair work, and a customized Triptik will help you avoid such pitfalls. Other automobile clubs offer similar services; check the Yellow Pages for listings.

We also recommend a road atlas of the United States—a single bound volume with maps of every state, plus an all-important map of the whole country.

If you're planning a long trip, take short trips of less than 2 hours to get smaller children used to their car seats, then gradually work your way up. Many parents get lulled into thinking their children will be model travelers on the basis of a 2-hour trip to Grandma's house. Most young kids fall asleep on trips of that length, so they're not an accurate test of what to expect on an all-day drive. You have to be prepared to entertain them while they're awake, and that's where frequent stops and the right packing come into play.

The Roads. America's cities are linked by fast, safe, exceedingly boring four-lane divided Interstate highways. Because there's little or nothing to see except the changing landscape, Mom and Dad have to supply breaks in the monotony. These come in the form of rest areas and exits.

Most rest areas designed and maintained by state highway departments offer, at the very least, bathrooms, water, a picnic table, and space to run around and let off steam. Some have historical markers and displays that provide local color; some have playground apparatus and snack-food machines. Rest areas are usually spaced at 50- to 100-mile intervals, and we recommend stopping at each one you come across, either for an impromptu picnic, a game of catch, or just to let the kids expend some energy.

If you're in a state with a scarce number of rest areas, exit the Interstate every 50 to 100 miles. Consult the map for places of interest lying only a few miles from the road, or stop for gas or burgers.

Because most gas stations these days are self-service, get the kids into the act by letting them wash the windows or check tire pressure. This goes a long way to making them feel like useful cogs in the family wheel.

Packing the Right Stuff. If you plan to picnic, take along as large a cooler as you can fit into the car. If you don't want to be driven crazy by that styrofoam squeak as the cooler scrapes against the side of the car, purchase a heavy-duty plastic or metal cooler. Besides offering the additional benefit of not cracking and leaking, heavy-duty coolers pay for themselves by keeping food colder and cutting down trips to convenience stores for overpriced ice cubes. Invest in a few of those blue ice packs that you freeze and slip into the cooler: They're pretty efficient but do require refreezing each night.

A cooler gives you the luxury of hauling nearly the entire range of food items you're used to eating at home. We like to stick to lunch-type fixin's—such as bread, sandwich meats and cheeses, mayo, mustard, chips, fruit, cookies, juices—and make sure we pack plenty of paper plates, cups, covered plastic cups, napkins, and knives. Include a small cutting board and a sharp serrated knife (kept separately away from prying hands, preferably in the glove compartment). For cleaning up, you can't beat premoistened wipes and plenty of plastic bags for storing left-overs and trash. Complement tailgate picnics with in-the-moving-car snacks like the ones we recommend for airplanes.

Take along the usual array of stuffed animals, coloring books, crayons, and storybooks, along with gift-wrapped presents, such as Silly Putty, dolls, and puzzles. Include pillows (Mom's and Dad's, too) and blankets, in case the kids surprise everyone by sleeping for more than 2 hours at a clip.

Consider taking an audio cassette player along so the kids can listen to fairy tales, Disney stories, and nursery rhymes on tape. Potentially less obtrusive are hand-held computer games, which are relatively noise-less and absorb kids' attention for hours at a time. For older children, there's always the old standby, binoculars.

When objects fail to amuse, try songs, word-association games, and other car games. If your children are small, songs and nonsensical rhyming word games should keep them occupied. For older children, don't forget the time-tested License Plate Game, in which you see how many states you can find.

Your Nightly Destination. Since road travel makes it necessary for you to seek shelter for the night, give some thought to the motels that will be your homes away from home along the way. Inexpensive chains—like Motel 6, (505) 891–6161; Scottish Inns, (800) 251–1962; and Red Roof Inns, (800) 843–7663—offer the basics for less than $30 per night. Nothing fancy here: Moderately firm mattresses, working bathrooms, and air conditioning are the mainstays. In most cases, these places also feature pools and some form of video entertainment (often cable-television movies).

Howard Johnson's, (800) 654–2000; Best Western, (800) 528–1234; and Comfort Inn, (800) 228–5150 cost a bit more (depending on the region and proximity to a major city), but provide coffee shops, an occasional indoor pool (kids like these even more), and in-room pay movies. Our favorite is Comfort Inn, a national chain with the most consistently clean facilities of any motels we've seen.

Renting a Car. Families interested in renting a car from a national chain can use the following list of toll-free telephone numbers to compare current rates.

Alamo: (800) 327–9633.
Avis: (800) 331–1212.
Budget: (800) 527–0700.
Dollar: (800) 421–6868.
Enterprise: (800) 325–8007.
Hertz: (800) 654–3131.
National: (800) 227–7368.
RPM: (800) 445–4776.
Snappy: (800) 669–4800.
Thrifty: (800) 367–2277.

For the telephone numbers of local rental agencies, check the telephone listings at the end of each city's chapter.

TRAVELING BY TRAIN

Once the only way to travel long distances, taking the train in the United States these days has become a short-distance proposition or one that's imited to a selective few who won't fly or who want to recapture the romance of the rails.

Planning Your Trip. Book through your travel agent or by telephoning Amtrak, (800) 872–7245. Amtrak will send you a nifty 88-page booklet, the *Amtrak Travel Planner*, which describes the different kinds of sleeping compartments, the routes, the food, and on-board amenities. Because there are fewer train compartments than seats on airliners, book your trip two to three months ahead of time during the off season and six months before a summer trip. Those planning a trip in coach (where there are no sleeping facilities) need not plan that far ahead. In many cases, a day ahead of time is adequate, and you can often buy a ticket within minutes of departure.

HOW TO READ THIS BOOK

Each chapter in this book is a presentation of a major American city, its amenities and the attractions it offers parents and their children. In the introductory section, parents will find information to use for family vacation roundtable discussions. Included are suggestions for budget museums and attractions and suggested three-day itineraries of the best the city has to offer. Each introduction includes information on climate and the address and phone number of the local Visitors Bureau. (As an integral companion to the book, obtain a detailed map of each city. Buy maps at bookstores or get them free if you're an auto club member.)

Attractions. Famous monuments, aquariums, amusement parks, and zoos are listed in this section. Along with a brief description of what the attraction has to offer your family, you'll find the address, phone number, the parking situation nearby, the nearest mass-transit station (where applicable), hours, and prices of admission. The section also highlights information of particular interest to families: stroller rentals, diaper-changing tables, restaurants, and, if they merit special mention, gift shops. Each entry concludes with our assessment of how children might enjoy the attraction and our ratings by age groups. The ratings, on a scale of A(excellent) to F(not recommended), are based on our personal experiences and observations of kids in action.

Museums. This section lays out the many and varied museums the city has to offer: science, industrial, historical, children's, and religious. It includes all the information and ratings listed under Attractions.

Hotels. Since we don't have space to list all the hotels in each city, we've chosen those that have something special to offer traveling families, whether extra space (there are many suite hotels), prime location, or especially good value. Each listing includes the address, phone number, the parking situation, rates at time of publication for a family of four (two children under age 12), a brief description, a list of hotel amenities, and the location of the closest emergency hospital.

Restaurants. While most kids would be content to eat three meals a day at fast-food joints, traveling parents are usually on the prowl for something with more variety. Our listings include restaurants with that something extra: children's portions of the local delicacies, entertaining visual distractions, balloons, even waitresses dressed in fairy tale costumes. Each listing includes the address, phone number, parking information, hours, a brief description, the availability of booster seats and high chairs, and the approximate cost.

Big Splurges. Sure it's fun to travel with your children; but it's also fun to get away from them at the end of a long day together. The splurge restaurant section is just for Mom and Dad. These restaurants offer good food, a relaxing (often romantic) atmosphere, and usually a full bar.

Shopping. Where do you go for unique souvenirs, toys, kids' books, and electronic games and gizmos? Selected shops are listed in this section, whether in malls or in quaint or historical areas of the city.

Transportation. From public transportation (buses, subways, ferry boats) to taxis, this section says what it costs, hours of operation, and whether we found it to be efficient or a waste of time. Where applicable, we include discount fares. Even if you drive, some forms of public transportation are worth riding just for the fun of it. (Turn back to page 9 for a list of telephone numbers for national car rental companies.)

Tours. Sometimes the best way to see a city is to start with a guided tour. Bus tours are most prevalent, but some cities have tours on boats, helicopters, trams, and old-fashioned trolleys.

Seasonal Events. Seasonal festivals are a great way to take in local culture and history, and to see a place with its happiest face. In this section, we list the name of the event, the approximate time of the month in which it takes place, and phone numbers for more information and reservations.

Children's Theater. Many cities offer theater designed especially for young people.

Babysitting Services. If your hotel doesn't offer babysitting referrals, to whom do you turn? In this section, we give the names, phone numbers, and prices of some of the local convention or in-hotel sitting services.

Publications. This section includes the top area newspapers and magazines, many of which publish calendars of events.

Local Telephone Numbers. Which pharmacies stay open late? How do you file a consumer complaint? More important, what's the number of the local poison-control hotline? These and other often-asked questions are answered in this portion of each chapter.

Note: Prices given in this book are subject to change. They were accurate at press time.

BOSTON

When you proudly announce Boston as the destination for the upcoming family vacation, get ready for the groans. The kids are grousing about the fact that, save for a touring carnival or two, there are no theme amusement parks or water slides within 35 miles of the city. But as visitors to the New England Aquarium, Science Museum, and Children's Museum—three of the best kid-oriented places on the East Coast—will readily attest, modern Boston is a city firmly rooted in the cosmopolitan, high-tech 20th century. Boston's most striking and popular attributes are the museums and sites devoted to events that shaped not only New England, but the United States as a whole. With more than fifty important historic attractions (from cemeteries to battlefields to repositories of important documents and artifacts), the Boston area is a cornucopia for history buffs both young and old. In fact, a 3-hour walk along the Freedom Trail through the oldest section of the city will teach your kids more about the first 150 years of American history than will ten years of school.

Boston has always been a frenzied place driven by citizens with little tolerance for those who would prevent the completion of their missions. This "edge" isn't new; it's a 350-year-old phenomenon that dates back to the Puritans, the first European residents of the city. Outcasts from both Britain and their adopted home of the Netherlands, Puritans stepped off the boat in Plymouth, Massachusetts in 1620 and founded Boston a decade later. Guided by their own stern code, the Puritans of Massachusetts had little or nothing to do with the other colonies in British North America until 1684, when their Massachusetts Bay Colony charter was revoked and they came under direct control of the British Crown.

After more than fifty years of doing things their own way, Boston residents never fully embraced direct British governmental rule and the responsibilities expected of all British subjects. Even though the city thrived under the Crown and its seaport became the busiest in all the colonies, tariffs and taxes were despised by the citizens and often went unpaid. In the 18th century, Boston became a hotbed for outspoken critics and angry protests, and Massachusetts was one of the earliest colonies to call for an end to British rule. With rabble-rousers like Samuel Adams and acts of defiance like the Boston Tea Party, it's no wonder that the first shots fired during the Revolutionary War were in Lexington, just outside Boston.

The "edge" carried over into the 19th century and ultimately set the stage for the Civil War. Massachusetts politicians like former President John Quincy Adams and Senator Daniel Webster stood nose to nose against the southern politicians who claimed that states' rights took precedence over the nation as a whole. Boston was also home to a growing movement calling for the abolition of slavery. When southerners sneered the word "Yankee," they usually were aiming their curled lips at Boston.

While Boston's years in the driver's seat of American history are reflected in its parks, historic harbor, and battlefields, its most popular collective nod to history is the Freedom Trail (see Attractions). The Freedom Trail connects the city's historic museums, churches, cemeteries, and meetinghouses. A 3-mile trek along sidewalks marked with an easy-to-follow red line (keeping the line in sight is a great game for younger kids), the Trail takes visitors from the multipurpose Boston Common, past two state houses (see Attractions), the site of the 1770 Boston Massacre, Faneuil Hall (see Attractions), Paul Revere's house (see Museums), the sailing ship U.S.S. *Constitution* (see Attractions), and the monument to the Battle of Bunker Hill (see Attractions).

With a metro-area population of about 2.8 million, Boston is also an important business center. In the early 1970s, the city was, like others in the declining industrial Rust Belt, a place that people moved away from. A living metaphor for Boston's economic woes was the John Hancock Tower, a 62-story office building that kept losing its massive thermopane windows due to a combination of engineering miscalculations, prevailing winds, and bad glue. The rise of the technology industries— which tap the abundant brainpower of the Massachusetts Institute of Technology, Harvard University, and the rest of the Boston area's nearly forty colleges—has made Boston once again a prosperous economic leader.

Among Boston's quieter marvels are its parks, many of which were designed in the 19th century by landscape architect Frederick Law Olmsted, the man behind New York City's Central Park. Along with Boston Common (first laid out in 1634) and the adjacent Public Garden (famous for its Swan Boat rides), Boston also boasts Franklin Park, the gorgeous Arnold Arboretum (see Attractions), and a ribbon of parkways and landscaped riverways that ring central Boston and make for scenic driving, walking, or bicycling.

Because Boston's pilgrim fathers were unable to foresee the automobile when they laid out the narrow streets, central Boston is not at all car-friendly. Parking is nonexistent, and Boston motorists are infamous for having heavy feet on their accelerators, heavy hands on their horns, and chips the size of railroad ties on their shoulders. Experts can't agree on why Bostonians drive like kamikaze pilots. Some say it's because Massachusetts is a no-fault insurance state. Our theory is that, instead of boring intersections where roads cross at right angles, Boston abounds with rotaries, insidious traffic circles in which cars enter, drive around counterclockwise at breakneck speeds, and spin off as soon as they can no longer hold the steering wheel in position.

Fortunately Boston has a public transportation system that effectively prevents most residents and visitors from becoming highway statistics. This integrated subway, rail, and bus system—popularly called the T—is under the supervision of the Massachusetts Bay Transportation Authority (MBTA) (see Transportation). Subway and bus stops are signified by a black letter T inside a white circle. The system serves all of central Boston and about a 10-mile radius from downtown. A commuter rail system that serves cities as far away as Providence, Rhode Island, makes it possible to reach nearly every attraction in the Boston area or eastern Massachusetts without a car.

FREEBIES AND CHEAPIES
(Free or $3.50 and under for adults)

❑ Freedom Trail (see Attractions and Museums)
❑ Massachusetts State House and Archives (see Museums)
❑ Faneuil Hall (see Attractions)
❑ U.S.S. *Constitution* (see Attractions)
❑ Bunker Hill Monument (see Attractions)
❑ Arnold Arboretum (see Attractions)
❑ Boston Public Library (see Attractions)
❑ Minute Man National Historical Park (see Attractions)
❑ Mapparium (see Attractions)
❑ Boston Public Garden Swan Boat Rides (see Attractions)
❑ Granary Burying Ground (see Attractions)

CLIMATE

Winters are often snowy, chilly, and damp; daytime highs are often below freezing and nights bring temperatures in the teens or below. Snow can cover the ground between late December and early March, with early-April blizzards always threatening to postpone opening day for the Boston Red Sox. The Atlantic Ocean keeps the city 10 degrees warmer in winter and cooler in summer than cities in the western part of the state.

Summer often finds Boston with high temperatures in the 70s and 80s. During hot spells, temperatures and relative humidity sometimes can climb into the 90s. With high temperatures in the 60s and 70s and lows in the 40s and 50s, spring and fall are glorious. To be on the safe side, always pack for weather that's cooler than normal—a warm sweater and lightweight jacket in summer, and a heavy jacket in spring and fall. With 52 inches of precipitation falling throughout the year, it's wise to pack an umbrella and rain parka during the warmer months and foul-weather outer garments in winter.

TOURIST INFORMATION

Contact the Greater Boston Convention and Visitors' Bureau, P. O. Box 490, Prudential Plaza, Boston, MA 02199, (617) 536–4100.

THE LONG WEEKEND

Day One

❑ Boston Museum of Science (see Museums)
❑ New England Aquarium (see Attractions)

Day Two

❑ Boston Tea Party Ship and Museum (see Museums)
❑ Boston Children's Museum (see Museums)
❑ Computer Museum (see Museums)

Day Three

❑ Freedom Trail (see Attractions and Museums)
❑ John F. Kennedy Museum and Library (see Museums)

ATTRACTIONS

FREEDOM TRAIL

The Freedom Trail is a 3-mile path that travels past old churches, meetinghouses, cemeteries, and monuments from the Boston Common, through downtown, the city's historic North End, and over the Charlestown Bridge to Charlestown. An easy-to-follow red line that runs along the sidewalks and within crosswalks through intersections, the trail follows an often zig-zag path that begins just outside the Park T station in Boston Common. Each listing in both the Attractions section and the Museums section will be identified with the words **Freedom Trail**. Maps of the Freedom Trail are available at the Boston National Historic Park Visitors Center, 15 State Street.

PRUDENTIAL TOWER SKYWALK

Boylston and Fairfield Sts. (617) 236–3318. Use the Prudential station on the Green T line. Pay lot parking.

Hours. Mon.–Sat., 10 A.M.–10 P.M.; Sun., 12 noon–10 P.M.

Costs. Adults, $2.25; ages 5–15, $1.25; ages 4 and under, free.

From the observation deck 50 stories above the city, on a clear day you can see close to 60 miles of Massachusetts, Rhode Island, and New Hampshire. Looking northeast through a coin-operated telescope, you can see how old Boston was mapped out in the 17th century. The Tower is also home to the computers and telecommunications equipment for Metro Traffic, the service that feeds all the local radio stations with the latest traffic information.

Kids' Facilities. No stroller rentals. No diaper-changing tables in restrooms (use lobby benches). No food or bottle-warming facilities.

Ratings. Your kids will enjoy the view of the city from this lofty perspective. 2–7, B; 8–11, A; 12–16, A.

JOHN HANCOCK TOWER OBSERVATORY

St. James Ave. and Trinity Pl. (617) 247–1976. Use the Copley station on the Green T line. Pay lot parking.

Hours. May 1 through October 31: Mon.–Sat., 9 A.M.–11 P.M.; Sun., 10 A.M.–11 P.M. Rest of the year: daily, 12 noon–11 P.M.

Costs. Adults, $2.75; ages 5–15, $2; ages 4 and under, free.

Completed in 1974, the Hancock Building became in the early 1970s a landmark of dubious distinction: Many of the windows were sucked off the building and sent crashing to the street below. The problem was later corrected with better glue and a strengthened building core. The observation deck is located on the 60th floor, 10 stories higher than the Prudential Tower Skywalk. The Hancock features some historical exhibits, including *Boston 1775*, a look at the city on the eve of the American Revolution.

Kids' Facilities. No strollers. No diaper-changing tables (use benches in lobby). No bottle-warming capability.

Ratings. Either tower (Hancock or Prudential) is worth the trip; however, seeing both is for skyscraper fanatics only. 2–7, B; 8–11, A; 12–16, A.

BOSTON PUBLIC LIBRARY

666 Boylston St. at Dartmouth St. (617) 536–5400. Use the Copley station on the Green T line. Pay lot parking.

Hours. Mon.–Thurs., 9 A.M.–9 P.M.; Fri. and Sat., 9 A.M.–5 P.M.; Open Sun., October 1 through May 31, 2 P.M.–6 P.M.

Costs. Free.

A recent addition has more than doubled the size of the nation's oldest public library, connecting the bright, ultramodern section with the Italian Renaissance repository (1888). The entryway rotunda in the old wing is decorated with marble columns and sculptured ceilings and the mazelike passageways between rooms display artwork and historical dioramas. The outdoor courtyard is a lovely place to take a breather, but keep the small kids away from the fountain. The staff conducts "Library Times" for children under 5, with Saturday programs and story hours every Tuesday afternoon at 3 P.M.

Kids' Facilities. No strollers, just books. No diaper-changing tables in restrooms (in summer, try the benches in the courtyard). No food or bottle-warming services.

Ratings. If your kids like books, the library is heaven. If not, the sheer size and majesty of the architecture is worth at least a quick look. "Library Times" activities are perfect for small children. All ages, A.

GRANARY BURYING GROUND

Tremont and Bromfield Sts., on the **Freedom Trail**. Use the Park station on the Green or Red T line. Pay lot parking.

Hours. Daily, 8 A.M.–4:30 P.M.

Costs. Free.

The slate headstones here read like a who's who of Revolutionary War Boston. So named because a granary once occupied the spot, the Granary Burying Ground holds the remains of Samuel Adams, the victims of the Boston Massacre, John Hancock, Paul Revere, Peter Faneuil, and Mary Goose, who became known as the storyteller Mother Goose. A map that pinpoints the famous graves is available for free at National Park Visitor Center.

Kids' Facilities. No strollers. No restrooms. No diaper-changing tables. No food or bottle-warming facilities.

Ratings. Some kids will enjoy the burying ground because it's a cemetery. Older children will appreciate the historical value of the place. Since you need only linger a few minutes, no one should complain too much. 2–7, B; 8–11, A; 12–16, A.

OLD SOUTH MEETING HOUSE

310 Washington St., on the **Freedom Trail**. (617) 482–6439. Use the State station on the Orange or Blue T line. Pay lot parking.

Hours. April 1 through October 1: daily, 9:30 A.M.–5 P.M. Rest of the year: Mon.–Fri., 10 A.M.–4 P.M.; Sat. and Sun., 10 A.M.–5 P.M.

Costs. Adults, $1.25; ages 6–18, 50¢; ages 5 and under, free.

Built in 1729 as a Congregational Church, the famed Old South Meeting House was the site of many impassioned town meetings during the pre-

Revolution years, including the events leading up to the Boston Tea Party and Massacre. There are a number of exhibits of period memorabilia, along with a lighted relief map of 18th-century Boston. An oral history of the building and its importance throughout history's turbulent times can be heard through headphones at various stations throughout the facility.

Kids' Facilities. No strollers. No diaper-changing tables. *No restrooms; Use the ones at the National Park Visitors Center two blocks away.* No food or bottle-warming facilities.

Ratings. Young children could be easily bored, especially if the parents wish to spend a lot of time here. Exhibits do command the attention of adults and older children. 2–7, D; 8–11, C; 12–16, A.

BOSTON NATIONAL HISTORIC PARK VISITORS CENTER

15 State St. at Devonshire St., on the **Freedom Trail**. (617) 242–5642. Use the State station on the Orange or Blue T line. Pay lot parking.

Hours. Daily, 9 A.M.–5 P.M.

Costs. Free.

The Visitors Center provides two welcome services: helpful park rangers to answer questions about historic Boston attractions, and bathrooms, (a major consideration among the older buildings along the Freedom Trail). It's also a place to pick up books, brochures, and free maps of downtown Boston and the Freedom Trail.

Kids' Facilities. No stroller rentals. No diaper-changing tables (use couches in the lobby). No food or bottle-warming services.

Ratings. Since the Center is a source of vital information, it scores an A for every age group, especially parents.

OLD STATE HOUSE

206 Washington St. at State St., on the **Freedom Trail**. (617) 242–5655. Use the State station on the Orange or Blue T line. Pay lot parking.

Hours. April 1 through October 31: daily, 9:30 A.M.–5 P.M. Rest of the year: Mon.–Fri., 10 A.M.–4 P.M.; Sat., 9:30 A.M.–5 P.M.; Sun., 11 A.M.–5 P.M.

Costs. Adults, $1.25; ages 6–16, 50¢; ages 5 and under, free.

Boston's oldest public building, the Old State House was built in 1657 and used as the colony's seat of government until 1713. It now displays memorabilia from the city's rich history. It has ship models, figureheads and scrimshaw from Boston's whaling past, weapons and uniforms from Colonial times, and, in a room overlooking the actual site, an exhibit of court records from the Boston Massacre.

Kids' Facilities. No strollers. No diaper-changing tables. *No bathrooms; use the facilities across the street at the National Historic Park Visitors Center.* No food or bottle-warming facilities.

Ratings. The boats and weapons will keep the younger children happy, while the older kids and Mom and Dad can concentrate on the fascinating material about the Boston Massacre. 2–7, B; 8–11, A; 12–16, A.

FANEUIL HALL

Dock Square, Congress, and North Sts., on the **Freedom Trail**. (617) 223–6098. Use the State station on the Orange or Blue T line. Pay lot parking.

Hours. Daily, 9 A.M.–4:30 P.M.

Costs. Free.

First built in 1742 by well-to-do businessman Peter Faneuil, Faneuil Hall has been the site of many important debates throughout the city's history, from Samuel Adams preaching independence in the 1770s to Daniel Webster preaching the value of a *United* States during the turbulent 1840s. The ground floor of the 3-story building is devoted to food and gift stalls (see Shopping). The second floor still functions as a meeting hall and as the repository of the famous mural ''Webster's Reply to Hayne.'' The 3rd floor is a military museum. The top 2 floors are staffed by National Park Service Rangers, who answer all historical questions.

Kids' Facilities. No stroller rentals. Restrooms, but no diaper-changing tables (and not much counter or bench space). Get bottles warmed at food service stalls on the first floor or across the plaza at Quincy Market.

Ratings. History, souvenirs, and food together? That's a combination that should please every member of the family. All ages, A.

PAUL REVERE HOUSE

19 North Sq., on the **Freedom Trail**, (617) 523–2338. Use the Haymarket station on the Orange T line. Pay lot parking.

Hours. Mid-April through late October: daily, 9:30 A.M.–5:15 P.M. Rest of the year: daily, 9:30 A.M.–4:15 P.M.

Costs. Adults, $2; college students, $1.50; ages 5–17, 50¢; ages 4 and under, free.

Paul Revere lived here when he made his famous ride to warn the countryside of a British invasion in April 1775. It's a notable tourist stop not only because the Revere family lived here between 1770 and 1800, but because it is also the oldest house still standing in Boston. Constructed in 1680, it has been refurbished and refurnished in late-18th-century style and exhibits a collection of memorabilia that includes a bell cast by Revere himself. Even without the Revere connection, it's interesting to walk down the narrow stairs and along the crude, squeaking floorboards.

Kids' Facilities. No stroller rentals. No diaper-changing facilities. No food or bottle-warming facilities.

Ratings. Since the top floor of the house is the one that is open to the public, parents of small, stroller-bound children may want to skip it (or take turns going upstairs). Because it's possible to see the whole house in 15 minutes or less, a stop here is worth the effort, even if you have younger kids or those who don't care about history. 2–7, C; 8–11, B; 12–16, A.

OLD NORTH CHURCH

193 Salem St., on the **Freedom Trail**, (617) 523–6676. Use the Haymarket station on the Orange T line. Pay lot and limited metered street parking.

Hours. Daily, 9 A.M.–5 P.M.

Costs. Free (donations accepted).

"One if by land, two if by sea . . ."—the signal sent from the steeple of the Old North Church to indicate the nature of the British invasion—launched Paul Revere on his history-making ride on the night of April

18, 1775. The original steeple is gone, blown over and rebuilt after a 1955 hurricane, but the church has remained intact. The oldest church in Boston (1723), it is home to an active parish today.

Kids' Facilities. No stroller rentals. No diaper-changing facilities in the small restrooms. No food or bottle-warming capabilities.

Ratings. Since it takes but a minute to see the church, none of the kids will mind a quick look inside. By itself, it's not that important an attraction, but taken as part of the Freedom Trail as a whole, a stop is almost mandatory. All ages, A.

CHARLESTOWN NAVY YARD— U.S.S. *CONSTITUTION*, U.S.S. *CASSIN YOUNG*, AND BOSTON NAVY YARD NATIONAL HISTORICAL PARK VISITORS CENTER

Constitution Rd. at the mouth of the Charles River, on the **Freedom Trail**, Charlestown. (617) 241–9078. Use the Haymarket station on the Green or Orange T line and take the number 93 bus across the Charlestown Bridge. Free parking.

The grounds of the Navy Yard include the National Historical Park Visitors Center, the U.S.S. *Constitution* ("Old Ironsides") the U.S.S. *Cassin Young*, and the U.S.S. *Constitution* Museum (see Museums). Each facility has its own hours of operation.

Ratings. The two ships are fascinating for all ages, especially in comparing the way shipbuilding and design changed in the 150 years between the commissioning of the *Constitution* and the *Cassin Young*. All ages, A.

NATIONAL HISTORICAL PARK VISITORS CENTER

Hours. June through August: daily, 9 A.M.–6 P.M. Rest of the year: daily, 9 A.M.–5 P.M.

Costs. Free.

The Visitors Center is staffed with green-uniformed park rangers who answer questions on the Navy Yard and its resident ships. The Center also hosts periodic special exhibitions of marine-related items and a 10-minute slide show on the *Constitution*.

Kids' Facilities. The Visitors Center has the only restroom facilities for the three attractions. No stroller rentals. No diaper-changing tables (use couches in the lobby). No food or bottle-warming facilities.

U.S.S. *CONSTITUTION*

Hours. Upper deck open daily, 9:30 A.M.–sunset. Lower decks open to organized tours only: daily, 9:30 A.M.–3:50 P.M.

Costs. Free.

"Old Ironsides," as the wooden, 44-gun frigate came to be known after successful engagements with British ships during the War of 1812, was built in Boston in 1797 and served with distinction for many years before getting a complete restoration and a permanent home at her present site. Still a commissioned fighting ship, she is staffed by United States Navy sailors who stand ready to answer questions and give tours.

Kids' Facilities. None (see Visitors Center, page 23).

U.S.S. *CASSIN YOUNG*

Hours. Summer: daily, 9:30 A.M.–6 P.M. Fall/spring: daily, 9:30 A.M.–4:30 P.M. January through March: weekends (tours only), 9:30 A.M.–4:30 P.M.

Costs. Free.

The *Cassin Young* is typical of the destroyers built for service during World War II. Battleship gray and nondescript, the *Cassin Young* provides a vivid picture of life at sea during a prolonged patrol. Living quarters seem cramped, even by the compact standards of children, and can make parents feel downright claustrophobic.

Kids' Facilities. None (see Visitors Center, page 23).

"THE WHITES OF THEIR EYES"

Constitution Rd., outside the Gate 1 entrance to the Charlestown Navy Yard, on the **Freedom Trail**, Charlestown. (617) 241–7575. Use the Haymarket station on the Orange or Green T line and take the number 93 bus across the Charlestown Bridge. Free parking.

Hours. June through August: daily, 9:30 A.M.–6 P.M. Rest of the year: daily, 9:30 A.M.–4:30 P.M.

Costs. Adults, $3; ages 5–16, $1.50; ages 4 and under, free; families, $8.

A multimedia reenactment of the Battle of Bunker Hill, the presentation makes full use of fourteen projectors, twenty-two mannequins, and a theater in the round. Often emotional and tinged with hyperbole, it provides a fairly accurate picture of the 1775 battle between local militia and seasoned British troops.

Kids' Facilities. No stroller rentals. No diaper-changing tables (do it in the lobby). No bottle-warming facilities.

Ratings. Since shows last only about a half hour (short enough for young children prone to fidgeting and older ones who already know the story), it's loud and colorful enough to placate most kids. All ages, A.

BUNKER HILL MONUMENT

Monument Sq. off Monument Ave., on the **Freedom Trail**, Charlestown. (617) 242–5641. Use the Haymarket station on the Orange or Green T line and take the number 93 bus across the Charlestown Bridge. Limited street parking.

Hours. Daily, 9 A.M.–5 P.M.

Costs. Free.

The Battle of Bunker Hill was actually fought on a Charlestown rise called Breed's Hill, which is today the site of the Bunker Hill Monument. Dedicated in 1825, the 221-foot granite obelisk marks the spot where the American militia killed or wounded more than 1,000 British soldiers on the sultry afternoon of June 17, 1775. The Americans were finally forced to retreat, but news of the damage inflicted upon the British regulars— along with the order "Don't shoot till you see the whites of their eyes"—gave a shot in the arm to the Revolutionary cause. Today, a 295-step climb to an observation deck atop the monument (no elevator) earns a commanding view of Boston Harbor, the Charles River, and downtown Boston. In the base of the monument, four historical dioramas depict the battle. The battle is reenacted yearly on June 17; on any other day, you may want to consider a picnic on the grounds.

Just below the monument, at the corner of Monument Square and Monument Avenue, a small, red-brick museum contains an assortment of Bunker Hill memorabilia.

Kids' Facilities. No strollers. No diaper-changing tables in restrooms (do it on the lawn). No food or bottle-warming facilities.

Ratings. Younger children may not comprehend the historical importance of the monument, but if they're old enough to make the climb, they'll relish the view. 2–7, B (A, if your kids can make it to the top under their own steam); 8–11, A; 12–16, A.

NEW ENGLAND AQUARIUM

Central Wharf, Atlantic Ave. and Central St. (617) 742–8870. Use the Aquarium station on the Blue T line. Pay lot parking.

Hours. Mon.–Thurs., 9 A.M.–5 P.M.; Fri., 9 A.M.–8 P.M.; Sat.–Sun., 9 A.M.–6 P.M.

Costs. Adults, $6; ages 4–15, $3.50; ages 3 and under, free.

Home to more than 2,000 fish, dozens of penguins, and loads of ocean-going mammals, the New England Aquarium displays marine life and also provides temporary exhibits that explain and enhance some of the larger exhibits. In the recent past, exhibits have included a presentation on strange animal behavior and an exhibition that focused on the Japanese art of breeding carp with specific colors and markings. The Aquarium's centerpiece is a 4-story, 180,000-gallon cylindrical tank filled with more than 800 species of salt-water tropical fish, sharks, eels, and sea turtles. Ramps allow visitors to view it from various locations and depths. Kids are encouraged to roll up their sleeves for a grope in the Aquarium's re-created New England tidal pool. Next door, in a floating marine pavilion, dolphin shows are presented at various times during the day.

Kids' Facilities. No stroller rentals. No diaper-changing tables in the bathrooms (use outdoor and indoor benches). No bottle-warming facilities at the outdoor fast-food snack bar.

Ratings. The Aquarium is tops for kids across the entire age spectrum. The favorite attraction among younger children is the tidal pool, where kids can get wet and drive their parents crazy. All ages, A.

MAPPARIUM

Massachusetts Ave. and Clearway St. (617) 450–2000. Use the Auditorium station on the Green T line. Pay lot parking.

Hours. Mon.–Fri., 8 A.M.–4 P.M.; Sat., 10 A.M.–3:45 P.M.; Sun., 12 P.M.–3:45 P.M.

Costs. Free.

Founded by Mary Baker Eddy, the Christian Science Church has been both an important religious institution and a landmark in downtown Boston since 1879. Today the church owns a huge chunk of real estate, adjacent to Prudential Center, that contains the original Mother Church, the Christian Science Publishing House (which publishes the Christian

Science *Monitor*), and the Mapparium, a world globe 30 feet in diameter. Built in 1935 out of more than 600 separate glass panels, the globe is illuminated by hundreds of lights and bisected by a tunnel that takes visitors on a journey to the center of the earth.

Kids' Facilities. Both the men's and ladies' restrooms have a lounge with a sofa that's perfect for changing diapers. No stroller rentals. No food or bottle-warming facilities.

Ratings. Older kids might be less than excited about the big globe; however, it takes but a few minutes to walk through it. The younger ones will be impressed. 2–7, A; 8–11, A; 12–16, B.

ARNOLD ARBORETUM

Arbor Way and V.F.W. Pkwy., Jamaica Plain. (617) 524–1717. Use the Arborway station on the Green T line. Free street parking.

Hours. Daily, dawn to dusk.

Costs. Free.

Established in 1872, Boston's largest public garden is a former tree farm that has been transformed into a 265-acre living botanical laboratory administered by Harvard University. It contains more than 7,000 species of North American flora, including huge gardens of roses, daffodils, magnolias, and rhododendrons. There are also greenhouses (open Wed., 1:30–4 P.M.), a Bonzai exhibit with specimens more than 300 years old, and a Visitors Center (Mon.–Fri., 9 A.M.–4 P.M.; Sat. and Sun., 10 A.M.–4 P.M.) where all your questions can be answered.

Kids' Facilities. No stroller rentals (*if you have children under 5, you should definitely bring your own*). Restrooms are found at the Visitors Center (no diaper-changing tables; use couches and chairs). No food or bottle-warming facilities.

Ratings. Parents of small, wandering children beware: the trails are long and there are some heavily wooded areas where kids can easily get lost. All ages, A.

BOSTON PUBLIC GARDEN SWAN BOAT RIDES

Boylston and Charles Sts. (617) 323–2700. Use the Park station on the Green or Red T lines. Pay lot parking.

Hours. Late April through late September: daily, during daylight hours.

Costs. Adults, 90¢; children under 13, 50¢.

One of Boston's great kids' activities, the Swan Boat rides have been a fixture on the Public Garden Pond since 1877. Constructed in the shape of a swan, each pedal-powered boat cruises the 3 ¾-acre pond in figure-eight fashion at a maximum speed of 3 MPH. That pace allows you to take in the sights: the carefully cultivated gardens, the algae clinging to the pond surface, and the ducks that inspired the classic children's book *Make Way for Ducklings*.

Kids' Facilities. No stroller rentals. No diaper-changing tables in restrooms (use benches in park; the deck of a Swan Boat isn't big enough). No bottle-warming facilities.

Ratings. Older kids have long passed the Swan Boat period, but the younger ones will have a ball. 2–7, A; 8–11, B: 12–16, D.

FRANKLIN PARK ZOO

Blue Hill Ave. and Columbia Rd., Dorchester. (617) 442–2005. Use the Forest Hills station on the Orange T line and then a number 16 bus east to the zoo entrance. Free parking.

Hours. Daily, 9 A.M.–5 P.M.

Costs. Adults, $1; children under 12, free.

Except for a mediocre children's zoo with some farm animals and a petting area, the Franklin Park Zoo is a disaster. With heaps of dirt and rubble from the construction of a new bird house and a new primate house that should be open by summer 1989, it looks more like postwar Berlin than Boston.

Kids' Facilities. No stroller rentals. Ample bench space, but no diaper-changing tables in children's zoo restrooms, which are often locked. No restrooms in the old section. Snack bar may be closed. No bottle-warming facilities.

Ratings. Until the new primate house opens, avoid the zoo at all costs. All ages, F.

BLACK HERITAGE TRAIL

Beacon Hill area. (617) 742–1854. Use the Bowdoin station on the Blue T line and walk 5 blocks to the west along Cambridge St. to Joy St. Pay lot parking.

Hours. Hours of access to different points of interest vary.

Costs. The walk is free, but some attractions charge admission.

Like the Freedom Trail, the Black Heritage Trail connects historical buildings that have been significant to black residents of Boston. It takes about 90 minutes to walk it if you stop at every location. The Trail starts at the Afro-American History Museum, 46 Joy Street at Smith Court (see Museums), and passes fourteen Beacon Hill sites. Stops include the African Meeting House, the oldest black church in the United States; the Smith Court Residences, home to 19th-century blacks; the Phillips School, one of the city's first interracial institutions; the Charles Street Meetinghouse; and the Lewis and Harriet Hayden House, a base for the political activities of Hayden, an abolitionist leader in the years before the Civil War.

Each stop on the Black Heritage Trail is marked with a black and silver logo.

MINUTE MAN NATIONAL HISTORICAL PARK

Along 6 miles of State Rte. 2A, between State Rte. 225, Lexington, and State Rte. 126, Concord. Battle Road Visitor Center, (617) 862–7753; North Bridge Visitor Center, (508) 369–6993 or (508) 484–6156. Take Interstate 90 west to the junction of Interstate 95; north on 95 to the Hwy. 2A exit; west about a mile to the Battle Road Visitor Center. Free parking.

Hours. The two Park Visitor Centers, Battle Road and North Bridge, are open daily from 8:30 A.M. to 5 P.M. The Battle Road Center is closed from December through March, while the North Bridge Center is open year-round.

Costs. Free.

The two visitor centers lie at opposite ends of the 6-mile strip of National Historical Park—the site of the Battle of Lexington and Concord, fought on April 19, 1775. Markers denote historic buildings and skirmishes between British regulars and local militia.

The Battle Road Vistor Center, just west of Lexington at the eastern edge of the park, is a modern wood-and-glass structure that displays battle memorabilia. There's also a 22-minute movie that details both the events of April 18 and 19, 1775, and the repressive British actions that provoked them. The Visitor Center also has a 10-minute electronic map and audio presentation with an hour-by-hour account of the British march to Concord, the midnight ride of Paul Revere, and the resulting all-day battle that was waged between Concord and Boston.

The North Bridge Visitor Center is located in an old Victorian building just north of the Concord River Bridge. The bridge and the Minuteman statue mark the spot where the "shot heard 'round the world" was fired. The Old Bridge Center features displays of Colonial weapons, uniforms, and memorabilia. A favorite stop for kids is an upstairs room containing plenty of replica Colonial clothes that children are encouraged to try on.

Kids' Facilities. At the visitor centers only. No strollers. No diaper-changing tables (use benches). No food service or bottle-warming facilities.

Ratings. With so much to do along the Battle Road and so much to see at the Visitor Centers, the Minuteman National Historical Park has something for everyone. All ages, A.

BUCKMAN TAVERN

Bedford St. across from the Lexington Common, Lexington. (617) 861–0928. Take Interstate 90 west to the junction of Interstate 95; north on 95 to the Hwy. exit 2A; go north to Massachusetts Ave. and turn right onto State Rte. 225; proceed a mile east to the Lexington Common. Free parking.

Hours. Mid-April through October 31: Mon.–Sat., 10 A.M.–5 P.M.; Sun., 1 P.M.–5 P.M.

Costs. Adults, $2; ages 6–16, 50¢; ages 5 and under, free.

Buckman Tavern was a rallying point for the militiamen who faced British troops marching to Concord on the night of April 18, 1775. Completely restored to its original state (even heating and plumbing were removed to make it authentic), the fragile condition of the furnishings mandates guided tours only.

Kids' Facilities. Absolutely none; go a half block east to the Lexington Visitors Center for restrooms.

Ratings. Keep kids under age 6 away: The temptation to grab antique glassware or sit on fragile period furniture could be too much. The tour takes about 20 minutes. 2–7, D; 8–11, A; 12–16, A.

LEXINGTON VISITORS CENTER

Bedford St. across from the Lexington Common, Lexington. (617) 862–1450. Take Interstate 90 west to the junction of Interstate 95; north on 95 to the Hwy. 2A exit; go north to Massachusetts Ave. and turn right onto State Rte. 225; proceed a mile east to the Lexington Common. Free parking.

Hours. April 15 through November 1: daily, 9 A.M.–5 P.M. Rest of the year: daily, 10 A.M.–4 P.M.

Costs. Free.

The Lexington Chamber of Commerce operates this small center to promote its tourist attractions and as a public convenience. A historical diorama of the battle on April 19, 1775, shows how seventy-seven colonial Militia fended off 700 British troops.

Kids' Facilities. No stroller rentals. No diaper-changing tables in restrooms. No food or bottle-warming capabilities.

Ratings. The restrooms at the Visitors Center are an oasis. The diorama usually commands the attention of small children. All ages, B.

SALEM WITCH DUNGEON

16 Lynde St. Salem. (508) 744–9812. Go north on Interstate 93 to the junction of Interstate 95; north on Interstate 95 until it becomes State Rte. 128; north on 128 to State Rte. 114; head east on 114 and follow signs into Salem. Metered lot and limited free street parking.

Hours. Daily, 10 A.M.–5 P.M.; shows about every half hour.

Costs. Adults, $2.75; ages 5–12, $1.75; ages 4 and under, free.

Shows dramatize a 1692 Salem witch trial. After the trial, the actors lead the audience on a tour of the grim basement dungeon filled with ghastly mannequins emitting recorded moans and groans. The witch dungeon is a replica of the dank, jaillike holding area that, in reality, stood only a few blocks away.

Kids' Facilities. No stroller rentals. No diaper-changing facilities. No bathrooms. No food or bottle-warming facilities.

Ratings. Kids like the scary dungeon, but it could cause nightmares. This attraction can teach a valuable lesson about justice, truth, and mob mentality. The gift shop offers some terrifically kitschy jewelry, witch yo-yos, and witch-shaped refrigerator magnets. 2–7, B; 8–11, A; 12–16, B.

MUSEUMS

INSTITUTE OF CONTEMPORARY ART

955 Boylston St. (617) 266–5151. Use the Auditorium station on the Green T line. Pay lot parking.

Hours. Wed.–Sun., 11 A.M.–5 P.M.; Thurs. and Fri., 11 A.M.–8 P.M. Closed on Mon. and Tues.

Costs. Adults, $4; students, $2.50; ages 14 and under, $1.50. Free on Fri., 5 P.M.–8 P.M.

The Institute of Contemporary Art may draw kids in like a magnet or repel them like a plate of cold brussels sprouts. It all depends on what is currently being displayed. However, the museum usually has something outrageous and kid-pleasing up its artistic sleeve.

Kids' Facilities. No stroller rentals. No diaper-changing tables (use the sofas in the lobby). No food or bottle-warming facilities.

Ratings. If not an absolute must-see, the Institute of Contemporary Art deserves at least a phone call to see what they have on tap at the moment. Ratings depend on the temporary exhibit.

MASSACHUSETTS STATE HOUSE AND ARCHIVES

Beacon and Park Sts., on the **Freedom Trail**. (617) 727–3676. Use the Park station on the Green or Red T line. Pay lot parking.

Hours. Mon.–Fri., 9 A.M.–5 P.M. Guided tours: Mon–Fri., 10 A.M.–4 P.M.

Costs. Free.

Always bustling with tourists and state employees, the State House (1797) boasts a gleaming golden dome and ornately inlaid marble floors. The large columned rooms off the main floor rotunda display portraits of former governors and all sorts of Colonial and state memorabilia. Older children may enjoy a peek at government in action when the legislature is in session. The basement-level archives hold the original Massachusetts Bay Company Charter and the original 1780 Massachusetts

State Constitution, the oldest anywhere in the world. Tours run about 45 minutes.

Kids' Facilities. No stroller rentals. No diaper-changing tables in restrooms (precious little bench space). No food or bottle-warming capabilities.

Ratings. If you're already on the Freedom Trail, it's worth a quick stop. Even kids who have no use for history quit complaining when confronted with documents signed by famous Founding Fathers. Young children shouldn't mind it either since it's always crowded enough to distract them for at least a short time. All ages, A.

U.S.S. *CONSTITUTION* MUSEUM

Charlestown Navy Yard, end of Constitution Rd. on the **Freedom Trail**, Charlestown. (617) 242–0543. Use the Haymarket station on the Green or Orange T line and take the number 93 bus across the Charlestown Bridge. Free parking.

Hours. Spring and fall: daily, 9 A.M.–5 P.M. Winter: daily, 9 A.M.–4 P.M. Summer: daily, 9 A.M.–6 P.M.

Costs. Adults, $2; ages 6–16, $1; ages 5 and under, free.

A museum dedicated to the ship moored nearby displays prizes and treasures taken off enemy ships by "Old Ironsides" in skirmishes with the Barbary pirates and in the War of 1812. There's also a large collection of swords, sidearms, and cannons. Kids love to climb the replica of the ship's fighting top and hoist the sail. They also flock to a computer game that lets them "captain" the ship. A huge collection of model ships occupies an entire gallery, and model ship–builders often hold demonstrations on weekends.

Kids' Facilities. No strollers. No diaper-changing tables (use well-placed benches throughout the museum). No food or bottle-warming facilities.

Ratings. There's something here for most kids. All ages, A.

BOSTON MUSEUM OF SCIENCE

Science Park on the Charles River Dam, between Cambridge and Boston. (617) 723–2500. Use the Science Park station on the Green T line. Pay parking lot.

Hours. Year-round: Tues.–Sun., 9 A.M.–5 P.M.; Fri., 9 A.M.–9 P.M. May through August: Mon., 9 A.M.–5 P.M.

Costs. Exhibit halls, Omnimax theater, and Laser shows (separate admission to each): adults, $5; ages 4–14, $3; ages 3 and under, free. Planetarium: adults, $4; ages 4–14, $2.50; ages 3 and under, free. Any combination of two of the above: adults, $7.50; ages 4–14, $5. Any combination of three of the above: adults, $10; ages 4–14, $7.

Along with typical science-museum fare—animal dioramas, a reconstructed Tyrannosaurus rex, and computers, the main exhibit hall contains a machine for tool making, a bizarre insect display, and a machine that manufactures ice crystals before your eyes. Our favorite was a 30-foot-tall Rube Goldberg-like installation that sends billiard balls along a wire track where they trip buzzers, bells, hammers, and wheels to perform outlandish physical feats. Kids like the physical-science demonstrations, and a discovery center for small kids has plenty of stuff to touch.

The Hayden Planetarium presents daily skyshows and regular lasarium programs. The Omnimax Theater shows two movies on a 4-story screen once every hour (check out the monster projector behind a glass wall). The museum has a huge gift shop and three restaurants offering everything from fast food and sodas to daily specials.

Kids' Facilities. No stroller rentals. Diaper-changing tables in each restroom. Nursing facilities available (ask at information booth). Bottles can be warmed at the restaurants.

Ratings. One of the finest facilities of its kind on the East Coast; everybody loves the Boston Museum of Science. All ages, A.

BOSTON TEA PARTY SHIP AND MUSEUM

Docked at the Congress St. Bridge. (617) 338–1773. Use the South station on the Red T line and walk one block east and one block north. Pay lot parking.

Hours. Daily, 9 A.M.–8 P.M.

Costs. Adults, $3.25; ages 5–12, $2.25; ages 4 and under, free.

The floating museum is moored next to the *Beaver II*, a replica of one of three tea ships visited by tea-dumping protesters in December 1773. The museum is filled with all sorts of merchant ship memorabilia, including an authentic tea chest. Lots of lithographs and a 10-minute slide presentation round out the depiction of the political climate during the last years of Colonial rule in Boston. You can board and explore the *Beaver II* but, sorry, no tea dumping.

Kids' Facilities. No stroller rentals. No diaper-changing tables in restrooms (which are tiny). No food or bottle-warming facilities.

Ratings. The subtle historical nuances might be lost on younger children; however, climbing aboard the tea ship is fun for the whole family. All ages, A.

BOSTON CHILDREN'S MUSEUM

300 Congress St., Museum Wharf. (617) 426–8855. Use the South station on the Red T line and walk one block east, one block north, and another block east. Limited free parking.

Hours. Mid-June through Labor Day: daily, 10 A.M.–5 P.M.; Fri. until 9 P.M. Rest of the year: Tues–Sun., 10 A.M.–5 P.M.; Fri. until 9 P.M. Closed on Mon. during the school year, unless a school holiday.

Costs. Adults, $4.50; ages 2–15, $3.50; under age 2, free. Free on Fri., 5 P.M.–9 P.M.

At a time when most cities have only recently opened children's museums, Boston's is celebrating more than seventy-five years in business. For toddlers, the BCM has a supervised play space where they can mess around with shapes and bounce on small pieces of apparatus. For kids under 5, there's an intricate 3-story climbing sculpture vertically situated near the stairway. For older children, there's a great interactive health exhibit. Our favorite displays are the ones that ask you to identify body noises and the mannequin with nylon rope intestines—pull the rope and see how long a human being's intestinal tract really is. Grandparents' House is a re-created 4-story building facade with rooms furnished as they might have been sixty years ago. Junior-high-aged kids can dance to pulsating rock 'n' roll music in the Clubhouse. The bubble room teaches kids new and ingenious ways to utilize soap and air. The gift shop has an incredible array of books, educational toys, and scientific games, and a resource center offers books and magazines for parents. The museum's directories are computerized—just punch up the floor you want and the floor plan spreads out before you on the screen.

Kids' Facilities. No stroller rentals. Diaper-changing tables in both men's and ladies' restrooms, one of each on every floor. No food or bottle-warming facilities (there's a McDonald's located in the same building).

Ratings. The BCM is by far the most comprehensive museum of its kind we've run across. A must for kids under age 12. 2–7, A; 8–11, A; 12–16, B.

COMPUTER MUSEUM

300 Congress St., Museum Wharf. (617) 426–2800 or (617) 423–6758. Use the South station on the Red T line and walk one block east, one block north, and another block east. Limited free parking.

Hours. Mid-June through Labor Day: daily, 10 A.M.–5 P.M.; Fri., until 9 P.M. Rest of the year: Tues.–Sun., 10 A.M.–5 P.M. Fri. until 9 P.M. Closed on Mon. during the school year, unless a school holiday.

Costs. Adults, $4; students, $3.

Located next door to the Boston Children's Museum, the only Computer Museum in the world displays some of the first computers and modern computers offering all sorts of games and high-tech diversions. Our favorite is a computer that creates a map showing the quickest route from the museum to any given Boston street address. You can even "fly" a plane courtesy of a computerized flight simulator.

Kids' Facilities. No stroller rentals. No diaper-changing tables in restrooms. No food or bottle-warming facilities (McDonald's is next door).

Ratings. To appreciate the Computer Museum, children need to have some familiarity with computers; if so, the hands-on computers can be a lot of fun. The historic exhibits tend to interest only adults and older kids. 2–7, C; 8–11, B; 12–16, A.

BOSTON MUSEUM OF FINE ARTS

465 Huntington Dr. (617) 267–9300. Use the Art Museum station on the Green T line. Limited paid parking in museum lot.

Hours. Entire museum: Tues.–Sun., 10 A.M.–5 P.M.; Wed. until 10 P.M. West wing only: Thurs. and Fri., 5 P.M.–10 P.M. Closed on Mon.

Costs. Adults, $5 when entire museum is open; $4 when only west wing is open; age 15 and under, free. Free on Sat. from 10 A.M. to 12 noon.

The most memorable artworks here are the Paul Revere silver collection and the portraits of Revolutionary War heroes. Best known are the portraits of George Washington by Gilbert Stuart; and Paul Revere, John

Hancock, John Quincy Adams, and Samuel Adams by John Singleton Copley.

The MFA has great European paintings and sculptures by Donatello, Goya, Monet, and Renoir. American favorites include works by Whittier, Cassatt, Sargent, Homer, Innes, and Eakins.

Kids' Facilities. No stroller rentals. No diaper-changing tables in restrooms. Bottles can be warmed at either of the museum's two dining areas, both comfortable, sit-down facilities complete with waiters and waitresses.

Ratings. While children under the age of 5 are usually good at art museums for an hour to an hour and a half (the more colorful the art, the better), you should not attempt a long visit with children under 10. Once that criterion is met, the MFA makes for a terrific outing. 2–7, C; 8–11, B; 12–16, A.

JOHN F. KENNEDY MUSEUM AND LIBRARY

Morrissey Blvd., Columbia Point. (617) 929–4523. Take Interstate 93/State Rte. 3 south to exit 15; follow signs to museum. Public transit: Use the J.F.K./U. Mass. station on the Red T line and free museum shuttle bus. Free parking.

Hours. Daily, 9 A.M.–5 P.M. (last movie shown at 3:50 P.M.).

Costs. Adults, $2.50; ages 15 and under, free.

Sitting on Dorchester Bay at the tip of Columbia Point, the futuristic glass and steel building designed by I. M. Pei houses memorabilia and artifacts from the life of the thirty-fifth President. Since 1979, people from around the world have come to pay homage to the chief executive who was assassinated in November 1963. Large crowds of visitors reverently pass the long, nine-exhibit "time line" that chronicles the Kennedy family history and the short life of JFK. A 30-minute movie documents his life. There are also exhibits and a film on John's brother, Robert Kennedy, who was assassinated in 1968.

Kids' Facilities. No stroller rentals. No diaper-changing tables in restrooms (use the sofas and benches outside the waiting area for the movie). No food or bottle-warming facilities.

Ratings. The JFK Museum may not have much meaning for children in the lower age range, but older kids and parents will find it terrific. 2–7, D; 8–11, C; 12–16, A.

COMMONWEALTH MUSEUM AT COLUMBIA POINT

Morrissey Blvd., Columbia Point. (617) 727–9268. Take Interstate 93/
State Rte. 3 south to exit 15; follow signs to JFK Museum. Public transit:
Use the J.F.K./U. Mass. station on the Red T line and free JFK Museum
shuttle bus. Free. parking.

Hours. Mon.–Fri., 9 A.M.–5 P.M.; Sat., 9 A.M.–3 P.M.

Costs. Free.

The exhibits in this futuristic facility trace the history of the people of
Massachusetts from the Indians and Pilgrims to the modern day. There
are slide and taped audio shows, a time tunnel to walk through, and
hands-on exhibits that make historical issues like freedom of speech and
civil disobedience come alive. An interactive exhibit on the Mayflower
Compact allows visitors to sign their names to the document. Hear history-
changing commentary "spoken" by famous Massachusetts citizens like
Samuel Adams, Chief Metacomet, who led the most serious Indian up-
rising in Massachusetts, abolitionist William Lloyd Garrison, and free
thinker Henry David Thoreau.

Kids' Facilities. No stroller rentals. No diaper-changing tables in restrooms. No food or bottle-warming facilities.

Ratings. While not for the very young, many exhibits are earmarked
for kids from about the third grade up. 2–7, D; 8–11, A; 12–16, A.

MUSEUM OF AFRO-AMERICAN HISTORY

46 Joy St., on the **Black Heritage Trail**. (617) 742–1854. Use the
Bowdoin station on the Blue T line. Pay lot parking.

Hours. Museum: Mon.–Fri., 9 A.M.–5 P.M. Old Meeting House: daily,
9 A.M.–4 P.M.

Costs. Free (donations appreciated).

Focusing on the history of blacks in the Beacon Hill area and the city
in general, the museum offers a perspective on Boston's role as a hotbed
of the pre–Civil War abolitionist movement. A wonderful interpretive
center, the Museum of Afro-American History should be the starting
point of walks along the Black Heritage Trail.

Kids' Facilities. No stroller rentals. No diaper-changing tables in restrooms. No food or bottle-warming facilities.

Ratings. The museum is too dry for smaller kids. School-aged children who've had some American history will benefit from a short stop even if the Heritage Trail is not on your itinerary. 2–7, D; 8–11, B; 12–16, A.

THE HARVARD MUSEUMS

Located just across the Charles River from Boston, Harvard is the nation's oldest university (founded in 1636). Over the years, Harvard has acquired lots of museum-quality art and artifacts. Most of those trinkets are on display at small museums and galleries throughout the campus. The main museums, however, come under two headings: the Harvard Art Museums and the Harvard Museums of Natural History. The art museums include the **Fogg Art Museum**, the **Busch-Reisinger Museum**, and the **Arthur M. Sackler Museum**. The five natural history museums are the **Botanical Museum**, the **Mineralogical and Geological Museums**, the **Museum of Comparative Zoology**, the **Peabody Museum of Archaeology and Ethnology**, and the **Semitic Museum**. The museums are listed by location.

Hours. Art museums: Mon.–Sat., 10 A.M.–5 P.M.; Sun., 1 P.M.–5 P.M. Natural history museums: Mon.–Sat., 9 A.M.–4:30 P.M.; Sun., 1 P.M.– 4:30 P.M. Semitic Museum: Mon.–Fri., 11 A.M.–5 P.M.; Sun., 1 P.M.– 5 P.M. Closed on Sat.

Costs. Art museums: adults, $3; ages 18 and under, free (one admission good for all art museums). Natural history museums: adults, $2; ages 5– 15, 50¢ (one admission good for all natural history museums); free on Sun., 9 A.M.–11 A.M.). Semitic Museum: free.

FOGG ART MUSEUM

32 Quincy St., Harvard University, Cambridge. (617) 495–4544 or (617) 495–9400. Use the Harvard station on the Red T line. Pay lot parking.

Founded in 1891, the Fogg is home to some of the world's finest classical paintings by Dutch, Spanish, and Italian artists from the 16th through the 18th centuries. The Fogg also displays paintings from the 19th and early-20th centuries, including the works of Renoir, Picasso, Matisse, Braque, Van Gogh, and Monet, plus modern efforts by Warhol and Lichtenstein. Your kids might get the opportunity to witness Harvard art students painting their own impressions of the great works.

Kids' Facilities. No strollers. No diaper-changing tables in restrooms. No food or bottle-warming facilities.

Ratings. The two-level museum can be seen in about an hour. 2–7, C; 8–11, B; 12–16, A.

BUSCH-REISINGER MUSEUM

29 Kirkland, Harvard University, Cambridge. (617) 495–4544. Use the Harvard station on the Red T line. Pay lot parking.

Once dubbed the "Germanic Museum," the BR features some terrific German paintings, lithographs, drawings, and prints from the modern era. One of its most famous pieces is a 1927 self-portrait of painter Max Beckmann. The museum also has a substantial collection of northern European art, including sculpture, decorative arts, and some fine 18th-century porcelain.

Kids' Facilities. No strollers. No diaper-changing tables in restrooms. No food or bottle warming-facilities.

Ratings. Quick and easy to see, the German paintings and lithos are terrific for Mom and Dad and represent only a half hour out of the lives of the kids. 2–7, C; 8–11, B; 12–16, A.

ARTHUR M. SACKLER MUSEUM

485 Broadway St., Harvard University, Cambridge. (617) 495–4544. Use the Harvard station on the Red T line. Pay lot parking.

The ultramodern Sackler building contains everything old, including ancient Greek and Roman statuary, 3,500-year-old Oriental sculpture, and Roman and Greek gold and silver coins.

Kids' Facilities. No stroller rentals. No diaper-changing tables in the restrooms (and few benches). No food or bottle-warming facilities.

Ratings. The museum's appeal for young children is its statuary. Kids are fascinated by anatomically correct body parts. It's easy to see everything in the Sackler within an hour. 2–7, B; 8–11, B; 12–16, A.

THE BOTANICAL MUSEUM
THE MINERALOGICAL AND GEOLOGICAL MUSEUMS
MUSEUM OF COMPARATIVE ZOOLOGY
PEABODY MUSEUM OF ARCHAEOLOGY AND ETHNOLOGY

24 Oxford St. and 11 Divinity Ave., Harvard University, Cambridge. Botanical, (617) 495–7602; Mineralogical, (617) 495–4758; Zoology,

(617) 495–2463; Peabody, (617) 495–2248. Use the Harvard station on the Red T line. Pay lot parking.

All four museums occupy a giant U-shaped building in the heart of the Harvard campus. The **Botanical Museum**'s claim to fame is its collection of glass flowers: more than 800 species and 3,000 total flowers. The **Mineralogical and Geological Museums** display more than 50,000 specimens of rare minerals, 75,000 different rocks and ores, and—a favorite for kids—514 meteors and extraterrestrial rocks.

The **Museum of Comparative Zoology** exhibits a large variety of fossils, vertebrates, invertebrates, extinct species, and representatives of the animal kingdom living today. Kids flock to the skeletons; the bigger and more primitive, the larger the flock. Favorites are the whale skeletons and the 42-foot-long Kronosaurus, a sea serpent that lived nearly 135 million years ago.

Opened in 1866, the **Peabody Museum of Archaeology and Ethnology** is the oldest museum of its kind in the Western Hemisphere. The permanent exhibits are the Hall of the North American Indian and the Pre-Columbian Gallery, which has one of the world's largest collections of artifacts from the Mayan Empire.

Kids' Facilities. No stroller rentals. No diaper-changing tables (plenty of bench space, however). No food or bottle-warming facilities.

Ratings. With the diversity of exhibits in the four museums, most children won't squawk if forced to spend three hours here. All ages, A.

THE SEMITIC MUSEUM

6 Divinity Ave., Harvard University, Cambridge. (617) 495–3123. Use the Harvard station on the Red T line. Pay lot parking.

The Semitic Museum has a tiny, but selective, collection of art and artifacts from the Middle East. Most of the region's ethnic and religious groups are represented. Besides lamps, urns, and vessels of both Jewish and Islamic origins, there are three kid-pleasing mummies and many photographs of the Holy Land taken during late-19th- and early-20th-century archaeological digs.

Kids' Facilities. No stroller rentals. No diaper-changing tables in restrooms. No food or bottle-warming facilities.

Ratings. When you have mummies, you have a winner. Twenty minutes is all that's needed to quickly see everything in this small and compact museum. All ages, A.

PEABODY MUSEUM OF SALEM

East India Sq., Liberty and Essex Sts., Salem (508) 745–1876 or (508) 745–9500. North on Interstate 93 to the junction of Interstate 95; north on Interstate 95 until it becomes State Rte. 128; north on 128 to State Rte. 114; head east on 114 and follow signs into Salem. Metered lot and limited free street parking.

Hours. Mon.–Sat., 10 A.M.–5 P.M.; Sun., 12 noon–5 P.M.; Thurs. until 9 P.M.

Costs. Adults, $4; students, $3; ages 6–16, $1.50; ages 5 and under, free.

The Peabody Museum of Salem (not to be confused with Harvard's Peabody Museum, listed earlier) is uniquely New England, not simply because of its regional maritime connection, but because during the 19th century Salem was home base for the lucrative China trade. Exhibits range from many of the riches brought to Salem from China, Japan, and the islands of the South Pacific, to ship models and tools used by both ship captains and those who remained on land and worked at the Customs House.

Kids' Facilities. No stroller rentals. No diaper-changing tables in restrooms (plenty of benches, however). No food or bottle-warming facilities.

Ratings. A feast of colorful artworks from around the Pacific, one can fault the Peabody only for having too much to see. We stayed two hours without looking at our watches. Children are easily captivated by the colorful, exotic artifacts on display. All ages, A.

HOTELS

Bargains are few and far between and, when found, often require a certain amount of hardship, such as noise, smoke stench in rooms, and less-than-perfect television sets. At present, Boston has only one all-suites hotel, the Embassy Suites.

Boston Central

EMBASSY SUITES HOTEL

400 Soldier's Field Rd. at the River St. Bridge. (617) 783-0090. Use the Central Square station in Cambridge on the Red T line. Hotel located about 10 blocks to the west of the station. (310 units.) Pay parking.

Rates. $165 to $190.

As with other Embassy Suites, this hotel is clean, roomy, and luxurious. Located on the Charles River across from Cambridge, the hotel allows kids under 18 to stay free in the same suite as the parents.
Cribs: Yes, no charge.
Rollaways: Yes, $10.
Babysitting: Yes, see guest services.
Pool: Yes, indoor.
Restaurants: Yes.
Kitchen facilities: Yes.
Room service: Yes.
Closest emergency hospital: Massachusetts General, 15 minutes away, (617) 726–2000.

Boston East

RAMADA HOTEL—EAST BOSTON

225 McClellan Hwy. (617) 569–5250. Use the Airport station on the Blue T line. 240 rooms. Pay parking.

Rates. $109.

If the muffled sound of jet plane traffic won't disrupt your sleep, this convenient Ramada offers reasonable rates. Kids 11 and under stay free with parents.
Cribs: Yes, no charge.
Rollaways: Yes, no charge.
Babysitting: No.
Pool: Yes, indoor plus Jacuzzis.
Restaurants: Yes.
Kitchen facilities: No.
Room service: Yes.
Closest emergency hospital: Winthrop Hospital, 10 minutes away, (617) 846–2600.

Cambridge

SHERATON COMMANDER HOTEL

16 Garden St. (617) 547–4800. Use the Harvard station on the Red T line. 174 units. Pay parking.

Rates. $139 to $149.

The Sheraton is located a stone's throw from the Cambridge Common near both Harvard University and Radcliffe College, and only a few blocks from the Harvard T station. Children 17 and under stay free in their parents' room.
Cribs: Yes, no charge.
Rollaways: Yes, $15.
Babysitting: No.
Pool: No.
Restaurants: Yes.
Kitchen facilities: No.
Room service: Yes.
Closest emergency hospital: Mt. Auburn Hospital, 10 minutes away, (617) 492–3500.

QUALITY INN CAMBRIDGE

1651 Massachusetts Ave. (617) 491–1000. Use the Harvard station on the Red T line. 135 units. Free parking.

Rates. $94.
Four blocks from the Harvard T station, this is a great bargain by Cambridge standards. Very close to public transportation. Kids 16 and under stay free in their parents' room.
Cribs: Yes, $8.
Rollaways: Yes, $8.
Babysitting: No.
Pool: Yes, outdoor.
Restaurants: Yes.
Kitchen facilities: No.
Room service: Yes.
Closest emergency hospital: Mt. Auburn Hospital, 10 minutes away, (617) 492–3500.

Newton

SUSSE CHALET—NEWTON

160 Boylston St. (State Rte. 9). (617) 527–9000. One-half mile west of the Chestnut Hill Mall station on the Green T line. 152 units. Free parking.

Rates. $44.70 to $49.03.
This is about as inexpensive as it gets in the Boston area without having to chain your toothbrush to the sink at night. If a clean (albeit small)

room with a television set is what you have in mind, this is the place. Kids under age 6 stay free with parents.

Cribs: Yes, $2.
Rollaways: No, biggest rooms have two double beds.
Babysitting: No.
Pool: Yes, outdoor.
Restaurants: Yes, a steak house and bar that does a land-office business at night.
Kitchen facilities: No.
Room service: No.
Closest emergency hospital: Newton-Wesley Hospital, 5 miles away on Rte. 16, (617) 243–6000.

RESTAURANTS

As far as national fast-food chains are concerned, they're all represented here. However, when it comes to restaurants with something extra for kids (balloons, singing Audio-Animatronic rodents, menus shaped like Bambi), you're out of luck.

THE RESTAURANTS OF THE FANEUIL HALL MARKETPLACE

Congress and North Sts., on the **Freedom Trail**. (617) 523–3886. Use the State station on the Orange or Blue T line. Pay lot parking.

Hours. Hours vary, but most restaurants are open Mon.–Thurs., 10 A.M.–10 P.M.; Fri. and Sat., 10 A.M.–11 P.M.; Sun., 12 noon–10 P.M.

From gooey chocolate donuts to lobster and thickly marbled prime rib, the Faneuil Hall Marketplace (see Shopping) offers something to tempt every palate. The marketplace includes five separate buildings: Faneuil Hall's ground level, Quincy Market, North Market, South Market, and Market Center. You can eat standing up or seated on a luxurious patio across from the site of the 1770 Boston Massacre. The restaurants are located at about the halfway point along the Freedom Trail and make a great lunchtime stop.

Kids' Facilities. Booster seats and high chairs are available at many, though not all, restaurants. No changing tables in restrooms.

NO-NAME RESTAURANT

15 ½ Boston Fish Pier, at Northern Ave. (617) 338–7539. Use the South station on the Red T line. Pay lot parking.

Hours. Daily, 11 A.M.–10 P.M.

One of the few places in town that serves an affordable lobster dinner, the dockside, no-frills No-Name has plenty of blue-collar charm and really packs in the customers on its two dining levels. While there are many single-family tables, some diners sit elbow to elbow with strangers at long communal tables. The seafood chowder is wonderful and a lobster dinner costs only about $14. No credit cards.

Kids' Facilities. High chairs and booster seats are available. No diaper-changing tables in restrooms. Special children's platters run $5.25 for dinner and $3.75 for lunch.

LEGAL SEAFOODS

One Park Plaza at Arlington, in Boston Park Plaza Hotel. (617) 426–4444. Use the Arlington station on the Green T line. Pay lot parking. (*Four other locations: Kendall Square in Cambridge; Chestnut Hill Mall in Newton; Worcester; and Burlington Mall.*)

Hours. Mon.–Thurs., 11 A.M.–10 P.M.; Fri. and Sat., 11 A.M.–11 P.M.; Sun., 12 noon–10 P.M.

Long famous for their take-home seafood operation at Boston's Logan Airport, the company has had a successful restaurant business for many years. Although the chalkboard lists the largest selection of seafood entrees in New England, tourists flock here for the lobster. The prices are on the top end of reasonable, with a lobster dinner about $18, depending upon availability. Always crowded. Credit cards.

Kids' Facilities. Booster seats and high chairs. No children's menus.

Big Splurges

UNION OYSTER HOUSE

41 Union St., on the **Freedom Trail**. (617) 227–2750. Use the State station on the Orange or Blue T line. Pay lot parking.

Hours. Sun.–Thurs., 11 A.M.–9:30 P.M.; Fri. and Sat., 11 A.M.–10 P.M.

The city's oldest restaurant (1826), the first floor is an oyster/clam bar where you can down a half dozen and listen to the button-down regulars engage in local gossip. Come in for the friendly, noisy, red-brick-and-dark-wood ambiance, and stay for a good seafood dinner at a moderate price (about $25 per person). Full bar. Reservations suggested. Credit cards.

MAISON ROBERT

45 School St., in the Old City Hall Building, on the **Freedom Trail**. (617) 227–3370. Use the Park station on the Red or Green T line. Pay lot parking.

Hours. Daily, 11 A.M.–10 P.M.

Despite its notoriety (it was one of the restaurants that replaced its regular coffee with Folger's instant in a television commercial), the two restaurants that make up Maison Robert—Bonhomme Richard and Ben's Cafe—are among the finest in Boston. A vagabond among restaurants, Maison Robert has moved three times in recent years and has settled in the Old City Hall building (1862) near the Granary Burial Ground. Ben's Cafe, on the first floor (with outdoor dining in the summer), is more informal and slightly less expensive. The salmon is wonderful as are any of the daily specials. Dinner for two (especially in the Bonhomme Richard) costs about $100, including drinks. The house wine is terrific, but there is also a huge cellar from which to order. Reservations urged. Major credit cards.

G'VANNI'S

2 Prince St. North End. (617) 720–3663. Use the Haymarket station on the Orange or Green T line. Pay lot or limited street parking.

Hours. Daily, 12 noon–12 midnight.

If intimate is what you want, G'vanni's is just what the marriage counselor ordered. With only about a dozen tables, strolling musicians, and soft lighting, it's the perfect place to get away for a quiet Italian dinner. Try the salmon piccata and the spinach in cream sauce with raisins and pine nuts. Dinner for two, with drinks, will run between $50 and $60. Full bar. Reservations recommended. Major credit cards.

SHOPPING

THE FANEUIL HALL MARKETPLACES

Congress and North Sts., on the **Freedom Trail**. (617) 523–3886. Use the State station on the Orange or Blue T line. Pay lot parking.

Hours. Mon.–Sat., 10 A.M.–9 P.M.; Sun., 12 noon–6 P.M.

The five buildings that comprise the Faneuil Hall Marketplace—Marketplace Center, Faneuil Hall, Quincy Market, North Market, and South Market—include hundreds of specialty shops and restaurants. While the marketplace as a whole covers every conceivable merchandise need, a few shops merit special mention.

Ever since the disappearance of whaling and the scarcity of legal sources of ivory, scrimshaw, the art of etching and staining ivory with intricate designs, has become almost nonexistent. Certain shops, however, can still import select pieces of ivory from animals exempted from the endangered lists. One of them is **Boston Scrimshanders**, in South Market Building, (617) 367–1552. Here you'll see some terrific engravings on the ivories of whales, elephants, long-extinct mastadons, and fossilized walruses. **Outermost Kites of Boston**, North Market Building, (617) 742–1455, specializes in all sorts of kites, from inexpensive assembly-line kites to one-of-a-kind, top-dollar flying gizmos. **Tales with Tails**, Quincy Market Building, (617) 227–8772, is a stuffed animal store that also sells children's books and toys.

Purple Panache, North Market Building (617) 277–0800, and **Hogwild**, (617) 367–9520, are stores with very specialized appeals. That's right, if you want an ever-changing array of merchandise with either a purple or porcine appeal, these two stores are for you. On the day we stopped by, neither store had a purple pig in stock. **Lefty**, in the North Market Building, (617) 523–2050, specializes in all sorts of gear, from scissors to measuring cups, for the left-handed among us. **Egyptian Bazaar**, Marketplace Center, (617) 951–0992, features all sorts of arts and crafts from Egypt. From rugs to jewelry to pottery, you can buy the merchandise and watch the artists creating their wares. You can also order custom-made items.

BOSTON CHILDREN'S MUSEUM GIFT SHOP

300 Congress St., Museum Wharf. (617) 426–8855. Use the South station on the Red T line and walk one block east, one block north, and another block east. Limited free parking.

Hours. Mid-June through Labor Day: daily, 10 A.M.–5 P.M.; Fri. until 9 P.M. Rest of the year: Tues.–Sun., 10 A.M.–5 P.M.; Fri. until 9 P.M. Closed on Mon. during the school year, unless a school holiday.

Boston's most creative kids' museum also has the city's best kids' store. Educational playthings are the ticket here, with all sorts of books, games, science toys, and puzzles topping the list. You can shop without paying a museum admission.

COMPUTER MUSEUM STORE

300 Congress St., Museum Wharf. (617) 426–2800 or (617) 423–6758. Use the South station on the Red T line and walk one block east, one block north, and another block east. Limited free parking.

Hours. Mid-June through Labor Day: daily, 10 A.M.–5 P.M.; Fri. until 9 P.M. Rest of the year: Tues.–Sun., 10 A.M.–5 P.M.; Fri. until 9 P.M. Closed on Mon. during the school year, unless a school holiday.

The Computer Museum's commercial outlet is open even to those who don't want to see the museum. There are lots of computer books and gifts for both the computer literate and the rest of us.

THE CHILDREN'S BOOK SHOP

237 Washington St., Brookline. (617) 734–7323. Use the Brookline Village station on the Green T line. Limited parking.

Hours. Mon.–Sat., 10 A.M.–5:30 P.M.; Thurs. until 8 P.M. During school year only: open Sun., 1 P.M.–5 P.M.

The owners of the decade-old Children's Book Shop remember well what it was like to discover the world of reading. Along with shelf upon shelf of terrific children's titles, they've designed the store with "reading holes," nooks and crannies kids can wedge themselves into and read.

TRANSPORTATION

If you can help it, try not to drive in Boston. There are few places to park that aren't exorbitantly expensive, the streets are narrow, and traffic always seems at a standstill.

BUSES, TROLLEYS, AND SUBWAYS

Boston may have some of the world's worst drivers, but it also has one of the nation's best public transportation systems. The system is administered by the Massachusetts Bay Transportation Authority (MBTA). Residents simply refer to the network as the T, which is signified by a black letter T in a circle, a symbol that is exhibited on the sides of buses, trolleys, subway cars, and at the entrances to subway stations. All public transportation is comfortable, clean, and safe.

A completely integrated system, the T subways operate almost exclusively underground within the downtown metropolitan area, with buses used in the few areas where subway lines are more than a couple of blocks away. Bus service is more extensive in the outlying suburbs, where the subways emerge from underground to travel on above-ground rails.

The subway is divided into four color-coded routes (red, blue, orange, and green), and radiates 10 miles outward from downtown where it connects with another light-rail system that serves areas as far away as Providence, Rhode Island.

MBTA charges only 60¢ for a bus or subway ride within the city, and $1.50 for service from outlying suburban stations into downtown Boston (an outward-bound ride costs only the basic rate of 60¢). Tokens or exact change are required. The MBTA runs between 5 A.M. and 12:30 A.M. Mondays through Saturdays, and on Sundays between 6 A.M. and 12:30 A.M. For more information, call (617) 722–5657, (617) 722–5672 or (617) 722–3200 between 6 A.M. and 11 P.M., or stop by the Park Street Boston Common Information Kiosk at the corner of Temple and Tremont Streets, located a few feet from the entrance to the Park T station.

TAXIS

In Boston, you can telephone for a taxi, hail a cruising cab from the sidewalk, or grab one at one of many cab stands around the city. The base rate is 90¢ for the first one-sixth of a mile and 20¢ for each additional one-sixth of a mile. That translates to $1.90 for the first mile. Within the downtown area, cabbing isn't that expensive a proposition. Just remember that traffic jams affect cabs, too, and the subway may be faster. Major cab companies include Town Taxi, (617) 536–5000, Checker, (617) 536–7000, and the Independent Taxi Operators Association, (617) 426–8700.

TOURS

BUS

Gray Line. (617) 426–8805. Tours range in scope from their 3-hour Greater Boston tour, which covers some of the best-known sites along the Freedom Trail, plus Harvard and M.I.T. (adults, $15; up to three children per family free), to trips to Lexington and Concord, Plymouth, Cape Cod, and a combination bus/ferry ride to Martha's Vineyard (adults, $42; children, free). Pickups are made at strategic hotels.

Beantown Trolleys and Brush Hill Tours. (617) 236–2148. Offers a 3-hour Boston Adventure tour (adults, $15; ages 6–12, $8) and excursions to Lexington and Concord, Cape Cod, Plymouth, and Salem. They also offer a 1½-hour Freedom Trail tour on an authentic 1920 trolley car that you can board and reboard at various stops along the way (adults, $11; ages 6–12, $5; ages 5 and under, free).

North Shore Tours. (617) 777–3288. Takes passengers on half and full-day tours of Boston and New England (from $15 to $20 for adults, depending on the trip; kids under 14, half fare).

Hub Bus Lines, (617) 776–0630, **and Boston Double Deckers,** (617) 739–0100. Offer competitively priced Freedom Trail tours between late spring and early fall.

BOAT

Bay State Cruises. (617) 723–7800. The area's largest steamship touring company offers everything from an hour-long Boston harbor sight-seeing cruise (adults, $4; kids, $2) to 3-hour excursions to Provincetown on the tip of Cape Cod (adults, $20; kids, $13). Bay State also provides medium-length excursions to some of the gorgeous islands in Boston Bay.

Best Tours, (617) 742–4265, **Mass Bay Lines,** (617) 749–4500, **and Boston Haor Cruises,** (617) 227–4320. Also offer competitively priced Boston Harbor sightseeing excursions.

Skyline Cruises. (617) 523–2169. Takes passengers on a 50-minute cruise (summer only) along the Charles River between the Boston Museum of Science and the Harvard (Massachusetts Avenue) Bridge. It gives passengers a unique view of the river, downtown Boston, and downtown Cambridge.

WALKING

Boston By Foot. (617) 367–2345, offers a 90-minute "Heart of the Freedom Trail" walking tour between May 1 and October 31 ($5). They also offer a scaled-down, hour-long walk for children between the ages of 6 and 12, dubbed "Boston by Little Feet" (a parent must tag along).

The Black Heritage Trail. (617) 445–7400. To dig deeply into the roots of Boston's 19th-century black community, make an appointment for a guided tour (adults, $5; children, $2.50).

The Make Way For Ducklings Tour. (617) 426–1898, traces the route of the ducks in Robert McCloskey's famed children's book. It begins on the Boston Common and ends with a ride in the popular Swan Boats. The Saturdays-only tour runs in late spring and throughout the summer.

Uncommon Boston. (617) 266–9768. Customized tours of Boston and vicinity. Personalized service is the key here (Prices vary depending on tour).

SEASONAL EVENTS

March

ST. PATRICK'S DAY

On March 17, the green beer flows all over metropolitan Boston, especially southeast of the Fort Point Channel in South Boston where most of the Irish reside. Parades punctuate the day's activities. The 17th is also celebrated as Evacuation Day: the day British troops were forced to pull out of Boston in 1776.

April

PATRIOTS' DAY

The midnight ride of Paul Revere and the Battle of Lexington and Concord are celebrated on the third Monday of April to commemorate the battle on April 18 and 19, 1775 that touched off the Revolutionary War. Patriot's Day also marks the annual running of the 26-mile Boston Marathon from suburban Hopkinton to Boston's Back Bay. Contact the Convention and Visitors Bureau, (617) 536–4100, for locations and times of activities.

June

BUNKER HILL REENACTMENT

On the Sunday before June 17, a large group of military hobbyists reenacts the 1775 battle that rallied patriots to the Revolutionary cause. All the action takes place on the streets of Charlestown and at the Bunker Hill Monument. For more information: (617) 242–5641.

July

HARBORFEST

The annual harbor festivities take place between the Thursday and Monday of the Fourth of July weekend. Along with an expanded schedule of harbor cruises, arts festivals, and musical events, there is the annual U.S.S. *Constitution* turnaround cruise—the only time the great old ship leaves her berth in the Charlestown Navy Yard. Events culminate on Monday night with a Boston Pops Orchestra concert at the Hatch Bandshell (at Mt. Vernon Street and Storrow Drive on the Charles River). The finale is always the *1812 Overture*, complete with cannon and fireworks.

December

BOSTON TEA PARTY REENACTMENT

The reenactment of the December 16, 1773, tea dumping takes place at the Tea Party Ship, permanently docked on the Congress Street Bridge next to the Boston Tea Party Museum. For more information: (617) 338–1773.

CHRISTMAS CAROLING

Check the local newspapers for annual Christmas activities, which include midmonth caroling services at Trinity Church on Copley Square and Christmas Eve caroling on Louisburg Square in Beacon Hill.

CHILDREN'S THEATER

PUPPET SHOWPLACE THEATRE

32 Station St., Brookline. (617) 731–6400. Use the Brookline Village station on the Green T line. Limited parking.

Established in 1974, the Puppet Showplace Theatre has become a Boston area institution, offering dozens of original programs and adaptations of fairy tales. During the school year, shows take place on Saturday and Sunday afternoons at 1 P.M. and 3 P.M.; during the summer months, shows are given on Wednesday and Thursday at 3 P.M. Shows are recommended for children over the age of 5. Tickets are $4 for both adults and children.

BABYSITTING SERVICES

PARENTS IN A PINCH
(617) 739–5437

Barbara Markus has been in the sitting business since 1984 and can access nearly 200 Boston area babysitters. All staff members are personally screened and receive first-aid training. Since hotel and convention business is their mainstay, the cost is considerably higher than their counterparts in other areas of the country: $10 per hour with a 4-hour minimum, plus transportation costs ($1.20 for subway during the day; cab fare after 8 P.M.). Each additional child is charged at a rate of 50¢ per hour.

PUBLICATIONS

Boston Globe. Daily newspaper; excellent weekend calendar of events.

Boston Herald. Daily newspaper; calendar of events in Friday "Weekend" section.

Boston Phoenix. Weekly alternative paper; entertainment listings.

The Boston Parents' Paper. Monthly paper, calendar of events plus discount coupons.

LOCAL TELEPHONE NUMBERS

Late-hours pharmacy: Phillip's Drug Co., 155 Charles St., Boston (at the Charles St. T station on the Red line), (617) 523–1028 or (617) 523–4372. Open 24 hours.
Consumer complaints: State: (617) 727–8400; city: (617) 725–3320.
Dental referral: Massachusetts Dental Society, (617) 651–7511 or (800) 342–8747.
Physician referral: Massachusetts Medical Society, (800) 322–2303.
Lawyer referral: Bar Association, (617) 661–1010.
Drug-abuse hotline: (617) 565–2800.
Poison-control hotline: (617) 232–2120.
Traveler's aid: (617) 542–7286.
Tourism office: (617) 536–4100.
Police: 911; some area cities are not on the 911 system.
Fire: 911; some area cities are not on the 911 system.
Ambulance: 911; some area cities are not on the 911 system.
Road conditions: (617) 973–7500.
Weather: (617) 936–1234.
Local car rental: Bob Brest Auto World, Lynn, (617) 599–1200.

◆

CHICAGO

Years before Chicago was recognized as a terrific family vacation spot, poet Carl Sandburg proclaimed it to be the "stormy, husky, brawling City of the Big Shoulders." If we are to take Sandburg at his word, those big shoulders would have toppled long ago without Chicago's granite feet—its bedrock anchor for three of the world's five tallest buildings. The very fact that Chicago brags about its big buildings (and everything else) says something about its character. The city's lust for being the busiest and biggest at everything from commerce to art has been apparent since the city's founding more than 150 years ago.

In the years preceding 1833, Chicago was known as Fort Dearborn, a United States military outpost that protected the Illinois Territory from the British and the Blackhawk Indians. Successful at both tasks, the city grew. A small town at the edge of a lake that was frozen most of the winter, Chicago bowed commercially to downstate Cairo at the junction of the Mississippi and Ohio rivers, until the advent of the railroad. Seeing a mighty opportunity, Chicago's city fathers courted the railroads. When the rails emerged as the most popular commercial mode of transport of the 19th century, Chicago became the Midwest hub. Cattle, farm produce and grains, and manufactured goods all came to Chicago first before being shipped elsewhere. Men got rich, primary manufacturing grew, and Chicago got bigger.

Chicago's resilience has been apparent ever since a fire in 1871 destroyed half the city. A massive rebuilding program produced 3,000 new structures in less than a year. While they were at it, Chicago engineers also changed the direction of the Chicago River to make it flow inward from Lake Michigan. In slightly more than twenty years after the fire, Chicago hosted the 1893 World's Columbian Exposition, that year's world's fair.

In the Chicago of the late 20th century, a four-sided gander at the Sears Tower—at 1,454 feet high, the world's tallest building—gives credence

FREEBIES AND CHEAPIES
(Free or $3.50 and under for adults)

- ❑ Museum of Science and Industry (see Museums)
- ❑ Oriental Institute (see Museums)
- ❑ Shedd Aquarium (see Attractions)
- ❑ Field Museum of Natural History (see Museums)
- ❑ Buckingham Fountain (see Attractions)
- ❑ Lincoln Park Zoo (see Attractions)
- ❑ Petrillo Music Shell (see Attractions)

THE LONG WEEKEND

Day One

- ❑ Museum of Science and Industry (see Museums)

Day Two

- ❑ Sears Tower Skydeck (see Attractions)
- ❑ Adler Planetarium (see Attractions)
- ❑ Shedd Aquarium (see Attractions)
- ❑ Art Institute (see Museums)

Day Three

- ❑ Lincoln Park Zoo (see Attractions)
- ❑ Expressways Children's Museum (see Museums)
- ❑ Chicago Academy of Sciences (see Museums)
- ❑ Mercury or Wendella Cruise of Chicago River (see Tours)

to the civic bombast. Always a top manufacturing center, the city has never limited itself in commercial pursuits. When one industry fades, a new one quickly replaces it. As the production of heavy machinery departed for Japan and Korea, high-tech industries grew. When the railroads began to fade, Chicago became the hub for air travel. Not content to let New York City possess the advertising industry, Chicago became a major force in the business. Recently, the city has even begun to lure television and movie production away from Hollywood.

Say what you will about the excesses of Chicago's entrepreneurs and first families, they concentrated on beautifying their city, making it a place worth its weight in vacation gold for travelers of every stripe, especially for families with children. Chicago's captains of industry built many of the parks and buildings that have become some of the most-visited attractions in the United States: the Field Museum of Natural History, the Museum of Science and Industry, and the University of Chicago, to name but a few.

CLIMATE

In spring, expect chills at night (sometimes freezes). In summer, daytime temperatures average in the 70s, but they can easily go into the 90s and at night can dip into the 50s. In autumn, daytime temperatures average between 70 and 40. With the deciduous trees ablaze in color, autumn is one of the nicest times to visit Chicago. In winter (December through March), temperatures often hang below freezing in the daytime and dip even lower at night.

Because of the presence of Lake Michigan, summers near the water tend to be a few degrees cooler than inland. Likewise, winters tend to be milder. Umbrellas and rain parkas should be part of any traveling family's ensemble all year long. Wool gloves and hats should accompany the family in spring, fall, and winter.

PARKING

Parking can be expensive. Most downtown parking garages charge $1 to $1.25 for 20 minutes, with a maximum from $8 to $10 per day. Most meters cost around 25¢ per half hour.

TOURIST INFORMATION

Contact the Chicago Tourism Council, 806 N. Michigan Ave., Chicago, IL. 60611, (312) 280–5740. The Visitor Eventline, (312) 225–2323, gives up-to-the-minute recorded information 24 hours a day.

ATTRACTIONS

ADLER PLANETARIUM

1300 S. Lake Shore Dr. (312) 322–0300. Limited meter parking available on-site; lot parking 2 blocks away.

Hours. Mon.–Thurs., 9:30 A.M.–4:30 P.M.; Fri., 9:30 A.M.–9 P.M.; Sat. and Sun., 9:30 A.M.–5 P.M. Closed on Christmas. Times vary for sky-shows.

Costs. General admission free. Planetarium skyshows: adults, $2.50; kids 6–18, $1.25; under age 6, not allowed except to a special children's show on Sat, at 10 A.M.

Adler Planetarium has plenty of colorful hands-on exhibits, including photos from the Voyager satellite missions, a Space Shuttle quiz with plenty of buttons to push, and scales that show your weight on the sun, the moon, Mars, and Jupiter. A number of telescopes are aimed at an artificial sky programmed to show all sorts of heavenly happenings. The Planetarium also displays loads of early navigational tools, quite a few antique telescopes, a moon rock, and space suits worn by NASA astro-nauts.

Kids' Facilities. A cafeteria on the lower level sells sandwiches and fast food. The dining area has recently been remodeled to impart an interstellar flavor. No diaper-changing tables or bottle-warming facilities. No stroller rentals.

Ratings. While science-minded grade schoolers and older kids will find it fascinating, most exhibits will leave preschoolers in the dark. 2–7, D; 8–11, B; 12–16, A.

BUCKINGHAM FOUNTAIN

Congress Ave. at Columbus Dr., in Grant Park. Parking at a number of city lots within a few blocks.

Hours. Memorial Day through Labor Day: daily, 11:30 A.M.–10:30 P.M.

Costs. Free.

Constructed in 1927, the Buckingham Fountain is a copy of the famed Versailles Fountain in France—only larger. At night, it's colorfully lighted. Close your eyes and imagine yourself either in pre-Revolutionary France or in the midst of the demonstrations during the 1968 Democratic Con-vention.

Kids' Facilities. No stroller rentals. No diaper-changing tables (plenty of benches, however). No food or bottle-warming facilities.

Ratings. One of the prettier fountains in the United States, it's well worth a stroll through the park. All ages, A.

JAMES C. PETRILLO MUSIC SHELL

Jackson Ave. at Columbus Dr., in Grant Park. (312) 294–2420. Parking at a number of city lots within a few blocks.

Hours. Summer evenings.

Costs. Free.

The focal point of the city's annual summer Lakefront Music Festival, this amphitheater setting amidst the beauty of Grant Park is an ideal place to spend a summer evening. Concerts that range from the classics to pop are presented from late June through August. Concert times vary; call for a listing of shows.

Kids' Facilities. No stroller rentals. No diaper-changing facilities. No bottle-warming facilities or food.

Ratings. This depends a lot on your children's appreciation for music. Since the concerts start rather late in the evening, it may not be suitable for young children. 2–7, C; 8–11, B; 12–16, A.

CHICAGO SUN-TIMES TOUR

401 N. Wabash Ave. (312) 321–2032. Parking at a number of pay lots in the area.

Hours. Mon.–Fri., 10:30 A.M.

Costs. Free, but reservations are required.

This is a great opportunity to see the workings of a large metroplitan newspaper. Visitors are taken to view the newsroom, composing room, and pressroom. If you're lucky, you may even catch a glimpse of movie critic Roger Ebert as he prepares to match wits with rival Chicago Tribune critic Gene Siskel, who works a block and a half away.

Kids' Facilities. No stroller rentals. No diaper-changing tables. No food or bottle-warming facilities.

Ratings. The tour is wonderful but is off-limits to children under age 10. 2–9, not allowed; 10–16, A.

CHICAGO TRIBUNE TOUR

777 W. Chicago Ave. (312) 222–3993. Metered street parking and pay parking in garages.

Hours. Mon.–Fri., 10:30 A.M. and 1:30 P.M.

Costs. Free, but reservations are required.

Not to be outdone by the Sun-Times, the Tribune offers two daily tours. Which is the better tour? It's a toss-up.

Kids' Facilities. No stroller rentals. No diaper-changing tables. No food or bottle-warming facilities.

Ratings. Great, but children under 10 not allowed; 10–16, A.

CHICAGO POLICE DEPARTMENT

1121 S. State St. (312) 744–5570. Limited to metered street parking, which is sometimes scarce.

Hours. Two tours Mon.–Fri. (no holidays), 10 A.M. and 2 P.M. Tour group size, 17–35 people.

Costs. Free.

The James J. Riordan Headquarters Building is a showplace of modern police technology. The most impressive sight on the tour is the communications center, where the cops field phone calls from all over the city. You'll never again wonder what happens when you dial 911.

Kids' Facilities. No stroller rentals. No diaper-changing tables in the restrooms. No food or bottle-warming facilities.

Ratings. This tour is wonderful but only for older kids: No one under age 12 is allowed. 2–11, not allowed; 12–16, A.

LINCOLN PARK ZOO

2200 N. Cannon Dr. (312) 294–4660. Meter and nonmeter parking available along street and in park.

Hours. Zoo area: daily, 8 A.M.–5:15 P.M. Zoo buildings: daily, 9 A.M.–5 P.M. Open 365 days a year.

Costs. Free.

The 35-acre Lincoln Park Zoo is one of the best (and last) free zoos in the country. Situated in a gorgeous lakeside park setting, it features world-class reptile, primate, great ape, and lion houses, as well as a children's zoo and the recently opened Farm in the Zoo, a scaled-down version of a real working farm.

Kids' Facilities. Three fast-food eating stations are located at the northern end of the zoo, as well as a sit-down restaurant. There are changing tables in a few of the ladies' restrooms. Strollers can be rented on Cannon Drive near the east entrance.

Ratings. Considering that most zoos charge admission, the Lincoln Park Zoo is a real deal. In summer, you're close enough to Lake Michigan to catch a breeze. All ages, A.

LINCOLN PARK CONSERVATORY

Stockton Dr. at E. Fullerton Ave. (312) 294–4770. Metered and nonmetered parking available on the street and in lots near entrance.

Hours. Daily, 9 A.M.–5 P.M.

Costs. Free.

Breathtaking outdoor and indoor gardens make the Conservatory a great companion to the zoo, which is only a block away. The indoor Tropical and Palm houses are terrific respites on a chilly day. The Conservatory features both permanent exhibitions and a number of yearly flower shows.

Kids' Facilities. Diaper-changing surfaces in restrooms. No stroller rental here, but available at the zoo. No food or bottle-warming facilities.

Ratings. Small kids can get bored; however, moving from tundra to the tropics usually holds the attention of the younger ones long enough for the rest of the family to enjoy a quick visit. 2–7, C; 8–11, B; 12–16, B.

BROOKFIELD ZOO

1st Ave. and 31st St., Brookfield. (312) 485–0263. Lot parking, $2.

Hours. May 1 through September 30: daily, 9:30 A.M.–6 P.M. Rest of the year: 10 A.M.–5 P.M.

Costs. Adults, $2.25; ages 6–11, 75¢: under age 6, free. Children's zoo: adults, $1; ages 3–11, 50¢. Seven Seas Panorama (dolphin show): adults, $1.50; ages 4–11, 75¢; under age 4, free.

This 204-acre zoo has more than 2,000 animals on view. Highlights include Tropic World, the world's largest indoor zoo exhibit, where indoor thunderstorms are staged three times a day; and the new Seven Seas Panorama, where dolphins and sea lions cavort. The children's zoo allows kids to pet the animals. What with all the exhibits, a motorized safari, and a 2-foot-gauge steam train (summer and fall), the Brookfield Zoo is an all-day affair.

Kids' Facilities. Diaper changing in restrooms. Plenty to eat and drink at snack bars and restaurants (bottle-warming available at sit-down restaurant). Stroller rentals available near zoo entrance.

Ratings. A terrific zoo for those who want to get out of the city for a day. All ages, A.

JOHN HANCOCK BUILDING OBSERVATION DECK

875 N. Michigan Ave. (312) 751–3681. Little street parking available, but expensive parking lots abound in the area, including inside the Hancock Building.

Hours. Daily, 9 A.M.–12 midnight.

Costs. Adults, $2.50; ages 5–15, $1.50; under age 5, free.

It almost seems silly to ride to the Hancock's 94th floor when you can go to the 103rd floor at the Sears Tower, the world's tallest. However, if you're in the neighborhood, the Hancock gives you pretty much the same view as Sears.

Kids' Facilities. No stroller rentals. No diaper-changing tables (but benches in lobby). No bottle-warming facilities.

Ratings. Kids young and old love the view. All ages, A.

SEARS TOWER SKYDECK

Wacker Dr. and Adams St. (312) 875–9696. Pay public parking garage located at the corner of Adams and Franklin.

Hours. Daily, 9 A.M.–12 midnight. Tickets sold until 11:30 P.M.

Costs. Adults, $3; ages 5–12, $2.50; under age 5, free with adult.

No doubt about it, this is as high you can go building-wise in the city, the country, or the world—103 stories and 1,350 feet above the pavement.

The elevator ride takes a mere 90 seconds. On a clear day, you can see four states. The price of admission includes a 7-minute multimedia slide show, the *Chicago Experience*. If you already know that Chicago is a great city and an ethnic melting pot, skip it and head directly to the elevator for the ear-popping ride to the top.

Kids' Facilities. No stroller rentals. No diaper-changing tables in the restrooms (use benches). Food and souvenirs are available in the lower lobby.

Ratings. The tower provides the best view in town of the boats on the lake and the planes landing at O'Hare Airport. All ages, A.

SHEDD AQUARIUM

1200 S. Lake Shore Dr. (312) 939–2426. Pay parking lots across Lake Shore Dr. at the Field Museum of Natural History.

Hours. Daily, 9 A.M.–5 P.M.

Costs. Adults, $2; ages 6–17, $1; ages 5 and under, free. Free on Thurs.

Thanks to a 1988 addition, the Shedd is now the world's largest indoor aquarium. Giant sea mammals have joined the 7,000-plus fish that swim in 200 display tanks. All the world's regions are represented. Caribbean fish are fed by staff divers every day at 11 A.M. and 2 P.M. at the aquarium's coral reef. Note: the galleries in which the tropical fish are viewed are quite warm, so dress accordingly.

Kids' Facilities. Diaper changing in ladies' restroom only. No stroller rentals. Also be aware of the twenty-two steps from the sidewalk to the main entrance. No bottle-warming facilities and no restaurant. The closest food is at McDonald's, across the street at the Field Museum.

Ratings. The Shedd is one of the best aquariums in the United States. At the coral reef exhibit, kids are allowed to touch some of the sea creatures, which either makes the littlest ones happy or puts them off fish sandwiches for a year. 2–7, B; 8–11, A; 12–16, A.

WATER TOWER AND VISITOR'S CENTER

Chicago Ave. and Michigan Ave. Street and garage parking available.

Hours. 24 hours a day.

Costs. Free.

While *Here's Chicago*, a slick, self-congratulatory multimedia show on the greatness of the city, packs them in at the old water pumping station across the street, the real attraction is the water tower itself. One of the few survivors of the infamous 1871 fire, the tower stands as a lone antique in the heart of the ultramodern Michigan Avenue shopping area.

Kids' Facilities. No stroller rentals. No diaper-changing tables. No food or bottle-warming facilities.

Ratings. Since you don't stop for long, the kids hardly know they're viewing an integral part of Chicago history. 2–7, B; 8–11, A; 12–16, A.

U.S.S. SILVERSIDES

Navy Pier, 600 E. Grand Ave. (312) 819–0055. Pay lot parking nearby.

Hours. 30-minute guided tours. Memorial Day to Labor Day: daily, 12 noon–6 P.M. Early March to May and September to early December: Sat. and Sun., 12 noon–6 P.M.

Costs. Adults, $2.50; under age 12, $1.

Navy Pier, Chicago's "Patio on the Lake" and home to a number of yearly festivals, is a wonderful place for strolls and lake's-eye views of the Chicago skyline. It's also the home of the U.S.S. *Silversides*, the most-decorated surviving World War II United States submarine. The tour takes visitors from stem to stern of the 312-foot vessel that, unlike the captured German U-boat at the Museum of Science and Industry, rests in the water and can still fire up her main engines.

Kids' Facilities. No stroller rentals. No diaper-changing tables. No restrooms. No bottle-warming or food facilities. Restrooms are located on the pier (changing table in ladies' rest room).

Ratings. Smaller kids may not appreciate the finer points of undersea travel, but the older ones, especially the boys, will. 2–7, C; 8–11, A; 12–16; A.

SIX FLAGS GREAT AMERICA

Interstate 94 and Rte. 132, Gurnee (located a few miles south of the Illinois-Wisconsin border, about midway between Chicago and Milwaukee). (312) 249–1776. Plenty of parking at $3 per car.

Hours. Hours vary from 10 A.M. to 8, 9, or 10 P.M. Mid-May through Labor Day: open daily. Early May and September: weekends only.

Costs. Adults and children ages 3 and up, $15.25; under 3, free.

Two-hundred-acre Six Flags Great America proves that what kids like best are junk food, gaudy trinkets, and stomach-churning rides. Great America has all that and more. The park recently opened an IMAX theater with movies on a 70-foot by 35-foot screen. It also has any number of stage shows and musical reviews.

Kids' Facilities. Plenty of places to buy fast food, change diapers, and get a bottle warmed. We suggest you take your own umbrella stroller.

Ratings. There is something here for every age. Plenty of food and plenty of fun. All ages, A.

RAVINIA MUSIC FESTIVAL

Ravinia Park, Highland Park (located approximately 20 miles north of the Loop on Interstate 94). (312) 728–4642. Limited parking in park lots.

Hours. Open June through September. Hours vary, depending on the concert.

Costs. Free.

Ravinia is a park where you can enjoy a picnic supper and let your children run ragged over 36 acres before and during concerts of classical music. Kids love the fact that they don't have to sit in uncomfortable seats. Concerts are given by the Chicago Symphony Orchestra and a number of visiting artists.

Kids' Facilites. No stroller rentals. Two restaurants (one indoor, the other outside) serve food if you choose not to pack your own. Plenty of bathroom facilities for older kids. Changing the little ones is best done on your own picnic blanket. Tip for parents: Take beach chairs for yourselves.

Ratings. Even though most little kids get antsy during regular concerts, the fresh air and exercise calms them down considerably by concert time. 2–7, C; 8–11, B; 12–16, A.

MUSEUMS

ART INSTITUTE OF CHICAGO

Michigan Ave. at Adams St. (312) 443–3622 for recorded message, (312) 443–3500 for general information. Underground parking available.

Hours. Mon., Wed., Thurs., Fri., 10:30 A.M.–4:30 P.M.; Tues., 10:30 A.M.–8 P.M.; Sat., 10 A.M.–5 P.M.; Sun., 12 noon–5 P.M.

Costs. Admission prices are only suggested, but you must pay something to enter. Adults, $4.50; under 18, $2.25; under age 6, free. Free on Tues. to all.

The Art Institute is one of the country's premier art showplaces. It is the happy repository of world-famous European paintings like Georges Seurat's *Sunday Afternoon on the Island of La Grande Jatte* and a wide assortment of Picassos, Renoirs, and Van Goghs; ancient Greek and Roman sculpture; select pieces of antique furniture; and an exhibit of weapons and suits of armor. Especially for kids is the Junior Museum, where children can view works of art at their eye level. Displays change and are varied. We saw two potters showing how to throw pots and allowing the kids to try their luck.

Kids' Facilities. Two museum stores, one in the Junior Museum. Three restaurants operate year-round, a cafeteria with sandwiches and two dining rooms with more formal menus. In the summer, an outdoor cafe is open. If a bottle needs warming, the restaurant staff can be of assistance. Changing facilities are relegated to a table in the ladies' restroom. Dads can use one of many gallery benches. You're allowed to bring in your own stroller (none for rent), but if it's large, you may have to fold it to get it through the narrow turnstiles.

Ratings. 2–7, B; 8–11, A; 12–16, A.

CHICAGO ACADEMY OF SCIENCES

2001 N. Clark St. at Lincoln Park. (312) 549–0606. Metered parking on street and in park.

Hours. Daily, 10 A.M.–5 P.M.

Costs. Adults, $1; kids under 18, 50¢. Free on Mon. to all.

The Academy's main exhibits are lifelike (but somewhat dated) dioramas depicting the forest, marshlands, and prairies of the upper Midwest. Walk-through exhibits featuring artists' renderings of local flora and fauna are like a nature hike without having to go outdoors. The Children's Gallery opened in 1987 and boasts interactive natural history activities for small children—plenty of live plants, live animals, and dead fossils to touch and examine.

Kids' Facilities. No stroller rentals. No diaper-changing tables in restrooms. No food or bottle-warming facilities. Strollers are permitted, but be prepared to carry them up three flights of stairs.

Ratings. The Children's Gallery has broadened the Academy's appeal to include children of every age. All ages, A.

FIELD MUSEUM OF NATURAL HISTORY

S. Lake Shore Dr. at Roosevelt Rd. (312) 922–9410. Lot parking available.

Hours. Daily, 9 A.M.–5 P.M.

Costs. Adults, $2; kids 6–17, $1; families, $4. Free on Thurs. to all.

The Field Museum is one of the most spectacularly large buildings you'll ever see: It has more than 10 acres of exhibits. The reassembled bones of two dinosaurs and the mummified remains of Jemutesonekh, a wealthy Egyptian woman who died about 1000 B.C., are the main drawing cards for older kids. Also, there are extensive Egyptology and American Indian exhibits. For smaller children, there's the hands-on Place for Wonder. A display called *Sizes* has the largest pair of Levi's ever made (size 76), a try-on pair of Chicago Bears shoulder pads, and a do-it-yourself standing broad jump that lets kids compare their jumping ability to that of other species.

Kids' Facilities. This place is user-friendly for small children. The lower level features a unisex diaper-changing and bottle-warming area. You can also rent a stroller, and there are plenty of places for worn-out parents to sit. There's a McDonald's restaurant downstairs.

Ratings. Great fun for all ages. All ages, A.

CHICAGO HISTORICAL SOCIETY

Clark St. at North Ave. (312) 642–4600. Metered parking on street and in park.

Hours. Mon.–Sat., 9:30 A.M.–4:30 P.M.; Sun., 12 noon–5 P.M.

Costs. Adults, $1.50; kids (6–17), 50¢; ages 5 and under, free on Mon. to all.

If you ever doubted that Abraham Lincoln was Illinois' favorite son, the Chicago Historical Society will correct that misconception. Lincoln memorabilia abounds here as do the trappings of early Chicago and both of the city's world's fairs. Well-preserved costumes and demonstrations of pioneer crafts make the Historical Society a must for history buffs. Older kids will enjoy sound booths where, with the touch of a button, they can hear old radio broadcasts and samples of Chicago jazz. There is also an audio-visual recreation of the 1871 Chicago fire.

Kids' Facilities. Diaper-changing tables in the ladies' restroom. Dads are left to their own devices. No stroller rental. No bottle-warming facilities.

Ratings. Excels educationally for older kids, but lacks enough audio-visual and tactile stimulation for the younger ones. 2–7, D; 8–11, C; 12–16, A.

EXPRESSWAYS CHILDREN'S MUSEUM

2045 N. Lincoln Park W. (312) 281–3222. Metered parking on street and in park.

Hours. Summer: Tues. and Wed., 9:30 A.M.–4:30 P.M.; Thurs. and Fri. 12:30 P.M.–4:30 P.M.; Sat. and Sun., 10 A.M.–3 P.M. Fall, winter, spring: Tues.–Fri., 12:30 P.M.–4:30 P.M.; Sat. and Sun., 10 A.M.–3 P.M. Closed on Mon.

Costs. Suggested donation: adults, $2; kids, $1.

Upstairs is *Touchy Business*, a place designed for kids from 3 to 7. Hands-on (and feet-on) exhibits include a kid-size furnished turn-of-the-century log cabin, a fantasy forest with mirrored walls, a vinyl-on-vinyl stick-'em wall for colored shapes, a crawl-through tunnel, and a rowboat filled with pillows. Kids just take off their shoes and run wild. Downstairs is *A Toddlin' Town*, a city-within-a-city featuring a newspaper office, a doctor's office, and an artist's gallery where kids can role play. Each "office" is a beautifully designed and painted miniature building. There's also a miniature city bus kids can "drive." This place is a favorite with the local preschool set.

Kids' Facilities. No problem with changing areas here: Tables in both men's and ladies' restrooms. No food or bottle-warming facilities. No stroller rentals.

Ratings. For children from 2 to 7, Expressways is probably the best attraction in Chicago. Above age 7, interest falls off quickly. 2–7, A; 8–11, D; 12–16, F.

MUSEUM OF SCIENCE AND INDUSTRY

57th St. and S. Lake Shore Dr. (312) 684–1414. Plenty of free parking in museum lot.

Hours. Memorial Day through Labor Day: daily, 9:30 A.M.–5:30 P.M.; Rest of the year: daily, 9:30 A.M.–4 P.M .; Sat. and Sun., 9:30 A.M.– 5:30 P.M.

Costs. Museum admission is free; however, certain attractions charge admission. Omnimax Theater: adults, $4; kids under 18, $2.50; the coal mine and the captured German submarine: adults, $1.50; kids under 18, $1.25.

This is easily one of the finest science and industry museums in the country and one of the most traveled-to attractions in the Midwest. There are more than 2,000 exhibits, many requiring pushing of buttons, in seventy-five large exhibition halls. Highlights include a simulated working coal mine, an IBM computer exhibit with a dozen terminals, the *Apollo 8* capsule, a dry-docked German submarine from World War II, and a 16-foot woolly mammoth. Junior-high-aged kids marvel at human cadavers sliced and preserved in sections between plates of glass (this exhibit is not for the squeamish). Curiosity Place, devoted to ages 6 and under, is a great touch-and-feel museum, but the hours are restricted: Mon., Tues., Thurs., Fri., 11:15 A.M.–3:30 P.M.; Wed., 10 A.M.–1:30 P.M.; Sat. and Sun., 10 A.M.–5 P.M.

Kids' Facilities. There is a snack bar and a restaurant, plus an area to eat bag lunches. Diapers can be changed at the first-aid station on the ground floor. No stroller rentals. No bottle-warming facilities.

Ratings. For smaller kids, remember that Curiosity Place has restricted hours (see above). With that in mind: All ages, A.

THE ORIENTAL INSTITUTE AT THE UNIVERSITY OF CHICAGO

1155 E. 58th St. (312) 962–9520. Street parking.

Hours. Tues.–Sat., 10 A.M.–4 P.M.; Sun., 12 noon–4 P.M. Tours (by appointment): Tues.–Sat., 10 A.M., 11:30 A.M., 1 P.M. and 2:30 P.M. Sun., 2:30 P.M.

Costs. Free.

This museum features archaeological artifacts dating back to 5000 B.C., many of which came from University of Chicago digs in the Middle East. Much of the collection comes from ancient Egypt, Persia, Palestine, and Mesopotamia.

Kids' Facilities. No stroller rentals. No diaper-changing tables in restrooms. No bottle-warming or food services.

Ratings. A must for archaeology buffs from age 12 up. If your kids aren't interested in the subject matter, you might be wise to pass it up. 2–7, F; 8–11, D; 12–16, A.

TELEPHONY MUSEUM

225 W. Randolph St. (in lobby of Illinois Bell Bldg.). (312) 727–2994. Pay parking lots nearby. No street parking to speak of.

Hours. Mon.–Fri., 8:30 A.M.–4 P.M. Closed on holidays.

Costs. Free.

This tiny museum shows you everything you want to know about the history of the telephone and does it quickly. You can see how electromechanical switching works (what happens when you dial) and a working demonstration of microwave communications. The museum displays all sorts of old phones, including experimental models that never made it into general production.

Kids' Facilities. No stroller rentals. No diaper-changing tables. No bathrooms. No food or bottle-warming facilities.

Ratings. There are a few hands-on exhibits that should appeal to ages 7 and up. If you're in a rush, you can do this musuem in less than a half hour and be on your way. 2–7, C; 8–11, B; 12–16 B.

HOTELS

LENOX HOUSE

616 N. Rush St. at E. Ontario. (312) 337–1000 or (800) 455–3669 (outside Illinois). 330 units. Pay parking.

Rates. Small suites, $95–$105; medium suites, $120–$130; 1-bedroom suites, $140–$150. Weekends: small suites, $59; 1-bedroom suites, $89.

This well-appointed 16-story converted apartment building is right in the heart of town, within walking distance of the Loop and Michigan Avenue shops. Each suite has a queen-size sofa sleeper and accommodates up to four adults without an extra charge. Kids 16 and under stay free.
Cribs: Yes, free.
Rollaways: Yes, $10 per night.
Babysitting: Yes, concierge referral.
Pool: No, but for $6 you have access to one at the nearby Marriott.
Restaurants: Two: a full-service restaurant and a coffee shop.
Kitchen facilities: Full kitchen and refrigerator.
Room service: Yes.
Closest emergency hospital: Northwestern Hospital, 5 minutes away, (312) 908–5222.

BARCLAY CHICAGO HOTEL

166 E. Superior St. (312) 787–6000. 120 suites. Pay parking.

Rates. Three styles of suites: deluxe, $145; parlor, $165; 1-bedroom, $195. Weekend rates as low as half the weekday price.

The Barclay is a beautiful hotel for the family with a few bucks to rub together. Each suite has a queen-size sleeper sofa. Nearly all the suites have full kitchens, and all have refrigerators and wet bars. Children under 12 stay free with parents.
Cribs: Yes, free.
Rollaways: Yes, free.
Babysitting: Yes, concierge referral.
Pool: Yes, outdoor roof pool.
Restaurants: Two: the Barclay Club (for hotel guests only) and Benihana of Tokyo.
Kitchen facilities: Yes, full kitchens in most suites.
Room service: Yes.
Closest emergency hospital: Northwestern Hospital, 1 block away, (312) 908–5222.

RESIDENCE INN CHICAGO—O'HARE

9450 W. Lawrence Ave., Schiller Park (located 20 miles northwest of the Loop off Interstate 90, 2 miles southeast of O'Hare Airport). (312) 678–2210. 174 units. Free parking.

Rates. Small suites range from $95 to $115; larger suites, from $115 to $135. Special weekend rates also available.

Part of the Marriott Residence Inn chain, this all-suites property offers nonsmoking suites, barbecues, Jacuzzis, and special activities for children. Their stock in trade is corporate executive relocation, but the 1-, 2-, and 3-bedroom suites are perfect for traveling families. Kids under 18 stay free with parents.

Cribs: Yes, $5 per night.
Rollaways: Yes, $10 per night.
Babysitting: Yes, concierge referral.
Pool: No.
Restaurants: No, but there's one next door.
Room service: No, but free continental breakfast and evening snack are served.
Kitchen facilities: Yes, full kitchens.
Closest emergency hospitals: Holy Family Hospital, in Des Plaines, 10–15 minutes away, (312) 297–1800, and Gottlieb Hospital, in Melrose Park, 10–15 minutes away, (312) 450–4905.

RADISSON SUITES HOTEL—O'HARE

5500 N. River Rd., Rosemont (located 20 miles northwest of the Loop off Interstate 90, 3 ½ miles northeast of O'Hare Airport). (312) 678–4000 or (800) 228–9822. 296 units. Free parking.

Rates. Suites range from $140 to $150. On weekends, the rates drop to $75 per night (based on two nights).

This all-suites hotel features an indoor pool and a game room for kids. The kitchens have microwave ovens, and each living room has a queen-size sofa sleeper. A free continental breakfast is served daily. Kids under 17 stay free with parents.

Cribs: Yes, free.
Rollaways: No.
Babysitting: Yes, concierge referral.
Pool: Yes, indoor.
Restaurant: Yes.
Kitchen facilities: Yes, full kitchens with microwave ovens.
Room service: Yes.
Closest emergency hospitals: Holy Family Hospital, in Des Plaines, 10–15 minutes away, (312) 297–1800, and Gottlieb Hospital, in Melrose Park, 10–15 minutes away, (312) 450–4905.

RESTAURANTS

Chicago has plenty of national chains like Burger King, Wendy's, and McDonald's. On top of that, the Windy City also offers up a local fast-food delicacy—deep-dish "Chicago style" pizza that, along with thicker dough, has nearly twice the amount of cheese found on thin-crust pizza. You'll find pizza parlors in every part of the city, and we've yet to find one that serves a substandard pizza.

MCDONALD'S

600 N. Clark St. (Ohio and Clark). (312) 664–7940. Plenty of free parking.

Hours. Open 24 hours. Delivery to local hotels between 9 A.M. and 3 P.M.

Normally we wouldn't mention the Golden Arches, but this place deserves your attention. It's huge and filled stem to stern with rock 'n' roll memorabilia: movie posters, neon lights, working (and free!) jukeboxes, and blazing movie screens. There's a vintage Chevrolet Corvette and life-size plaster statues of the Beatles. And because it's McDonald's, the price is right! Cash only.

Kids' Facilities. Plenty of high chairs and booster seats. No diaper-changing tables.

THE HARD ROCK CAFE

63 W. Ontario. (312) 943–2252. Pay valet parking and limited metered street parking.

Hours. Sun.–Fri., 11:30 A.M.–12:30 A.M.; Sat., 11 A.M.–1:30 A.M.

The first things you notice in this carbon copy of the London, Los Angeles, and New York Hard Rocks are the unmistakable odor of charcoaled meat and the pulsating sounds of loud rock 'n' roll. Despite the noise, you'll enjoy the people-watching, and the menu is chock-full of inexpensive to moderately priced sandwiches. Dinners run about $10. Alcohol available. Credit cards.

Kids' Facilities. For kids over 5. No high chairs, no booster seats, and no kid's menu. No diaper-changing tables in the restrooms.

ED DEBEVIC'S

640 N. Wells St. (312) 664–1707. Valet parking and limited metered street parking.

Hours. Mon.–Thurs., 11 A.M.–12 midnight; Fri. and Sat., 11 A.M.–1 A.M.; Sun., 11 A.M.–11 P.M.

Fifties-style dining is in these days, and Ed Debevic's is at the cutting edge of movement. Like sister restaurants in Torrance and Beverly Hills, California, and Phoenix, Arizona, Ed's flagship operation specializes in vintage American cuisine (burgers, milk shakes, blue plate specials, etc.) served by sassy waitresses in starched uniforms. Juke box controls are installed in each booth. Prices for dinner run between $10 and $20. No credit cards, cash only—just like in the 1950s.

Kids' Facilities: High chairs and booster seats are available, but no children's menus and no changing tables in the restrooms.

THE ORIGINAL MITCHELL'S

101 W. North Ave. at Clark St. of (312) 642–5246. Metered parking available.

Hours. Sun.–Thurs., 6 A.M.–1:30 A.M.; Fri. and Sat., open all night.

This family restaurant claims "We pamper all kids." Their stock in trade is breakfast; however, they serve fish, daily specials, steaks, and vegetarian specialties. Costs are moderate—breakfast and lunch run in the neighborhood of $5, dinners $7 to $10—and the hours are right for any dining whim, They also deliver. It's a great place to go after the Lincoln Park Zoo or the Expressways Children's Museum. No credit cards.

Kids' Facilities: High chairs and booster seats are available. No diaper-changing tables.

Big Splurges

PUMP ROOM

Ambassador East Hotel, 1301 N. State Pkwy. (312) 266–0360. Pay lot parking.

Hours. Sun.–Thurs., 6 P.M.–9:45 P.M.; Fri., 6 P.M.–11:45 P.M.; Sat., 5 P.M.–11:45 P.M.

The Pump Room is a landmark in Chicago, having served customers for fifty years. The food is still terrific—we had an incredible prime rib dinner the night we were there. Save room for dessert: They make their own ice cream. Prices: $25 and up per person. Full bar. Jackets required. Reservations required. Major credit cards.

LE FRANCAIS

269 S. Milwaukee Ave., Wheeling (Interstate 94 to Dundee exit, west to Milwaukee Ave.). (312) 541–7470. Valet parking.

Hours. Tues.–Sun., two seatings nightly: 6:15 P.M. and 9:15 P.M. Closed on Mon.

Although a bit of a drive from Chicago, Le Francais is worth the trip. One of the few five-star restaurants in the country, everything on the menu is incredible. Their fresh fish entrees are out of this world, as is their chocolate souffle for dessert. Great food, but the prices are on the steep side—$80 per person (with wine). Full bar. Jackets required. Call at least three weeks in advance for reservations. Major credit cards.

SHOPPING

WATER TOWER PLACE

835 N. Michigan Ave. (312) 440–3165. Metered street parking (scarce) and pay parking garage under mall.

Hours. Daily, 10 A.M.–6 P.M., Mon. and Thurs. until 7 P.M.

Occupying a full city block, gargantuan Water Tower Place has 125 shops, ten restaurants, and seven movie theaters spread over eight levels. The stores face out on an atrium. It's all gleaming brass, marble, and greenery. Shoppers ride escalators and glassed-in elevators. Two super department stores are featured: **Lord and Taylor** and **Marshall Field** (not to be confused with MF's flagship store at State and Randolph). Of special interest to children are the **F.A.O. Schwarz** toy store, (312) 787–8894, which showcases a vast array of fine European toys and stuffed animals; **Gamesters**, (312) 642–0671, a store devoted to board games; and **This Little Piggy**, (312) 943–7449, a shop offering a wide selection of kids' footwear and socks.

SATURDAY'S CHILD

Two locations. 50 E. Washington Blvd., (312) 372–8697, pay garage parking. 2146 N. Halsted St., (312) 525–8697, metered street parking.

Hours. Washington Blvd.: Mon.–Sat., 10 A.M.–6 P.M. Halsted St.: Mon.–Sat., 10 A.M.–6 P.M., Thurs. and Fri. until 7 P.M.; Sun., 12 noon–5 P.M.

These stores specialize in toys that "are not advertised on television."

Instead, they offer creative, educational—and more expensive—toys, games, and puzzles. They also have a large selection of infant toys and science gizmos for older kids.

MARSHALL FIELD

111 N. State St. (312) 781–1000. Pay garage parking.

Hours. Mon.–Sat., 9:45 A.M.–5:45 P.M., Mon. and Thurs. until 7 P.M.

With an impressive 1850s exterior and 73 acres of shopping space, Marshall Field is one of America's great department stores. From its restaurant (where they bake their own pastries and make their own candy) to its bargain basement, shoppers can turn a little shopping into an all-day affair. The giant clock (1907) at the corner of State and Washington is a Chicago landmark, as are the Christmas display windows. During the Christmas season, Field's toy department becomes one of the most popular spots in the city.

CUT RATE TOYS

2424 W. Devon Ave. (312) 743–3822. Street parking.

Hours. Mon.–Wed., 9:30 A.M.–8 P.M. (until 9 P.M. during the Christmas season); Thurs. and Fri., 9:30 A.M.–9 P.M.; Sat., 9:30 A.M.–7 P.M.; Sun., 11 A.M.–5 P.M. (until 8 P.M. during the Christmas season).

In business since 1952, Cut Rate Toys showed Toys 'R Us how to sell in high volume for less. They offer just about everything under the sun, and for a bargain surprise, look for the cardboard boxes marked "3 for $1."

THE LEARNING STORE

165 Green Bay Rd., Wilmette. (312) 251–7168. Street parking.

Hours. Mon.–Fri., 10 A.M.–5 P.M.; Sat., 10 A.M.–4 P.M.; Sun., 12 noon–4 P.M.

The Learning Store focuses on toys and books for kids from 6 months to 6 years of age and offers a sampling of their wares for kids to play with.

THE BOOKWORM

1722 Central St., Evanston. (312) 328–4660. Plenty of street parking and on Saturdays you can park in the rear of the building.

Hours. Tues.–Sat., 10 A.M.–5 P.M. During the Christmas season: Mon., 10 A.M.–5 P.M. and Thurs. until 8:30 P.M.

Books account for only half of this relatively new store's sales; the rest is devoted to records and educational games. The management also conducts reading workshops and has designated a large area where the kids can play while Mom and Dad shop. Only a mile or so separate the Bookworm from the Learning Store, so plan to visit both.

TRANSPORTATION

BUSES

The Chicago Transit Authority (CTA) operates one of the largest bus and rapid-transit networks in the country. The base fare is 90¢ and transfers cost 25¢. Some routes run 24 hours a day. For information: (312) 836–7000

CULTURE BUS

One of the best bargains on Sundays and holidays from early May until late September is the Culture Bus. There are three—the South, North, and West—and they travel three different circuitous routes past the major museums and attractions. All three begin at the Art Institute in Grant Park between 10:30 A.M. and 10:55 A.M. and run every 30 minutes until 5:40 P.M. At $2.50 for adults and $1.25 for kids 7 to 11 (under 7 free), one fare is good for the entire day. For more information: (312) 836–7000.

SUBWAYS AND "ELS"

The CTA also handles rapid transit, which costs the same as the buses (90¢/25¢). Within the city, trains run underground and on tracks above street level—these are "els," or "elevated railways." As they approach the suburbs, trains run on expressway median strips. If you choose not to drive in Chicago, the trains are wonderful for getting to and from the Loop. Once downtown, however, you might want to walk or use buses or taxis. Trains run 24 hours a day. For more information: (312) 836–7000.

TAXIS

Cabs are a bargain if you don't ride too far. The base rate is $1, plus 90¢ per mile, plus 50¢ for each additional passenger. Cabs from O'Hare Airport to the Loop cost around $18. You can hail cabs on the street or phone for them. Cab companies include American United, (312) 248–7600; Checker and Yellow, (312) 829–4222; and Flash, (312) 561–1444.

TOURS

BUS TOURS

Six companies offer a vast assortment of bus tours, from a short 2-hour daytime hop throughout the Loop, downtown, and the lakefront, to a 6-hour trip that includes most of the city plus a trip up to the observation deck of the Sears Tower. There are also night tours and tours that include Lake Michigan boat rides. While the greatest variety and number of tours are offered during May through September, most companies also offer a greatly reduced schedule of activities during the rest of the year. Prices range from about $10 to $30 for adults, and about half that for children between 5 and 11. Tours depart from selected hotels.

Gray Line Tours. (312) 346–9506. The largest and best-known company. Offers the largest variety of tours.

Adelei Chicago Tours. (312) 781–0081. Offers individual and group tours, with bilingual service in Spanish and Portugese.

American Sightseeing Tours. (312) 427–3100. Gives tours of both the north and south sides of the city, and includes a Chinatown tour and a "nightclubbing" tour for after the kids are put to bed.

Art Safari Tours. (312) 338–7310. Gives half- or full-day tours for any size group or special interest.

Chicago Motor Coach Tours. (312) 989–8919. Operates in open-air double-decker buses in the summer.

My Kind of Town Tours. (312) 432–6060 or (312) 432–4966. Not only offers forty different tour packages but also throws parties.

On the Scene Tours. (312) 661–1440. Also offers a full range of tours and throws parties.

BOAT TOURS

Water tours are a must in a city that takes as much pride in its waterfront as Chicago does. Tour companies operate on a full schedule between June and August, and on a somewhat limited one in May and September.

Mercury Sightseeing Boats. (312) 332–1353. One-hour, 1 ½-hour, and 2-hour tours. The 1-hour trips leave six times a day between 10:20 A.M. and 11 P.M.; 1 ½-hour excursions depart five times a day between 10 A.M. and 7:30 P.M.; and 2-hour trips leave once a day at 7:30 P.M. Adult trips cost from $5 to $8, with kids under 12 half price. Mercury tours depart from the south side of the Chicago River at Wacker Drive and Michigan Avenue. Mercury also offers a 1-hour Wacky Pirate Cruise for kids every Saturday at 10:30 A.M. The cruise, which features a sing-along, runs between Memorial Day and Labor Day.

Wendella Sightseeing Boats. (312) 337–1446. Approximately the same tours, at the same times and for the same prices, as Mercury (see above). The Wendella dock is at 400 N. Michigan Avenue, at the northwest corner of the Michigan Avenue bridge.

Shoreline Marine Co. (312) 673–3399. Thirty-minute tours departing from the Shedd Aquarium dock, the Buckingham Fountain dock, and the Adler Planetarium dock—all in Grant Park. Aquarium dock tours run six or seven times a day, between 12:20 P.M. and 6:20 P.M. Planetarium dock tours run ten times a day between 12:20 P.M. and 9:20 P.M. Buckingham Fountain dock tours run three times a night, Monday, Tuesday, and Thursday evenings between 8:15 and 10:15, and four times a night Wednesday, Friday, Saturday, and Sunday evenings between 7:45 and 10:45 when there are Grant Park evening concerts. (Adults, $4; kids under 10, $1.50.)

SEASONAL EVENTS

February

CHINESE NEW YEAR

This event varies with the Chinese calendar, but is always celebrated with a parade in Chinatown. Colorful (and sometimes scary) dragons, masks, and fireworks are the hallmarks of the celebration. The parade starts at Chinatown City Hall, S. Wentworth Avenue and W. 22nd Street. Have dinner at an area restaurant before the parade. For more information: (312) 225–6198.

March

ST. PATRICK'S DAY

Some cities settle for green food coloring in the beer on March 17. Chicago dyes the Chicago River green. The yearly parade is one of

Chicago's most musical events, with a great number of marching bands. For more information: (312) 744–3315.

June

CHICAGO WOODEN BOAT FESTIVAL

Navy Pier, 600 E. Grand Ave., is the site of this crowd-pleasing lakeside festival. Highlights include new and restored wooden boats and lots of nifty sailboats. For more information: (312) 787–6858.

July

TASTE OF CHICAGO

Chefs from the local restaurants come to the Buckingham Fountain at Grant Park to prepare their specialties. This week-long food fest is usually held around July 4. For more information: (312) 744–3315.

JULY 4 CONCERT AND FIREWORKS

Grant Park's Petrillo Music Shell (see Attractions) is the location of a free concert and the free fireworks display that explodes on the lakefront. For more information: (312) 744–3315.

AIR AND WATER SHOW

Typically held on the third weekend in July, the air show features aerial acrobatics by standard and experimental aircraft. It's held at the eastern end of Chicago Avenue at the lakefront. For more information: (312) 294–2493.

August

VENETIAN NIGHT

This mid-August event is a parade of illuminated yachts in the Monroe Street harbor. A fireworks display follows the parade. For more information: (312) 744–3315.

September

GERMAN AMERICAN PARADE AND FESTIVAL

If you saw the movie *Ferris Bueller's Day Off*, you know what fun this is. It coincides with the traditional German Oktoberfest. For more information: (312) 478–7915.

INTERNATIONAL FOLK FESTIVAL

Held at Donnelley Hall, just east of McCormick Place, this two-day fest is held the last weekend of September and features ethnic food, dancing, music, and crafts from more than fifty countries. For more information: (312) 744–3315.

November

CHRISTMAS AROUND THE WORLD

From just after Thanksgiving through New Year's Day, the Museum of Science and Industry (see Museums) hosts a display of Christmas trees and crèches from around the world. For more information: (312) 684–1414.

CHRISTMAS TREE LIGHTING

At Daley Plaza (Randolph and Clark in the Loop, the home of the big Picasso sculpture), the 80-foot-high Christmas tree is lighted annually on the day after Thanksgiving. For more information: (312) 744–3315.

CHILDREN'S THEATER

PUPPET PARLOR THEATER

5301 N. Damen Ave. (312) 774–2919. Street parking available.

The Puppet Parlor is no amateur sock puppet outfit. It produces full-blown *operettas*. The last time we visited, *Hansel and Gretel* was being performed on weekends, and *Faust* was being presented in German by Puppentheater Berlin. Productions, ticket prices, and times vary, so call ahead.

GOODMAN THEATER

200 S. Columbus Dr. (312) 443–3800. Pay parking garage under the Art Institute and at pay lots in Grant Park.

The Goodman is home to the oldest locally produced theater in Chicago. As a regional theater, it ranks with the best in the country, mounting productions that often make their way to Broadway and Washington's National Theater. Special, often seasonal, children's productions are presented here as well. Call for show and ticket information.

SECOND CITY THEATER

1616 N. Wells St. (312) 337–3992. Street parking.

The training ground for comedians like John Belushi, Bill Murray, Mike Nichols, and Elaine May also presents children's theater. Call for information.

CINEMA FACETS MULTIMEDIA

1517 W. Fullerton Ave. (312) 929–KIDS. Street parking.

On weekends, this theater shows movies for both younger and older kids.

CHICAGO PUBLIC LIBRARY CULTURAL CENTER

78 E. Washington Blvd. (312) 346–3278. Pay garage parking and lot parking in Grant Park.

Completed in 1897, the ornate old building used to be the main building of the Chicago Public Library. Today it serves as a branch library, meeting facility, and site for children's weekend events like storytelling hours, puppet shows, and kid-oriented lectures. Call for a recorded schedule of upcoming events.

BABYSITTING SERVICES

AMERICAN REGISTRY FOR NURSES AND SITTERS
(312) 248–8100

In the business since 1950, Mary Jane Sellers provides licensed and bonded sitters. The basic rate charged is $5 per hour, with a 4-hour minimum plus cab fare or a ride home after 9 P.M. Ms. Sellers requests as much advance notice as possible.

PUBLICATIONS

Chicago Tribune. Daily newspaper; Friday calendar section.

Chicago Sun-Times. Daily newspaper; Friday calendar section.

Chicago Reader. Free weekly (Thursday) paper; excellent events guide; available at stores, restaurants, and bars all over the city.

Chicago Magazine. Monthly magazine; calendar of events; restaurant listings.

Chicago Parent. Free monthly newspaper; large events calendar; available at toy stores and kids' boutiques.

LOCAL TELEPHONE NUMBERS

Late-hours pharmacy: Walgreen's, 757 N. Michigan Ave. (312) 664–8686. Open 24 hours.
Alco Drug, 347 E. 35th St., (312) 225–4660. Open 24 hours.
Consumer complaints: City of Chicago, (312) 744–9400.
Consumer information: State of Illinois, (312) 917–2754.
Dental emergency: Chicago Dental Society, (312) 726–4321.
Doctor's home referral: (312) 880–6655.
Drug abuse: Mercy Hospital alcohol and drug programs, (312) 567–2486.
National Health Information Clearinghouse: (800) 336–4797.
Poison control: Rush Presbyterian–St. Lukes Hospital, (312) 942–5969.
Traveler's aid: (312) 435–4500.
Tourism office: Chicago Tourism Council, (312) 280–5740.
Police: 911.
Fire: 911.
Ambulance: 911.
Road conditions: (312) 283–6204.
Weather: (312) 976–1212 (toll call).
Car rental companies: Econo car, (312) 951–6262; Altra, (312) 736–8630.

LOS ANGELES

"Looks like another perfect day. I love L.A."

—RANDY NEWMAN

While Los Angeles has been viciously criticized by many who live east of the Rocky Mountains, many of the city's worst critics secretly dream of a life in—or at least a visit to—southern California. Los Angeles is home to world-class museums, a great symphony, and renowned institutions of higher learning. Think about the glitz and glamour of the entertainment industry, wide beaches, and world-class amusement facilities, and you understand why it's a prime destination for vacationers, especially those traveling with children.

The Spanish first settled in Los Angeles in 1781 when, with the stroke of his pen, the governor of Mexico ordered the area populated and incorporated. El Pueblo de Los Angeles (see Attractions), founded near what is today's Chinatown, began with forty-four permanent residents. During the late 18th century, the Los Angeles area was merely a second thought, one of many way stations the Spanish needed to connect their prosperous settlements of San Diego and Monterey. Without a natural harbor or even close proximity to the ocean (it was about 10 miles away), the pueblo held little attraction except as a place to raise horses and cattle, convert Indians to Catholicism, and garrison a few Spanish troops.

Los Angeles remained a sleepy ranching area through most of the early 19th century, hardly batting an eye when Mexico gained its independence from Spain in 1821. Of slightly more importance was the 1846 invasion and subsequent annexation of California by the United States during the Mexican War. Agriculture was still king and only with the coming of the railroad in the 1880s did Los Angeles start to pick up steam.

Despite Los Angeles' growth as the western center of the citrus industry in the late 19th century, it remained little more than a cow town until the first decade of the 20th. L.A.'s wake-up call came in the form of men with cameras escaping from New York. Independent producers, on the lam from creditors and New York's strict motion picture patent laws, began to arrive in droves. Soon the big companies followed. Attracted by the warm year-round climate, the bright California light, and inexpensive labor, the fledging motion picture industry had all but evacuated New York by 1915. By 1923, movies accounted for 20 percent of California's manufactured goods, more than 20,000 actors were at work, and there were 260 studios in production. Hollywood, a sleepy little community northwest of downtown Los Angeles, had become the motion picture capital of the world.

Movies led to the growth of other industries. Its position on the edge of the Pacific Ocean, coupled with cheap real estate and ideal building weather, made L.A. a natural choice for the aircraft industry. That, plus southern California's natural oil reserves, made the location prime as the United States built up its war machine in the late 1930s. Suddenly, Los Angeles was a boomtown for four big industries: oil, aircraft, agriculture, and the movies. With banking as a growing fifth major industry, Los Angeles was on its way to becoming the second largest city in the United States and a world economic power.

As attractions go, most vacationing families these days come to Los Angeles for the big three: the movie studios, the amusement parks, and the beach. But, as we'll show you in the following pages, the city has a lot more to offer than the obvious.

CLIMATE

Los Angeles is pleasant year-round with an average mean temperature of 64 degrees. In summer, temperatures can soar to around 100 degrees but usually reside in the comfortable mid-80s. At night, the summertime mercury can dip into the mid-60s. During the winter months, the average daily highs hover in the mid-60s, with nighttime lows dipping into the low 40s. Fall and spring temperatures average in the 70s during the day and drop down to the low 50s at night.

When traveling to L.A. during any season, it's a good idea to take a jacket along. While summer travel will avail you some of the most consistent weather (sunny and warm), winter is the rainy season, and most of the city's 14 inches fall between November and April. If you plan to head up to the local mountains, be prepared for winter snows and temperatures that fall to the teens at night and rise into the 40s during the day.

Los Angeles' wide beaches are a draw any time of the year, but if you plan on going into the water, be prepared for a shock. The currents that run along southern California are cold, and, in summer, don't expect water temperatures to rise any higher than the low 70s. In the winter, water temperatures are often in the low 50s.

FREEBIES AND CHEAPIES
(Free or $3.50 and under for adults)

❑ California Museum of Science and Industry (see Museums)
❑ El Pueblo de Los Angeles Historical Monument (see Attractions)
❑ Kidspace (see Museums)
❑ Griffith Park Pony and Train Rides (see Attractions)
❑ Griffith Park Observatory, Planetarium, and Hall of Science (see Attractions)
❑ Los Angeles County Museum of Art (see Museums)
❑ George C. Page Museum of La Brea Discoveries and La Brea Tar Pits (see Museums)
❑ Wells Fargo Museum (see Museums)

THE LONG WEEKEND

Day One

❑ Los Angeles Children's Museum (see Museums)
❑ El Pueblo de Los Angeles Historic Monument (see Attractions)
❑ Mon Kee's Sea Food Restaurant (see Restaurants)
❑ California Museum of Science and Industry (see Museums)
❑ Natural History Museum of Los Angeles County (see Museums)

Day Two

❑ Disneyland (see Attractions)
❑ *or* Universal Studios Tour (see Attractions)

Day Three

❑ Griffith Park Pony Rides (see Attractions)
❑ Los Angeles Zoo (see Attractions)
❑ NBC Studio Tour (see Attractions)
❑ Venice and Santa Monica Ocean Walk (see Attractions)

TOURIST INFORMATION

Contact the Greater Los Angeles Visitors and Convention Bureau, Manulife Plaza, 515 S. Figueroa Street, 11th Floor, Los Angeles, CA 90071, (213) 624–7300.

ATTRACTIONS

GRIFFITH PARK

Visitors Center at 4730 Crystal Springs Dr. (213) 665–5188. Take the Los Feliz Blvd. exit off Interstate 5. Free parking.

Hours. *Park:* daily, 5 A.M.–10 P.M. *Visitors Center:* daily, 7 A.M.–5 P.M.

Costs. Park use is free; certain attractions charge admission.

With 4,107 acres, Griffith Park is the largest city park in the United States. At the eastern terminus of the Santa Monica Mountain range, Griffith Park combines well-groomed lawns and beautifully landscaped flatland meadows with mountainous areas covered with native southern California scrub bushes and grasses. Its highest point, Mount Hollywood, rises to an impressive 1,652 feet. With such a variety of landscaping, the park offers a long list of activities, including golf, softball, wilderness hikes, a bird sanctuary, horseback riding, campgrounds, and picnic areas. For more information, call park headquarters. (*The park also boasts the Los Angeles Zoo and the Griffith Park Observatory, Planetarium, and Hall of Science. See separate attractions listings. It is also the home of the new Gene Autry Western Heritage Museum. See separate museums listings.*)

Griffith Park offers a number of specialized activities within a short distance of the Visitors Center:

Travel Town, (213) 662–5874, is an outdoor collection of out-of-service locomotives and train cars, including a retired Hawaiian narrow-gauge sugar train, old Los Angeles streetcars, and a monstrous old Union Pacific steam locomotive. The exhibit also features some vintage World War II and Korean War airplanes. Many of the railroad relics are there for kids to climb aboard, but the aircraft are just for looking at. An inside exhibit area displays old fire-fighting equipment, a collection of antique cars and trucks, and horse-drawn buggies and wagons. Travel Town is located on Zoo Drive near Griffith Park Drive in the northwest corner of the park (use the Forest Lawn Drive exit off Highway 134). It's open Monday through Friday, 10 A.M.–4 P.M., and Saturday and Sunday, 10 A.M.–5 P.M. No admission is charged. Restrooms nearby.

Pony Rides, (213) 664–3266, are a delight for younger children. The youngest are strapped to the saddle and walked slowly around an oval.

Older, more adventurous kids can ride around a larger oval at a gallop. Stagecoach and wagon rides are also offered. The cost per ride is $1. The ponies are located at Crystal Springs Drive near Los Feliz Boulevard (use the Los Feliz entrance to the park). Winter hours are Tuesday through Friday, 10 A.M.–4 P.M.; Saturday and Sunday, 10 A.M.–5 P.M. Summer hours are Monday through Friday, 10 A.M.–5:30 P.M.; Saturday and Sunday, 10 A.M.–6:30 P.M. Snack stand and restrooms nearby.

The park's **Miniature Train**, (213) 664–6788, is located a few yards from the pony rides. The narrow-gauge miniature train winds its way through a small strip of land in the Park's southeastern section. The whole trip takes about 10 minutes, and kids love it. The hours are the same as for the pony rides. The costs: ages 11 and up, $1.50; ages 10 and under, $1.25. Snack stand and restrooms nearby.

The Griffith Park **Merry-Go-Round**, (213) 665–3051, is one of our favorite carousels. Currently undergoing a slow refurbishing process (they've been working on it for years but continue to operate), this 1926 beauty offers four concentric rings of brightly painted animals, and one of the best pneumatic band organs on any carousel anywhere. The rides are long, and the carousel is fast. It's located a few hundred yards south of the Visitors Center. During the winter, it operates on Saturdays, Sundays, and holidays, 11 A.M.–6 P.M. During the summer, it operates daily, 11 A.M.–6 P.M. Rides cost 75¢ for all ages. Restrooms nearby.

Kids' Facilities. No stroller rentals in the park. No diaper-changing facilities at the above attractions, but plenty of park benches. Food concession stands (hot dogs, popcorn, sodas) are scattered throughout the park. No bottle-warming facilities.

Ratings. Griffith Park has something for everyone. All ages, A.

LOS ANGELES ZOO

5333 Zoo Drive, Griffith Park. (213) 664–1100. Take the Zoo Drive exit off Interstate 5. Free parking.

Hours. Winter: daily, 10 A.M.–5 P.M. Summer: daily, 10 A.M.–6 P.M.

Costs. Adults, $4.50; ages 2–12, $2; under age 2, free.

This is a gem that's often overshadowed by the reputation of the huge San Diego Zoo 120 miles to the south. Located in a scenic, hilly, 113-acre section of Griffith Park, it's home to 2,000 animals, clustered by continent and presented in naturelike environments. Two of the best exhibits are the very animated gorillas (in a wonderful outdoor exhibit area) and the zoo's nocturnal animal house (night is simulated during the day). The brand-new children's zoo, dubbed Adventure Island, offers a number of innovative exhibits, including a plexiglass dome from which kids can observe a marmot den, a hunt section where children can look through the eyes of various animals, and the always-popular animal nursery. Petting areas are included.

Kids' Facilities. Strollers rented for $2. Special diaper-changing areas at children's zoo. No bottle-warming facilities. Lots of fast-food stands, including one that sells healthier foods like peanut butter sandwiches, fruit, and vegetables.

Ratings. We consider the Zoo one of the city's best-kept secrets. Be prepared for lots of hilly walking. See it all in a day. All ages, A.

GRIFFITH PARK OBSERVATORY, PLANETARIUM, AND HALL OF SCIENCE

2800 E. Observatory Rd., Griffith Park. (213) 664–1191. Take the Los Feliz exit on Interstate 5; go west on Los Feliz to Vermont Ave. and turn north to observatory. Free parking.

Hours. *Observatory and Hall of Science:* Winter: Tues.–Fri., 2 P.M.–10 P.M.; Sat., 11:30 A.M.–10 P.M.; Sun., 1P.M.–10 P.M. Summer: daily, 1 P.M.–10 P.M. *Planetarium shows:* mid-September through mid-June: Tues.–Fri., 3 P.M. and 8 P.M.; Sat. and Sun., 1:30 P.M., 3 P.M., 4:30 P.M., and 8 P.M. Summer: Mon.–Fri. 1:30 P.M. children's show.

Costs. *Observatory and Hall of Science:* free. *Planetarium shows:* adults, $2.75; ages 5–15, $1.50; under age 5 not admitted, except to special children's shows.

Movie buffs will remember the Art Deco observatory as the site where outsider James Dean battled with meanies like Nick Adams and Dennis Hopper in *Rebel Without a Cause*. Astronomy buffs will enjoy other aspects, including the state's largest public telescope (open at night between 7 P.M. and 10 P.M.), a Foucault pendulum, and exhibits on the moon and the planets. The planetarium presents wonderfully choreographed skyshows, complete with light and music. Call ahead for a schedule as shows change every few months. They shouldn't be missed.

Kids' Facilities. No stroller rentals. No diaper-changing tables in restrooms. No food or bottle-warming facilities.

Ratings. The youngest kids will probably not understand much of what the Hall of Science has to offer, nor can they attend most planetarium shows. However, children over age 5 will love it. The Hall of Science can be seen in about a half hour. 2–7, B; 8–11, A; 12–16, A.

EL PUEBLO DE LOS ANGELES HISTORIC MONUMENT

Visitor Center, 622 N. Main St. (park is located between Alameda and Main Sts., and Macy and Arcadia Sts.). (213) 628–1274. Use the Alameda St. exit off the 101 Freeway. Pay lots, $5 per day.

Hours. See individual attractions, below.

Costs. Free.

This was the center of Los Angeles when it became a pueblo (community) in 1781. Today, the site is home to a handful of attractions that celebrate the city's Mexican heritage. The **Plaza**, just to the south of Olvera Street (see below) was the early settlement's ground zero. Today it contains a monument to the city's first families and is the location of a number of yearly events of special interest to the Hispanic community.

Sepulveda House, 622 N. Main St., a refurbished Victorian house (1887) is the Pueblo's visitor center. Here park employees will provide you with information on the park and present an 18-minute film on the history of Los Angeles. The center is open Monday through Friday, 10 A.M.–3 P.M., and Saturday, 10 A.M.–4:30 P.M. Restrooms available.

The **Avila Adobe**, 10 E. Olvera St., is the oldest residence now standing in Los Angeles. Built of adobe in 1818 by Francisco Avila, it was restored in 1971 to look as it did in the 1840s, when it was home to a well-to-do California family. Constructed around a central patio garden, the rooms are filled with period furnishings. Kids will enjoy the children's room with a cowhide bed and a doll collection. It's open Tuesday through Friday, 10 A.M.–3 P.M.; Saturday and Sunday, 10 A.M.–4:30 P.M. Restrooms nearby.

The two-story, red-brick **Firehouse #1**, 134 Paseo de la Plaza, was the city's first firehouse (1884) and has been converted into a showplace for antique fire-fighting equipment. The collection includes an 1880s fire engine, a pumper wagon, and a chemical vehicle. Also on display are old fire hats, photographs, alarms, and other fire-fighting memorabilia. The hours are the same as for the Avila Abode. Restrooms nearby.

Olvera Street, between Main and Alameda Sts., is one of Los Angeles' oldest roadways. Now converted into a traditional Mexican bazaar, the narrow brick street is home to all sorts of commercial shops, stalls, and restaurants. On most days it's possible to watch craftspeople making tortillas, dipping candles, and blowing glass. Most shops are open daily from 10 A.M.–8 P.M. Restrooms available at restaurants.

Kids' Facilities. No stroller rentals. No diaper-changing tables in restrooms. Bottles warmed at some of the restaurants on Olvera Street. Food also available at stalls.

Ratings. With all the colors, crowds, crafts, and food, El Pueblo de Los Angeles has something for every taste. It will take a solid 90 minutes to see everything quickly. All ages, A.

VENICE AND SANTA MONICA OCEAN WALK

Pacific Ocean, between Venice Blvd. and the Santa Monica Pier, though the main commercial activity is found between Windward Ave. and the Pier. Use the Venice Ave. exit off the 405 Freeway; drive west to the ocean and park. Free street and pay lot parking; on weekends, spaces fill up fast, so leave early.

Hours. Daily from about 10 A.M.–dusk. Weekends are the best times to go.

Costs. The beach and boardwalk are free. Be prepared to buy food and trinkets for the kids along the way.

While beaches all along the coastline are suitable for swimming and water sports, only the stretch from Windward Avenue north to the Santa Monica Pier offers so much more. On weekends throughout the year, this infamous ribbon of sidewalk becomes a people-watching paradise. The best way to describe it is as a combination outdoor marketplace/restaurant row/talent showcase/roller rink. It's the gathering point for street hawkers, street musicians, near-professional roller skaters, and comedians. Have lunch or breakfast at one of the many restaurants along the beach and just watch the parade of humanity, or rent skates or bicycles and join the parade yourself. It's a great place to buy mounted lithographs, inexpensive clothing, or a decent $2 pair of sunglasses.

Kids' Facilities. No stroller rentals: Definitely bring your own. No diaper-changing tables. Public restrooms available, but they're pretty dirty; we suggest using restaurant restrooms. Bottles warmed at restaurants.

Ratings. A great place for all ages during the daylight hours (the neighborhood's rough at night). A brisk walk one way will take about an hour. All ages, A.

MANN'S [FORMERLY GRAUMAN'S] CHINESE THEATER

6925 Hollywood Blvd., Hollywood. (213) 464–8111. Use the Hollywood Blvd. exit off the 101 Freeway and drive west. Pay lot and metered street parking.

Hours. Daily, 9 A.M.–11 P.M.

Costs. Free.

Back in the 1920s and 1930s, theater owner Sid Grauman had a brainstorm. The idea was to cast in cement the hands, feet, and signature of every Hollywood movie star outside the front entrance to his ornate Chinese-influenced movie theater. Those hand and foot prints were an instant sensation then and today remain one of Hollywood Boulevard's biggest tourist attractions.

The theater is a good place to get free tickets to tapings of television game shows and situation comedies. They're distributed on the sidewalk in front of the theater.

Kids' Facilities. No stroller rentals. No diaper-changing tables. No restroom facilities. No bottle warming. There are plenty of souvenir gift shops and restaurants nearby.

Ratings. Even though younger kids won't understand the significance of the hand and foot prints, they'll enjoy matching hands and feet with the great stars of the cinema. Figure on a half hour to shake hands and feet with them all. 2–7, B; 8–11, B; 12–16, A.

HOLLYWOOD IN MINIATURE

6834 Hollywood Blvd., Hollywood. (213) 466–7758. Take the Hollywood Blvd. exit off the 101 Freeway and drive west. Street and pay lot parking.

Hours. Sun.–Thurs., 10 A.M.–10 P.M.; Fri. and Sat., 10 A.M.—1 A.M.

Costs. Adults, $2.50; ages 6–12, $1; ages 5 and under, free.

Much has been made of the glamour of Hollywood during the 1930s and 1940s, especially in contrast to the seediness you find in some areas today. Hollywood in Miniature is a collection of painstakingly accurate models created by artist Joe Pellkofer in 1940. From the tiny foot and hand prints on the sidewalk of Grauman's (now Mann's) Chinese Theater to every streetlight and theater marquee, Pellkofer's models provide the only three-dimensional look at the Hollywood of fifty years ago. An audio tape explains what you are seeing as you view each of four model neighborhoods.

Kids' Facilities. No stroller rentals. No diaper-changing tables in restrooms. No bottle warming. Restaurant and gift shop in lobby.

Ratings. Younger children will probably want these "toys" for their very own. Older kids and parents will enjoy both the detail and the historical significance. It takes about a half hour to view all the models. 2–7, B; 8–11, A; 12–16, A.

LOS ANGELES TIMES TOUR

202 W. 1st St. (213) 972–5757. Use the Temple Street exit off the 101 Freeway; drive south to 1st St. and turn left to Times. Pay lot parking.

Hours. Tours: Mon.–Fri., 11:15 A.M. and 3 P.M.

Costs. Free.

The largest newspaper on the West Coast, the Times has been published continuously since the 1880s. The 1-hour tour takes you through the newsroom, the wire room, through the composing area, past the high-speed presses, and the area from which the papers are distributed. The Times' lobby features a pictorial "time line" going back 100 years, some historical printing equipment, and an impressive 10-foot brass-and-marble world globe.

Kids' Facilities. No stroller rentals. No diaper-changing tables. No food or bottle-warming facilities.

Ratings. *No children under 10 are allowed.* Older children and teenagers will find the tour fascinating. 2–9, not allowed; 10–11, A; 12–16, A.

WILL ROGERS STATE HISTORIC PARK

14253 Sunset Blvd., Pacific Palisades. (213) 454–8212. Take the Sunset Blvd. exit off the 405 Freeway; go west on Sunset to park entrance. Parking, $2.

Hours. *Park:* daily, 8 A.M.–6 P.M. (7 P.M. during Daylight Savings Time). *Will Rogers House:* daily, 10 A.M.–5 P.M.

Costs. Only cost is $2 charge per car.

Located on 187 acres of grasslands and woods, Rogers' former estate (from the 1920s through 1935) today is home to hiking trails, polo fields and picnic areas, and the famed humorist's California home. Polo matches are still played on the fields on weekends during the spring, summer, and early autumn at 2 P.M., and spectators are welcome. At other times, the fields are given over to makeshift softball diamonds. Rogers' home is open to the public and is furnished much as it was in 1935 when Rogers and pilot Wiley Post died in an Alaska plane crash. For want of a better term, the house is appointed in cowboy rustic: cowhides, western rugs, and wood furnishings.

Kids' Facilities. No stroller rentals; bring your own if you want to hike. No diaper-changing tables in restrooms (plenty of bench space, however). No food or bottle-warming facilities.

Ratings. It's a wonderful place for a family outing: The trails are great, often leading to terrific ocean vistas. The house can be viewed in about 20 minutes. All ages, A.

NBC STUDIO TOUR

3000 W. Alameda Ave. at Olive Ave., Burbank. (818) 840-3537. Use the Barham Blvd. exit off the 101 Freeway; go north on Barham to W. Olive and turn right; go east on Olive to Alameda and park. Free parking.

Hours. Mon.–Fri., 8:30 A.M.–4 P.M.; Sat., 10 A.M.–4 P.M.; Sun., 10 A.M.–2 P.M.

Costs. Adults, $6; ages 5–14, $4; ages 4 and under, free.

NBC is the only major television network to open its doors to the public. The tour takes you through sound stages (where game shows, the local news, and the *Tonight Show* are produced) as well as makeup rooms, the prop, set-construction, and wardrobe departments, and a specially designed miniature studio where kids and parents can see themselves on television and watch how some special effects are created. An added bonus is being able to catch a glimpse of the stars (Johnny Carson, for example, arrives in the early afternoon on show days). You can obtain free tickets for upcoming game shows, but kids under 16 are not permitted in audiences).

Kids' Facilities. No stroller rentals (bring your own umbrella stroller as there's lots of walking). No diaper-changing tables in restrooms. No bottles warmed. The Peacock Garden Cafe serves fast food and salads. Gift shop.

Ratings. The tour helps unfold some of the mysteries of television production. The guides, some of whom are hoping to break into show business, are extremely informative and patient with children's questions. The tour takes about 75 minutes. All ages, A.

DISNEYLAND

1313 Harbor Blvd., Anaheim (located about 27 miles southeast of downtown Los Angeles). (714) 999–4565 or (213) 626–8605 ext. 4565. Take the Harbor Blvd. or Katella Ave. exits off Interstate 5 and follow the signs. Parking, $3.

Hours. June through early September plus selected school holiday periods: daily, 9 A.M.–12 midnight. Rest of the year: Mon.–Fri., 10 A.M.–6 P.M.; Sat. and Sun., 9 A.M.–12 midnight.

Costs. Single day admission: adults, $21.50; ages 3–11, $16.50; ages 2 and under, free. Two-day pass: adults, $38.75; ages 3–11, $29.75. Three-day pass: adults, $51.50; ages 3–11, $39.50.

"The Happiest Place on Earth," in operation since 1955, is the prototype that other amusement parks have attempted to copy. Until the opening of Orlando's Disney World in the early 1970s, the 80-acre park was also the most-traveled-to place of its kind in the world. Today, Disneyland maintains its reputation by providing the public with the cleanest and best-run park this side of central Florida. The model for Disney World's Magic Kingdom, Disneyland is split into seven theme lands, most of which capitalize liberally on the use of Audio-Animatronics to create computerized talking and singing robots.

Adventureland. Its themes come from Asia, Africa, and the South Pacific. It's here you'll find attractions like the Enchanted Tiki Room, the Swiss Family Robinson Tree House, and African river rides.

Critter Country. Until recently called Bear Country, this theme land re-creates the Northwest wilderness. Attractions include the musical Country Bear Playhouse and Disneyland's newest ride, Splash Mountain. A 40-MPH log ride that includes a 50-foot, 45-degree drop, Splash Mountain will appeal to the older thrill seekers in the family.

Fantasy Land. Disney's storybook land is for younger children. The rides are tame and the themes are familiar. The best-known attraction is It's a Small World, where visitors ride past lots of life-size dolls from different countries, all singing the same song over and over.

Frontierland. Filled with pioneers and characters from the Wild West, this area boasts excursions on a huge replica stern-wheel paddle boat and the runaway mining-cart ride called Big Thunder Mountain.

Main Street U.S.A. Disneyland's entrance is an idealized version of small-town America at the turn of the 20th century. Famous for its Main Street Electrical Parade most nights, it also features lots of shops and an Audio-Animatronic visit with some former United States Presidents.

New Orleans Square. This is Walt Disney's version of what 19th-century New Orleans would have looked like if Disneyland's efficient custodial staff had been around to keep the city well scrubbed. The most famous of this area's attractions is Pirates of the Caribbean, a subterranean water ride filled with Audio-Animatronic buccaneers.

Tomorrowland. A look at the world of the future, this is one of Disneyland's most popular spots. Not only can you catch showings of Michael Jackson's 3-D movie *Captain Eo*, but it offers up the wraparound movie *America the Beautiful* and super-ride Space Mountain, where passengers career down the inside of a mountain in near-pitch-black conditions.

With food and souvenirs literally at every turn, the only reasons to leave the park are to sleep and to earn more spending money. (*Note: Families sometimes get into trouble when their expectations of Disneyland are too high. Kids expect to do everything and often can't because the lines are too long to get to everything in a day. Prepare yourselves to head off their disappointments and everyone will have a terrific time.*)

Kids' Facilities. Strollers are rented just inside the park entrance for $3, with a $3 deposit. Diaper-changing tables are located at restrooms throughout the park. The Gerber Baby Center, on Main Street U.S.A., provides changing tables, bottle warming, and rooms for nursing mothers. Baby food, formula, and diapers are provided for a small charge. There are many fast-food stands, including a couple devoted to health foods. Sit-down restaurants dot the landscape. There are dozens of gift-buying areas.

Ratings. It's every American child's birthright to go to Disneyland. Fun is guaranteed. Spend a whole day. All ages, A.

SIX FLAGS MAGIC MOUNTAIN

26101 Magic Mountain Blvd., Valencia (located about 40 miles north of downtown Los Angeles). (805) 255–4111 or (818) 367–5965. Take the

Magic Mountain Blvd. exit off Interstate 5 and follow the signs to the park. Parking, $3.

Hours. June through August plus selected school holiday periods: daily, 10 A.M.–10 P.M. (some nights till 12 midnight). Rest of the year: Sat. and Sun., 10 A.M.–6 P.M. (some nights until 8 P.M. or 10 P.M.).

Costs. Adults, $20; kids under 48″ tall, $10; ages 2 and under, free.

Of the major theme parks near Los Angeles, Magic Mountain has the scariest, most thrill-oriented roller coasters. From Ninja, a roller coaster in which you travel at 55 MPH and dangle from a track above your head, to Shock Wave, where you ride upside down and standing up, this park is tailor-made for fearless older kids. At the same time, Magic Mountain offers younger children the tame rides of Bugs Bunny World. A full-service amusement park, it also provides a crafts village, musical shows, a petting zoo, picnic areas, a dance club for teenagers, a trained dolphin show, fireworks, and at least five separate electronic-game arcades. Like most theme parks, Magic Mountain is populated with people in cartoon character costumes. In this case it's Bugs, Daffy Duck, and company. (*Note: Be aware that because of the park's distance from the ocean, it can get extremely hot in the summer, often around 100 degrees.*)

Kids' Facilities. Strollers are rented near the entrance for $2 (with $5 deposit). The Pampers Baby Care Center is located near Bugs Bunny World: lots of changing tables and bottle warming. A first-aid facility with a nurse and paramedic on duty are available near the Back Street section of the park. Many fast-food stands, as well as a handful of sit-down restaurants. Plenty of gift and toy shops.

Ratings. Because many of Magic Mountain's rides appeal to older kids, you may have to contend with roving packs of teenagers, especially at night. Still, there's fun for everyone here. All ages, A.

KNOTT'S BERRY FARM

8039 Beach Blvd., Buena Park, Orange County (located about 23 miles southeast of downtown Los Angeles). (714) 220–5200 or (714) 827–1776. Take the Beach Blvd. exit off Interstate 5. Free parking for the first 3 hours.

Hours. June through August and certain school holiday periods: Sun.–Thurs., 10 A.M.–11 P.M.; Fri., 10 A.M.–12 midnight; Sat., 10 A.M.–1 A.M. Rest of the year: Mon.–Fri., 10 A.M.–6 P.M.; Sat., 10 A.M.–10 P.M.; Sun., 10 A.M.–7 P.M.

Costs. Adults, $17.95; ages 3–11, $13.95; pregnant mothers, $12.95; ages 2 and under, free.

From its humble beginnings as a fruit stand on 10 acres of rented land in the 1920s, Knott's Berry Farm has grown into one of the largest independently owned amusement parks in the country. Capitalizing on an Old West theme, the park features more than 165 rides, live musical shows, and attractions. Realizing early on that they had to fill needs that neighboring Disneyland didn't, Knott's chose to concentrate on thrill rides. The two best-known rides are the Corkscrew (with two 360-degree loops) and Montazooma's [sic] Revenge, a roller coaster that sprints from 0 to 55 MPH in 5 seconds. For the dinosaur maniacs in the family, there's Kingdom of the Dinosaurs, an indoor ride where giant Audio-Animatronic dinosaurs roam as they did 200 million years ago. In addition to fast rides, the park features a park within the park: **Camp Snoopy** caters to young children with characters from the *Peanuts* comic strip wandering about. The Camp offers tamer versions of the park's hairier rides, plus boat trips, pony rides, a simulated hot-air-balloon trip, and a petting zoo.

Kids' Facilities. Strollers are rented just inside the main entrance for $3, plus $20 deposit or driver's license. There are three baby stations scattered about the park in secluded cabins. Each includes diaper-changing tables, free diapers and wipes, private nursing areas, microwave ovens for bottle warming, and even rocking chairs for tired kids and parents. (Our only objection was the loud piped-in banjo music blaring in the facilities.) The park features lots of fast-food joints and Mrs. Knott's Chicken Dinner Restaurant, a sit-down facility that's located just outside the main entrance. Gift shops at Knott's Marketplace, also outside the main entrance.

Ratings. Standing in Disneyland's formidable shadow, Knott's Berry Farm holds its own. Spend an entire day. All ages, A.

QUEEN MARY AND SPRUCE GOOSE

Pier J and Queens Hwy., Port of Long Beach (located approximately 20 miles south of downtown Los Angeles). (213) 435–3511. Take the Long Beach Freeway (710) south to the end; exit onto Harbor Scenic Drive to Queens Highway. Parking, $3.

Hours. Daily, 10 A.M.–5 P.M. (box office closes at 4 P.M.).

Costs. Both attractions for one price: adults, $14.95; ages 5–11, $8.95; ages 4 and under, free.

One of the world's greatest ocean liners, the *Queen Mary* was a first-class passenger ship from the 1930s through the late 1960s. At one time, she was the fastest ship afloat: top speed 36 MPH. Completely refurbished, the ship today is a floating hotel as well as a maritime museum. Visitors can take self-guided tours, viewing the captain's quarters and displays on World War II, and even observing regular lifeboat drills. For an extra $5 per person, the 90-minute Captain's Tour will take you behind the scenes. It's also possible to dine on board or rent a stateroom for the night.

The *Spruce Goose* was one of eccentric millionaire Howard Hughes' boondoggles. During World War II, Hughes began constructing the seaplane as a model for a fleet of super troop carriers. Built entirely of wood, the plane's wingspan is 320 feet. It's as tall as an 8-story building, and, fully loaded, it would weigh 400,000 pounds. In 1947, amid rumors it wouldn't fly, Hughes himself took the controls. He got it to rise out of the water for only a few seconds; having technically proved the plane air worthy, he taxied to the shore and had it mothballed. The warehoused plane is absolutely breathtaking to look at. Companion exhibits explain its engineering, and there are movies on the plane and Hughes.

Londontowne, a shopping and restaurant area near the attractions, offers British-made souvenirs and cuisine.

Kids' Facilities. No stroller rentals. No diaper-changing tables in the restrooms (though there are plenty of sofas and benches). No bottle-warming facilities. Plenty of restaurants and gift shops.

Ratings. While for young children the only thing the ship and plane have going for them is mind-boggling size, older children with a sense of proportion and history will have a terrific time. Take a minimum of 3 hours to see everything. 2–7, C; 8–11, A; 12–16, A.

UNIVERSAL STUDIOS TOUR

100 Universal Plaza, San Fernando Valley, Universal City. (818) 508–9600. Take the Lankershim Ave. or Universal Center Dr. exits off the 101 Freeway. Parking, $3.

Hours. Summer and selected holiday periods: daily, 8:30 A.M.–5 P.M. Rest of the year: Mon.–Fri., 10 A.M.–3:30 P.M.; Sat. and Sun., 9:30 A.M.–3:30 P.M.

Costs. Adults, $17.95; ages 3–11, $12.95; ages 2 and under, free.

The Universal Studios Tour is one of the most successful tourist stops in the Los Angeles area. The tour, via a tram bus, takes visitors behind the scenes to show many of the tricks of the movie trade, including special effects, prop construction, and stunts. There's an impressive array of crowd-pleasing attractions, including the giant shark from the movie *Jaws*, a huge Audio-Animatronic King Kong, a simulated flash flood, a parting of the Red Sea, and an audience participation filming of a *Star Trek* adventure. After the tram tour, you can view any or all of the studio's open-air theater programs, including a *Miami Vice* stunt show, a *Conan the Barbarian* action program, a western-movie stunt presentation, and a performance by a talented group of animal actors.

Kids' Facilities. Strollers rented for $1.50 (however, you can't take strollers on the trams). Diaper-changing counters in most restrooms. No bottle-warming facilities. Fast-food stands at various locations on tour route. Sit-down restaurants outside the tour area.

Ratings. Kids of all ages will be fascinated. The tram tour takes about 3 hours. If you add all the after-tour shows, figure on staying 7 to 8 hours. All ages, A.

MUSEUMS

GENE AUTRY'S WESTERN HERITAGE MUSEUM

4700 Zoo Dr., Griffith Park. (213) 667–2000. Take the Zoo Drive exit off the 5 Freeway. Free parking.

Hours. Tues.–Sun., 10 A.M.–5 P.M.

Costs. Adults, $4.75; students, $3.50; ages 2–12, $2.

The new $54 million museum salutes both the history of the American West and the movies that glorified it (often inaccurately). Named for the movies' famed singing cowboy Gene Autry, the 140,000-square-foot facility houses exhibits of authentic weapons, clothing, and equipment used by real-life cowboys, as well as the Hollywood hardware sported by John Wayne, William (Hopalong Cassidy) Boyd, Roy Rogers, and Autry. There's a large exhibit of Western art and literature, an impressive Colt handgun collection, and even an authentic stagecoach. The Museum also offers interactive video exhibits that show clips from old western movies. On Saturday afternoons, a movie theater presents showings of old westerns.

Kids' Facilities. No stroller rentals. Diaper-changing tables in both men's and ladies' restrooms. No bottle warming. Fast-food cafeteria. Gift shop.

Ratings. The museum offers a good balance between what the West was really like and the way the movies depicted it. Fun for all. It takes at least 90 minutes to see it all. 2–7, B; 8–11, A; 12–16, A.

CALIFORNIA AFRO-AMERICAN HISTORY MUSEUM

600 State Dr., Exposition Park. (213) 744–7432. Take the Exposition Blvd. exit off the 110 Freeway and head west to the Park. Parking $1 in all-day lot, or metered street parking.

Hours. Daily, 10 A.M.–5 P.M.

Costs. Free.

This fine museum is home to temporary exhibitions on the history of blacks in Los Angeles, as well as exhibits by contemporary and historically important black artists. Along with the nearby Natural History Museum and the Museum of Science and Industry, it should not be missed.

Kids' Facilities. No stroller rentals. No diaper-changing tables in restrooms. No food or bottle-warming facilities. Gift shop.

Ratings. It's difficult to rate, since the exhibits change. However, all the exhibits we've seen have been consistently top-notch.

NATURAL HISTORY MUSEUM OF LOS ANGELES COUNTY

900 Exposition Blvd., Exposition Park. (213) 744–3411 or (213) 744–3414. Take the Exposition Blvd. exit off the 110 Freeway. Parking $1 in pay lot or metered street parking.

Hours. Tues.–Sun., 10 A.M.–5 P.M.

Costs. Adults, $3; students with ID, $1.25; ages 5–12, 75¢; ages 4 and under, free.

Huge and packed to the rafters with fossils, minerals, and gemstones, the Natural History Museum is perhaps best known in the city for its beautiful dioramas of both North American and African animals. History galleries depict life in California and the Southwest from the early 16th century through the 1940s, as well as the United States in general from Colonial times through the early 20th century. They also feature a wonderful collection of antique cars and a discovery center gallery where young children can get their hands on fossils, rocks, stuffed animals, and a myriad of costumes for dress-up. All this in a monumental building that looks like it should be on the campus of Harvard University instead of in southern California.

Kids' Facilities. No stroller rentals. No diaper-changing tables in restrooms (plenty of benches, however). No bottle-warming facilities. Cafeteria serves fast food and sandwiches. Gift shop.

Ratings. One of the West Coast's great natural science museums, it gets top marks in all areas. All ages, A.

CALIFORNIA MUSEUM OF SCIENCE AND INDUSTRY

700 State St., Exposition Park. (213) 744–7400. Take the Exposition Blvd. exit off the 110 Freeway. Parking $1 in all-day lot, or metered street parking.

Hours. Daily, 10 A.M.–5 P.M.

Costs. *Museum:* free. *IMAX Theater:* adults, $4.75; ages 3–17, $3; ages 2 and under, free.

Hands-on interactive exhibits on computers, energy, math, health, and space are highlights of the Museum of Science and Industry. The popular Hall of Health features a large number of stations where visitors can test their hearts, blood pressure, eyesight, and other senses with use of a computer credit card; at the end of the visit, turn your card in for a computer printout of your health status. An interactive display (in the form of a lunchroom counter and sassy video waitress) helps you to make the correct dietary choices. The Air and Space Center is a relatively new addition to the museum. It displays NASA space memorabilia, communications satellites, real airplanes, and a replica of a Space Shuttle. The IMAX Theater presents motion pictures on a screen that stands 5 stories high.

Kids' Facilities. No stroller rentals. Diaper-changing areas in most restrooms. No bottle warming. There's a McDonald's restaurant on the premises. Gift shop.

Ratings. With all the buzzers, bells, and visual stimuli, it's a terrific place for all ages. Devote at least two hours. All ages, A.

LOS ANGELES COUNTY MUSEUM OF ART

5905 Wilshire Blvd. (213) 857–6000. Use the La Brea Ave. exit off the 10 Freeway; go north on La Brea to Wilshire and turn left to museum. Pay parking lot across street, maximum $5, or metered street parking.

Hours. Tues.–Fri., 10 A.M.–5 P.M.; Sat. and Sun., 10 A.M.–6 P.M.

Costs. Adults, $3; students with ID, $1.50; ages 5–12, 75¢; ages 4 and under, free. Free to all on second Tues. of every month.

The L.A. County Museum is a gargantuan facility with nearly every kind of art from every corner of the earth from every time period. Highlights include the recently opened Robert O. Anderson Gallery, an ultramodern building that features 20th-century paintings and sculpture. The bizarre-looking Pavilion for Japanese Art has major permanent exhibitions of netsuke sculptures and screen paintings. Throughout, you'll find the West Coast's largest collections of Far Eastern art, American and European paintings, decorative arts from all periods, and pre-Columbian artifacts, as well as Islamic and Indian art.

Kids' Facilities. No stroller rentals. No diaper-changing tables in restrooms, but plenty of benches. No bottle-warming facilities. A terrific cafeteria serves up sandwiches and salads. Gift shop.

Ratings. The visual stimuli are so plentiful that kids of all ages are bound to see something they like. It will take a good 2 hours to make your way throughout the Museum complex. All ages, A.

GEORGE C. PAGE MUSEUM OF LA BREA DISCOVERIES AND LA BREA TAR PITS

5801 Wilshire Blvd. (213) 936–2230. Use the La Brea Ave. exit off the 10 Freeway; go north on La Brea to Wilshire and turn left to the Museum. Pay parking lot at 6th and Curson Sts., maximum $3, or metered street parking.

Hours. Tues.–Sun., 10 A.M.–5 P.M.

Costs. Adults, $3; ages 13–17, $1.50; ages 5–12, 75¢; ages 4 and under, free. Free to all on second Tues. of every month.

Prehistory is the general theme here, with a special focus on the ice-age period in the area that became Los Angeles. Kids love the bones of age-old animals, and the Page Museum doesn't disappoint. Here you'll discover reconstructed saber tooth tigers, prehistoric wolves, mastodons, bison, and birds. Murals and dioramas re-create the period and a well-made 15-minute documentary film and slide show explains why the area is so rich in fossils. Kids can visit a laboratory where technicians clean, tag, and catalog fossils. Just outside the museum are the famed Rancho La Brea Tar Pits, the bubbling asphalt beds that preserved many of the relics on view inside. Replicas of the mammals that once lived in the area surround the oozing bog.

Kids' Facilities. No stroller rentals. No diaper-changing tables in rest-rooms, but plenty of benches. No bottle-warming facilities. Fast food at La Brea Lunch Stand. Gift shop.

Ratings. While there are no dinosaurs (they were long gone by the time the tar pits appeared), the bones on view are still enough to tantalize kids of all ages. Set aside a good hour to see the museum, and 20 minutes to see the tar pits. All ages, A.

HOLLYWOOD STUDIO MUSEUM

2100 N. Highland Ave., Hollywood. (213) 874–2276. Use the Highland Ave. exit off the 101 Freeway. Free parking.

Hours. Tues.–Sun., 10 A.M.–4 P.M.

Costs. Adults, $2; students with ID, $1.50; ages 11 and under, $1.

The first major Hollywood movie production was Cecil B. DeMille's 1913 silent epic *The Squaw Man*. Much of the indoor filming of that motion picture took place in the barn that now houses the Museum. Along with memorabilia from that movie are artifacts, costumes, and movie props from films, stars, and studios throughout the silent era in Hollywood (1913–1928). You'll see personal items owned by screen icons like Charlie Chaplin, Mabel Normand, and Rudolph Valentino. To get you in the mood, there's a 20-minute video presentation on the facility and the early days of movie-making in the area.

Kids' Facilities. No stroller rentals. No diaper-changing tables in rest-rooms (use benches). No food or bottle-warming facilities. Gift shop.

Ratings. If you or your children are movie lovers, this museum cannot be topped. It takes about an hour to see it all. 2–7, C; 8–11, A; 12–16, A.

J. PAUL GETTY MUSEUM

17985 Pacific Coast Hwy., Malibu. (213) 458–2003. Take the 10 Freeway west until it empties on Pacific Coast Hwy.; proceed north along coast to museum. Free lot parking. (*Note: Parking space is limited. Reservations for parking must be made in advance. In summer, the wait for a space is often a week; in winter, three days or more.*)

Hours. Tues.–Sun., 10 A.M.–5 P.M.

Costs. Free, but parking reservations must be made prior to admission.

A re-created ancient Roman villa overlooking the Pacific Ocean, the Getty's building design and landscaping are accurate right down to the colors of the paint and the flowers in the garden. A large portion of the items on display are Greek and Roman antiquities, with an ample supply of European Medieval and Renaissance paintings, sculptures, and manuscripts. It all makes for a beautiful step back in time.

Kids' Facilities. No stroller rentals. Diaper-changing table in ladies' basement restroom. No bottle warming. Fast-food cafeteria with indoor and outdoor seating.

Ratings. Even if your kids don't like the art, the opulent Roman-style building and gardens should be enough to hold their curiosity for an hour. 2–7, B; 8–11, B; 12–16, A.

MUSEUM OF CONTEMPORARY ART (MOCA) AND THE TEMPORARY CONTEMPORARY

MOCA: 250 S. Grand Ave. (213) 621–2766. Take the Temple St. exit off the 101 Freeway; go south to 1st St. and turn left; turn right on Grand to Museum. Pay lot and metered street parking. *Temporary Contemporary:* 152 N. Central Ave., Little Tokyo. (213) 621–2766. Take the Temple St. exit off the 101 Freeway; go south to 1st. St. and turn left; go 9 blocks to Central Ave. and turn left. Pay lot and metered street parking.

Hours. Both facilities: Sat., Sun., Tues., and Wed., 11 A.M.–6 P.M.; Thurs. and Fri., 11 A.M.–8 P.M.

Costs. One charge for both facilities: adults, $4; students with ID, $2; ages 12 and under, free.

The beautiful MOCA building, designed by architect I. M. Pei, is a sight to behold from the exterior. The problems are inside. An ultramodern museum, its interior lacks warmth and visual stimulation. Large rooms are devoted to a single neon light bulb or a large canvas painted in one color. There are some interesting sculptures, but they are too few and far between to hold anyone's interest, let alone that of an 8-year-old. The Temporary Contemporary, on the other hand, is a treasure, featuring an eclectic grouping of lithographs, sculptures, paintings, and some amazing constructions. There's something new and stimulating to see at every turn. Anything goes at the Temporary Contemporary.

Kids' Facilities. *MOCA:* No stroller rentals. Countertops in all restrooms suitable for diaper changing. No bottles warmed. Italian restaurant in museum courtyard. *Temporary Contemporary:* No stroller rentals. No diaper-changing tables in restrooms. No food or bottle-warming facilities. Gift shops in both places.

Ratings. *MOCA:* Dull for children. The only compelling aspects are the beautiful wooden floors and great echoes in most of the sparse rooms. 2–7, D; 8–11, D; 12–16, D. *Temporary Contemporary:* A great museum, alive with clutter that will appeal to every age and taste. All ages, A.

WELLS FARGO HISTORY MUSEUM

444 S. Flower St., ground level. (213) 253–7166. Take the Temple St. exit off the 101 Freeway; go south on Hope St. past 1st St.; veer to right onto Flower; stay on Flower and turn left into pay parking lot. Parking lot at 400 S. Flower.

Hours. Mon.–Fri., 9 A.M.–5 P.M.

Costs. Free.

This wonderful little museum, in the main branch of the Wells Fargo Bank, features two stagecoaches: an authentic, restored mid-19th-century coach and a recently constructed facsimile. The old coach is just for viewing, but you're invited to climb aboard the facsimile and listen to an audio tape describe an 1859 stagecoach journey. Other exhibits include gold nuggets taken from the California gold fields, Gold Rush memorabilia, and a re-created Wells Fargo office from the era, complete with telegraph office and a working telegraph kids can try.

Kids' Facilities. No stroller rentals. Large countertop in ladies' room for diaper changing. No bottle-warming facilities. Restaurants located in Well's Fargo Center (shopping area in building). Gift shop.

Ratings. The museum offers an interesting slice of history. Kids love to ''ride'' in the stagecoach and work the telegraph. See it all in a half hour. 2–7, A; 8–11, A; 12–16, B.

KIDSPACE MUSEUM

390 S. El Molino Ave., Pasadena. (818) 449–9143. Take the 11 (Pasadena) Freeway to its northern end (Arroyo Pkwy.); turn right on California St.; turn left on El Molino Ave. Free street parking; free lot parking on weekends.

Hours. Wed., 2 P.M.–5 P.M.; Sat. and Sun., 12 noon–4:30 P.M.

Costs. $2.50; under age 2, free.

Kidspace is a hands-on museum aimed at children between the ages of 2 and 12, although most of the exhibits will be of little interest to kids over 10. Flights of fancy and imagination are encouraged, and permanent fixtures include a real race car, a television studio, a radio booth in which to play records and talk on a microphone, and a dress-up trunk filled with uniforms. In addition, children can climb on and through a number of structures designed to teach mobility and agility. We loved the Dr. Feelbetter exhibit with X-rays, a hospital room, and soft-sculpture doll with removable vital organs.

Kids' Facilities. No stroller rentals. Diaper-changing table in ladies' restroom only. No bottle-warming facilities. Soda machine only. No food service.

Ratings. Younger kids dive right into the activities, but kids over 10 could be bored stiff. 2–7, A; 8–11, C; 12–16, F.

LOS ANGELES CHILDREN'S MUSEUM

310 N. Main St., Los Angeles Mall. (213) 687–8800. Take the Temple St. exit off the 101 Freeway; turn left at Temple; turn left at Main. Pay lot parking underneath building.

Hours. Summer: Mon.–Fri., 11:30 A.M.–5 P.M; Sat. and Sun., 10 A.M.–5 P.M. During school year: Wed. and Thurs., 2 P.M.–4 P.M.; Sat. and Sun., 10 A.M.–5 P.M.

Costs. $4 per person; under age 2, free.

In operation since 1979, the two-level 13,000-square-foot Museum is chock-full of hands-on exhibits and activities. Attractions include a miniature version of the city streets with street signs, lights, a bus, a police motorcycle and uniforms to try on, an exhibit on the many ethnic cultures of L.A., face painting, a doctor's and dentist's office, a giant Lego building set, a working recording studio, a soft-sculpture play area for toddlers, a television station, and lots of craft workshop areas. All exhibits encourage kids to roll up their sleeves and get involved.

Kids' Facilities. No stroller rentals. Diaper-changing tables in both ladies' and men's restrooms. No food or bottle-warming facilities. Fast-food restaurant downstairs in the Los Angeles Mall. Gift shop.

Ratings. Younger children, up to age 12, will enjoy this museum. 2–7, A; 8–11, A; 12–16, D.

LOS ANGELES MARITIME MUSEUM

Berth 84, Foot of 6th St., San Pedro. (213) 548–7618. Take the Harbor Blvd. exit off the 110 Freeway; turn right on Harbor Blvd. and drive south to 6th St. Free parking.

Hours. Tues.–Sun., 10 A.M.–5 P.M.

Costs. $1 donation accepted.

First built in 1941 as a ferry terminal, this streamlined Art Deco building overlooks the Los Angeles Harbor. Exhibits include the original bridge of the cruiser *Los Angeles* and lots of scale models of famous historical vessels. In addition, there are many authentic naval artifacts including ships' bells, navigation equipment, and even an amateur radio room where visitors can listen to ship-to-shore radio communication. It's located next door to Ports 'O Call shopping village and the harbor cruise ship docks.

Kids' Facilities. No stroller rentals. Diaper-changing table in ladies' restroom. No bottle-warming or food service. Gift shop.

Ratings. A nice stop if you're in the neighborhood to take a sightseeing cruise of Los Angeles Harbor. See it all in about 45 minutes. 2–7, B; 8–11, A; 12–16, A.

MOVIELAND WAX MUSEUM

7711 Beach Blvd., Buena Park, Orange County, (located about 23 miles southeast of downtown Los Angeles). (714) 522–1155. Take the Beach Blvd. exit off the 5 Freeway; head south on Beach to the museum. Free parking.

Hours. Summer: daily, 9 A.M.–8 P.M. Rest of the year: daily, 10 A.M.–8 P.M.

Costs. Adults, $9.95; ages 4–11, $5.95; ages 3 and under, free.

One of the finest wax museums we've run across, Movieland features more than 240 celebrities in familiar movie and television settings. As much work has gone into re-creating the sets as the look-alike wax figures. The famous include the whole *Star Trek* crew on the bridge of the *Enterprise*; Dorothy, Toto, and the rest of her traveling partners in *The Wizard of Oz*; and three of the Cartwrights in front of the Ponderosa ranch house from *Bonanza*. There's even a figure of singer Michael Jackson before he had the plastic surgeon add a cleft to his chin. The museum's perfunctory chamber of horrors includes Dracula, Frankenstein, and the Phantom of the Opera. The inside joke, of course, is a scene of Vincent Price from his early-1950s classic *House of Wax*.

Kids' Facilities. No stroller rentals. No diaper-changing tables in restrooms (some benches, but they're in areas that are almost too dark to be of help). No food or bottle-warming facilities. Three gift shops.

Ratings. Kids with any exposure to movies or television are bound to recognize most of the wax figures. 2–7, B; 8–11, A; 12–16, A.

HOTELS

Because the Los Angeles area is so large, when making a reservation you should give serious thought to the activities you're planning. Geographically speaking, you don't want to be too far away. If your plans will keep you close to most of Los Angeles' most popular museums and attractions (Hollywood, Beverly Hills, and the movie studios), accommodations can be expensive, especially when you add the costs of restaurant meals. We've tailored our hotel suggestions to provide the greatest number of services for the most reasonable cost.

PLAZA SUITE HOTEL—BEVERLY HILLS

141 S. Clark St., Beverly Hills. (213) 278–9310. 102 units. Free parking.

Rates. $115; special rates sometimes available.

A terrific all-suite hotel, the Plaza Suite caters to business people and their families who are in Los Angeles on extended stays. It's not unusual to find motion picture crew members and directors from other parts of

the country. A no-frills outfit that belies the Beverly Hills address, it is close to downtown Beverly Hills and West Hollywood. Children under 18 stay free with parents.
Cribs: Yes, no charge.
Rollaways: Yes, no charge.
Babysitting referrals: Yes.
Pool: Yes.
Restaurant: No.
Kitchen facilities: Yes.
Room service: Yes.
Closet emergency hospital: Cedars Sinai Medical Center, 5 minutes away, (213) 855–6512.

PLAZA SUITE HOTEL—HOLLYWOOD

7230 Franklin Ave., Hollywood. (213) 874–7450. 79 units. Free parking.

Rates. $95; special lower rates sometimes available.

The Plaza caters to the entertainment industries, with an emphasis on the music business. The atmosphere and staff are friendly and helpful. It's near Mann's Chinese Theater, Hollywood in Miniature, and Griffith Park. Children under 18 stay free with parents.
Cribs: Yes, no charge.
Rollaways: Yes, no charge.
Babysitting referrals: No.
Pool: Yes.
Restaurant: No.
Kitchen facilities: Yes.
Room service: Yes.
Closest emergency hospital: Cedars Sinai Medical Center, 20 minutes away, (213) 855–6512.

LE REVE HOTEL

8822 Cynthia St., West Hollywood. (213) 854–1114 or (800) 424–4443. 80 units. Free parking.

Rates. $115 to $145 per night; special weekend rates available.

Part of the L'Ermitage all-suite hotel chain, Le Reve is a small, quiet facility in a sleepy neighborhood. The hotel is popular with out-of-town screenwriters hammering out final screenplay drafts. It's sandwiched between Beverly Hills and Hollywood. Children under 12 stay free with parents.
Cribs: Yes, no charge.

Rollaways: Yes, no charge.
Babysitting referrals: Yes.
Pool: Yes.
Restaurant: No.
Kitchen facilities: Yes.
Room service: Yes.
Closest emergency hospital: Cedars Sinai Medical Center, 10 minutes away, (213) 855–6512.

LE DUFY HOTEL

1000 Westmount Dr., West Hollywood (213) 657–7400 or (800) 424–4443. 121 units. Free parking.

Rates. $160; special weekend rates available.

The Le Dufy is also part of the L'Ermitage chain. A quiet neighborhood surrounds the hotel, which is close to the shopping and restaurants of Sunset Boulevard. Kids under 12 stay free with parents.
Cribs: Yes, no charge.
Rollaways: Yes, no charge.
Babysitting referrals: Yes.
Pool: Yes.
Restaurant: No.
Kitchen facilities: Yes.
Room service: Yes.
Closest emergency hospital: Cedars Sinai Medical Center, 10 minutes away, (213) 855–6512.

LE PARC HOTEL

733 N. Westknoll Ave., West Hollywood. (213) 855–8888 or (800) 424–4443. 154 units. Free parking.

Rates. $180; special weekend rates available.

The Le Parc is one of our favorite hotels. Also part of the L'Ermitage chain, it not only is situated in a quiet neighborhood, it features a very good little French restaurant and tennis courts on the roof. It's located near shopping, restaurants, and Beverly Hills. Kids under 12 stay free with parents.
Cribs: Yes, no charge.
Rollaways: Yes, no charge.
Babysitting referrals: Yes.
Pool: Yes.
Restaurant: Yes.

Kitchen facilities: Yes.
Room service: Yes.
Closest emergency hospital: Cedars Sinai Medical Center, 10 minutes away, (213) 855–6512.

DISNEYLAND HOTEL

1150 W. Cerritos Ave., Anaheim. (714) 778–6600 or (800) 642–5391. 1174 units. Parking $7 per day.

Rates. $125 to $180.

A huge four-building structure, the Disneyland Hotel stands just across the parking lot from Disneyland and is the only hotel that features Disneyland Monorail service (a thrill for kids). A luxury hotel, it boasts ten tennis courts, three swimming pools, and a tropical beach on a huge inland waterway. Children under 18 stay free with parents.
Cribs: Yes, no charge.
Rollaways: Yes, $15.
Babysitting referrals: Yes.
Pool: Yes.
Restaurant: Yes.
Kitchen facilities: No.
Room service: Yes.
Closest emergency hospital: University of California–Irvine Medical Center, 10 minutes away, (714) 634–6158.

RESTAURANTS

Los Angeles is the unabashed fast-food capital of the world. A drive down any boulevard and it seems like there are McDonald's, Burger Kings, and Wendy's at 1-mile intervals. If your kids are hankering for burgers, we recommend In-N-Out, a drive-through chain, which makes all their burgers fresh (no frozen beef) and to your order. Their french fries are wonderful.

ED DEBEVIC'S

134 N. La Cienega Blvd. near Wilshire Blvd., Beverly Hills. (213) 659–1952. Valet parking, $1.50.

Hours. Mon.–Thurs., 11:30 A.M.–12 midnight; Fri. and Sat., 11:30 A.M.–1 A.M.; Sun., 11:30 A.M.–11 P.M.

A carbon copy of its Chicago namesake, Ed's is a throwback to the

1950s. Sassy waitresses in starched uniforms shout to be heard above the blaring jukebox music. All this shouting and blaring multiplied by the fifty or so tables and booths makes for a raucous good time that kids are sure to enjoy. The menu offers burgers, fries, meatloaf, chili, and soda fountain creations. The blue plate specials include lots of lumpy mashed potatoes, iceberg lettuce salads, and enriched white bread. For parents, the bar serves beer (try Ed's own brand). Figure on spending $5 to $7 per person. Be prepared for elbow-to-elbow crowds at dinner. Reservations taken for lunch only. MasterCard and Visa.

Kids' Facilities. Booster seats and high chairs available. No children's menus. No diaper-changing tables in restrooms.

CHUCK E. CHEESE PIZZATIME THEATER

Many locations all over the greater Los Angeles area including: 8425 Reseda Blvd., Northridge, (818) 993–3446; 8357 Laurel Canyon Blvd., Sun Valley, (818) 768–2104; and 2821 Pacific Coast Hwy., Torrance, (213) 326–8470. Free parking.

Hours. Sun.–Thurs., 11 A.M.–10 P.M.; Fri. and Sat., 10 A.M.–11 P.M.
    Nothing you can say to a child between 18 months and 7 years will whip him or her into a frenzy like the words "Chuck E. Cheese." Perhaps it's something in the cheese they use or the setting, a cavernous arcade filled with electronic games, shooting galleries, and rides. The establishment's namesake and a smiling group of fellow Audio-Animatronic rodents play musical instruments and serenade you while you dine. The pizza is cheap and pretty good, but beware of the games arcade. Those 25¢ tokens add up. Food will run less than $5 per person. No reservations (except for birthday parties). Major credit cards.

Kids' Facilities. Booster seats and high chairs available. Diaper-changing counters in ladies' restrooms. No children's menus.

MON KEE'S SEA FOOD RESTAURANT

679 N. Spring St., Chinatown. (213) 628–6717 or (213) 628–1090. Valet parking, $1.50; also metered street parking.

Hours. Sun.–Thurs., 11:30 A.M.–9:45 P.M.; Fri. and Sat., 11:30 A.M.–10:15 P.M.
    While the decor is a bit on the tacky side at Mon Kee's (formica tables, linoleum floors and a huge hand-painted undersea mural on the north wall), it hasn't stopped them from serving what we feel to be some of

the best Chinese seafood dishes in Los Angeles. We recommend their shrimp with garlic, pepper, and onion; the double-fry scallops; and, in spring and early summer, their sauted fresh asparagus. For lunch on any given day, the establishment is filled with local Chinatown residents, well-dressed attorneys, and City Hall workers. At dinner, you'll find some of the same people, with their families in tow. Figure on spending about $10 per person for food. Beer and wine served. Make reservations for dinner. Major credit cards.

Kids' Facilities. Booster seats and high chairs available. No children's menus; however, the personnel dote on kids, often giving them handfuls of fortune cookies. No diaper-changing tables in restrooms.

MICELI'S ITALIAN RESTAURANT

3653 Cahuenga Blvd. W., Studio City. (213) 851–3344. Free parking.

Hours. Mon.–Thurs., 5 P.M.–12 midnight; Fri. and Sat., 5 P.M.–1 A.M.; Sun., 4 P.M.–12 midnight.

Miceli's is one of the few remaining Italian restaurants in Los Angeles that offers singing waiters and waitresses. The result is excellent entertainment that younger children really love and older ones tend to find embarrassing, especially if Mom and Dad sing along. The food's pretty good, and the bread they serve is some of the best in the city. Entrees run $7 to $15. Full bar. Reservations suggested. Major credit cards.

Kids' Facilities. Booster seats and high chairs available. No diaper-changing tables in restrooms. No children's menus, but portions are large, and you're allowed to split orders with children at no extra cost.

EL CHOLO

1121 S. Western Ave. at 11th St. (213)734–2773. Free parking across the street; valet parking, $1.50.

Hours. Mon.–Thurs., 11 A.M.–10 P.M.; Fri. and Sat., 11 A.M.–11 P.M.; Sun., 11 A.M.–9 P.M.

A favorite star hangout during Hollywood's silent movie days, El Cholo has been packing in Mexican food fans since before 1920. The ambiance is early California, with beige stucco walls and large darkly stained wooden tables. Waiters and waitresses dress in traditional costumes, and music is provided by a wandering mariachi band. The atmosphere is loud and festive, and the food is good and not too expensive (dinners from

$6 to $15). Full bar (try the margaritas!). Reservations a must for dinner. Major credit cards.

Kids' Facilities. Booster seats and high chairs available. No diaper-changing tables in restrooms. No children's menus.

Big Splurges

MICHAEL'S

1147 3rd St., Santa Monica. (213) 451–0843. Valet parking.

Hours. Lunch: Mon.–Fri., 12 noon–2 P.M.; Sat. and Sun., 10:30 A.M.–2 P.M. Dinner: nightly, 6:30 P.M.–10 P.M.

One of the city's best restaurants, Michael's is also one of the more expensive. New menus are printed each day based on whatever fresh ingredients happen to be available. Typically, the fare in this quietly elegant restaurant consists of fresh pasta appetizers and salads, and entrees of duck, lamb, and fresh seafood. Dishes are strictly a la carte with appetizers priced at around $16, entrees $32, and desserts $10. Full bar. Reservations recommended. Major credit cards.

SPAGO

1114 Horn Ave., West Hollywood. (213) 652–4025. Valet parking.

Hours. Nightly, 6 P.M.–11:30 P.M.

For the last decade or so, Wolfgang Puck has been the hottest chef in town. Spago, with its fancy nouvelle pizza, is one of the city's most-traveled-to nighttime eateries and one of the toughest reservations to get if you want to eat any time before 10 P.M. Bizarre and exotic pizza and pasta dishes are the mainstay. Expect the dishes to be made with non-traditional ingredients like pesto, prawns, and goat cheese, or whatever strikes Chef Puck's mood for the night. The food is good, and the people-watching is great. It's the one place in Los Angeles where you're almost assured of seeing movie and television personalities. We suggest making a meal out of appetizers. Figure on spending about $35 per person, without wine. Full bar. Reservations for dinner should be made 4 to 5 days in advance. Major credit cards.

SHOPPING

CHILDREN'S BOOK AND MUSIC CENTER

2500 Santa Monica Blvd. at 26th St., Santa Monica. (213) 829–0215 or (800) 443–1856. Free parking.

Hours. Mon.–Sat., 9 A.M.–5:30 P.M., Wed. until 7 P.M.

The largest children's bookstore in the United States, Children's Book and Music offers a wonderful selection of books for kids from infancy through teenage, parenting books for adults, musical instruments, video cassettes, and compact discs.

SAN MARINO TOY AND BOOK

2475 Huntington Dr., San Marino. (818) 795–5301. Free parking.

Hours. Mon.–Sat., 10 A.M.–5 P.M.

A medium-size, well-stocked store, San Marino Toy and Book features a large selection of children's reading materials, puzzles, science experiments, and educational toys, including Brio and Lego building sets.

CHILDREN'S BOOK WORLD

10580 ½ W. Pico Blvd. near Overland Ave., (213) 559–2665. Metered street parking.

Hours. Mon.–Fri., 10 A.M.–5:30 P.M.; Sat., 10 A.M.–5 P.M.

In business only since 1986, Children's Book World is already a stop for children's book authors on the autographing circuit. A smallish shop, it features a large selection of children's books as well as a few toys and puppets. The store boasts a couch and a number of nooks and crannies for reading.

POWER OF PLAY

14425 Ventura Blvd. near Van Nuys Blvd., Sherman Oaks. (818) 906–2123. Free parking.

Hours. Mon.–Sat., 10 A.M.–6 P.M.

Located in a busy shopping center, Power of Play specializes in educational toys and features a large area for children to "test" them. Their formidable book section has a hands-on reading area. Manufacturers often give toy demonstrations.

BEVERLY CENTER SHOPPING MALL

8500 Beverly Blvd., corner La Cienega and Beverly Blvds. (213) 854–0070. First 3 hours of parking free.

Hours. Mon.–Sat., 10 A.M.–9 P.M.; Sun., 11 A.M.–6 P.M.

The Beverly Center is a shopping mall for the well-to-do. While you may not have the needed funds for buying those bizarre-looking European outfits, it's fun to walk by and look in the windows. Aside from expensive, high-fashion stores, the Beverly Center features two well-known southern California department stores, **The Broadway**, (213) 854–7200 and **Bullocks**, (213) 854–6655, as well as **By Design**, (213) 652–9230, a wonderful high-tech store with the latest gadgets and gifts.

GRAND CENTRAL MARKET

Between Broadway and Hill St., and 3rd and 4th Sts. (213) 624–2378. Pay lot and metered street parking.

Hours. Daily, 9 A.M.–6 P.M.

Grand Central is one of the last great indoor farmers' markets left in Los Angeles. It contains more than fifty stalls that offer everything from fresh vegetables and fish to sandwiches and prepared Mexican delicacies. Even if you don't intend to buy, a walk-through is an educational experience for kids whose only shopping experience has been the neighborhood supermarket. Spanish is the first language here, although all the vendors speak English, too.

TRANSPORTATION

Before the mid-1950s, Los Angeles had one of the finest mass transit systems in the United States. The swift and efficient light-rail cars of the Pacific Red and Yellow lines were scrapped in favor of a massive plan to build freeways and encourage two-car garages. However, by the late 1990s, the first two legs of a long-proposed subway system are scheduled to be in operation. Nevertheless, it will probably be decades before Los Angeles has a subway system that fills the needs of a majority of citizens and tourists. Until then, visitors will have to drive cars or take buses—both of which are subject to traffic delays.

BUS

The Southern California Rapid Transit District (RTD) operates most of the buses in L.A. Operating on a 24-hour schedule, RTD services most of the county. The base fare is $1.10 (exact change) with transfers selling for 25¢. Downtown Area Short Hop (DASH) minibuses run Mondays through Saturdays from 6 A.M. to 6 P.M. and service downtown L.A.'s business and shopping areas. DASH rides cost $1.50 (exact change). RTD also offers a Freeway Flyer bus service that connects passengers in Los Angeles with some of the outlying tourist attractions. The RTD operates a very helpful information line for help in route plotting; call (213) 626–4455.

TAXIS

Because of the vast distances between points of interest, taxis in Los Angeles can be very expensive. The initial cost for climbing aboard is $1.90, with an additional cost of $1.40 per mile. Dollars add up quickly, with a taxi from a downtown hotel to Venice Beach running from $25 to $30 and from a West Hollywood hotel to Universal Studios topping out at between $15 and $20. Cabs are almost never hailed in Los Angeles. Unless you pick one up at a local hotel or at the airport, you must telephone. Companies include Independent Cab Company, (213) 385–8294; L.A. Taxi, (213) 627–7000; and United Independent Taxi, (213) 653–5050.

TOURS

BUS

Gray Line. (213) 481–2121. Offers a large number of daily sightseeing tours. Their most popular are their half-day tour of the Beverly Hills and Bel Air homes of the movie stars (adults, $23; ages 3–11, $17) and their big, 1-day Los Angeles tour with stops at hot spots like Hollywood, Beverly Hills, and downtown L. A. (adults, $27; ages 3–11, $18). They also offer excursions to Universal City, the San Diego Zoo, and Tijuana, Mexico.

Oscar J's. (818) 501–2217. Sells a big 4-hour City Tour that includes downtown, the Music Center, Beverly Hills, the stars' homes, Melrose Avenue, Century City, and Westwood (adults, $33; ages 3–11, $25). In tandem with the City Tour, they offer the Universal Studios Tour to make it an all-day affair. The cost for the combination package is $56 for adults and $42 for ages 3–11. Their 7-hour Beach Tour takes in Marina Del Rey, Santa Monica, Venice, Will Rogers State Park, and the Getty Museum (adults, $46; ages 3–11, $36). They also offer excursions to Disneyland.

Starline Tours. (213) 463–3131. Offers a 2-hour tour of movie star homes (adults, $19; ages 3–11, $11) and a 5-hour City Tour that includes downtown, Olvera Street, Korea Town, Chinatown, the La Brea Tar Pits, and Beverly Hills' Rodeo Drive (adults $26; ages 3–11, $15). Starline offers twelve additional tours.

Grave Line Tours. (213) 392–5501. For those families who are macabre at heart. Passengers on the 2 ½-hour tour become "guest mourners" as they climb inside a vintage Cadillac hearse for a trip back through "100 years of Hollywood death and scandal." It's a tongue-in-cheek look at the city's colorful past through visits to famous cemeteries and sites of deaths and suicides. Tours run Tuesdays through Sundays from Mann's Chinese Theater at 12 noon. Call ahead for reserved $30 seats or standby $25 seats. Reservations should be made by calling between 6 P.M. and 8 P.M. Pacific Time. Due to the often dark subject matter, we recommend this tour for parents and kids over age 12.

BOAT

Los Angeles Harbor Cruises. (213) 831–0996. Takes passengers on 1-hour tours of the Los Angeles Harbor (both inner and outer harbors). You see the docks, the Pacific cruise ships, and the large supertankers. Tours depart several times a day between 12 noon and 5 P.M. from Ports 'O Call Village, San Pedro, Berth 77. (Adults, $6; ages 2–12, $3.)

Catalina Express. (213) 519–1212. Provides 90-minute one-way hops between Los Angeles Harbor and Catalina Island, about 26 miles out into the Pacific Ocean. The large boats have airline-type seats and cabin attendants. You can buy drinks and snacks on board. Boats leave every 2 hours during the summer and on weekends throughout the year (adults, $27.40, round trip; ages 3–11, $20.20). In summer 1989, Catalina Express will inaugurate a hydrofoil service that will take around 45 minutes to reach Catalina.

MOVIE LOCATIONS

Hollywood on Location. (213) 659–9165. Offers a unique service to tourists who wish to get a first-hand glimpse of their favorite stars currently filming television shows and movies on location on the streets of Los Angeles. For $29, Hollywood on Location provides clients with a list of the day's and night's shooting schedule, the names of the stars who'll be there, exact times, exact street locations, and maps on how to get there. To obtain the list, stop by their offices, 8644 Wilshire Boulevard, Beverly Hills, and ask for a free rundown of the shows and stars shooting that day. You pay only if you want the addresses and exact timetables.

WALKING

The Los Angeles Conservancy. (213) 623–2489. Conducts weekly Saturday morning walks through the historic areas of downtown Los Angeles. Some tours incorporate interesting downtown locations like the old Broadway theater district and the city's financial district. The main thrusts are buildings and architectural styles. Tours leave the Biltmore Hotel Saturdays at 10 A.M. Call ahead for reservations and directions. These tours will probably be of interest to parents and children over 12. ($5 per person.)

SEASONAL EVENTS

January

TOURNAMENT OF ROSES PARADE

This floral extravaganza, held on January 1 (January 2, if the 1st falls on Sunday), has been occurring annually for the last century. The grand-daddy of all parades, it begins at 8 A.M. To secure a good vantage point, you should get to the 5-½ mile parade route along Pasadena's Colorado Boulevard by 5 A.M. It's free for a spot on the street. As good as it looks on national television, it looks better in person. For more information: (818) 449–4100 or (818) 449–ROSE for a recorded message.

WHALE WATCHING

One of the great joys in southern California is putting out to sea to watch a few hours of the 4-month migration (through early April) that Pacific gray whales make between their summer home in the Gulf of Alaska and their wintering place in the Sea of Cortez off Baja California. Boats leave daily for a 3-hour cruise from the Catalina Landing in downtown Long Beach. For more information: (213) 514–3838.

February

CHINESE NEW YEAR

A week-long celebration (usually in February, depending on the lunar calendar), Chinese New Year in Los Angeles entails a beauty pageant, a 10k run, a weekend carnival (complete with firecrackers), and a big nighttime parade. The restaurants get crowded, so make reservations early. For more information: (213) 617–0396.

March

SANTA MONICA PIER KITE FESTIVAL

Spring arrives early in southern California as the stiff March winds blow off the ocean. This colorful late-March weekend festival takes place just north of the Santa Monica Pier, with some amazingly intricate kites to watch as their owners put them through their paces. Almost everybody in the crowd launches a kite of his or her own, sometimes causing great air disasters. It's all in good fun, and kids love it. For more information: (213) 822–2561.

May

CINCO DE MAYO

Olvera Street and El Pueblo de Los Angeles Historical Monument are the locales for the annual festival that celebrates the May 5, 1862, victory of Mexican troops over the French at the Battle of Puebla. Music, food, and colorful costumes highlight the week-long activities. For more information: (213) 687–4344.

July

JULY FOURTH FIREWORKS

While fireworks displays occur all around Los Angeles, one of the best takes place at Marina del Rey, just south of Venice. The fireworks are doubly impressive when reflected in the calm waters of the Marina. The first explosion is at 9 P.M. For more information: (213) 305–9545.

FESTIVAL OF ARTS AND PAGEANT OF THE MASTERS

Throughout July and August, Laguna Beach (along the coast, halfway between Los Angeles and San Diego) hosts this world-famous art festival. One of the festival's most incredible sights is the nighttime Pageant of the Masters, in which local citizens pose motionless amid lavish backdrops to re-create famous paintings by the Old Masters. For more information (and Masters tickets): (714) 494–1145.

September

MEXICAN INDEPENDENCE DAY

El Pueblo de Los Angeles Historic Monument is the site of this mid-month fiesta celebrating the independence of our neighbor to the south. For more information: (213) 687–4344.

LOS ANGELES COUNTY FAIR

A two-week blowout at the end of the month, the L.A. County Fair at the fairgrounds in Pomona (east of the city), features carnival rides, cooking contests, livestock judging, horse racing, arts and crafts displays, flower shows, and musical concerts by famous performers. It's the largest county fair in North America and ranks number six in size among all fairs and expositions on the continent. For ticket information: (714) 623–3111.

November

HOLLYWOOD CHRISTMAS PARADE

Usually occurring on the Sunday after Thanksgiving, the Hollywood Christmas Parade features all sorts of stars and celebrities from the entertainment world, plus Santa, of course. Kicking off at about 6 P.M., the parade winds along Hollywood Boulevard. It's free to those who line the sidewalks. For more information: (213) 462–2394.

DOO DAH PARADE

While this event, designed to poke fun at the Tournament of Roses parade, doesn't occur every year, it has taken place like clockwork over the last few, usually on the Sunday after Thanksgiving. Paraders dress in all sorts of funny costumes. A perennial favorite is the Precision Briefcase Drill Team, a group of men wearing conservative suits and carrying briefcases who perform intricate drills and maneuvers. The turnout is healthy for the 2-hour parade, which begins at 12 noon, so its wise to show up around 10 A.M. For recorded information on times and exact route: (818) 796–2591.

December

MARINA DEL REY CHRISTMAS BOAT PARADE

This boat parade gets bigger and bigger every year. Local yacht owners deck their hulls with holly, lights, and colorful ornamentation for the annual spin through the many channels of the Marina. A real delight for children, it takes place on a Saturday night two weeks before Christmas. For more information: (213) 821–7614.

CHILDREN'S THEATER

BOB BAKER MARIONETTE THEATER

1345 W. 1st St. (213) 250–9995. Free parking.

The longest-running marionette theater in the nation, the Bob Baker company has been in operation for twenty-five years. The troupe puts on shows at various times seven days a week. Your $7 admission ("for kids of all ages") buys you a 1-hour show plus refreshments, as well as a guided tour of the marionette workshop. The whole package takes about 2 hours and is fascinating for the whole family. Call ahead for show times.

THEATREWEST'S STORYBOOK THEATER

3333 Cahuenga Blvd. W., Hollywood. (818) 761–2203. Free street parking.

The Storybook Theater's ever-changing repertoire of productions is aimed at children of different age groups. Most plays have original story lines with characters familiar to most kids. Shows are presented Saturdays and Sundays at 1 P.M. Call ahead for a schedule and reservations. Tickets are $5.

SANTA MONICA PLAYHOUSE

1211 4th St. near Wilshire Blvd., Santa Monica. (213) 394–9779. Park free in Santa Monica Place shopping mall parking lot; also metered street parking.

A terrific theater for young children, Santa Monica Playhouse's Saturday and Sunday afternoon performances are given at 1 P.M. and 3 P.M. Their changing repertoire often includes familiar fairy tale characters. Each show lasts about an hour and costs $5 per ticket. These plays are so popular that reservations are a must.

LOS ANGELES PHILHARMONIC SYMPHONIES FOR YOUTH

Dorothy Chandler Pavilion, 135 N. Grand Ave. (213) 972–7211 or (213) 972–0702. Pay lot parking.

Each year, the L.A. Philharmonic Orchestra presents a five-concert Saturday morning series for children between November and April. The musical programs offer choices that are easily accessible for kids and feature interpretative remarks by the conductor. Phone ahead for schedule and reservations. Tickets cost $5.

BABYSITTING SERVICES

WE SIT BETTER
(818) 997–1421

Twenty years in the business, We Sit Better sends state-licensed and bonded sitters to hotels throughout the Los Angeles area. Their base rate for one or two children is $28 for a 4-hour minimum stay, with a $6 charge for each additional hour. For more than two children, they charge an additional 50¢ for each hour per child. Rates are slightly higher during high-demand holiday periods, and the customer is responsible for the sitter's parking costs.

ALL AROUND CHILD CARE AGENCY
(818) 710–8151

Serving the west San Fernando Valley (the northern half of Los Angeles), Mary Diaz's agency has been in business for more than a quarter century. She charges $5.50 per hour for one small child (toddler or younger) or two older children, with a 4-hour minimum. Additional children are billed at a rate of 50¢ per child per hour. She levies an additional $3.50 for parking and agency fees, and covers hotels west of Van Nuys Boulevard.

PUBLICATIONS

L.A. Parent Magazine. Monthly magazine; filled with advertisements for clothing and toy stores, articles on parenting, and a hefty monthly calendar of events.

Los Angeles Times. Daily newspaper, with the area's most comprehensive calendars of events; each Thursday, the "View" section includes "54 Hours," a rundown of the most interesting events for the upcoming weekend; on Fridays, the "Calendar" section lists movies, plays, concerts, and children's theater presentations for the weekend; on Sundays, the "Calendar" section offers a comprehensive list of entertainment events for the upcoming week.

Los Angeles Herald Examiner. Daily newspaper; publishes a weekend calendar of events in Friday's entertainment section.

Los Angeles Daily News. Daily newspaper; offers an outstanding entertainment calendar every Friday.

Los Angeles Magazine. Monthly magazine; good calendar of events listing theater, concerts, and children's programs.

California Magazine. Monthly magazine; features a great calendar of events for both Los Angeles and San Francisco.

L.A. Weekly. Free newspaper; its calendar lists most of the concerts, museum shows, movies, plays, and lectures in the greater Los Angeles area; pick it up Thursday evenings at boutiques and restaurants city wide.

LOCAL TELEPHONE NUMBERS

Late-hours pharmacy: Horton & Converse Pharmacy, 6225 Van Nuys Blvd., Van Nuys, (818) 782–6251. Open 24 hours.
Consumer complaints: (213) 620–4360.
Dental referrals: (213) 481–2133 or (800) 336–8478.
Physician referrals: (213) 483–6122.
Lawyer referrals: (213) 622–6700.
Drug-abuse hotline: (213) 650–6736.
Poison-control hotline: (213) 484–5151.
Traveler's aid: (213) 686–0950.
Tourism office: (213) 624–7300.
Police: 911.
Fire: 911.
Ambulance: 911.
Weather: (213) 554–1212.
Local car rental agencies: AutoExotica, (213) 652–2834; MPG Car Rental, (213) 746–2421; Ace Rent-a-Car, (213) 417–2220.

NEW YORK

The only substantial difference between the hustle and bustle of Manhattan at 3 A.M. and at 3 P.M. is the presence or absence of sunlight. According to the famous song, New York is a "city that doesn't sleep." It's not because it doesn't want to; it can't: It's too darn noisy. Night and day, you're serenaded by a a discordant mix of ear-piercing sirens and the unrelenting drone of taxi horns. Taken at face value, that noise is an annoying intrusion. However, a closer listen tells another story. The noise is a by-product of the drive, the fast-lane intensity that makes New York as exciting and invigorating as any place on earth.

While many consider New York City too unwieldy for a family vacation, we urge you to reconsider. Not only does New York have world-class museums, galleries, and entertainment of every stripe, it teems with history—and not only the kind you have to pay admission to see. The streets, often grimy and choked with traffic, are a museum. The tall buildings create granite canyons as formidable as those in any national park. The capital of American commerce and the arts for over a century, New York's monuments are located all over the city!

Central Park, designed by Frederick Law Olmsted in 1857, is a rolling, 840–acre island of tranquillity in a city that's dense with tall buildings. It's where you'll find the refurbished Central Park Zoo, the Children's Zoo, and much more (see Attractions).

The **Brooklyn Bridge**, designed and built by John and Washington Roebling in 1883, was the largest and most ambitious bridge of its time.

The **Flatiron Building**, at the intersection of Broadway and 23rd Street and 5th Avenue, was one of Manhattan's first (1902) steel-reinforced limestone skyscrapers.

The 77-story Art Deco **Chrysler Building** (1930), at 42nd Street and Lexington Avenue, has snarling gargoyles and a hubcap frieze near the top that make it one of the most distinctive structures in Manhattan.

At 102 stories, the Art Deco **Empire State Building** (1931) (see Attractions) at 5th Avenue and 34th Street was the tallest building in the world for forty years before the World Trade Center and Chicago's Sears Tower topped it. It's difficult to look at without thinking of King Kong.

The medieval-style **Cloisters** (see Museums), in Fort Tryon Park at the northern tip of Manhattan, contains sections of French monastic buildings constructed in the Renaissance. A former Rockefeller estate and now part of the Metropolitan Museum of Art, the Cloisters overlooks rolling parkland and the Hudson River.

Ellis Island is the former fort and powder magazine that from 1892 to 1943 served as the United States' main immigration station. It is now closed for a face lift that should be completed by 1990. But you get a stirring glimpse of the main building from the Staten Island Ferry. (See transportation.)

The beautiful **Statue of Liberty** (see Attractions) was presented to the United States by France in 1884 and has recently undergone a major face (and body) lift. It has long been one of the country's most traveled-to attractions.

The **New York City subway** (see Transportation) is the marvel of the transportation world. A bit seedy with stations on the grimy side, it nonetheless remains one of the largest underground transportation systems in the world . . . and a ride costs only a buck.

If commerce and an ability to attract it are essential for a successful town, then big citydom was always in the cards for New York. Its great natural harbor was claimed for the Dutch in 1609 when Henry Hudson sailed up the river that would ultimately bear his name. A permanent settlement called New Amsterdam was established in 1613 around a grouping of four Dutch trading houses. Peter Minuit was installed as governor in 1626, after allegedly buying the island of Manhattan for $24 worth of beads. By 1653 New Amsterdam was a thriving metropolis of 800 people.

By 1664, the successful colony came to the attention of the British, and the Duke of York sent a fleet to seize it. The Dutch, who had a greater distaste for their governor Peter Stuyvesant than the invading British, capitulated without a fight. During the British Colonial period, New York, named for the conquering duke, became a center for free-wheeling, laissez-faire capitalism. It also became a center for political freedom (John Peter Zenger won a landmark case establishing freedom of the press in 1735), and a hotbed of revolt (British troops occupied the city throughout the Revolutionary War).

By the time the Constitution was ratified by the state of New York in 1788, the city was the third largest in North America, after Philadelphia and Boston. It was the country's first capital (1789–1790) and the site of Washington's first inaugural. By 1790, New York was the country's most populous city (33,000), and by 1810 it had surpassed Philadelphia in domination of foreign trade. Throughout the 19th and the early 20th century, New York was the entry point for the greatest influx of immigration any nation has ever seen.

Today, despite a general population shift to the South and West, New York City continues to dominate commerce. It is headquarters for many major United States corporations, major television networks, the advertising and publishing businesses, banking, and shipping. It's the home of the United Nations and, as New Yorkers will readily brag, the world capital of art, music, dance, and theater.

It also covers a lot of territory, thanks to the creation in 1898 of Greater New York, which unified the five separate boroughs of Manhattan, the Bronx, Queens, Brooklyn, and Staten Island into one city. In tourist terms, each borough possesses its own charms. Cosmopolitan Manhattan, the smallest of the five, is the main attraction, and as such will be the main focus of this chapter. Brooklyn, the most populous of the boroughs, leads the country in foreign trade and ranks fifth nationally in manufacturing. A microcosm of New York as a whole, it has rough slums (in Bedford-Stuyvesant) and expensive brownstones (in beautiful Brooklyn Heights, the television home of the *Cosby Show*'s Huxtable family).

Queens, a middle-class bedroom community, is where you'll find Shea Stadium, home of the New York Mets, and New York's two major airports, La Guardia and Kennedy. The Bronx is best known as an urban battleground where citizens are attempting to reclaim their community from drug dealers and general decay. Oddly enough, the Bronx is also home to the wonderful Bronx Zoo (see Attractions) and Yankee Stadium. Staten Island, which geographically seems to belong more to New Jersey

---

FREEBIES AND CHEAPIES
(Free or $3.50 and under for adults)

- ❏ Staten Island Ferry (see Transportation)
- ❏ New York Stock Exchange (see Attractions)
- ❏ New York City Fire Museum (see Museums)
- ❏ World Trade Center (see Attractions)
- ❏ The New York Subway (see Transportation)
- ❏ St. Patrick's Cathedral (see Attractions)
- ❏ Museum of the City of New York (see Museums)
- ❏ Central Park (see Attractions)
- ❏ Brooklyn Children's Museum (see Museums)
- ❏ American Museum of Natural History (see Museums)
- ❏ American Craft Museum (see Museums)

than to New York, is the terminus for the famed Staten Island Ferry (see Transportation) and the hilly home to suburban housing tracts.

Despite its size, New York City in general and Manhattan in particular should be walked to be fully appreciated, and exploration on foot is a good way to get children involved. *We strongly urge you not to drive in Manhattan.* By walking (and using public transportation or cabs as a backup), you experience a freedom you miss when driving: You don't have to park or retrieve a car and can go wherever and whenever the mood strikes you. Walking also gives you a real perspective on the scale and scope of the city—the gargantuan buildings, the smells of the restaurants (and other things), and the diversity of the neighborhoods that, like foreign borders, can change swiftly and dramatically.

Some areas of the city practically cry out for exploration. The financial center of Wall Street (between Fulton and Wall near the southern tip of Manhattan) is a mixture of tall, modern buildings and historic old ones set along narrow streets. Chinatown (between Worth and Canal Streets, east of Broadway), teeming with outdoor markets, restaurants, and Chinese language signs, is about as foreign as you can get. Little Italy (just north of Canal Street from Chinatown) has great Italian restaurants and neighborhood groceries. SoHo (short for "South of Houston Street," between

---

THE LONG WEEKEND

Day One: Lower Manhattan

❏ Statue of Liberty (see Attractions)
❏ World Trade Center (see Attractions)
❏ Umberto's Clam House in Little Italy (see Restaurants)
❏ Museum of Holography (see Museums)
❏ New York City Fire Museum (see Museums)

Day Two: Midtown Manhattan

❏ Rockefeller Center and NBC Tour (see Attractions)
❏ F. A. O. Schwarz (see Shopping)
❏ Central Park (see Attractions)
❏ American Museum of Natural History (see Museums)

Day Three: Upper Manhattan and the Bronx

❏ Museum of the City of New York (see Museums)
❏ The Bronx Zoo (see Attractions)

Houston—pronounced "house-ton"—and Canal and west of Broadway) and Greenwich Village (between Houston and W. 14th Street) are home to funky shops, expensive boutiques, and flea markets. Midtown (east of Broadway between 42nd and 59th Streets) contains the bulk of Manhattan's skyscrapers, fancy stores, and topnotch hotels.

Note: When escorting children under age five, be sure to take a lightweight umbrella stroller if you're going to be walking longer than a half hour.

CLIMATE

While New York experiences a full measure of seasonal change, winter is relatively mild: Highs can reach 40 degrees with lows in the 20s. Snow does fall but seldom amounts to more than 6 inches at a clip. In spring and fall, expect highs in the 50s and 60s, and lows in the 40s. Summer isn't unbearable (highs in the 70s and 80s, lows in the 60s), but there may be long stretches with temperatures in the upper 90s and high humidity. These periods are characterized by occasional brownouts from the overuse of air conditioners, and inversion layers of hot, stagnant air cling to the city like a dirty plastic bag. Rain (41 inches annually) in New York falls throughout the year, so pack an umbrella. In winter, heavy coats are a must; in fall and spring, pack medium parkas; and in summer, light jackets are a good idea because of air conditioning.

TOURIST INFORMATION

Contact the New York Convention and Visitors Bureau, 2 Columbus Circle, New York, NY 10019, (212) 397–8222.

ATTRACTIONS

CENTRAL PARK

Between 59th and 110th Sts. and 5th Ave. and Central Park West, Manhattan. (212) 397–3156. Use various stations on the 1, 2, 3, 4, 5, 6, A, C, K, B, N, or R subway; or the M1, M10, M18, M19, M29, or M79 bus. Very limited street parking.

Hours. 24 hours a day (*Note: Use the park only during daylight hours*).

Costs. Park is free; however, some attractions charge admission.

Designed in 1857 by famed landscape architect Frederick Law Olmsted, Central Park is 840 acres of pastoral beauty in the heart of the city. With its lakes, trees, and pathways, the park is the favorite destination for New

York families. On fair-weather weekends, you can easily spend the entire day there. Food and souvenir vendors can be found at every turn, and you can rent bicycles, boats, and skates.

The park's smorgasbord of special activities includes:

The Dairy, (212) 397–3156, a restored 19th-century dairy building with interactive exhibits. It's located in the center of the park's southern section, at about 64th Street, north of the Wollman Skating Rink (enter park at E. 60th Street and walk northwest). Open Tuesday through Thursday and Saturday and Sunday, 11 A.M.–5 P.M.; Friday, 1 P.M.–5 P.M.

Wollman Rink, (212) 517–4800, has ice skating from mid-November through late March. It's located in the center of the park's southern section at about 63rd Street (enter the park at E. 60th Street and walk northwest). It's open Monday through Thursday, 10 A.M.–5 P.M.; Tuesday through Thursday, 7 P.M.–9:30 P.M.; Friday, 10 A.M.–9 P.M. and 9:30 P.M.–12 midnight; Saturday, 12 noon–9 P.M. and 9:30 P.M.–12 midnight; Sunday, 10 A.M.–5 P.M. and 7 P.M.–9 P.M. Adults, $4.50; children under 12, $2.25; skate rentals, $2.

Mineral Springs Pavilion Roller Skating, (212) 861–1817, rents skates (size 1 and up, no half sizes) Monday through Friday, 10 A.M.–5 P.M. and weekends until 6:30 P.M., weather permitting. Mineral Springs is located in the middle of the southern section of the park at Sheep Meadow and 69th Street (enter at E. or W. 72nd Street). Rentals cost $4 for the first hour and $1.50 per additional half hour ($10 plus ID required). Fast food and restrooms available.

Loeb Boathouse, (212) 517–3697, rents rowboats for self-propelled excursions on Central Park Lake, weather permitting (not in winter), between 9 A.M. and 5 P.M. daily. The boathouse is located on the northeast corner of the Lake at 74th Street (enter at E. 72nd Street and follow the road west, then north). Minimum age for renting is 16, and up to five people are allowed in each boat. Life jackets provided. Rentals cost $5 per hour with a $20 deposit. The restaurant at the boathouse offers fast-food and sit-down service. Restrooms available.

Belvedere Castle, (212) 397–3156, holds educational workshops (at Central Park Learning Center) for children between ages 5 and 11. It also houses a National Weather Service station. The Castle is located mid-park at 79th Street, south of the Great Lawn (enter park at W. 81st Street path and walk east). It's open Tuesday through Thursday and Saturday and Sunday, 11 A.M.–5 P.M; Friday, 1 P.M.–5 P.M. (October 15 through April 15, it closes at 4 P.M.).

The **Carousel**, (212) 879–0244, is located in the center of the park's southern section at about 64th Street (enter park at W. 65th Street path and walk east). Open Monday through Friday, 10:30 A.M.–4:45 P.M.; Saturday and Sunday until 5:45 P.M. (October 15 through April 15, till 4:45 P.M.). Rides cost 50¢.

Kerb's Boathouse, at 74th Street and 5th Avenue (enter park at 72nd Street and walk north along path), is a mecca for radio-controlled boat fanatics. The small lake, Conservatory Water, opposite the boathouse is the spot for races on Saturday at 10 A.M., but racing aficionados put boats through their paces all weekend long most of the year. A snack bar next door to the boathouse serves hot dogs and ice cream.

The **Children's Zoo**, (212) 408–0271, a fixture in Central Park for decades, is located at 5th Avenue between 65th and 66th Streets (enter at 64th Street path and walk north). It features small animals (ducks, goats, chickens, and raccoons) plus a llama for petting. Small, storybook-styled buildings are there for children to crawl inside. The kid's zoo is open daily from 10 A.M. to 5 P.M. (Tuesday until 8 P.M.) and the admission is still only 10¢. Restrooms available.

Central Park Zoo, (212) 220–5111, has recently been renovated to include a wildlife conservation center, a tropical rain forest exhibition, animals from the temperate region, birds and bears of the polar regions, and a seal and sea lion pool. A small facility, it takes only about 45 minutes to see it all. A zoo shop sells souvenirs, and the Zoo Cafe serves sandwiches and salads. The zoo is located in the park's southern section at 5th Avenue and 64th Street (enter at the E. 64th Street path). Open daily: 10 A.M.–5 P.M. (4 P.M. during Eastern Standard Time). Adult admission, $1; ages 3–13, 25¢; ages 2 and under, free. (*Note: on fair-weather weekends, go early in the day; in the afternoon, the lines are long.*) Restrooms available.

Kids' Facilities. No stroller rentals in the park, so bring your own. The only bona fide diaper-changing table is located in the ladies' restroom of the Central Park Zoo; otherwise, use the benches. No bottle-warming facilities at any of the restaurants. Restrooms are scattered throughout the park.

Ratings. For sheer good times, it's hard to top Central park. There's literally something for kids of every age. All ages, A.

ROCKEFELLER CENTER (NBC TOUR, SKATING RINK, RADIO CITY MUSIC HALL TOUR)

48th to 52nd Sts. between 5th and 6th Aves. (Ave. of the Americas), Midtown Manhattan. (212) 664–4000. Use the 47th–50th St. station on the F, D, or B subway; or the the 49th St. station on the R or N subway; or the M5, M6, M7 bus. Limited pay lot parking.

Hours. *NBC tours:* Mon.–Sat., 10 A.M.–4 P.M: *Ice skating rink:* October through April: daily, 9 A.M.–1 P.M.; 1:30 P.M.–5:30 P.M.; and 6 P.M.–10 P.M., plus extended hours at special times. *Radio City tour:* daily at "frequent times during the day," except Sun. during the Christmas holidays.

Costs. *NBC tour:* $6.50. *Ice skating rink:* Mon.–Thurs., adults, $7 per session; children under 12, $6; Fri.–Sun., adults $8 per session; children under 12, $6.50. *Radio City tour:* $3.95.

Art Deco Rockefeller Center, built between 1931 and 1940, is a linked grouping of nineteen separate buildings covering 22 acres. The center is the home of the National Broadcasting Company, the Radio City Music Hall, the outdoor skating facility, and an underground concourse of shops and boutiques. The best way to really see the inner workings of the place is to take either of the tours.

The **NBC Tour**, (212) 664–7174, takes visitors upstairs to the offices and network studios where shows like *Saturday Night Live, Today*, and *The David Letterman Show* are produced. The fascinating 1-hour walkthrough gives visitors an inside look at the studio facilities, all sorts of technical devices, props used in television production, and the network's makeup facilities. Children under the age of 6 are not permitted.

The **Skating Rink** is an integral part of winter in Manhattan. If you or your kids are novices on the ice, you may want to steer clear of this one: it's often overcrowded and Central Park's Wollman Rink is much cheaper. However, the rink-side tables are perfect for sitting and watching.

The **Radio City Music Hall Tour**, (212) 541–9436, takes you throughout the theater (home of the high-kicking Rockettes) and its ornate foyer, past the largest theater organ in the world, and underground for a look at the massive hydraulic system that raises and lowers theater props (and actors) into place. The whole tour takes about an hour. Tours are offered "frequently throughout the day"—phone for current schedule. (*Note: During the Christmas season, tours are sometimes canceled.*)

Kids' Facilities. No stroller rentals. No diaper-changing tables in the restrooms. No bottle-warming facilities.

Ratings. *NBC Tour:* While no children under age 6 are allowed, the tour can be fascinating for the older kids. 7–11, A; 12–16, A. *Skating rink:* If you want to spend the money, your kids will have a ball. 2–7, C; 8–11, A; 12–16, A. *Radio City Music Hall:* If your kids like theaters, this is the place. 2–7, C; 8–11, B; 12–16, A.

ST. PATRICK'S CATHEDRAL

5th Avenue at 50th St., Midtown Manhattan. (212) 753–2261. Use the 47th–50th St. station on the F, D, or B subway; or the M5, M6, or M7 bus. Pay lot parking.

Hours. Daily, 6:30 A.M.–8 P.M.

Costs. Free (donations accepted).

One of the nation's largest and, thanks to famous funerals (Senator Robert F. Kennedy's comes to mind) most recognizable religious buildings in the country, St. Patrick's 330-foot twin spires are easy to spot from blocks away. Inside the Gothic, 13th-century-inspired church, visitors are overcome by the grand scale of the ceilings and stained glass windows. If you visit on a weekend, you might witness a wedding or some other religious service. Daily masses.

Kids' Facilities. No stroller rentals. No diaper-changing facilities. No food or bottle-warming facilities.

Ratings. As churches go, this is one of the biggies. You may not want to bring younger kids; once they discover how well their voices echo, they may be inclined to shout while a service is going on. See it all in about 20 minutes. 2–7, D; 8–11, C; 12–16, B.

EMPIRE STATE BUILDING

5th Ave. and 34th St., Midtown Manhattan. (212) 736–3100. Use the 33rd St. station on the 6 subway; or the 34th St. station on the B, D, F, N, or R subway; or the M1, M2, M3, M4, M5, M6, M7, M16, or M32 bus. Pay lot parking.

Hours. Daily, 9:30 A.M.–12 midnight.

Costs. Adults, $3; under age 12, $1.75.

For years America's tallest building, the Empire State (built in 1931) is currently number three, just behind Chicago's Sears Tower and New York's World Trade Center. The wonderfully ornate Art Deco structure offers magnificent views from two observation decks, but you have to put up with some minor inconveniences to get there. First, take an escalator to the basement to buy your ticket. Then queue up for an elevator ride to the 80th floor. Stand in line again for a ride to the 86th-floor observation deck (indoor and outdoor views). Finally, line up for a trip to the 102nd floor, where there's a small room with tiny windows. On a weekend, the whole process can take an hour.

Located in the building's lower concourse, the **Guinness World Records Exhibit Hall**, (212) 947–2339, displays models of the world's fattest man, tallest woman, and biggest vegetables, among many other exhibits. The entrance fee is $3 ($2 for children) and the exhibit make up for all that waiting in line. Open daily, 9:30 A.M.–6 P.M.

Kids' Facilities. No stroller rentals. No diaper-changing tables in restrooms (they're on the 86th floor). No bottle-warming facilities. The 86th floor has a gift shop and a fast-food snack bar.

Ratings. The view is great, but you may not want to subject small kids to the wait on weekends. 2–7, D; 8–11, A; 12–16, A. Guinness Hall: All ages, A.

STATUE OF LIBERTY

Liberty Island in Upper New York Bay, New York. Ferry from Battery Park at the southern tip of Manhattan. (212) 269–5755 or (212) 563–3590. Use the Bowling Green station on the 4 or 5 subway; or the Whitehall St. station on the R subway; or the M6 bus. Limited free parking.

Hours. Daily, 9 A.M.–5 P.M. (last ferry at 4 P.M.). Ferries leave every hour on the hour. Closed in January and February.

Costs. Park is free. Ferry: adults, $3.25; ages 1–11, $1.50.

Cleaned up and repaired to commemorate her 100th birthday in 1986, the Statue of Liberty remains one of the *great* attractions in New York. Lady Liberty's 156-foot-tall base houses the terrific American Museum of Immigration, a tribute through pictures, sound recordings, costumes, and artifacts to nearly every nationality in the United States melting pot. The base also has an outdoor observation platform and an inter-active computer that exhibits with photographs of a family with your last name living in the country of your ancestors. The statue itself stands 151 feet high and sports a new elevator that takes passengers about halfway up. From there, you walk up a stairway that gets progressively narrower and steeper (claustrophobic, overweight, and 6-foot-plus folks beware) as it approaches the windows at the base of Liberty's crown. The view from the crown is not of the Manhattan skyline, but rather of the harbor. (*Note: During summer vacations, the line to get to the top of the statue can be long. If there's no line outside the statue base, it will take you about 45 minutes to climb to the top and make your way back down again. Should the line stretch to a marker about 50 yards from the statue's base, the wait could be as much as 3 hours. In summer, the un-air-conditioned stairway can get unbearably hot.*)

Kids' Facilities. No diaper-changing tables. No stroller rentals and you can't use your own on the stairs. No bottle-warming facilities. Fast food and gifts in building between statue and boat dock.

Ratings. As magnificent as the statue is, if the wait is going to be over an hour and a half (ask a park ranger), you may want to avoid the climb to the top. Likewise, if you have a child who's between the toddler stage and 4 years old, you may also want to avoid the climb: those kids are too heavy to hold, and they often get too tired to walk by themselves. Conversely, older kids usually enjoy the walk more than their parents. The whole excursion can take a half day. 2–5, F; 6–11, A; 12–16, A.

CASTLE CLINTON

State St. and Battery Place, Battery Park, Lower Manhattan. (212) 344–7220. Use the Bowling Green station on the 4 or 5 subway; or the Whitehall St. station on the R subway; or the M6 bus. Limited free parking.

Hours. Mon.–Fri., 8:30 A.M.–4 P.M.; Sat. and Sun., 8:30 A.M.–5 P.M.

Costs. Free.

Built on the site of a 1624 Dutch fort, Castle Clinton was constructed in 1811 to protect New York harbor from attack by the British. In the 1820s, it was renamed Castle Garden and became a major showplace for symphony and opera. Later, it served as a processing station for new immigrants and finally as a public aquarium. Today, Castle Clinton is a ring of connected brick rooms containing exhibits that detail its history. It's a good place to wait for the next ferry to the Statue of Liberty.

Kids' Facilities. No stroller rentals. No diaper-changing tables. No food or bottle-warming facilities. Gift shop and ticket office for the Circle Line ferries to the Statue of Liberty.

Ratings. The exhibits are interesting. Those who linger are a captive audience just killing time while waiting for the Statue of Liberty Ferry: You can see it all in 15 minutes. 2–7, D; 8–11, B; 12–16, B.

WORLD TRADE CENTER

2 World Trade Center (Church and Liberty Sts.), Lower Manhattan. (212) 466–4170/4233. Use the Cortland St. station on the 1, N, or R subway; the Chambers St.–World Trade Center station on the A, C, E, or K subway; or the M1, M6, M9, M10, or M22 bus. Limited pay lot parking.

Hours. Daily, 9:30 A.M.–9:30 P.M.

Costs. Adults, $2.95; ages 6–12, $1.50; ages 5 and under, free.

The Empire State Building may have the history, but the indoor and outdoor observation decks on the 107th floor the World Trade Center provide the best views of the harbor, the five New York boroughs, Long Island, and New Jersey. To help you better appreciate what you're seeing, the tower windows have outlines of the Manhattan skyline noting famous landmarks. Inside, a nifty *History of Trade* exhibit explains some of the finer points of finance and trade, plus there's a scale model of the first ship built in Manhattan in 1614. During the Christmas season, Santa puts in an appearance, and there are daily puppet shows at noon. A week before Easter, the Easter Bunny makes his presence known.

Kids' Facilities. No stroller rentals. No diaper-changing tables in restrooms. No bottle-warming facilities. The deck has a massive snack shop offering pizza, hot dogs, bagels, and drinks.

Ratings. The best view and easiest elevator ride in Manhattan. Whip through it all in 45 minutes. All ages, A.

THE UNITED NATIONS

1st Ave. between 42nd and 48th Sts. (visitors entrance at 1st and 45th), Midtown Manhattan. (212) 754–7625. Use the Grand Central Terminal Station on the 4, 5, 6, or 7 subway; or the M15, M27, M42, or M104 bus. Limited pay lot parking.

Hours. Tours daily, 9 A.M.–4:45 P.M.

Costs. Adults, $4.50; students, $2.50; ages 12 and under, $2.50; children under 5 not permitted.

The hour-long tour of the giant Le Corbusier structure includes stops at many of the world organization's council rooms and the giant General Assembly chamber. The most exciting time of the year is when the U.N. is in session (late-September through mid-December). Exhibits explain how the U.N. functions and, along the way, you'll see gifts from member countries, such as the impressive giant ivory carving from China and a ¹⁄₁₀ scale model of the Thai royal barge. One very solemn exhibit contains artifacts from the rubble of the 1945 Nagasaki and Hiroshima atom bomb blasts. The tour's final stop is the basement. You can buy souvenirs, eat in the cafeteria, or visit the U.N. Post Office, where you can buy U.N. stamps and mail letters and postcards; it's the only post office on United States soil where U.N. stamps are honored. For a real treat, there are often a few spaces available for eating in the delegate's dining room; ask your tour guide.

Kids' Facilities. No stroller rentals. No diaper-changing tables. No bottle-warming facilities. The cafeteria can be great fun, especially when you're seated near foreign delegates and tourists from other countries.

Ratings. The tour doesn't provide enough visual stimulation for kids under 10; however, older children will really enjoy the experience. 2–5, not admitted; 6–10, D; 11–16, A.

NEW YORK STOCK EXCHANGE

20 Broad St., Lower Manhattan. (212) 656–5168. Use the Wall St. station on the 2, 3, 4, or 5 subway; the Rector St. station on the N or R subway; the Broad St. station on the J or M subway; use the M1, M6, M15, X23, or X25 bus. No parking.

Hours. Mon.–Fri., 9:20 A.M.–4 P.M.

Costs. Free.

From the time the New York Stock Exchange was created in 1792 (dealers met under a buttonwood tree nearby), Wall and Broad Streets have been the center of American commerce. The Stock Exchange Visitors Center tour includes audio-visual presentations, tour guide explanations of how the Exchange works, and inter-active computer displays. The payoff is a view of the frenzied activities on the Stock Exchange trading floor, accompanied by taped explanations in English and five other languages. Cameras must be checked before entering, and you must go through a very sensitive metal detector. (*Note: By about noon, the lines for the Visitors Center can get quite long. Go early in the day.*)

Kids' Facilities. No stroller rentals. No diaper-changing tables. No bottle-warming facilities. Gift shop.

Ratings. The Stock Exchange doesn't allow kids under 12 on the tour, and it's no wonder: Much of the material was way over *our* heads. Junior executives will find it fascinating. Allow an hour if there's no crowd. 12–16, B.

THE AT&T INFOQUEST CENTER

550 Madison Ave. at 56th St., Midtown Manhattan. (212) 605–5555. Use the 59th St. station on the 4, 5, 6, N or R subway; the 5th Ave. station on the E or F subway; or the M1, M2, M3, M4, M5, M6, M7, M10, M27, M28, M32, or M104 bus. Limited pay lot parking.

Hours. Tues.–Sun., 10 A.M.–6 P.M.; Tues. until 9 P.M.

Costs. Free.

If your kids love computers, the Infoquest Center is the place in New York to take them. Begin by getting a magnetic credit card, upon which you enter your name: You'll use it throughout the center to activate a series of fantastic information-filled computer stations. Each station focuses on a different aspect of the information age, from lasers (lightguides) to microelectronics to computer software. About midway through the 4-floor trek, you come to the payoff: a large grouping of computerized machines that allows you to make your own music video, take your picture and scramble your face, play photo guessing games, and guides a mouse through a maze with voice commands. Your last stop is a group of video stations that look like New York cabs, where actor Harry Anderson (your driver) takes you on a tour of the city via the magic of video.

Kids' Facilities. No strollers. Restrooms have large counters suitable for diaper changing. No food or bottle-warming facilities. Small gift shop.

Ratings. If your children are over 5, you won't be able to drag them away from this place. See it all in about an hour, but be prepared to stay longer when your kids request it. 2–7, B; 8–11, A; 12–16, A.

BRONX ZOO

Fordham Rd. and Southern Blvd., Bronx, (212) 220–5100 or (212) 367–1010. Subway and bus: Take the 2 express subway to Pelham Pkwy. and walk west to the Bronxdale entrance; *or* the D express subway to Fordham Rd. and the Bx12 bus to the Rainey Gate entrance. Parking, $4.

Hours. Mon.–Sat., 10 A.M.–5 P.M.; Sun., 10 A.M.–5:30 P.M. (November, December, and January: closes at 4:30 P.M. every day.)

Costs. April through October: adults, $3.75; ages 2–12, $1.50; under age 2, free. Rest of the year: adults, $1.75; ages 2–12, 75¢; under age 2, free.

The biggest urban zoo in the United States, the Bronx Zoo houses more than 4,000 animals on 265 wooded acres. In addition to pastoral North American landscapes, many of the animals reside in specially designed habitats like JungleWorld, a tropical rain forest; Himalayan Highlands, a mountainous habitat for snow leopards and red pandas; the

World of Birds, a tropical aviary afflicted by thunderstorms every day at 2 P.M.; a nocturnal mammal house where day turns into night; and a fabulous reptile house. There are also separate admission attractions like the Children's Zoo for feeding and petting tame animals (adults, $1.50; kids 2–12, $1); the Bengali Express monorail ($1.50/$1); and camel rides ($2 for all). All rides closed during the winter.

Kids' Facilities. Strollers are available for rental. Diapers can be changed in most ladies' restrooms. No bottle-warming facilities. Three sit-down restaurants and loads of fast-food snack carts. Gift shop.

Ratings. Despite its age, the Bronx Zoo is a wonderfully fresh, modern, and interesting attraction. Allow a good half day or more. All ages, A.

MUSEUMS

CON EDISON ENERGY MUSEUM

145 E. 14th St., Downtown Manhattan. (212) 860–6868. Use the 14th St. station on the 4, 5, or 6 subway; the 14th St.–Union Square station on the N or R subway; or the M1, M2, M3, or X25 bus. Limited pay parking.

Hours. Tues.–Sat., 10 A.M.–4 P.M.

Costs. Free.

The Con Edison Energy Museum focuses on the history of electric power in general, and New York's use of it in particular. Through models, interactive computer exhibits, and appliances from the early days of electric power, visitors get an idea of the enormity of Thomas Edison's task: He wired up much of downtown Manhattan only three years after inventing the light bulb in 1879. The multimedia presentation *Energy Today* depicts the various electric, gas, sewer, and steam lines beneath the streets of Manhattan.

Kids' Facilities. No stroller rentals. No diaper-changing tables. No restrooms. No bottle-warming facilities.

Ratings. Young children will probably not grasp the power concept, but older ones will be able to write a school report about it, especially after grabbing some of the free literature in the lobby. See it all in about 45 minutes. 2–7, D; 8–11, B; 12–16, A.

NEW YORK CITY FIRE MUSEUM

278 Spring St., SoHo, Lower Manhattan. (212) 691–1303. Use the Canal St. station on the 1 subway; the Spring St. station on the C or K subway; or the M10 bus. Limited street and pay lot parking.

Hours. Tues.–Sat., 10 A.M.–4 P.M.

Costs. Donations: adults, $3; children, 50¢ (the firemen manning the door are pretty flexible about this).

Open only since October 1987, the 2-story former fire station contains a large number of turn-of-the-century fire wagons and an 1820 hand pump. There are plenty of model trucks, antique fire hats, fire insurance emblems, colorful old lithographs, paintings, commendations, and a great collection of New York fire alarm boxes. A filmed documentary and a cartoon presentation for young children detail the history of firefighting.

Kids' Facilities. No stroller rentals. Counters in restrooms are big enough for diaper changing. No food or bottle-warming facilities. Small gift counter.

Ratings. The firefighting equipment is top-notch, and the video presentations are tailor-made for children. Allow at least an hour. All ages, A.

MUSEUM OF HOLOGRAPHY

11 Mercer St., SoHo, Lower Manhattan, (212) 925–0581 or (212) 925–0526. Use the Canal St. station on the B, D, N, Q, or R subway; or the M8 bus. Extremely limited street and pay lot parking.

Hours. Tues.–Sun., 11 A.M.–6 P.M.

Costs. Adults, $3; students, $2.75; under age 12, $1.75.

Opened in 1976, only five years after holography was invented, this funky warehouse in the center of the SoHo art district presents ever-changing exhibits on the art of three-dimensional picture-making. A 20-minute video presentation explains how holograms are made, and ongoing demonstrations for kids all but insure a new generation of holographers. Call for schedule.

Kids' Facilities. No stroller rentals. No diaper-changing tables in restrooms (use benches). No food or bottle-warming facilities. Large gift shop.

Ratings. Kids really enjoy the pictures and are especially taken by the fact that, as the viewer's perspective changes, so does the image. Your kids will want to spend an hour here. 2–7, B; 8–11, A; 12–16, A.

NEW YORK POLICE ACADEMY MUSEUM

235 E. 20th St. (2nd floor), Downtown Manhattan. (212) 477–9753. Use the 23rd St. station on the 6, N, or R subway; or the M15, M28, M31, M32, and M103 bus. Limited pay lot parking (do not park on street in front of academy; spaces are for police vehicles only).

Hours. Mon.–Fri., 9 A.M.–3 P.M.

Costs. Free.

Along with a wide variety of police equipment used by New York's Finest over the years, the museum displays ''hardware'' used by infamous criminals. The most celebrated weapon is a machine gun once owned by 1930s gangster Al Capone. There are plenty of guns on display, each with its own bizarre story. The academy also offers a 2-hour tour of the facilities, including a look at recruits in training.

Kids' Facilities. No stroller rentals. No diaper-changing tables in restrooms. No bottle-warming facilities. Food vending machines located on the 3rd floor.

Ratings. Young children will probably find the museum a tad on the boring side. However, older children will get a kick out of the experience. The tour is limited to kids age 11 and older. See the museum in a half-hour. 2–7, C; 8–11, A; 12–16, A.

SOUTH STREET SEAPORT MUSEUM

207 Front St., Lower Manhattan. (212) 669–9416 or (212) 669–9424. Use the Nassau St. station on the 2, 3, 4, or 5 subway; the Broadway–Nassau station on the J, M, or R subway; the Fulton St. station on the A or C subway; or the M15 bus. Pay lot parking.

Hours. Museum: daily, 10 A.M.–6 P.M. Harbor boat tours: Call ahead for daily schedule.

Costs. Museum general admission (good for entry to all buildings and docked ships): Adults, $5; students, $3; ages 4–12, $2; ages 3 and under, free. Harbor boat tours: Adults and students, $7.50; ages 4–12, $6; ages

3 and under, free. Combination museum admission and boat tour: Adults, $11.50; students, $9.50; ages 4 to 12, $6; ages 3 and under, free.

The South Street Seaport is a cluster of museums, 19th-century-style shops, and historic ships spread over 6 square blocks of historic East River frontage and Pier 16. Combined, the facilities trace New York's commercial connection with the sea.

Museums and shops include the **A. A. Low Building**, 171 John Street, which has changing exhibits on ships and shipbuilding. A 20-minute video describes the *Peking*, the 1911 steel sailing ship docked on Pier 16. (Restrooms in building.) The **Children's Center**, 165 John Street, offers hands-on workshops on sailors' crafts: pulling in a sail on an authentic mast, knot tying, signal flag language, and cooking aboard ship. Kids must sign up for workshops early in the day. Phone ahead for schedule. (Restroom in building.) The **Boat Building Shop**, corner John and South Streets, features boat-building demonstrations by artisans using old-time construction methods. Call ahead for schedule. (No restrooms.) The **Museum Gallery**, 213 Water Street, has ocean-related exhibits that change about every six months. (Emergency restroom only.) **Browne & Co. Stationers**, 211 Water Street, is a working print shop that shuns modern printing techniques in favor of old-fashioned letterpress printing (setting type by hand). They offer workshops on the process and sell their wares. (No restrooms.) The **Museum Visitors Center**, 207 Water Street, features changing exhibits. (No restrooms.)

Ships include the *Peking*, Pier 16, a steel-hulled boat (1911) that, at 347 feet, is the second-largest sailing ship afloat. Today it's a museum with refurbished cabins and a large photographic exhibit on vessels that, like her, hauled cargo around Cape Horn before the opening of the Panama Canal. (No restrooms.) The *Ambrose*, Pier 16, is a motorized lightship whose beacon guarded the outer reaches of New York Harbor until 1963. (No restrooms.) The *Wavertree*, Pier 15, is a sailing ship (1885) that is currently being refurbished. A guided tour daily at 1 P.M. provides insight into the work that goes into making an old ship seaworthy after years of disrepair.

The South Street Seaport also provides daily 90-minute harbor boat tours from March through December. The excursions are offered aboard three of the museum's historic ships.

The Seaport Experience, 210 Front Street, is a 60-minute multimedia presentation on the history of the seaport area and life on 19th-century sailing ships. With umpteen projectors, plenty of screens, loads of special effects, and lots of speakers, the action surrounds the viewer. It's presented every hour on the hour, daily from 11 A.M. Closing times vary, so call ahead, (212) 608-7888. Adults, $3.75; under age 12, $2.50. (Restrooms in building.)

Kids' Facilities. No stroller rentals. No diaper-changing tables (large counters in restrooms at A. A. Low Building). No food (restaurants aplenty at Pier 17 shopping mall and Fulton Market building nearby). Gift shops throughout area.

Ratings. There's so much here, you're bound to find something for kids of all ages. At the very least, there's a dynamite view of the Brooklyn Bridge from the Pier 17 shopping mall. It'll take at least a half day to see it all. All ages, A.

AMERICAN CRAFT MUSEUM

40 W. 53rd St., Midtown Manhattan. (212) 956–3535. Use the 5th Ave. station on the E or F subway; or the M1, M2, M3, M4, M5, M6, M7, or M32 bus. Extremely limited pay lot parking.

Hours. Tues., 10 A.M.–8 P.M.; Wed.–Sun., 10 A.M.–5 P.M.

Costs. Adults, $3; students, $1.50; ages 12 and under, free.

The bright, spacious American Craft Museum is *the* New York showplace for the latest in ceramics, furniture, and multimedia artworks. Most of the work is colorful, futuristic, and a bit bizarre, from oddly shaped desks and chests to jewelry made from industrial materials. The Eventspace has a number of visitor-participation artworks. When we were there, visitors were encouraged to rearrange the tiles on a large ungrouted ceramic mosaic, play with a photo jigsaw puzzle, and add bits of cloth and yarn to a tapestry still in the weaving process.

Kids' Facilities. No stroller rentals. No diaper-changing tables in restrooms (plenty of chairs and slatted benches, however). No food or bottle-warming facilities. Gift shop.

Ratings. At first, kids don't know what to make of Eventspace—after those years of hearing Mom and Dad tell them not to touch things in an art gallery. But they quickly adjust to the idea. Allow at least an hour. All ages, A.

AMERICAN MUSEUM OF NATURAL HISTORY

Central Park West and 79th St., West Side, Manhattan. (212) 769–5100; planetarium, (212) 769–5920. Use the 81st St. station on the B, C, or K subway; or the M10 or M17 bus. Limited pay lot parking.

Hours. Mon., Tues., Thurs., Sun., 10 A.M.–5:45 P.M.; Wed., Fri., Sat., 10 A.M.–9 P.M.

Costs. Suggested admissions: *museum:* adults, $3.50; children to age 17, $1.50 (free on Fri. and Sat. 5 P.M.–9 P.M.). *Naturemax Theater:* adults, $3.75; children to 17, $1.75. *Hayden Planetarium:* adults, $3.75; students, $2.75; through age 12, $2; planetarium fee covers admission to museum.

One of the nation's best-known and best-loved natural history museums, it's collections have set the standard for museums. Its life-like dioramas (African and American native animals and people) are large and comprehensive. The Hall of Meteorites houses the world's largest collection of rocks from the sky, including a huge 15-by-6-footer that kids can touch. The darkened Hall of Minerals is a favorite place for children. Not only are the displays colorful, but the terraced exhibit space has carpet-covered nooks and crannies where kids can sit, and display cases at kid level for easy viewing. The Discovery Room has special hands-on exhibits and two dinosaur exhibits that are real children pleasers. One of the best exhibits is the *Life on the Forest Floor* diorama, an enlarged view of all the creepy crawlers (worms, centipedes and ants), dirt, and roots in your own back yard. The planetarium and huge-screen Naturemax theater show a changing array of programs daily.

Kids' Facilities. No stroller rentals. Diaper-changing tables in ladies' restroom on the lower level. Bottles warmed at the American Museum Restaurant (a sit-down facility). The Food Express cafeteria serves fast food. Two gift shops: one for the adults and one just for kids.

Ratings. It's hard not to love this museum. Be prepared to spend a half day. All ages, A.

MUSEUM OF BROADCASTING

1 E. 53rd St. Midtown Manhattan. (212) 752–7684 or (212) 752–4690. Use the 5th Ave. station on the E or F subway; or the M1, M2, M3, or M4 bus. Extremely limited pay lot parking.

Hours. Tues.–Sat., 12 noon–5 P.M.; Thurs. until 8 P.M.

Costs. Adults, $4; students, $3; under age 13, $2.

Finally, a museum tailor-made for the baby boom generation. Its collection of more than 10,000 television shows and scads of commercials from the last forty-five years is available for private viewing (an hour at a time) in comfortable modular consoles. Here's the chance to show your kids the kind of television you were raised on! The museum presents daily selections on the big screen in a 63-seat theater. The variety of the programming is wide, so call ahead for a schedule of upcoming presentations. The museum has special Saturday screenings for kids. Besides television, you can also audit tapes from a library of more than 60,000 radio programs.

Kids' Facilities. No stroller rentals. No diaper-changing tables in the restrooms. No food or bottle-warming facilities. Gift shop in lobby.

Ratings. Kids love television and will enjoy seeing you react to your favorite old shows. Screenings last about an hour. All ages, A.

MUSEUM OF MODERN ART

11 W. 53rd St. Midtown Manhattan. (212) 708–9500 or (212) 708–9480. Use the 5th Ave. station on the E or F subway; or the M1, M2, M3, M4, M5, M6, M7, M27, M28 or M32 bus. Limited pay lot parking.

Hours. Fri.–Tues., 11 A.M.–6 P.M.; Thurs., 11 A.M.–9 P.M.; closed on Wed.

Costs. Adults, $6; students, $3.50; under age 16, free.

The five-level museum is a premier showplace for modern art in the United States. From films (call for schedule) to the best of modern photography, painting, sculpture, drawings, prints, and architectural and industrial design, MOMA has one of the best collections in the world. Highlights include paintings by Degas, Picasso, Klimt, and Seurat; sculptures by Rodin and Picasso; and large collections of Soviet paintings. The industrial designs include streamlined 1940s sewing machines and typewriters, postmodern furniture, and a helicopter suspended from the ceiling of the top floor.

Kids' Facilities. No stroller rentals; you must check your own stroller. The Museum no longer lends baby carriers, so you'd better bring your own along for infants. No diaper-changing tables (some benches in lounge areas, however). No bottle-warming. The Garden Restaurant provides sit-down meal service. Large gift shop.

Ratings. The museum doesn't really cater to small children, but if your child likes bright, colorful art, this place is worth a visit. To see everything quickly, set aside two hours. 2–7, C; 8–11, B; 12–16, A.

METROPOLITAN MUSEUM OF ART

5th Avenue at 82nd St., Uptown, Manhattan. (212) 535–7710 or (212) 879–5500. Use the 86th St. station on the 4, 5, or 6 subway; or the M1, M2, M3, M4, M18, or M79 bus. Limited pay lot parking (fills up early in the day).

Hours. Tues.–Sun., 9:30 A.M.–5:15 P.M.; Tues. until 8:45 P.M.

Costs. Suggested admission: adults, $5; students, $2.50; under age 12, free.

Nearly everything the world of art has ever offered has some sort of representation here. The gold of Egypt and ceramics and sculpture from Greece highlight the collection of ancient artifacts. The medieval period is represented by religious paintings, sculptures, and religious objects. Whole rooms—including walls, ceilings, floors, furniture, and artwork —from 15th- and 16th-century European buildings have been reconstructed. Also, the best of the last 200 years of American and European art and furniture are on display. Highlights include a large collection of French Impressionist paintings. The Junior Museum on the lower level functions as a hands-on art gallery, where younger kids and their parents can draw and experiment with shapes. On Saturdays, the Uris Center for Education offers workshops for kids from ages 5 to 12 (call for more information).

Kids' Facilities. No stroller rentals. Ladies' restroom on lower level has diaper-changing table. No bottle-warming facilities. One sit-down restaurant and one self-serve fast-food cafeteria. Large gift shop.

Ratings. You could spend days here and not see everything: It's that overwhelming. With something for everyone, you should be able to stay at least 2 hours before small children get too antsy. All ages, A.

THE CLOISTERS

Fort Tryon Park, Ft. Washington Ave. near 190th St., Upper Manhattan. (212) 923–3700. Use the 190th St. station on the A subway. (*Note: The subway station is a 10-minute walk from the museum. The park is beautiful but not considered terribly safe.*) Or use the M4 bus, which takes you right to the front door. Free parking.

Hours. Tues.–Sun., 9:30 A.M.–5:15 P.M. (during Eastern Standard Time, 4:45 P.M.).

Costs. Suggested admission: adults, $5; students, $2.50; under age 12, free.

This branch of the Metropolitan Museum of Art, once part of a Rockefeller estate, was built in the style of a Gothic monastery. Filled with medieval and early-Renaissance tapestries, sculptures, religious paintings, and wooden carvings, its most impressive displays are the sepulchral (tomb) carvings and stone walls and gardens from 12th- to 15th-century European cloisters. The museum also features some terrific 9th- and 10th-century ivory carvings and beautiful hand-lettered and -painted medieval books. With medieval music playing in the background, it's easy to believe you've stepped back in time.

Kids' Facilities. No stroller rentals. No diaper-changing tables. No food or bottle-warming facilities. Gift shop.

Ratings. Younger children might not fully comprehend this magnificent structure and its art, but older kids with even a rudimentary knowledge of the period will love it. It'll take a minimum of 90 minutes to see everything. 2–7, C; 8–11, A; 12–16, A.

JEWISH MUSEUM

1109 Fifth Ave. at E. 92nd St., Manhattan. (212) 860–1863. Use the 96th St. station on the 4, 5, or 6 subway; or the M1, M2, M3, or M4 bus. Limited pay lot parking.

Hours. Sun., 11 A.M.–6 P.M.; Mon., Wed., Thurs., 12 noon–5 P.M.; Tues., 12 noon–8 P.M.; closed on Fri. and Sat.

Costs. Adults, $4; students, $2; ages 6 and under, free.

Dedicated to interpreting the Jewish experience in America, the Jewish Museum presents changing exhibits (usually a half dozen or so a year) on Jewish culture and history. Permanent exhibits include a large collection of coins and medals dating back to the 5th century B.C.; sculptor George Segal's "The Holocaust," life-size plaster figures in a concentration camp; and a large display of Biblical archaeology. The museum also offers a series of family programs and activities for kids (call ahead for schedule).

Kids' Facilities. No stroller rentals. No diaper-changing tables (use benches scattered throughout). No food or bottle-warming facilities. Gift shop.

Ratings. The museum's appeal is contingent upon the current exhibits. Exhibits usually have a wide appeal: being Jewish is not a prerequisite for enjoyment. It takes about an hour see it all. 2–7, C; 8–11, B; 12–16, A.

MUSEUM OF THE CITY OF NEW YORK

5th Ave. and E. 103rd St., Manhattan. (212) 534–1672. Use the 103rd St. station on the 6 subway; or the M1, M2, M3, or M4 bus. Limited street parking.

Hours. Tues.–Sat., 10 A.M.–5 P.M.; Sun., 1 P.M.–5 P.M.

Costs. Adults, $3; students, $1.50; children, $1; families, $5.

Like New York City itself, this museum offers visitors a little bit of everything. Highlights include John D. Rockefeller's bedroom and dressing room, a gallery of costumes, antique toys, model ships, fire equipment, and displays on Dutch and English colonial life in New York. The biggest kid pleaser is ITT's *The Big Apple*, a 30-minute multimedia presentation on the history of New York projected on a movie screen inside a giant plastic apple.

Kids' Facilities. No stroller rentals. Small diaper-changing stand in ladies' restroom; covered radiator in men's room (don't use in winter!). No food or bottle-warming facilities.

Ratings. With something for kids of all ages, the museum is a wonderful place to spend a morning or an afternoon. All ages, A.

WHITNEY MUSEUM OF AMERICAN ART

945 Madison Ave. at E. 75th St., Manhattan. (212) 570–3676. Use the 77th St. station on the 6 subway; or the M1, M2, M3, or M4 bus. Limited pay lot parking.

Hours. Tues., 1 P.M.–8 P.M.; Wed.–Sat., 11 A.M.–5 P.M.; Sun., 12 noon–6 P.M.

Costs. Adults, $4.50; under age 12, free.

The Whitney's collection of important works of American art includes a large number of paintings by Edward Hopper and Jasper Johns. Changing exhibits of modern art can be delightful or leave you wondering if the air-conditioning ducts have crashed to the floor. The best draw for small kids is Alexander Calder's mobile, *Circus*, near the entrance on the 1st floor. It's made from wire coat hangers and bits of wood and cork. A changing series of movies are shown daily (call ahead).

The Whitney also has satellite museums in several office-building lobbies and courtyards: **Whitney Museum at Federal Plaza**, 33 Maiden Lane (just south of the South Street Seaport), Lower Manhattan, (212) 570–3633, displays some of the Whitney's permanent collection. **Whitney Museum at Equitable Center**, 787 7th Ave. (between 51st and 52nd Streets), Midtown Manhattan, (212) 554–1113, has a Thomas Hart Benton mural and the biggest Roy Lichtenstein painting in the world. **Whitney Museum at Philip Morris**, 120 Park Avenue (at 41st St.), Midtown Manhattan, (212) 878–2550, presents changing exhibits on the ground floor and in the courtyard. The satellite museums are open during business hours, Monday through Saturday.

Kids' Facilities. *Whitney:* No stroller rentals. No diaper-changing tables (not much bench space either). No bottle-warming facilities at the museum's sit-down restaurant. Gift shop. *Satellites:* No facilities.

Ratings. *Whitney:* Except for Calder's *Circus*, there isn't much to appeal to small children except the large elevators. It also is top-heavy with minimalist modern paintings and sculpture, which don't really hold the interest of children. You can see it all in about 90 minutes. 2–7, C; 8–11, C; 12–16, B. *Satellites:* Worth a quick look if you happen to be passing by. 2–7, C; 8–11, C; 12–16, B.

INTREPID SEA AIR SPACE MUSEUM

12th Ave. and W. 46th St. (Pier 86), Manhattan. (212) 245–0072 or (212) 245–2533. Use the 42nd St. station on the C, E, or K subway (8-block walk); or the M5, M15, or M42 bus. Pay lot parking.

Hours. Wed.–Sun., 10 A.M.–5 P.M. (box office closes promptly at 4 P.M., no negotiating).

Costs. Adults, $4.50; ages 7–13, $2.50; ages 6 and under and uniformed military personnel, free.

An ambitious undertaking, the museum is the decommissioned World War II aircraft carrier *Intrepid* afloat in the Hudson River. Not only has the museum foundation refurbished the ship, but it has stocked her with the military aircraft—propeller planes, helicopters, and jets—that flew from her decks between 1944 and 1974. Other highlights include five exhibit halls, rockets and satellites, dioramas, restored command centers, and crew quarters. Movies, videos, and multimedia presentations are shown continuously.

Kids' Facilities. No stroller rentals. No diaper-changing tables in the restrooms. No bottle-warming facilities. Food vending machines.

Ratings. Kids, especially boys over age 5, will get a real kick out of this slice of military history. Give yourselves 2 hours to see it all. 2–7, C; 8–11, A; 12–16, A.

NEW YORK CITY HALL OF SCIENCE

47-10 111th St., Flushing Meadows–Corona Park, Queens. (718) 699–0675. Use the 111th St. station on the 7 subway; or the Q23, Q48, or B58 bus. Free parking.

Hours. Wed.–Sat., 10 A.M.–5 P.M.

Costs. Adults, $2.50; children, $1.50. Free on Wed. and Thurs.

Built on the grounds of both the 1939 and 1964 World Fairs, the Hall of Science is a futuristic place with all sorts of hands-on activities including bubble-making and a microscopic look at atoms. A nifty demonstration of the use of gears (coupled with centrifugal weights for extra help) allows a child pedaling a bicycle to turn an airplane propeller. The building alone is worth a visit.

Kids' Facilities. No stroller rentals (you must check yours and receive a carrier in return). Diaper-changing surfaces available. No bottle-warming facilities. Fast-food cafeteria.

Ratings. With lots of buttons to push and equipment to touch, this museum is worth the hour subway ride from Midtown Manhattan if you are spending more than several days in the city. All ages, A.

BROOKLYN CHILDREN'S MUSEUM

145 Brooklyn Ave., Brooklyn. (718) 735–4432 or (718) 735–4400. Use the Kingston Ave. station on the 3 subway; or the B7, B44, B47, or B65 bus. Free street parking.

Hours. During school year: Mon., Wed.–Fri., 2 P.M.–5 P.M.; Sat. and Sun., 10 A.M.–5 P.M.; closed Tues. During summer vacation: Wed–Mon., 10 A.M.–5 P.M. Closed Tues.

Costs. General admission, $2.

A bit off the beaten Manhattan path, the Brooklyn Children's Museum is an attraction you don't want to miss. Founded in 1899 and built underground, its unifying corridor is a sloping tunnel through which a rushing river of recycled water flows. At 25-foot intervals, the tunnel opens onto different hands-on activity stations. These include a play space for kids aged 2 to 5; an area where fun activities introduce the concept of weights and measures; a section where kids can make music on a handful of exotic instruments like a walking piano and a computer; and a natural science area with a working greenhouse, microscopes, and live animals. The theater, which presents lectures and live theater, is housed in an old water tank.

Kids' Facilities. No stroller rentals. Diaper-changing tables in men's and ladies' restrooms. No food or bottle-warming facilities.

Ratings. Despite a 6-block walk from the Kingston Avenue subway station (the neighborhood is so-so), it's well worth a visit for adventuresome families. You'll need at least an hour to experience it all. 2–7, A; 8–11, A; 12–16, C.

CHILDREN'S MUSEUM OF MANHATTAN

Two locations: 314 W. 54th St. between 8th and 9th Aves., Manhattan. Use the 59th St. Station on the A subway; or the 50th St.–8th Ave. station on the C, E, or K subway; or the M10, M11, M27, M28, or M104 bus. Limited pay lot parking. 212 W. 83rd St., Manhattan. Use the 79th St. station on the 1, 2, or 3 subway; the 81st St. station on the A, C, or K subway; or the M7, M10, M11, or M79 bus. Limited pay lot parking. (212) 765–5905.

Hours. Tues.– Fri. 1 P.M.–5 P.M.; Sat.–Sun., 10 A.M.–5 P.M.

Costs. Tues.–Fri.: adults, $1; children, $2. Sat. and Sun.: adults, $2; children, $3; under age 2, free at all times.

The original children's museum location on 54th Street has housed some impressive changing exhibits. But because of the space limitations, the whole place had to close down while each new exhibit was built. That will all change in fall 1989, when a new 4-story location opens on W. 83rd Street. It will be one of the largest and most technologically advanced children's museums in the country. The Brainatorium will be filled with electronic gadgets to help kids learn about the brain. There will be an outdoor theater, an arboretum, and an art studio where painting, sculpture, and calligraphy will be taught. The Nature and Pet Studio will stress hands-on pet care with real animals. Also included will be a working television studio, a miniature Manhattan cityscape, and a step-by-step hands-on demonstration of how books are made. A 250-seat indoor theater will present plays, concerts, and workshops. The 54th Street location will continue to serve as a showplace for changing exhibits. Workshops and children's theater presentations will continue there.

Kids' Facilities. W. 54th Street: No stroller rentals. Diaper-changing areas. No food or bottle-warming facilities. W. 83rd Street: No stroller rentals. Diaper-changing tables in restrooms. Nursing area for mothers and babies. Bottle-warming available. No food.

Ratings. *W. 54th Street:* A beehive of activity where changing exhibits are always popular with the small fry. Geared to younger kids; after age 7, interest starts to wane. Seeing it takes nearly an hour. 2–7, A; 8–11, B; 12–16, D. *W. 83rd Street:* Should be great and will undoubtedly appeal to a wider age group. Allow at least 2 hours. 2–7, A; 8–11, A; 12–16, C.

ACCOMMODATIONS

If you're determined to stay at a hotel during your New York trip, be prepared for a shock. Most decent hotels in the city cost at least $150 to $175 per night for a family of four. If that sounds like a lot (and it is), at least you have a choice about how to spend it. You can spend that money on a hotel room with everyone in the family living on top of one another, or try one of the many suite hotels that dot the Manhattan landscape. We think a suite hotel is the way to go: our hotel listings include three "reasonably priced" suite hotels and one "reasonable" standard hotel.

Be careful of so-called bargain hotels. While some in Manhattan cost less than $100 per night, there may be some serious drawbacks for families. They may have less-than-savory locations, have services that leave much to be desired, or give no discounts for children. When it comes to the final tally, that bargain hotel could cost you a whopping $50 to $60 more than you expected. Suburban hotels, which are increasingly popular in most metropolitan areas, have some drawbacks for New York. First, there aren't as many as you'd expect for a city this size; most are near LaGuardia and Kennedy airports. Second, a suburban hotel makes a car necessary, and a car is a royal pain in Manhattan.

Bed and breakfast hospitality

This is a decades-old phenomenon with a very New York application. In many parts of the country, the term denotes a quaint Victorian inn, with doilies on the tables and daily high tea. In New York, bed and breakfasts (B and Bs) have a more practical application: They're found in the homes and apartments of New Yorkers.

Whether it's a spare bedroom in a Midtown Manhattan high rise where you share a bathroom with your host, or an entire 3-bedroom brownstone in fashionable Brooklyn Heights, with the owner nowhere in sight, a number of New York agencies can match your family with the right accommodations. The cost is half or less than the price of a hotel room and you get a lot more of the amenities of home. A single bedroom with a shared bath (good for single parents or couples with one child) costs as little as $45 to $60 per night. Two bedrooms with a connected bath (great for a family of four) can cost less than $100. It's not unusual to find an unhosted two-bedroom apartment for less than $175 per night. And you get breakfast, which not only gets you out on the town in the morning without that false start caused by stopping for breakfast but saves you money on restaurants.

There are two procedural differences between arranging for a bed and breakfast and a hotel. (1) You should call the agency a few weeks in advance to be sure you get the best possible accommodations. You will usually have to remit a check for a deposit. (2) Credit cards are out; you must pay with cash or travelers checks. Having tried B and B's in New York, we'll never again pay for a hotel room in the city. Here's a partial list of B and B agencies:

AT HOME IN NEW YORK

P.O. Box 407
New York, NY 10185
(212) 956–3125

BED AND BREAKFAST CITY LIGHTS, INC.

P.O. Box 20355, Cherokee Station
New York, NY 10028
(212) 737–7049

BED AND BREAKFAST, A NEW WORLD

150 5th Ave.
New York, NY 10010
(800) 443–3800

URBAN VENTURES

306 W. 38th St.
New York, NY 10018
(212) 594–5650

Hotels

PLAZA 50 SUITE HOTEL

155 E. 50th St. at 3rd Ave., Midtown Manhattan. (212) 751–5710 or (800) 637–8483. 206 units. Parking, $20 per day.

Rates. $140 to $165; weekend rate packages approx. ⅓ less.
  Small by Manhattan standards, the Plaza 50 is part of the Manhattan East Suite Hotels chain. The junior suites can sleep four family members. It's close to Rockefeller Center, the United Nations, and St. Patrick's Cathedral. Children under age 13 stay free with parents.
Cribs: Yes, $20.
Rollaways: Yes, $20.
Babysitting: No.
Pool: No.
Restaurant: No.
Kitchen facilities: Yes.
Room service: Yes, from nearby deli.
Closest emergency hospital: New York Hospital, 10 minutes away, (212) 472–5050.

SHELBURNE MURRAY HILL HOTEL

303 Lexington Ave. at 37th St., Murray Hill, Manhattan. (212) 689–5200 or (800) 637–8483. 240 units. Parking, $20 per day.

Rates. $150 to $175; weekend rate packages approx. ⅓ less.
  Also part of the Manhattan East Suite Hotels chain, the Shelburne is located not far from the United Nations and the Empire State Building. Children under age 13 stay free with parents.
Cribs: Yes, $20.
Rollaways: Yes, $20.
Babysitting: No.
Pool: No.
Restaurant: Yes.
Kitchen facilities: Yes.

Room service: Yes.
Closest emergency hospital: New York Hospital, 15 minutes away, (212)
472–5050.

SOUTHGATE TOWER HOTEL

371 7th Ave. at 31st Street, Chelsea, Manhattan. (212) 563–1800 or
(800) 637–8483. 527 units, Parking, $20 per day.

Rates. $145 to $175 per day.

The largest hotel in the Manhattan East Suites chain, the Southgate is
not far from the Empire State Building, Times Square, and Pennsylvania
Station. Children under 13 stay free with parents.
Cribs: Yes, $20.
Rollaways: Yes, $20.
Babysitting: No.
Pool: No.
Restaurant: Yes.
Kitchen facilities: Yes.
Room service: Yes.
Closest emergency hospital: Beth Israel Hospital, 15 minutes away, (212)
420–2840.

HOTEL LEXINGTON

511 Lexington Ave. at 48th St., Midtown Manhattan. St. (212) 755–
4400 or (800) 228–5151. 715 rooms. Parking, $22 per day.

Rates. $140 to $155.

Part of the reasonably priced Quality Inn chain, the Lexington is located
near the United Nations, Rockefeller Center, and St. Patrick's Cathedral.
It is *not* a suite hotel. Children under 16 stay free with parents.
Cribs: Yes, free.
Rollaways: Yes, free.
Babysitting: No.
Pool: No.
Restaurant: Yes.
Kitchen facilities: No.
Room service: Yes.
Closest emergency hospital: New York Hospital, 15 minutes away, (212)
472–5050.

RESTAURANTS

When it comes to fast-food franchises, New York isn't much different from most major cities in the United States. Finding McDonald's, Burger King, Pizza Hut, or Roy Rogers isn't at all difficult: There's a cluster of them on Broadway near Times Square. But New York's best fast food is as close as the nearest street corner. We're talking about steamed hot dogs ("franks") from one of the thousands of steam carts that dot the landscape. A gastronomic experience, New York dogs snap when you bite into them and have a flavor that holds its own against a mound of sauerkraut, onions, and mustard. They cost only $1 to $1.50—a small price for a lunch that will stay with you for the rest of the day.

MANHATTAN CHILI COMPANY

302 Bleecker St. near 7th Ave., Greenwich Village, Manhattan. (212) 206–7163. Use the Christopher St. station on the 1, 2, or 3 subway. Very limited street parking.

Hours. Mon.–Thurs., 12 noon–12 midnight; Fri.–Sat. until 1 A.M.; Sun. until 11 P.M.

If your kids haven't had the pleasure of wrapping their lips around spicy Tex-Mex chili, bean, and jalapeño dishes, take them to Manhattan Chili. While residents of Santa Fe and San Antonio might quibble over a few points (like waiters with Brooklyn accents), they'd have to agree that the food is good and authentic-tasting. If spiciness is a consideration, ask your waiter to indicate the milder dishes. Meals are in the $7 to $12 range. Full bar. Reservations suggested. Credit Cards.

Kids' facilities. High chairs and booster seats available. No diaper-changing tables in restrooms. No children's menus.

TWO BOOTS

37 Avenue A near 4th St., Lower East Side, Manhattan. (212) 505–5450. Use the 2nd Ave. station on the F subway. Very limited street parking.

Hours. Tues.–Sun., 12 noon–12 midnight; Sat., Sun. brunch, 12 noon–4 P.M.

Two Boots is an extraordinarily inexpensive Italian restaurant with a full range of entrees for Moms and Dads and the famed "pizza face" pizza, a small pie with the ingredients arranged in a happy face, for the kids. If you're there during the heavy family times (lunch and dinner), admonish your kids to "be quiet and eat your face" and pretty soon every kid within earshot will be echoing the line. Pizzas run from $4.50 to $18.50; entrees between $4.95 and $8.95. No reservations. No credit cards.

Kids' Facilities. Booster seats and high chairs available. No diaper-changing tables in restaurants. Kids' menu consists of pizza face.

SERENDIPITY

225 E. 60th St. between 2nd and 3rd Aves., Manhattan. (212) 838–3531. Use the Lexington Ave. station on the B, N, or R subway; or the 59th St. station on the 4, 5, or 6 subway; use the M103 bus. Very limited pay lot parking.

Hours. Mon.–Thurs., 11:30 A.M.–12.30 A.M.; Fri. until 1 A.M.; Sat. until 2 A.M.; Sun. until 12 midnight.

Well into its fourth decade, Serendipity is famous for foot-long hot dogs and fabulous desserts—specifically, a world-class hot fudge sundae. Located in a brownstone, the restaurant is as well-known for its quiet elegance and Tiffany lamps as its food. In fact, the management places such an emphasis on ambiance and proper decorum that parents may wonder if their kids will measure up. A la carte items run from $2.50 to $12.50, lunches around $10, and dinners about $15. No alcohol. Reservations suggested. Major credit cards. *Beware of Saturdays, the most popular day of the week.*

Kids' Facilities. No high chairs or booster seats. No diaper-changing tables in restrooms. No children's menus.

CARNEGIE DELI

854 7th Ave. between 54th and 55th Sts., Manhattan. (212) 757–2245. Use the 7th Ave. station on the B, D, or E subway; or the 57th St. station on the B, N, or R subway. Limited pay lot parking.

Hours. Daily, 6:30 A.M.–4 A.M.

The Carnegie offers a great mix of jovial service, good food, and humongous portions. It played a pivotal role in the Woody Allen movie *Broadway Danny Rose* and is still a hangout for comedians like Henny Youngman. During lunch hour, you may have to wait outside for a table. Inside, they pack customers in like sardines, so chances are you'll share a table with strangers. If you're the least bit shy, your waiter will break the ice with loud editorial comments about your menu choices. Be aware of sandwich sizes: a half sandwich is almost too much for an adult. The corned beef and pastrami are world famous, and the potato pancakes are sublime. Figure on spending about $10 per person. No reservations. Credit cards.

Kids' Facilities. Booster seats available. No high chairs. No kids' menus. No diaper-changing tables in restrooms.

UMBERTO'S

129 Mulberry St. near Canal Street, Little Italy, Lower Manhattan. (212) 431–7545. Use the Canal St. station on the 6, B, D, J, N, or R subway. Very limited pay lot parking.

Hours. Daily, 11 A.M.–6 A.M.

One of the great Italian seafood restaurants in Little Italy, Umberto's prepares clams, mussels, oysters, and calamari to perfection. Added to Umberto's red spaghetti sauce (mild or hot, but order mild) and linguine, it becomes a lunch worth its weight in Maalox tablets. The decor is no-nonsense nautical, with wooden tables slathered in marine varnish and sturdy wooden chairs. Kids love the sodas served in old-fashioned miniature, 7-ounce bottles. After lunch or dinner, walk down Mulberry Street and stop at one of the many Italian pastry shops. Entrees run from $5 to $15. Alcohol. American Express only.

Kids' Facilities. Booster seats available. No highchairs. No children's menus. No diaper-changing tables. Restrooms down a narrow stairway.

ASTI'S

13 E. 12th St., Manhattan. (212) 741–9105. Use the 14th St–Union Square station on the 4, 5, or 6 subway; or M2, M3, M5, or M7 bus. Pay garage next door.

Hours. Tues.–Sun., 5:30 P.M.–12:30 A.M.

Music and general frivolity are what Asti's is all about. It's an Italian restaurant that serves up great pasta and veal dishes, as well as terrific entertainment. All the waiters are singers, and they delight both kids and adults with old standards and selections from operas and musical comedies. Showtime starts at 6:30 P.M. and continues through the evening. Prices are moderate: $12.75 and up from an a la carte menu. Full bar. Credit cards.

Kids' Facilities. No children's menu, but they do have booster seats and high chairs.

HARD ROCK CAFE

221 W. 57th St. between Broadway and 7th Ave., Manhattan. (212) 459–9320. Use the 57th St. station on the B, D, N, Q, or R subway; or the M5, M6, or M7 bus. No parking facilities.

Hours. Daily, 11:30 A.M.–2:30 A.M.

Throbbing with the latest rock 'n' roll music, walls festooned with pop star memorabilia, the Hard Rock Cafe is a favorite of teenagers, but be prepared to shout. The food is standard fare but quite good, mostly sandwiches, burgers, and grilled chicken. Prices range from $6 to $18.50 on entrees. Full bar. Major credit cards.

Kids' Facilities. No kid's menu but plenty of low-price choices. They do have high chairs and booster seats.

Big Splurges

TROIKA

148 W. 67th St., Manhattan. (212) 724–0709. Use the 66th St.–Lincoln Center station on the 1 subway. Limited pay lot parking.

Hours. Lunch: Tues.–Sat., 12 noon–3 P.M. Dinner: Tues.–Sun., 5 P.M.–12 midnight. Brunch: Sun. 12 noon–4 P.M.

Near Lincoln Center, Troika is a small, intimate place with fabulous Russian food, good wines, and a talented piano player who sets a romantic mood. The menu features all standard Russian dishes from borscht to chicken kiev, plus daily specials. Chicken dishes are glorious and the before-theater prix-fixe dinner is a winner at only $24. For dinner for two (not prix fixe) plus wine, expect to pay about $70. Try this "unknown" restaurant before the secret gets out. Reservations are urged. Full bar. Jackets suggested at dinner. Major credit cards.

TAVERN ON THE GREEN

W. 67th St. and Central Park West, Manhattan. (212) 873–3200. Use the 72nd St. station on the A, B, C, or K subway; or the M10 bus. Limited pay lot parking.

Hours. Lunch: Mon.–Fri., 11:30 A.M.–3:30 P.M. Dinner: daily, 5:30 P.M.–12 midnight. Brunch: Sat.–Sun., 10 A.M.–3:30 P.M.

Famous for those coffee ads ("We secretly replaced their fine coffee . . ."), Tavern on the Green is the only restaurant in the lower western quadrant of Central Park. One of the city's most romantic dining locales, the Tavern's new chef has made the menu equally attractive. The specialties of the house include rack of lamb, sautéed shrimp with ginger, and veal chops. Dinner for two with wine costs about $80. The before-theater prix-fixe dinner is a real bargain at $14.50. Request a table near a window overlooking the park. Full bar. Reservations a must. Major credit cards.

HATSUHANA

17 E. 48th St., Manhattan. (212) 355–3345. Use the 51st St. station on the G subway; or the M1, M2, M3, M4, or M32 bus. No parking facilities.

Hours. Lunch: Mon.–Fri., 11:45 A.M.–2:30 P.M.; Dinner: Mon.–Fri., 5:30 P.M.–10 P.M.; Sat., 5 P.M.–10 P.M.; Closed on Sun.

In Manhattan for eleven years, Hatsuhana serves some of the best Japanese food we've come across. They specialize in sushi and sashimi, and list more than twelve appetizers for every possible taste. The restaurant is quiet, intimate, and decorated in traditional Japanese style. Even though it may sound like an oddity, try the green tea ice cream for dessert—it's great. Lunch is $20 and up; dinner, $25 and up. Full bar. Dinner reservations are required. Major credit cards.

SHOPPING

THINK BIG!

Two locations: 313 Columbus Ave. at W. 76th St., Manhattan; (212) 769–0909; use the 81st St. station on the B, C, K, or A subway. Limited street parking. 390 West Broadway, SoHo; (212) 925–7300; use the Spring St. station on the C, E, or K subway. Limited street parking.

Hours. Mon.–Thurs., 11 A.M.–7 P.M.; Fri.–Sat, 10 A.M.–10 P.M.; Sun., 10 A.M.–8 P.M.

Everything on display at Think Big! suffers from hyperbole: 6-foot pencils, 2½-gallon Coca Cola glasses, wall switches the size of small refrigerators, and aspirin tablets as big as your head. Whether you buy (the merchandise is pretty pricey) or just browse, your kids will marvel at the sheer size of everything. It's great fun.

MYTHOLOGY

370 Columbus Ave. at W. 77th St., Manhattan. (212) 874-0774. Use the 81st St. station on the B, C, K, or A subway. Limited street parking.

Hours. Mon.–Sat., 11 A.M.–11 P.M.; Sun., 12 noon–6 P.M.

Among its crazy, bizarre toys and books from all over the world, Mythology has art books filled with strange paintings, reprinted post cards with grotesque messages, inexpensive Japanese toys, and strange stuffed animals. The pulsating techno-pop music on the store's speaker system will put you into the wacky frame of mind to buy.

THE LAST WOUND-UP

290 Columbus Ave. at W. 74th St., Manhattan. (212) 787–3388. Use the 72nd St. station on the B, C or K subway. Limited pay lot parking.

Hours. Mon.–Thurs., 10 A.M.–9 P.M.; Fri.–Sat., 10 A.M.–10 P.M.; Sun., 11 A.M.–7 P.M.

It's amazing what they're doing with wind-up toys: from little jumping mice, to gargantuan monsters that cost half a week's paycheck. To catch up on the latest the industry has to offer, check out this store.

EEYORE'S BOOKS FOR CHILDREN

Two locations: 2212 Broadway at W. 79th Street, Manhattan; (212) 362–0634; use the 79th St. station on the 1 subway. Limited pay lot parking. 1066 Madison Ave. at E. 80th Street, Manhattan; (212) 988–3404; use the 77th St. station on the 6 subway; or the M1, M2, M3, or M4 bus. Limited pay lot parking.

Hours. Mon.–Sat., 10 A.M.–6 P.M.; Sun., 10:30 A.M.–5 P.M.

Named for Winnie the Pooh's donkey friend, Eeyore's is a small hole-in-the-wall that makes up in quality what it lacks in size. Aimed at children under 10, it stocks the latest in kids' literature along with time-honored standards. A corner reading area becomes a storytelling space on Sundays at 11 A.M. at the West side store and 12:30 P.M. at the East side store: Employees, or sometimes the writers themselves, read to the kids lucky enough to squeeze in. The staff is helpful and friendly. (*Note: Sometimes story hours are different, so phone ahead.*)

ZABAR'S

2245 Broadway at W. 80th St., Manhattan. (212) 787–2000. Use the 79th St. station on the 1 subway. Limited pay lot parking.

Hours. Mon.–Fri., 9 A.M.–7:30 P.M.; Sat. until 12 midnight; Sun. until 6 P.M.

Homemade apple strudel, chocolate croissants, smoked salmon, whole corned beefs, cheeses with names you can't pronounce, cordless electric irons, microchip toasters . . . if it has to do with household activities or cooking, you're bound to find it at Zabar's. Your kids will love the tastes and smells and sights of this old-fashioned European market. Weekends are the busiest and most entertaining time of the week. (*Note: Strollers not allowed on weekends. Weekend crowds can be so large that small kids under age 6 might panic in the crush.*)

I.S. 44 FLEA MARKET

Schoolyard on Columbus Ave. between W. 76th and W. 77th Sts., Manhattan. (212) 316–1088. Use the 81st St. station on the B, C, or K subway. Limited street parking.

Hours. Sun., 10 A.M.–5:30 P.M. (6 P.M. in summer).

Who says you can't find a flea market or a farmers' market in New York City? On any Sunday, this schoolyard is loaded with antiques, old magazines and books, toys, clothing, and farm-fresh produce trucked in from the country.

F. A. O. SCHWARZ

767 5th Ave. between E. 58th and E. 59th Sts. in General Motors Building, Manhattan. (212) 644–9400. Use the 59th St. station on the B, N, or R subway; or the M1, M2, M3, M4, M5, or M7 bus. Pay parking in building.

Hours. Mon.–Sat., 10 A.M.–6 P.M.; Thurs. until 8 P.M.; Sun., 12 noon–5 P.M.

Kids are encouraged to play with the merchandise at this "granddaddy" of New York toy stores. F. A. O. Schwarz holds special children's programs and book signings. They also have an extensive selection of children's books. The most impressive sight is the giant 28-foot clock tower in the middle of the store: it sings and moves its eyes, and at the top of the hour, a ballerina dances, toy soldiers march, and Humpty Dumpty appears on the clock base.

TRANSPORTATION

SUBWAY

The New York subway system consists of 237 miles of tracks in Manhattan, Brooklyn, Queens, and the Bronx (Staten Island has no subway). Unfortunately, the system can be confusing to newcomers. A total of twenty-six different subway lines often have overlapping service and share station platforms. There are also stations that have the same name, but are served by different subway lines and are actually a few blocks apart. If you plan to use the subway at all, obtain a free color-keyed map from the New York Convention and Visitors Bureau or subway token booths.

The subway operates 24 hours a day throughout the year, but we'd be remiss if we didn't add a word of caution: For all that convenience, there is at least some potential danger. Many subway stations are dark, dirty places where, often at night there are few passengers, transit personnel, or police. Because purse snatchings and muggings occur regularly on the subways, we strongly urge you not to travel alone at night and to stay alert during the day. If you're traveling in a group that includes more than your family, you should have no trouble. When waiting for a train, especially at night, stand only in the special after-hours waiting areas designated by yellow signs on the platform ceiling. Those areas are monitored regularly by police.

The subways cost $1, with children under 6 riding for free. That's quite a bargain when you realize you can ride the entire 237-mile system for that buck. A daytime subway ride is real treat for kids. The subway turnstiles accept only tokens, which can be purchased at booths near the turnstiles. Since some stations don't sell tokens, it's wise to buy several when you have the opportunity. These tokens can also be used on buses.

Much has been made about graffiti and vandalism. While you still might catch a glimpse of a spray-painted train, they are a vanishing breed. The surfaces of newer cars repel paint and are, for the most part, clean and comfortable. Be prepared to stand up while riding during rush hours. Should you have any questions, ask a transit cop, or a uniformed subway driver, or try your luck with a usually helpful New Yorker.

For more information, contact the New York City Transit Authority 24 hours a day at (718) 330–1234 (a local call from Manhattan).

BUSES

New York City Transit Authority buses offer an alternative to subways. Like the subways, a city bus ride is $1 (under 6, free), token or exact change (no bills) only. Bus stops are clearly marked and usually have diagrams of the route the bus takes. The big drawback to these modern, comfortable, and clean vehicles is that they must operate in New York traffic, which is subject to gridlock. Buses generally run uptown or downtown (north-south) on all the avenues; and crosstown (east-west) on major streets. The crosstown buses using Central Park transit roads (65th, 81st, 86th, 96th, and 110th Streets) are the quickest way to travel between the East and West sides of Manhattan. For information: (718) 330–1234.

FERRIES

The Staten Island Ferry is still one of the best tourist bargains in New York: 25¢ round trip from Manhattan only; the return trip is free. You get a wonderful 20-minute ride past Ellis Island and the Statue of Liberty, with the Manhattan skyline as a backdrop. On Staten Island, visit the Ferry Museum right inside the ferry terminal (the schedule is sporadic, but you might get lucky). The boats are fast (13–14 knots) and have indoor seating and large outdoor decks, snack bars that serve hot food, and restrooms. The cost for ferrying a car is $2 (plus 25¢ for extra passengers). Motorcycles cost $1.25 and bicycles 25¢. The ferry terminal is located at the tip of Manhattan next to Battery Park at Whitehall Street (Use the South Ferry station on the 1 subway). Ferries run 24 hours a day: at half-hour intervals during the day, at hour intervals late at night. For information: (212) 806–6940.

TAXIS

New York taxicabs are painted yellow and prowl the city streets constantly: Some run all day long, changing drivers every 12 hours. Don't be shy about hailing taxis. The best way is to stand a few feet into the street and raise your arm or point to the driver. They won't stop if they have a passenger or if their "off duty" light is turned on. Almost without exception, taxi drivers will not accept more than four passengers.

Compared with some cities, taxis are a bargain in New York. It costs $1.15 for the first eighth of a mile and 15 cents for each additional eighth and for each minute of waiting time. There's a 50¢ surcharge between 8 P.M. and 6 A.M. and all day on Sunday; no charge for extra passengers. A tip of 15–20 per cent is customary. For complaints about service, note the driver's license number and name, (displayed above the glove compartment) and call the Taxi and Limousine Commission complaint line, (212) 382–9301.

Tours

BUS

Gray Line Tours. (212) 397–2600. Offers fourteen different bus excursions around Manhattan and the rest of New York City. They include a 2-hour trip around upper Manhattan and Harlem ($13.25), a 5-hour grand tour of Manhattan ($19.75), and an all-day tour of Lower Manhattan and the Statue of Liberty ($25). They also offer combination trips to places like the Metropolitan Museum of Art, the South Street Seaport, and an evening tour of the city. All tours depart the Gray Line offices on 8th Avenue between W. 53rd and W. 54th Streets.

BOATS

The Circle Line. (212) 563–3200. The 3-hour cruise around Manhattan takes in the skyline and points of interest along the waterfront, including the city's fabulous bridges, the Cloisters Museum, and any ocean liners that happen to be in port. Tours leave daily from mid-March through late November. Adults, $15; children under 12, $7.50. Schedule fluctuates seasonally; call.

The Seaport Line. (212) 669–9082 or (212) 669–9416. Has two reproduction steamboats, the *DeWitt Clinton* and the *Andrew Fletcher*, which offer daily 90-minute tours of New York Harbor and the East River. They depart several times a day from Pier 16, adjacent to the South Street Seaport Museum in Lower Manhattan from April through November and Fridays through Sundays in December. Adults, $8; children under 12, $5. The *Pioneer*, the Seaport's vintage cargo schooner, conducts daily 2- and 3-hour trips around Manhattan from May through mid-September. Two-hour trip: adults, $16; under age 13, $11. Three-hour excursion: $21 and $16.

WALKING

The Museum of the City of New York. (212) 534–1672. Holds regularly scheduled Sunday walks through interesting and historical neighborhoods all over the city, from March through early November. Tours run from 11 A.M. to 3 P.M. with a stop for lunch (not included in price). The cost is $10 per person. Reservations are recommended. Call ahead for schedule and meeting site. Children age 10 and up are welcome.

The Municipal Art Society. (212) 935–3960. Offers a different conceptual tour every Sunday afternoon between 1 P.M. and 4 P.M. Sometimes the thrust is famous buildings; at other times, specific neighborhoods are singled out. Call for a reservation, a tour schedule, and the departure point. For most tours, children should be age 11 and up; however, the Society sometimes schedules trips that are perfect for the younger ones. The cost is $10 per person.

Talk-a-Walk. (212) 686–0356. 30 Waterside Plaza, 10D, New York, NY 10010. Will send you a cassette tour tape and a map for $11.95 apiece. Tours include "Across the Brooklyn Bridge," "Customs House to Seaport Museum," "World Trade Center to Bowling Green," and "Seaport Museum to World Trade Center." Call or write for a list or buy tapes at a Barnes and Noble bookstore. Ages 8 and up will enjoy these walks

HELICOPTER

Manhattan Helicopter Tours. (212) 247–8687. Offers several sky tours over Manhattan from 9 A.M. to 5:30 P.M daily. Prices range from $30 to $139, depending on the length of the trip. Flights leave from the heliport at W. 30th Street and 12th Avenue along the Hudson River.

Gray Line. (212) 397–2600. Offers a short hop aboard a helicopter as part of a Lower New York tour package ($43.75). The chopper departs from the E. 34th Street and East River Heliport.

HANSOM CABS

Central Park South between 5th and 8th Avenues is the place to climb aboard a horse-drawn carriage for a ride around Central Park. In summer, it can be refreshing and romantic; in winter, the drivers provide plenty of blankets. Rates aren't cheap: Official rates are $17 for the first half hour and $5 for each additional 15 minutes. Confirm this with the driver before embarking.

SEASONAL EVENTS

Unless otherwise noted, contact the New York Convention and Visitors Bureau, (212) 397–8222, for information pertaining to the following listings.

January

CENTRAL PARK WINTER FESTIVAL

This 1-day festival includes ice skating, cross-country skiing, snowman making, and more in sites throughout the park. If January proves to be brown instead of white, the park hooks up its snow-making machinery. For more information: (212) 397–3156 or (212) 360–1333.

February

CHINESE NEW YEAR

New York's Chinese population is one of the largest in the United States. It's fitting then that its Chinese New Year celebration be the biggest. It means big dinners at Chinatown restaurants, firecrackers, and a big parade.

March

ST. PATRICK'S DAY PARADE

Because the city has one of the nation's largest Irish populations, March 17 is a big day in New York. The bars dye the beer green, and paraders line up on 5th Avenue and 44th Street and move uptown to 86th Street. The prime location for viewing is St. Patrick's Cathedral at 5th Avenue and 50th Street.

April

CENTRAL PARK EASTER EGG ROLL

This event takes place the day before Easter (weather permitting) on Central Park's Great Lawn (enter park at 81st Street). Primarily a photo opportunity for Mom and Dad, young children can roll eggs between 9 A.M. and 3 P.M. For more information: (212) 397–3156 or (212) 360–1333.

May

BROOKLYN BRIDGE DAY PARADE

New York's oldest and most famous bridge is the site for this annual walk-over by marching bands.

NINTH AVENUE INTERNATIONAL FOOD FESTIVAL

This weekend party along 9th Avenue from 37th to 57th Streets features foods and people of every ethnicity. There are lots of visual distractions for the kids, including street mimes and musicians and balloons. It gets mighty crowded.

July

INDEPENDENCE DAY

Two fireworks spectaculars stand out: Macy's sponsors the explosions along the East River between 14th and 51st Streets; Battery Park at the southern tip of Manhattan has an all-day celebration followed by fireworks with the Statue of Liberty as a backdrop.

CENTRAL PARK'S KIDS' SUMMER ENTERTAINMENT

Throughout July and August, mobile entertainment units fan out over the park bringing sports equipment, street entertainers, and art supplies to the kids at various playgrounds. For more information: (212) 408–0100 or (212) 397–3156.

September

FEAST OF SAN GENNARO

Little Italy's Mulberry Street is the site for the 10-day mid-September Italian street festival. The theme is religious, but the realities are food, street entertainment, and a flea market crammed onto narrow Mulberry Street each day between 12 noon and 12 midnight. For more information: (212) 226–9546.

November

MACY'S THANKSGIVING PARADE

You've all seen it on TV: the crowds and those gigantic cartoon character balloons as big as 5-story buildings. In person, they look even bigger and more colorful. The Thanksgiving morning parade kicks off at 77th Street and Central Park West and heads south past Columbus Circle and down Broadway to 34th Street and Macy's. For an added treat, you can watch them inflate the balloons the night before near the parade's starting point.

December

ROCKEFELLER CENTER CHRISTMAS TREE LIGHTING

With the smell of roasting chestnuts in the air, the Rockefeller Center tree is ceremonially lit in early December at Rockefeller Plaza just off 5th Avenue and 50th Street. The crowds for the initial sunset lighting are large, but it's a beautiful sight any night throughout the Christmas season. For more information: (212) 489–4300.

NEW YEAR'S EVE

With fireworks fired off in Central Park and the crowds that gather at Times Square, New York is an exciting place on New Year's Eve. While you probably won't want to drag a 6-year-old to Times Square, older kids will really enjoy it. Hold on tight so you don't get separated.

CHILDREN'S THEATER

LINCOLN CENTER

140 W. 65th St. at Broadway, Manhattan. (212) 877–1800. Use the Lincoln Center station on the 1 subway; or use the M5, M7, M10, M11, M29, M30, M103, or M104 bus. Pay lot parking on premises.

Lincoln Center presents a wealth of children's entertainments throughout the year. Most are performed by outside companies in Lincoln Center's seven theater facilities.

Happy Concerts for Young People. A five-concert Saturday series between October and April at Avery Fisher Hall. The concerts are aimed at children between age 6 and 12. Tickets cost from $10 to $20 per performance and must be purchased in advance.

The Big Apple Circus. (212) 391–0767. A New York institution. Performed in a tent set up on the grounds of the Lincoln Center complex, this one-ring circus runs from early November through the New Year's holiday. It's one of the most anticipated events of the winter and, of late, has become one of the hottest tickets in town. It's expensive—in the $30 range.

Young People's Concerts. Most baby boomers remember Leonard Bernstein's broadcasts on public television in the 1960s. Those concerts are still presented at Avery Fisher Hall by the New York Philharmonic Orchestra. There are usually four concerts per year with the season running from January through April. Tickets range from $4 to $15 per seat: a great bargain.

Lincoln Center offers a number of free concerts in the summer and special events throughout the year. It's also possible to obtain $4 tickets for Philharmonic dress rehearsals, held on Thursday mornings at 9:45 before the opening of a concert's four- or five-day run. Call ahead for a monthly schedule, or stop by the Center and pick up free calendars and brochures.

NEW YORK PUPPET FESTIVAL

At the Museum of the City of New York, 5th Ave. and E. 103rd St., Manhattan. (212) 534–1672 ext. 206. Use the 103rd St. station on the 6 subway; use the M1, M2, M3, or M4 bus. Very limited street parking.

This terrific museum offers occasional early-afternoon puppet shows. Tickets cost $2.50, and children must be over 3 years of age. Call for schedule.

PUPPET PLAYHOUSE

555 E. 90th St., Manhattan. (212) 396–8890. Use the 86th St. station on the 4 or 6 subway. Very limited pay lot and street parking.

Puppet shows are presented Saturdays and Sundays at 11 A.M. and 1 P.M. Most performances at this popular theater are by guest puppeteers. Call for a schedule and reservations. Tickets cost $3.

SWEDISH COTTAGE MARIONETTE THEATER

In Central Park at W. 79th St. and Central Park West (enter park at W. 81st St.), Manhattan. (212) 988–9093. Use the 81st St. station on the B, C, or K subway line. Limited pay lot parking.

Reservations are urged for these wonderful 1-hour marionette productions. Productions are staged Saturdays and Sundays at 12 noon and 3 P.M., from late fall through May. Admission is $2. Call ahead for a schedule of upcoming productions.

13TH STREET REPERTORY COMPANY

50 W. 13th St. near 5th Avenue, Greenwich Village, Manhattan. (212) 675–6677. Use the 14th St. station on the F and S subway line. Very limited pay lot parking.

This troupe performs old standards and original plays using well-known storybook characters and themes. They target ages 2 through 10, and performances are usually on Saturdays and Sundays at 1 P.M. and 3 P.M. Admission is $3. Call ahead for a schedule and to make reservations.

CHILDREN'S MUSEUM OF MANHATTAN

See Museums for locations and telephone.

The "old" 54th Street museum continues to offer special programs in music, storytelling, dance, and art about once a month. Performances are often scheduled for Saturdays and Sundays at 2 P.M. and are free with a $3 museum admission. Call ahead for schedule. The "new" 83rd Street museum will perform regular shows when the facility opens in late 1989.

BABYSITTING SERVICES

AVALON REGISTRY
(212) 245–0250

In business for more than 35 years, the Avalon Registry will provide hotel babysitters on the day you call but prefers 24-hours notice. They charge $7 per hour with a minimum of four hours. If your child is under 7 months old, the rate is $8 per hour; infants cost $9 per hour. You also pay for car fare at a rate of $2 during the day, $5 after 8 P.M., and $10 after midnight. All sitters are bonded.

BABYSITTER'S GUILD
(212) 682–0227

This 50-year-old agency charges $7 per hour with a 4-hour minimum. They prefer 24-hours notice but can often get someone the same day. You pay taxi fare after dark.

If there's a convention in town and the above services can't help out, try the following services. They are reputable and their prices are comparable.

GILBERT CHILD CARE AGENCY
(212) 757–7900

PART TIME CHILD CARE
(212) 879–4343

PUBLICATIONS

New York Family. Free bi-monthly magazine; loads of children's store advertising and exceedingly fine calendar of events; pick it up at children's toy and clothing stores.

New York Press. Free weekly newspaper; very good calendar of events tackles the week on a day-by-day basis and includes ample activities for children; available at boutiques and stores throughout Greenwich Village and lower Manhattan.

Village Voice. Weekly newspaper; marvelous calendar of events; "Kid's Stuff" section is amply packed; published Wednesday.

New York Times. Daily newspaper; lots of children's activities in Friday "Weekend Guide."

New York Daily News. Daily newspaper; "Friday" calendar section has entertainment listings for the whole family, and "City Kids" has specific weekend listings for children.

New York Post. Daily newspaper; a large Friday "City Weekend" feature lists theater, movie, and restaurant happenings; Saturday paper includes "Happenings for Kids."

New York Magazine. Weekly magazine; includes the granddaddy of events calendars for the upcoming week; children's calendar appears under "Other Events."

Where Magazine. Free monthly magazine; includes calendar of events, shopping guide, restaurant listings, and Manhattan map; available in hotel lobbies.

LOCAL TELEPHONE NUMBERS

Late-hours pharmacy: Kaufman's Beverly Pharmacy (in Beverly Hotel), Lexington Ave. and 50th St., Midtown Manhattan, (212) 755–2266. Open 24 hours, and they deliver.
Consumer complaints: (212) 587–4908 or (212) 557–0111.
Dental referrals: Dental Association of New York, (212) 772–1661.
Physician referrals: (718) 745–5900.
Lawyer referrals: (212) 382–6625 or (212) 577–3300.
Drug-abuse hotline: (800) 522–5353.

Poison-control hotline: (212) 764–7667 or (212) 340–4494.
Travelers' aid: (212) 944–0013.
Tourism office: (212) 397–8222.
Police: 911.
Fire: 911.
Ambulance: 911.
Weather: (212) 976–1212.
Local car rental: U-Drive, (212) 348–5152; East Side Rent-a-Car, (212) 410–3100; Rent-A-Wreck, (212) 769–1160.

ORLANDO

When the Orlando area was first settled in the 1840s, men were men and mice weren't named Mickey. The first white citizens were army volunteers whose spoils for fighting Seminole Indians were the swamplands and forests vacated by their native enemies. The cattle industry helped keep the region financially solvent until the citrus industry came along.

Started in the years following the Civil War, the orange and grapefruit business didn't thrive until the 1890s, when the railroads began to sell off their extensive land holdings for a dollar an acre: converted to 1960s dollars that's not that much less than what Walt Disney paid for the land seventy years later. By the mid-1890s, the whole Orlando area was booming, and all went well until 1895, when one of the worst freezes in history held central Florida in its grip. As profits went south, so did the growers, effectively leaving boomtown Orlando to founder.

Although the citrus-processing industry remained, Orlando was only a speck on the Florida map until the 1950s, when the city's proximity to Cape Canaveral Space Center spurred renewed growth. Walt Disney had kept his eye on the area and in the late-1950s quietly began to buy up land that would eventually total more than 28,000 acres. Although Disney died in 1966, his Magic Kingdom, a larger version of the California Disneyland, opened in 1971. Epcot Center, Disney's showcase of the world and the future of technology, opened in 1982.

These days first-time visitors are surprised at what they find. Although it's hot and humid in the summer, it's not as subtropical as southern Florida. The Orlando area is actually a string of medium- to small-size cities surrounded by pine forests, grassland, and lots of fresh-water lakes. It covers about 400 square miles and is bordered by the Seminole/Orange County line to the north, the city of Kissimmee to the south, Disney World to the west, and the Orlando Airport to the east (and Cape Canaveral is only 50 miles to the east). The population, estimated at almost one million, is an eclectic mix of native Floridians, escapees from the

**FREEBIES AND CHEAPIES
(free or $3.50 and under for adults**

❑ Cornell Fine Arts Center (see Museums)
❑ Orange County Historical Museum (see Museums)
❑ Loch Haven Art Center (see Museums)
❑ Tupperware Museum (see Museums)
❑ Cartoon Museum (see Museums)
❑ Places of Learning (see Attractions)
❑ Spaceport USA (see Attractions)

Rust Belt, and retired people. Today Orlando natives under the age of 10 are about as scarce as California natives in Los Angeles.

To accommodate the booming tourist industry, hotels, restaurants, and attractions are going up like weeds. That presents a number of problems, not the least of which is traffic. Interstate 4 and a number of four-lane state highways help alleviate the traffic crunch, but during peak tourist periods (Christmas vacation, spring break, and summer), rush hour turns into gridlock. While the highway department is constantly widening and improving roads, it's a good idea to make traffic consciousness part of your game plan. Avoid travel during the early-morning and late-afternoon rush hours, and be prepared to drive long distances as many attractions are at the far reaches of the Orlando area.

THE LONG WEEKEND

Day One
❑ Disney World (see Attractions)

Day Two
❑ Spaceport USA (see Attractions)

Day Three
❑ Epcot Center (see Attractions)

CLIMATE

Except for hot and humid conditions in the summer (low 90s during the day with 90 percent humidity, dropping to the mid-70s at night), the area is pleasant with a year-round average of 72 degrees. In the winter, the mercury hovers in the mid-60s. The rainy season is from July to September, with frequent showers. Winters are drier, but weather fronts from the northwest bring rain that is often followed by a cool air mass that makes the skies azure blue. On rare occasions, those nippy cold fronts drop the mercury to below freezing at night. During those periods, the days seldom make it much past the high 40s. It's always a good idea, therefore, to keep an umbrella handy. For winter visits, bring at least one warm jacket or coat per person.

TOURIST INFORMATION

Contact the Orlando/Orange County Convention and Visitors Bureau, 7680 Republic Dr., Suite 200, Orlando, FL 32819, (407) 345–8882.

ATTRACTIONS

For our purposes, the greater Orlando area includes Kissimmee, Winter Park, Lake Buena Vista, and Walt Disney World. We've also included a few attractions outside this area (notably in Clermont, 20 miles to the west, and Cape Canaveral, 50 miles to the east). Because distances and travel times will vary, pay attention to the addresses and cities. If no city is specified in the address, it's Orlando.

WALT DISNEY WORLD

Interstate Route 4 and US Hwy. 192, Lake Buena Vista. (407) 824–4500. Follow the signs to the Magic Kingdom or Epcot; each is easily reached from the entrance of the other by monorail. Parking, $3 per day.

Hours. Hours of specific attractions vary according to season and proximity to school holidays; however, throughout the year, count on the Magic Kingdom being open at least from 9 A.M. to 6 P.M. and Epcot Center from 9 A.M. to 8 P.M.

Costs. Prices continue their upward spiral, rising sharply about every six months. A 1-day pass for *either* the Epcot Center *or* the Magic Kingdom (excluding River Country and Discovery Island): adults, $28; ages 3–9, $22; 2 and under, free. There are also 3-, 4-, and 5-day passes that include admission to both Epcot and the Magic Kingdom. Three-day passes: adults, $78; ages 3–9, $63. Four-day passes: adults, $98; ages 3–9, $77. Five-day passes: adults, $110; ages 3–9, $88.

Disney World and its multiple attractions are spread over 28,000 acres. The park offers hundreds of diversions, along with four golf courses, a shopping center, a resort with eight major hotels, a movie and television studio, and a complete vacation center, including an RV campground. Six major divisions make up Disney World: the Epcot Center, the Magic Kingdom, Fort Wilderness recreation center, the Disney MGM Studios, Typhoon Lagoon, and Discovery Island.

You begin to realize the immensity of the place as you drive onto the Disney property from US 192 from Kissimmee or Interstate 4 from Orlando. First, you're encouraged to tune your AM radio to 1030 for updated information. Don't worry if you tune in during the middle of the recorded message. It repeats. And with Epcot 2 miles from each highway and the Magic Kingdom 4, there's plenty of time to hear all the broadcast.

EPCOT CENTER

Located 2 miles south of the Magic Kingdom, Epcot Center is a late-20th-century vision of the what the 21st century has in store. Short for Experimental Prototype Community of Tomorrow, Epcot is actually home to two major attractions: World Showcase and Future World.

The Future World attractions include impressive exhibits sponsored by major corporations. They include:

Spaceship Earth. A 180-foot-high geosphere that outlines the history of communication. You also ride through a mock star field and view earth from outer space.

Communicore East and West. Features an extensive view of computer technology, including a history of computing and lots of computers for visitors over age 6 to play with. There's also a robot show and demonstrations of Audio Animatronics, the process Disney uses to create its lifelike robots.

The Living Seas. Takes you under the ocean (actually the world's largest saltwater tank—5.7 million gallons) to see hundreds of species of tropical fish and mammals and an underwater human environment. Kids can also try on a high-tech diving suit and play interactive video games.

The Land. Features a ride through a tropical rain forest, an African desert, and American farm country. The Harvest Theater shows a movie on man and his relationship with the land. The Kitchen Kabaret is an

Audio-Animatronic singing and dancing salute to foods found in every kitchen. Young kids will love the singing vegetables and condiment containers.

Journey into Imagination. Features a tram ride through an Audio-Animatronic salute to the creative process. Younger kids especially will enjoy the songs and antics of the bearded Dreamfinder and his dinosaur sidekick, Figment. An exhibit called the Image Works lets you ''paint'' with electronics, role play in Dreamfinder's School of Drama, and play electronic musical instruments. Journey's most popular attraction is the 3-D movie *Captain Eo*, starring Michael Jackson.

World of Motion. Takes you on a ride through the history of transportation. It has one of Epcot's largest Audio-Animatronic casts and is often quite hilarious. There's also an exhibit of futuristic vehicles and hands-on computer exhibits.

Horizons. A look at the future through the eyes of 19th-century visionaries like Jules Verne. It also features a look at four future home environments, complete with robots and ultramodern conveniences.

Universe of Energy. Looks at both the history and the future of energy. The past is viewed in a unique theater setting in which the audience, theater seats and all, is transported back to the days when dinosaurs roamed the earth. Afterward, a multimedia movie on the current status and probable future of energy is presented on a 210-foot wraparound screen. It will probably go right over the heads of kids under 7 or 8.

The Wonders of Life. Set to open in fall 1989, this attraction offers a filmed flight-simulator ride through the human body.

World Showcase. Beautifully situated on a lake, this is a gathering of exhibits sponsored by eleven nations. Each features structures built in an architectural style representative of the host country. Despite the educational bent, this is mostly a glorified way to sell ethnic food and souvenirs. There is also, at times, lots of singing, dancing, and comedy by ethnically dressed performers. World Showcase includes:

Canada, which features a terrific wraparound movie showing Canadian cities and countryside. Also includes restaurants and souvenirs.

The **United Kingdom** showcase boasts two restaurants and six souvenir shops.

France's exhibit features a movie tour of the French countryside, plus five food attractions and six shops.

Morocco has a Moroccan travel service office, a gallery of native art, and Fez House, an example of early Moroccan architecture. Also included is a restaurant and eight crafts shops.

Japan features an exhibit of antique kites, four restaurants, and a Japanese department store.

The American Adventure has an Audio-Animatronic Ben Franklin and Mark Twain hosting a sentimental multimedia look at America and its people. There's also live outdoor entertainment and a United States Constitution exhibit.

Italy offers a restaurant and four souvenir shops.

Germany features an Oktoberfest beer garden and seven souvenir shops.

China's showcase includes a wraparound motion-picture travelog of the country and a great exhibit of 18th-century clocks and watches. There are also two restaurants and a gift shop that sells items made in the People's Republic.

Norway, the newest World Showcase attraction, features restaurants, shops, a 10th-century Viking village, and boat rides on 16-passenger Viking ships.

Mexico's showcase offers a boat ride, *El Rio de Tiempo*, which takes passengers through Mexican history to the present, and an exhibit of art from 300 years of Spanish rule. There are also two restaurants and four souvenir shops.

Kids' Facilities. While a number of the restrooms feature diaper-changing tables, World Showcase also boasts a complete nursery service located at the east-side entrance of World Showcase (in the Odyssey Restaurant, between Mexico and Future World's World of Motion). Diapers are available from a vending machine. There's a closed room for nursing mothers, plenty of changing counters, and a place to warm a bottle, plus a lounge with comfortable chairs and sofas for pooped parents. Right next door is the first-aid station, with a nurse on duty ready to supply headache, nausea, and cold medications for adults and kids.

Rent strollers and wheelchairs on the left side of Epcot's Entrance Plaza. The charge is $4 for each, but be sure you come early, as they are in limited supply. If the weather is hot and sunny and your own stroller doesn't have a canopy, rent one of theirs.

As the seats at the restaurants at World Showcase are limited and there's usually a line at mealtime, make your reservations upon your arrival. Call (407) 824–4321.

If questions about facilities or attractions arise during the day, go to World Key Information Satellites (there are two each in World Showcase and Future World) and use the computers for assistance. It's amazingly simple to get answers to your basic questions, and kids get a kick out of the interactive computers.

THE MAGIC KINGDOM

Most folks who visit Disney World come for the Magic Kingdom—the place with all the rides and the attractions. The big attractions here are the nighttime Main Street Electrical Parade (depending on the time of year), Pirates of the Caribbean, Big Thunder Mountain, and Space Mountain. The MK is broken down into a number of "lands" that most parents have memorized.

Main Street USA. The first place you see upon entering the Magic Kingdom. Done up in Victorian style, it's the home of attractions like the Walt Disney Railroad, a steam train that runs around the MK; Main Street Cinema, which shows continuous silent movies; the Walt Disney Story, a film on the man's life; and a penny arcade where pennies, nickels, dimes, and quarters will buy you all kinds of amusement fun. There are also horse-drawn carriage rides and rides on old automobiles, jitneys, omnibuses, and fire engines.

Tomorrowland. Features some of the best rides, including Mission to Mars; *American Journey*'s wraparound movie of some of the wonders of the American landscape; *If You Could Fly*," a travelog to vacation sites; the WEDway People Mover; Star Jets; the Audio-Animatronics Carousel of Progress, a look at the benefits of electrical power; Skyway, an aerial tramway that takes you to Fantasy Land; Space Mountain, a thundering roller-coaster ride through the darkness of space (there's a minimum height restriction); Grand Prix Raceway, where you can drive a racecar on a European track; Dreamflight, a flight through the history of aviation (opened in late 1988); and the Tomorrowland Theater, a stage show with Disney characters.

Fantasyland. A great place for little kids because it features an abundance of kiddie rides that aren't too taxing on the young ones—but *are* taxing on the adults. They include the Mad Hatter's giant teacups; the 20,000 Leagues Under the Sea submarine ride; the Dumbo Flying Elephant ride; Cinderella's Golden Carrousel; It's a Small World, the ride through a land of singing dolls; Peter Pan's flight over London; Skyway (see Tomorrowland); and Fantasy Faire where Disney characters perform. There are also attractions for slightly older kids (all warning parents of small kids that they may be too intense) including Mr. Toad's Wild Ride, a mini–roller coaster; Snow White's Adventure; and Fantasyland Theatre, featuring a 3-D movie.

Frontierland/Liberty Square. Here is one of the best roller coasters around: Big Thunder Mountain, a runaway train that zigs and zags through ''gold mine country'' (height and health restrictions apply). But there are plenty of attractions for all ages, including: Tom Sawyer Island and Fort Sam Clemens; Country Bear Jamboree, an Audio-Animatronic music show; Frontierland Shooting Gallery; and the Diamond Horseshoe Jamboree, a live stage show (make reservations for this upon your arrival at the Hospitality House on Main Street USA). Liberty Square attractions include the Hall of Presidents, where former chief executives come to life via Audio Animatronics, and the entertaining Haunted Mansion. There are also two boat rides: the Mike Fink Keelboats, small craft that take passengers around Tom Sawyer Island, and the Liberty Square Riverboat, a real paddle-wheel steamer that also chugs around Tom Sawyer Island.

Adventureland. This tropics-flavored attraction features Pirates of the Caribbean, a boat ride through the coastal stronghold of some Audio-Animatronic 18th-century pirates; the Swiss Family Treehouse, a facsimile of the house used by the characters in the 1960 Disney movie *Swiss Family Robinson*; the Jungle Cruise, a boat ride down the world's most famous tropical rivers; and a favorite of most younger kids, Tropical Serenade, where Audio-Animatronic birds, plants, and tikis encourage you to sing along.

Kids' Facilities. The Magic Kingdom Baby Center has changing tables, baby food, bottle-warming facilities, and a sitting area. Diapers are available from a vending machine. There is also a nurse-staffed first-aid station next door.

Strollers can be rented for $4 per day from the stroller shop just to the right of the Magic Kingdom entrance. To get one, it's best to come early, as they often run out during especially busy days.

Make reservations for the Diamond Horseshoe Jamboree at the Hospitality House, on the right as you enter the Magic Kingdom.

For further information, check with the City Hall Information Center to the left after entering the Magic Kingdom.

THE OTHER ATTRACTIONS

Other additional-cost amusement areas on the Disney property include:

River Country at Fort Wilderness. Features white sand beaches, a swimmin' hole, water slides, a nature trail, and a heated swimming pool. Adults, $9.95; ages 3–12, $7.25; ages 2 and under, free.

Discovery Island. An 11-acre wildlife preserve and zoo with ninety animal species and 250 different kinds of plants. Adults, $6; ages 3–12, $3; ages 2 and under, free. A combined fee of $12.25 (adults) and $8.25 (3–12) covers River Country and Discovery Island.

Disney MGM Movie Studios. Workmen have been working feverishly to complete a number of studio attractions and a studio tour; these are slated to be completed and operational by summer, 1989.

Typhoon Lagoon. A tropically oriented water attraction, featuring the world's largest man-made watershed and pools for snorkling, surfing, swimming, and sliding, is scheduled to open in mid-1989.

To top it all off, Disney World features moving sidewalks, monorails, a massive shopping center, a huge camping and RV facility, and resort hotels on the premises.

Families with kids under 10 beware: Because of the immensity of this place, we suggest buying a multiday pass. Don't worry if you don't use all the days the passes are good for—unused passes are good FOREVER. Arrive early in the day, stay for a few hours, and head back to the hotel for a swim and a nap. As long as you get your hands stamped, you can re-enter the park. In the hot weather, afternoons can be unbearable. And, if you come back in late afternoon, you'll be fresh for the evening's activities, like the Main Street Electrical Parade in the Magic Kingdom.

Disney World abounds with glassy-eyed tourists dragged haphazardly around by their kids and angry parents swatting the behinds of terminally cranky children. These are the folks who didn't prepare as well as they should have. That's what the Disney organization's Guest Relations department is for. Write to them at P.O. Box 40, Lake Buena Vista, FL 32830 or call (407) 824–4500 to request a general package of information (allow six to eight weeks for delivery of literature).

Ratings. No question about it. Even manic depressives love the Disney attractions. Your kids will be humming "It's a Small World" for the next six months. All ages, A.

HARRY P. LEU GARDENS

1730 Forest Ave. (407) 894–6021. Free parking.

Hours. Daily, 9 A.M.–5 P.M. Guided tours of the Leu house are available Mon.–Sat., 10 A.M. and 3:30 P.M.; Sun., 1 P.M. and 4 P.M. Closed on Christmas.

Costs. Adults, $3; ages 6–16, $1; ages 5 and under, free.

Central Florida, with its moist, nearly tropical climate is blessed with knockout formal gardens. The 47-acre Leu Gardens on the shores of Lake Rowena encompass meandering asphalt trails and a new gazebo and dock on the shore. Along with the gardens, the Leu House, built in the 1890s, is a fine example of period architecture. Trees provide a great shelter from the rain, as does the Leu House's screened-in porch.

Kids' Facilities. No changing tables; however, there are plenty of benches. No stroller rentals and no bottle-warming facilities. There are three wheelchairs available at no cost.

Ratings. Since outdoor tropical gardens abound in Florida (and the kids would rather be at Disney World), the younger members of the family may not get that big a kick out of this place. 2–7, C; 8–11, C; 12–16, B.

LOCH HAVEN PARK

Mills Ave. (US 17/92) and Lake Formosa Dr. N. Free parking.

Loch Haven Park, Orlando's cultural hub, is home to the Loch Haven Art Center (see Museums), the Orange County Historical Museum (see Museums), the Central Florida Civic Theatre (see Theaters), and the Orlando Science Center.

THE ORLANDO SCIENCE CENTER

810 E. Rollins St. (407) 896–7151. Free parking.

Hours. Mon.–Thurs., 9 A.M.–5 P.M.; Fri., 9 A.M.–9 P.M.; Sat., 12 noon–9 P.M.; Sun., 12 noon–5 P.M. Closed on New Year's Day, Thanksgiving, and Christmas. *Planetarium shows:* Mon.–Fri., 2:30 P.M.; Sat. and Sun., 2 P.M. and 3:30 P.M.

Costs. Adults, $3; ages 4–17, $2; ages 3 and under, free.

This catch-all science museum features a good selection of natural history exhibits plus a large area devoted to space science. The Tunnel of Discovery features hands-on exhibits, including magnets, bubble-making with unusual instruments like hula hoops, and a sound exhibit complete with tuning forks and a steam whistle. Curiosity Corner, for toddlers, boasts baby chicks, hamsters, magnets, and puzzles. The new Natural History Hall displays four different ecosystems.

Kids' Facilities. No stroller rentals. Changing tables in ladies restroom (dads can go next door to Orange County Historical Museum). Fast food is available at the Lunching Pad, where they'll be glad to warm a bottle.

Ratings. There's something here for everyone. And it's right next door to the Historical Museum and across the parking lot from the Orlando Art Museum. All ages, A.

SEA WORLD OF FLORIDA

7007 Sea World Dr. (407) 351–3600 or (800) 327–2420 (nationwide) or (800) 432–1178 (in Florida). Free parking.

Hours. Daily, 9 A.M.–7 P.M.; longer hours during peak seasons.

Costs. *Daily pass:* adults, $23.05; ages 3–11, $18.90; ages 2 and under, free. *Weekly pass:* adults, $26.50; ages 3–11, $23.50; ages 2 and under, free. *Guided tours of behind-the-scenes operations:* adults, $5.50; kids, $4.50. *Sky Tower ride*, $1.25.

Sea World consists of four theme areas: Ocean Friends, Beneath the Sea, Sea Lions and Otters, and Shamu Stadium/Atlantis. Some of the highlights include:

The **Baby Shamu Celebration**, a water show featuring killer whale Baby Shamu (the first born in captivity).

Sea Lions of the Silver Screen, a sea lion and otter show that apes Hollywood movies of the 1920s and 1930s. It's really goofy, but small kids eat it up.

The **Tropical Reef**, where divers enter a 160,000-gallon tropical reef to feed thousands of fish.

The **Shark Encounter**, an exhibit that utilizes two multimedia theaters and an underwater viewing area where customers see three dozen sharks swimming above them.

Cap'n Kids World, a playground for the little ones that features a games arcade and a pirate ship.

The **Sky Tower**, a 400-foot-high observation platform from which to take in all the sites.

The **Whale and Dolphin Show**, where marine mammals cavort on command.

The **Penguin Encounter** featuring 200 penguins from the Antarctic.

Sea World also has marine exhibits, feeding pools, alligators, a Florida tidal pool, water ski shows, general merriment, and lots of junk food. In the summer and during select school holiday periods, there are special shows and fireworks displays.

Kids' Facilities. This place is ready for kids. There are a vast number of strollers and wheelchairs (for $3.50 per day). Diaper changing can be done in the ladies' restrooms. Nursing facilities are available adjacent to the restrooms at the Penguin Encounter. Nurses are available at all times: Just alert any employee and help will be on the way. For bottle warming, ask the waiters and waitresses at any of the sit-down restaurants.

Ratings. If you see nothing in the Orlando area but this place and Disney World, the kids will go home fulfilled. All ages, A.

PLACES OF LEARNING

6825 Academic Dr. (407) 345–1038. Free parking.

Hours. Daily, 9 A.M.–6 P.M.

Costs. Free.

While the children's book and toy store (called the Parent Store: see Shopping) is what people on their way to and from Sea World come here for, Places of Learning does have an interesting free attraction: a 1-acre map of the United States. Boundaries, lakes, rivers, and dams are all here, as are the Gulf of Mexico, the Great Lakes, and the Pacific Ocean, which are actually filled with water. Add to that the flags of all fifty states, fifteen four-foot-high children's books, and a giant chess board, and you've got something to keep the kids occupied while you shop.

Kids' Facilities. No stroller rentals, no changing tables, and no bottle-warming capabilities.

Ratings. For a quick stop, it's pretty impressive. 2–7, B; 8–11, A; 12–16, B.

BOARDWALK AND BASEBALL

Interstate 4 and US Hwy. 27, Baseball City. (407) 648–5151 or (800) 367–2249 (in Florida) or (800) 826–1939 (nationwide). Free parking.

Hours. Fluctuate seasonally; however, at the very least it's open: Mon.–Thurs., 9 A.M.–6 P.M.; Fri.–Sun., 9 A.M.–11 P.M.

Costs. Adults, $16.95; under 48″ tall, $12.95; under 3, free.

Harcourt Brace Jovanovich has combined turn-of-the-century ocean-front amusement boardwalk with a number of exhibits with a baseball theme. The result is a place to ride roller coasters and one of the world's tallest ferris wheels (10 stories), get pitching and hitting instruction, and whack away at balls in batting cages. There are also kiddie rides (a great selection!), arcade games, all sorts of dining choices, a giant-screen IMAX theater, a miniature Cooperstown baseball museum, a live-action Wild-West musical show and a movie showing great moments in major league baseball.

As a bonus, B&B's 7,000-seat stadium is now the spring training home of the Kansas City Royals and, during the summer, the Class A Florida State League Baseball City Royals. For a few bucks more each game day, you can see 'em play.

Kids' Facilities. There are two special diaper-changing rooms that sell disposable diapers. Strollers and wheelchairs rent for $3. Bottles can be warmed at restaurants, and baby food is available.

Ratings. Although the combination of baseball and boardwalk attractions may sound incongruous, it works and provides diversions for every member of the family. All ages, A.

WET 'N WILD

6200 International Dr. (407) 351–3200. Free parking.

Hours. June through late August: daily, 9 A.M.–9 P.M. Mid-February through early June and late August through October 31: daily, 10 A.M.–5 P.M.

Costs. Adults, $14.95; ages 3–12, $12.95; 2 and under, free.

At 25-acre Wet 'N Wild, you can bob around in the wave pool waiting for "the big one" to ride into the beach, race across a wild rapids, or plummet down one of many water slides. You can also picnic on a private beach (you can bring your own food). There are amusement park rides, but some have a height restriction. There is an area designated for small children called Dr. Pepper Park and a 6-story water slide for 5- to 10-year-olds dubbed Bubble Up.

Kids' Facilities. Plenty of diaper-changing areas, and the fast-food vendors will be happy to warm a bottle. No stroller rentals, but you're free to bring your own.

Ratings. Kids of all ages like to get wet and since Wet 'N Wild offers so many ways to do it, it's a real winner. All ages, A.

FUN 'N WHEELS

6739 Sand Lake Rd. (407) 351–5651. Free parking.

Hours. Mon.–Thurs., 4 P.M.–12 midnight; Fri.–Sun., 10 A.M.–12 midnight.

Costs. Free admission. Tickets are sold for individual rides and attractions at a rate of 20 for $20. Individual tickets cost $1.25 each. Most rides cost between one and three tickets.

For miniature golf, go-carts, bumper cars, and fast food it's hard to top Fun 'N Wheels. The rides tend to be on the expensive side, but, because of its no-admission-fee policy, it's one of the few area attractions that doesn't penalize you for leaving after only 45 minutes.

Kids' Facilities. No diaper-changing facilities. Bottles gladly warmed at food stands. Strollers available for $2.

Ratings. There are amusements for kids from age 2 to adult. All ages, A.

SPACEPORT USA

State Hwy. 405, Kennedy Space Center. (407) 425–2121. Take State Hwys. 50 and 405 *or* State Hwys. 528 and 407 (toll) and 405. Free parking.

Hours. Daily, 9 A.M.–dusk.

Costs. Free admission. Bus tours of Kennedy Space Center *or* Cape Canaveral: adults, $4; ages 3–12, $1.75. IMAX Theater presentation of *The Dream is Alive*, a movie about the Space Shuttle: adults, $2.75; ages 3–12, $1.75

Even during the months following the January 1986 *Challenger* disaster, Spaceport USA often attracted 23,000 visitors per day. The museum runs the space gamut from lunar modules and Apollo space suits to a "garden" that offers a full historical array of Titan and Saturn rockets. Along with hundreds of historical space artifacts, there are two 2-hour bus tours: of the Kennedy Space Center launching pads and operations buildings, and of historic Cape Canaveral's manned and unmanned launching sites.

There are a number of hands-on demonstrations for younger kids and a few interactive exhibits that allow kids to sit in a lunar rover and be photographed wearing a space suit.

Topping off your visit is the IMAX feature *The Dream is Alive*, a look at the Space Shuttle program with some nifty in-space shots of Shuttle flights.

Kids' Facilities. No stroller rentals. Changing tables in ladies' restrooms in cafeteria. The cafeteria staff will warm bottles for you.

Ratings. Spaceport USA is not really for kids under 3; however, kids in strollers can easily tolerate it. A couple of tips: Arrive before 11 A.M. and buy tickets for both the IMAX Theater and the bus tours. Tickets are good for a specific time and, as the day wears on, many tours and theater showings are sold out. Bus tours may be just the ticket for young children: The motion of the bus puts them to sleep (no car seats allowed in the buses). Also, if you forget your camera, the gift shop will loan you one when you buy film. 2–7, B; 8–11, A; 12–16, A.

CHURCH STREET STATION

129 W. Church St. (407) 422–2434. Metered lot and street parking.

Hours. Daily, 10 A.M.–12:30 A.M.; some stores are open fewer hours.

Costs. Free during the day; $11.95 at night for live entertainment.

While Church Street Station and Church Street Exchange are commercial ventures that house restaurants and shops, the owners have done a great job restoring these 2-block-long facilities in what was Orlando's commercial hub 100 years ago. Various restaurants and shops boast period furnishings like stained glass windows, pool tables, and gun collections that are worth seeing. The Station also has a 1912 steam engine parked next door, and many of the restaurants, including Rosie O'Grady's, the Cheyenne Saloon, and Phineas Phogg's Balloon Works, feature top-name entertainment.

Kids' Facilities. No changing tables (although there are plenty of indoor benches). No stroller rentals. Ask at the restaurants for bottle warming.

Ratings. As long as you go during daylight hours, it costs nothing to get in. In those instances, the kids might enjoy it for an hour or so, especially for getting some lunch or shopping for souvenirs. All ages, B.

XANADU

US Hwy. 192 and State Hwy. 535, Kissimmee. (407) 396–1992. Free parking.

Hours. Daily, 10 A.M.–10 P.M.

Costs. Adults, $5.95; ages 4–17, $3.75; age 3 and under, free.

Xanadu's owners obviously feel that 21st-century homes will be sculpted from polyurethane plastic foam that resembles dollops of hardened shave cream. Actually, Xanadu is quite a marvel and a showcase for all kinds of computerized gadgets designed for trouble-free living. There are computer screens at every turn, a futuristic bathroom, a high-tech kitchen, and a children's play area with a small video game arcade and plenty of nooks and crannies where the little ones can amuse themselves while Mom and Dad take a serious look around. Xanadu is worth a good hour.

Kids' Facilities. No strollers (none needed, even though Xanadu is more than 6,000 square feet), no bottle-warming facilities, and no changing tables. Restrooms are in a separate structure next to the parking lot.

Ratings. This place packs in all ages, but kids need to be 8 and older to really appreciate it. 2–7, C; 8–11, A; 12–16, A.

GATORLAND ZOO

14501 S. Orange Blossom Trail. (407) 857–3845 or (407) 855–5496. Free parking.

Hours. Summer: daily, 8 A.M.–7 P.M. Winter: 8 A.M.–6 P.M.

Costs. Adults, $5.25; ages 3–12, $3.75; under age 3, free.

"Are those real?" asked our 4-year-old. And, after the plethora of Audio-Animatronic creatures at Disney World, it seemed like a reasonable question. The 5,000-or-so gators on the premises are indeed real, especially the ones that jump out of the water to snatch chickens out of the hands of an attendant. But jumping alligators aren't the only crowd pleasers here. Along with a zoo that includes monkeys, birds, zebras, and sheep, Gatorland features a photo area where you or the kids can pose holding a 3-foot alligator or a 10-foot boa constrictor, ride a miniature steam train, and ride a 2,000-foot-long elevated walk through an authentic Florida swamp. The gift shop offers alligator-hide boots and leather goods, as well as canned gator meat and chowder.

Kids' Facilities. No stroller rentals, no changing tables, and no bottle warming. The snack bar features chili dogs and cokes.

Ratings. When you're used to seeing only one or two alligators at any one time, this many all at once is mind boggling. Kids, especially young ones, really love this place. 2–7, A; 8–11, A; 12–16, B.

ALLIGATORLAND SAFARI ZOO

4580 W. US Hwy. 192, Kissimmee. (407) 396–1012. Free parking.

Hours. Daily, 9 A.M.–sunset.

Costs. Adults, $4.25; ages 3–11, $3.15; under 3, free.

While Alligatorland has a gaudy giant cement gator in the parking lot and a facade that looks like the world's largest gift shop, this is actually one of the cleanest, best-kept zoos in Central Florida. Most of the alligators are confined to a fenced-in lake just past the entrance. The zoo has a number of exotic animals, including jaguars, llamas, an ostrich, deer, monkeys, a Siberian tiger, hyenas, African lions, sassy baboons, and even lemurs and a couple of coatimundis. In the absence of an Orlando/Kissimmee municipal zoo, this one will do nicely.

Kids' Facilities. No stroller rentals, no changing tables (restrooms are small, but there are plenty of benches), and no bottle-warming service. Snacks in the gift shop.

Ratings. All ages, A.

MUSEUMS

BEAL-MALTBIE SHELL MUSEUM

Corner of Park and Holt aves., Winter Park. (407) 646–2364. Free parking.

Hours. Mon.–Fri., 10A.M.–12 noon and 1 P.M.–4 P.M. Closed weekends and holidays. Call ahead as this museum is sometimes closed.

Costs. Adults, $1; ages 6–12, 50¢; ages 5 and under, free.

As incredible as it may sound, Beal-Maltbie has over two million shells and more than 200,000 species on display.

Kids' Facilities. No changing tables, no stroller rentals but it's not big enough to need them. No bottle-warming facilities.

Ratings. Shells tend to send younger kids into fits of ecstasy, especially those old enough to realize that Florida shell collecting is an activity in which they can participate. 2–7, A; 8–11, A; 12–16, C.

CORNELL FINE ARTS CENTER

Holt Ave. on Rollins College Campus, Winter Park. (407) 646–2526. Free parking.

Hours. Tues.–Fri., 10A.M.–5 P.M.; Sat. and Sun., 1 P.M.–5P.M. Closed on holidays.

Costs. Free.

A small museum with few permanent artworks on display. Since almost every square foot is devoted to traveling exhibitions, call ahead to see if there's anything of current appeal to you or your kids.

Kids' Facilities. No stroller rentals. No changing tables. No food or bottle-warming facilities.

Ratings. The ratings here depend on the particular exhibit; however, the general sophistication level would interest teenagers on up.

MORSE GALLERY OF ART

133 E. Welbourne Ave., Winter Park. (407) 644–3686. Free and metered street parking.

Hours. Tues.–Sat., 9:30 A.M.–4 P.M.; Sun., 1 P.M.–4 P.M.

Costs. Adults, $2.50; students, $1.

This small storefront gallery holds one of the world's top collections of the glassworks of Lewis Comfort Tiffany. There are other Art Nouveau works, such as Rookwood pottery, and period paintings by Gilbert Stuart and Samuel F. B. Morse. Allow a half hour, tops.

Kids' Facilities. No stroller rentals. No changing tables. No facilities for warming a bottle.

Ratings. Despite the multicolored light created by the lamps and windows, this place is not for the younger ones. Older kids, especially those with an artistic bent, might enjoy it, 2–7, D; 8–11, C; 12–16, B.

ORANGE COUNTY HISTORICAL MUSEUM

812 E. Rollins St. (407) 898–8320. Free parking.

Hours. Wed.–Fri., 10 A.M.–4 P.M.; Sat.–Sun., 2 P.M.–5 P.M. Closed Mon. and Tues.

Costs. Free.

This museum provides a taste of Orlando as it was during the citrus boom of the 1890s. There are displays of period clothing, quilts, and even a country store. There's even an old hot-type printing press and a mock-up of a decades-old Orlando *Sentinel* office. Kids like Fire Station No. 3, the vintage 1926 firehouse behind the museum.

Kids' Facilities. Bottles can be warmed next door at the Orlando Science Center. There are changing tables in *both* men's and ladies' restrooms. No stroller rentals available (or needed).

Ratings. This is one of the area's more enjoyable free attractions, with something for every age group. All ages, A.

LOCH HAVEN ART CENTER

2416 N. Mills Ave. (407) 896–4231. Free parking.

Hours. Tues.–Fri., 10 A.M.–5 P.M.; Sat., 12 noon–5 P.M.; Sun., 2 P.M.–5 P.M.

Costs. Free.

This gallery contains a reasonable collection of pre-Columbian pottery as well African tribal sculpture, both of more interest to kids than the American paintings.

Kids' Facilities. No changing tables. No stroller rentals. No place to warm a bottle. Walk across the parking lot to the Orlando Science Center.

Ratings. Close proximity to the Science Center and Historical Museum (and free admission) make this a worthwhile stop while in Loch Haven Park. All ages, B.

TUPPERWARE EXHIBIT AND MUSEUM

At the Orange-Osceola County line on Orange Blossom Trail (US 441). (407) 847–3111. Free parking.

Hours. Mon.–Fri., 9 A.M.–4 P.M.

Costs. Free.

Tupperware, the resting place of unfinished meals, is the main attraction at this museum located at the company's world headquarters. Along with a 20-minute guided tour through an all-American home filled with handy

Tupperware, a museum displays containers that date back to 4000 B.C, and a Tuppertoys section where kids from age 1 to 8 can play. On top of this, you walk out with a free souvenir container.

Kids' Facilities. No changing tables (however, there are plenty of couches in the waiting area). No bottle-warming facilities. No stroller rentals.

Ratings. Kids who have not yet observed first-hand a Tupperware party in their own living room may not understand the relevance. But Moms and Dads with either a love for the product or a sense of humor will have a riot. 2–7, B (for the Tuppertoys); 8–11, C; 12–16, C.

ELVIS PRESLEY MUSEUM

5931 American Way. (407) 345–8860. Free parking.

Hours. Daily, 9 A.M.–9 P.M.

Costs. Adults, $4; ages 7–12, $3; ages 6 and under, free.

At this, the largest of three Elvis museums (the others are in Memphis and Honolulu), you'll see hundreds of the King's personal possessions, including a 1969 Mercedes limousine, the race car he drove in the movie *Spinout*, lots of his jewelry, plenty of clothing, an early driver's license, even his birth records.

Kids' Facilities. No stroller rentals. No changing tables. No bottle-warming facilities.

Ratings. Younger kids would rather see a shrine to Big Bird or Mister Rogers. The older the kids, the more they'll like it. 2–7, C; 8–11, B; 12–16, A.

THE CARTOON MUSEUM

4300 S. Semoran Blvd., Suite 103. (407) 273–0141. Free parking.

Hours. Mon.–Sat., 11 A.M.–6 P.M.; Sun., 11 A.M.–4 P.M.

Costs. Free.

Here you'll find comic books, Little Golden Books, old television premiums, and magazines. Teach your kids about the good old days with the books and magazines your parents used to say would turn your brain to mush.

Kids' Facilities. No stroller rentals. No changing tables. No bottle-warming capabilities.

Ratings. Owner Jim Ivy discourages kids under 11 because they finger the merchandise, and because he feels the exhibits are relevant only to teenagers and adults. 2–7, F; 8–10, F; 11–16, A.

HOTELS

With more than 60,000 hotel rooms in the greater Orlando area (and more opening all the time), there is no shortage of space as long as you plan ahead—especially during the busy school vacation periods of spring, Christmas, and summer. Quite a few establishments fall into the $40- to $50-per-night range, with specials offered on a regular basis. Suite hotels and motor inns provide the most bang for your buck.

Orlando—North

RESIDENCE INN ORLANDO—ALTAMONTE SPRINGS

270 Douglas Ave., Altamonte Springs. (407) 788–7991.

Rates. $79 to $104.

As with most Residence Inns, this one provides a terrific suite for a reasonable price. The atmosphere is homey and the staff is dedicated. There's a free continental breakfast daily. Kids under 18 stay at no extra charge.

Cribs: Yes, no charge.
Rollaways: Yes, $10
Babysitting: Yes, referrals.
Pool: Yes, plus two Jacuzzis.
Restaurants: No.
Kitchen facilities: Yes.
Room service: No.
Closest emergency hospital: Florida Hospital, 5 miles away, (407) 897–1940.

PARK SUITE HOTEL ORLANDO NORTH—ALTAMONTE SPRINGS

225 E. Altamonte Dr., Altamonte Springs. (407) 834–2400. 210 units.

Rates. $85 to $95.

This hotel features 1-bedroom suites and a pretty garden courtyard. Kids 16 and under stay free with parents.

Cribs: Yes, no charge.
Rollaways: No.
Babysitting: Yes, referrals.
Pool: Yes, indoor pool plus sauna and whirlpool.
Restaurants: Yes.
Kitchen facilities: Yes.
Room service: Yes.
Closest emergency hospital: Florida Hospital, 5 miles away, (407) 897–1940.

Orlando—West

PARK SUITE HOTEL

8978 International Dr. (407) 352–1400. 245 units.

Rates. $85 to $105.

This hotel features 1- and 2-bedroom suites. It's close to the Wet 'N Wild water park, the Elvis Presley Museum, and Sea World. Kids 16 and under stay free with parents.

Cribs: Yes, no charge.
Rollaways: No.
Babysitting: Yes, referrals.
Pool: An indoor pool, a wading pool, and a whirlpool.
Restaurants: Yes, coffee shop and dining room.
Kitchen facilities: Yes.
Room service: Yes.
Closest emergency hospital: Sand Lake Hospital, 3 miles away, (407) 351–8500.

EMBASSY SUITES HOTEL

8250 Jamaican Ct. (407) 345–8250. 246 units.

Rates. $85 to $95.

This hotel features 1-bedroom suites with wet bars. It's close to the Wet 'N Wild water park, Elvis Presley Museum, and Sea World. Complimentary beverages are served each evening. Kids 12 and under stay free with parents.

Cribs: Yes, no charge.

Rollaways: Yes, no charge.
Babysitting: Yes, referrals.
Pool: An indoor/outdoor pool, a sauna, and a whirlpool.
Restaurants: No.
Kitchen facilities: Yes.
Room service: Yes.
Closest emergency hospital: Sand Lake Hospital, 3 miles away, (407) 351–8500.

RESIDENCE INN AT ORLANDO INTERNATIONAL

7610 Canada Ave. (407) 345–0117. 176 units.

Rates. $79 to $119.

This Residence Inn features 1- and 2-bedroom suites. It's close to the Wet 'N Wild water park, the Elvis Presley Museum, and Sea World. Along with its homey atmosphere and cheerful accommodation to guest requests, it features a free continental breakfast every day. Kids under 18 stay free with parents.
Cribs: Yes, no charge.
Rollaways: Yes, $10.
Babysitting: Yes, referrals.
Pool: Yes.
Restaurants: No.
Kitchen facilities: Yes.
Room service: No.
Closest emergency hospital: Sand Lake Hospital, 2 miles away, (407) 351–8500.

Orlando—South

QUALITY INN EXECUTIVE SUITES

4855 S. Orange Blossom Trail. (407) 851–3000.

Rates. $56 to $96.

Located in an up-and-coming area near Florida Mall and other smaller centers, this hotel is a great bargain. The bulk of the rooms are studio suites with a smattering of 1-bedroom units. Kids 16 and under stay free with parents.
Cribs: Yes, no charge.
Rollaways: No.
Babysitting: Yes, referrals.

Pool: Yes.
Restaurants: No.
Kitchen facilities: Yes.
Room service: No.
Closest emergency hospital: Orlando Regional Medical Center, 15 minutes away, (407) 841–5210.

DAYS INN AT FLORIDA MALL

1221 W. Landstreet Rd., (407) 859–7700. 449 units.

Rates. $43 to $80.

Located on the southern outskirts of Orlando, this is one of the best bargains among the area suite hotels. Two-hundred-forty-five of the hotel's units are suites. While the decor is unspectacular, the suites have plenty of space, full kitchens, and basic utensils for rent ($2 per day). Kids under 18 stay free with parents.
Cribs: Yes, no charge.
Rollaways: Yes, no charge.
Babysitting: No.
Pool: Yes.
Restaurants: Yes, coffee shop.
Kitchen facilities: Yes.
Room service: No.
Closest emergency hospital: Orlando Regional Medical Center, 20 minutes away, (407) 841–5210.

Kissimmee

RESIDENCE INN—KISSIMMEE

4786 W. Irlo Bronson Memorial Hwy. (US 192), Kissimmee. (407) 396–2056.

Rates. $82 to $129.

This lakeside property features 1- and 2-bedroom suites. It's adjacent to Xanadu and 4 miles from Disney World. It has a great staff, free continental breakfast every day, and a kids' playground facility. Kids under 18 stay free with parents.
Cribs: Yes, no charge.
Rollaways: Yes, $10.
Babysitting: Yes, referrals.
Pool: Yes.

Restaurants: No.
Kitchen facilities: Yes.
Room service: No.
Closest emergency hospital: Kissimmee Memorial Hospital, 20 minutes away, (407) 827–6271.

RESTAURANTS

There are plenty of fast-food emporiums, including all the national chains: McDonald's, Wendy's, Burger King (which began in Florida in the 1960s), Domino's Pizza, and Arby's, to name a few. There are also chains like Red Lobster for seafood, the Waffle House for breakfast, and Subway for quick, inexpensive submarine sandwiches. Restaurants that demand special recognition for kid appeal are dinner theaters **Medieval Times**, **Fort Liberty**, **King Henry's Feast**, and **Mardi Gras** (see Children's Theater.)

Big Splurges

CHRISTINI'S

7600 Doctor Phillips Blvd. (in the Marketplace Mall.) (407) 345–8770. Free lot parking.

Hours. Mon.–Sat., 6 P.M.–12 midnight. Closed Sun.

A gourmet Italian restaurant that received the prestigious Ivy Award for food excellence, Christini's is well worth a visit. Their homemade pasta dishes are all wonderful, and we also recommend their seafood, which is flown in fresh daily. It's a romantic change from the commercial side of Orlando. Dinner costs about $30 per person. Full bar. Reservations required. Credit cards.

LA COQUINA

1 Grand Cypress Blvd., in the Grand Cypress Hotel. (407) 239–1234, ext. 6362. Valet parking $2.

Hours. Sun.–Thurs., 6:30 P.M.–11 P.M.; Fri.–Sat., 6 P.M.–11 P.M.

An intimate French restaurant that serves an extensive menu of steaks, seafood, and other entrees. Try their Mocha or Grand Marnier soufflé for dessert. They have their own bakery, so eat light at Disney World. It's expensive; about $50 per person (with wine). Full bar. Jackets required. Reservations suggested. Credit cards.

SHOPPING

Orlando and Kissimmee specialize in discount factory outlets. While literally dozens of single-store outlets dot the map (especially on International Drive in Orlando and on US Hwy. 192 just west of Kissimmee), we'll focus on the the area's biggest outlet mall.

BELZ FACTORY OUTLET AND ANNEX

5401 W. Oak Ridge Rd. (407) 352–9611. Free parking.

Hours. Mon.–Sat., 10 A.M.–9 P.M.; Sun., 10 A.M.–6 P.M.
More than ninety stores occupy the mall and the annex across the street. Most stores sell merchandise for 50 percent off the retail price. Along with parent-type outlets for clothes, shoes, and electronics, there are toy stores and kids' clothing stores as well. There are stores that sell products from a single manufacturer, as well as outlets that combine products made by a number of different companies.

THE PARENT STORE

6825 Academic Dr. (407) 345–1038. Free parking.

Hours. Daily, 9 A.M.–6 P.M.
Places of Learning has an impressive United States map for kids to play on and explore (see Attractions). But most of the fun is indoors at the Parent Store, where parents and kids are encouraged to use hands-on demonstration computers, read books, and shop for nearly every educational toy available in this country. The large staff is very attentive and not easily provoked by rambunctious kids.

WALT DISNEY WORLD VILLAGE

Buena Vista Drive and State Hwy. 535, Lake Buena Vista. (407) 828–3058. Free parking.

Hours. Daily, 9:30 A.M.–10 P.M.
This shopping center geared to kids has toy shops, stores specializing in Disney character items, places to buy kids' clothing, and artists' stalls where you can have your caricature drawn. WDWV features a number of fast-food stands, as well as a handful of moderate-to-expensive full-service restaurants. On a regular, though often unannounced basis, singing groups and entertainment troupes perform at a lakeside outdoor stage.

CHURCH STREET ANNEX

129 W. Church St. (407) 849–0901. Metered lot and street parking.

Hours. Daily, 10 A.M.–12:30 P.M.
See listing for Church Street Station in Attractions.

TRANSPORTATION

BUSES

About thirty bus routes cover the Orange-Seminole-Osceola area. The Transit Authority bus system charges a 75¢ basic fare and 10¢ for a transfer. Although it is possible to bus it to many of the major attractions, the wait (especially with antsy kids) can be troublesome. For information: (407) 841–8240.

TAXIS

Taxicabs can be found at the major hotels and at taxi stands around the metro area. Taxis are on the pricey side: $1.80 to $2 for the first mile and $1.20 thereafter, an expensive ride to far-flung attractions like Spaceport USA, Boardwalk and Baseball, and Disney World. Taxi companies include White Rose, (407) 855–0564; Yellow, (407) 422–4455; City (407) 422–5151; and Ace, (407) 859–7514.

TOURS

BUS

Gray Line Tours. (407) 422–0744 or (800) 433–0330. Handles their touring slightly differently in the Orlando area than in other parts of the country. Instead of providing guided tours, Gray Line acts as a jitney service to major area attractions. They provide shuttle service from hotels to the Mercado Shopping Center (see Shopping). From there, big Gray Line buses depart for major attractions like Sea World, Boardwalk and Baseball, Disney World, even Busch Gardens in Tampa. One fee to Gray Line includes admission. The only exception is Disney World, where you pay for transportation only and buy your own tickets upon arrival. Not including admission costs, transportation costs between $7 and $10.

BOAT TOURS

Scenic Boat Tours of Winter Park. (407) 644–4056. Offers daily 1-hour tours of the pretty lakes surrounding Winter Park, Orlando's patrician neighbor to the north. The short trip in 15-seat open boats takes in three lakes, a couple of narrow canals, plenty of expensive homes, and a fair number of water birds. Trips leave every hour on the hour between 10 A.M. and 4 P.M. from the landing located at 312 Morse Blvd., on the shore of Lake Osceola, approximately 5 miles north of Church Street Station via Orange Avenue (State Route 527). (Adults, $4.40; ages 2–11, $2.20.)

BALLOON TOURS

Rise and Float Balloon Tours. (407) 352–8191. Offers hour-long, early-morning scenic balloon rides over western Orlando. For $125 for adults and $75 for kids 10 and under, you get a ride, champagne (the traditional drink of aeronauts) orange juice, and fresh pastries. Some find the hour (6:15 A.M.) painful, but it provides riders with a view seldom seen by mere mortals: empty parking lots at Disney World and Sea World. Riders meet at 5931 American Way (approximately 9 miles southwest of Church Street Station via Interstate 4). Call well in advance for reservations.

HELICOPTER TOURS

J. C. Helicopters. Inc. (407) 857–7222. In business since 1977, J. C. offers 5- to 15-minute rides in 4-passenger, jet-turbine choppers that take in all the sites of Orlando and Kissimmee. Prices range from $20 to $50 for adults and from $10 to $20 for kids. Rides are offered daily between 9:30 A.M. and dusk and leave from the Orlando Hyatt Heliport at 6385 Space Coast Hwy., Kissimmee (located near Disney World at the intersection of Interstate 4 and US 192). Call in advance for reservations.

SEASONAL EVENTS

January

SCOTTISH HIGHLAND GAMES

Bagpipes, costumes, and other Scottish trappings are all there for the annual one-day event in mid-January. It usually takes place at the Central Florida Fairgrounds off Colonial Drive. For more information: (407) 422–8226 or (407) 657–9735.

February

CENTRAL FLORIDA FAIR

Here is typical fair fare: agricultural exhibits plus rides and games for the kids. The almost two-week-long event, during the last week of February and the first week of March, takes place at the Central Florida Fairgrounds. For more information: (407) 295–3247.

March

BASEBALL SPRING TRAINING

Three spring-training facilities are located in the Orlando area. The Minnesota Twins train in Orlando at Tinker Field, at Tampa Avenue and South Street, (407) 849–6346. The Houston Astros train at Osceola Stadium in Kissimmee, on US Hwy. 192/441, (407) 933–5500. The Kansas City Royals play at Baseball City in the Boardwalk and Baseball theme park at the junction of Interstate 4 and US Hwy. 27, (407) 648–5151. Each team plays an average of sixteen games in the home stadiums between early March and early April. Call to place ticket orders.

ST. PATRICK'S DAY STREET PARTY

Church Street Station (see Attractions) is the location for this annual Irish blowout on March 17. For information: (407) 422–2434.

May

ZELLWOOD CORN FESTIVAL

You don't have to wait until late summer to enjoy fresh sweet corn. Here, late May is corn season, and in rural Zellwood, the annual Corn Fest has plenty of ears and lots of music. For more information: (407) 886–0014.

July

JULY FOURTH AT DISNEY WORLD

Disney World (see Attractions) presents one of the most spectacular fireworks displays in the world.

September

OKTOBERFEST

Orlando has major blowouts at two popular locations: the Bavarian Schnitzel House, 6159 Westwood Boulevard, and Church Street Station (see Attractions). For more information and reservations, call the Schnitzel House, (407) 352–8484, or Church Street Station, (407) 422–2434.

October

FLORIDA STATE AIR FAIR

All sorts of conventional and experimental aircraft are on display, as well as an exhibition by the United States Navy Blue Angels precision flying team. All the action takes place at the Kissimmee Municipal Airport between US Hwy. 192 and State Rte. 531. For more information: (407) 847–5000 or (800) 432–9199 (in Florida).

December

CHRISTMAS AT WALT DISNEY WORLD

A living nativity and all sorts of special programs and decorations make this almost seem like Christmas in the colder, snowier climes. Call (407) 824–4500 for more information.

CHILDREN'S THEATER

THEATRE FOR YOUNG PEOPLE

At the Tupperware Theater in Loch Haven Park, 1001 E. Princeton St. (407) 896–7365. Free parking.

The only local theater group dedicated to special theater for kids. Each season (September through May), they offer approximately five plays geared to ages 5 through 8, and four plays for kids between 8 and 10. The performances often include music, dance, and puppetry. Call for current schedule and ticket prices.

DINNER THEATERS

FORT LIBERTY WILD WEST SHOW

5260 US Hwy. 192, Kissimmee. (407) 351–5151. Free parking.

Hours. Vary according to season; often two seatings a night.

All the action takes place on a stage set up in the middle of a United States cavalry mess hall, ca. 1875. There are troopers (the waiters), a commanding officer, an Indian chief and his dancing tribe, and a traveling Wild-West medicine show. There's singing and dancing, acrobatics, and comedy. The food is uninspired but filling. Bottomless pitchers of beer, wine, and soft drinks are served. There's audience participation, and, once each show, the kids are brought on stage to participate. Adults, $23.95; ages 3–11, $15.95. Reservations suggested. Credit cards.

Kids' Facilities. High chairs and booster seats are provided, and kids eat from the adult menu.

MARDI GRAS

8445 S. International Dr. (407) 351–5151. Free parking.

Hours. Vary according to season; often two shows per night.

It's New Orleans Mardi Gras every night of the year with can-can dancers, clowns, singers, and comedians performing a 2-hour show. Dining consists of a couple of entrees, salad, soup, and beer, wine, and soft drinks. Adults, $23.95; ages 3–11, $15.95. Reservations suggested. Credit cards.

Kids' Facilities. High chairs and booster seats available, as well as a children's menu.

KING HENRY'S FEAST

8984 International Dr. (407) 351–5151. Free parking.

Hours. Vary according to season; often two shows per night.

Stout King Henry VIII presides over this 15th-century banquet complete with singing troubadours, court jesters, jugglers, a magician, and fighting knights. Serving wenches cater to your gluttony with lots of food and beer, wine, and soft drinks. The great dining hall serves about 600 cheering, jeering patrons. Kids really get into it, especially eating with their hands. Adults, $23.95; ages 3–11, $15.95. Reservations suggested. Credit cards.

Kids' Facilities. High chairs and booster seats available. Kids eat from the adult menu.

MEDIEVAL TIMES DINNER THEATER

US Hwy. 192, Kissimmee. (407) 239–0214. Free parking.

Hours. Vary according to season; always at least one show per night.

Opened in 1983, this is the oldest and best of the Orlando theme dinner theaters. The setting is an 11th-century castle, with dinner seating for 960 people. There's jousting, sword fighting, magicians, costumed lords and ladies, and impressive displays of horseman (and -woman) ship. The audience is split into six groups, each with a rooting interest in one of the six competing knights. The food is better than the usual dinner theater fare. Kids appreciate that there's not a spoon, knife, or fork to be found anywhere. Adults, $25; ages 3–11, $17. Reservations are a must. Credit cards.

Kids' Facilities. Their excuse for having no kids menus, no high chairs, and no booster seats is almost acceptable: "There weren't any in the 11th century."

BABYSITTING SERVICES

FAIRY GODMOTHERS
(407) 277–3724 and (407) 275–7326

In business since 1983, Gertrude Ridgeway provides licensed and bonded babysitters to all hotels within a 50-mile radius of Orlando. Fairy Godmothers also provides sitters to accompany kids to area attractions. Services are available 24 hours a day, seven days a week. For a single family, one to three kids cost of $5 per hour, with a 4-hour minimum. For additional children, add an extra $1 per hour. Transportation costs are $4 per visit. Fairy Godmothers also has rates for combined families. Cash or travelers checks are accepted.

PUBLICATIONS

Orlando Sentinel. Daily newspaper; Friday entertainment guide.

Orlando Magazine. Monthly magazine; "The Guide" includes listings of museums, shopping, the arts, restaurants, and night life.

LOCAL TELEPHONE NUMBERS

Late-hours pharmacy: Gooding's Pharmacies, located in Gooding's supermarkets: 7053 Orange Blossom Trail (US 441), (407) 857–4883; 4520 S. Semoran Blvd., (407) 658–1349, and 1024 Semoran Blvd., Casselberry, (407) 331–1714. All are open Mon.–Sat., 9 A.M.–9 P.M.; Sun., 11 A.M.–7 P.M.

Physician referral: (407) 857–2814 or (407) 841–5221.

Dental referral: (407) 628–4363.

Drug abuse: (407) 426–6611.

Poison control: (800) 282–3171.

Consumer complaints: (800) 342–7940.

Community services: (407) 894–1441.

Convention and Visitors Bureau: (407) 345–8882.

Police: 911.

Fire: 911.

Ambulance: 911.

Road conditions: Highway Patrol, (407) 423–6400.

Weather: (407) 851–7510.

Local car rental: Jim Lash, (407) 295–2614; Classy Chassies, (407) 294–2746; Delta, (407) 851–0289 and (800) 423–0702.

PHILADELPHIA

Founded 300 years ago by William Penn as a haven of tolerance, Philadelphia has over the years been tolerant of persecuted Quakers, oppressed Jews, and runaway slaves. These days, with its rutted roads and sloppy trash removal, the city of Philadelphia shows that its citizens are still a tolerant lot—tolerant of shoddy public services. Philadelphia nevertheless can make for a rewarding vacation experience. History is its biggest and best commodity. Not only was it at one time the country's largest city, it was also the United States capital for a decade (1790–1800) and the birthplace of the Declaration of Independence.

Thanks in great part to Penn's conversion to the fair-minded Quaker religion, the Pennyslvania colony was founded in 1681 under a charter that, far ahead of its time, established a general assembly, guaranteed freedom of religion, and mandated fair treatment for the native Indian population. By 1682, Philadelphia was established as Pennsylvania's capital. Although Penn spent a total of only four years in the colony, he was there long enough to see it grow by leaps and bounds.

Located between the wide Delaware and Schuylkill (SCHOOL-kul) rivers, Philadelphia stood almost at the center of the eastern seaboard British Colonies. This "keystone" position (Pennsylvania is known as the Keystone State) made the city a hub of agricultural commerce and spurred its phenomenal growth. By 1699, Philadelphia had grown from a frontier outpost to a city of 10,000, and by the 1770s, the city had a population of more than 30,000, the largest in America and the third-largest in the entire British Empire. Philadelphia's deep freshwater port became a center for oceanic trade. Pennsylvania timber was traded in the West Indies for sugar and rum, and those commodities were traded in England for goods that were not produced in the Colonies.

Because of its large population and tolerance for all sorts of political thought, Philadelphia sprouted the seeds of revolution. America's discontented leaders flocked to the centrally located city for the First and

Second Continental Congresses in 1774 and 1775–1776. In 1776, Thomas Jefferson wrote the Declaration of Independence here; in 1787, Philadelphia hosted the Constitutional Convention; and in 1790, Philadelphia became the second federal capital.

Among the city's early cultural contributions were the United States' first free library, which was founded by Benjamin Franklin, the first hospital; and the first society of letters (the American Philosophical Society). Some of American history's best-known artists—Charles Willson Peale, Rembrandt Peale, Gilbert Stuart, and Benjamin West—lived here.

Today Philadelphia is the United States' fourth-largest city, with a population of 1.6 million (4.7 million in the metropolitan area). Ethnic neighborhoods, while still apparent in certain isolated pockets of the city, have begun to homogenize. Gentrification has been under way in many neighborhoods for the last twenty years. The process of converting formerly rough neighborhoods into yuppie havens has made Philadelphia more picturesque.

The Philadelphia metamorphosis is great for tourists. The revitalized sections include the area around the Independence Mall, an L-shaped chunk of land between 6th and 2nd Streets that contains Independence Hall and most of the buildings of the Independence National Historical Park. In fact, nearly all the real estate between Chestnut and Walnut Streets from the Schuylkill River on the west to the Delaware River on the east is prime, picturesque turf. Add to that a long green space from

---

FREEBIES AND CHEAPIES
(Free or $3.50 and under for adults)

☐ Independence Hall National Historical Park (see Attractions and Museums)
☐ Betsy Ross House (see Attractions)
☐ U.S. Mint (see Attractions)
☐ Atwater Kent Museum (see Museums)
☐ The Ships at Penn's Landing (see Attractions)
☐ National Museum of American Jewish History (see Museums)
☐ Afro-American Historical and Cultural Museum (see Museums)
☐ Mummer's Museum (see Museums)
☐ Elfreth's Alley Museum (see Museums)
☐ Fireman's Hall Museum (see Museums)

the formidable City Hall northwest to the Philadelphia Museum of Art in Fairmount Park and you've got some great vacation diversions.

Even though ethnic neighborhoods are disappearing, the ethnic restaurants and the foods they serve are alive and well. Philadelphia's two most famous food features are the cheesesteak hoagie sandwich and the neighborhood Italian restaurant. Each is available in abundance throughout the city in numerous locations (we mention some in the Restaurant section). The bottom line: While you may need new shocks on the family Buick, nobody goes hungry in Philadelphia.

PARKING

With pay parking lots dotting the landscape, it is possible to drive a car in downtown Philadelphia—as long as you don't mind narrow streets pockmarked with ruts and constant road construction. To avoid the high fees charged at the large downtown parking structures, use lots on the perimeter of the downtown area. When parking for Independence National Historical Park, for example, use the lots along Front Street opposite Penn's Landing on the Delaware River. When parking for the Franklin Institute of Science Museum and the Academy of Natural Sciences, use the small parking lots north and east of Logan Circle.

THE LONG WEEKEND

Day One

❑ Independence National Historical Park (see Attractions and Museums)
❑ Betsy Ross House (see Attractions)

Day Two

❑ Please Touch Museum (see Museums)
❑ Franklin Institute Science Museum (see Museums)
❑ Fireman's Hall Museum (see Museums)
❑ U.S. Mint (see Attractions)

Day Three

❑ Sesame Place (see Attractions)
❑ Mummer's Museum (see Museums)
❑ Civil War Library and Museum (see Museums)
❑ Philadelphia Maritime Museum (see Museums)

CLIMATE

Although average summer temperatures range from a high during the day in the high 80s to a low in the upper 60s, July and August often find downtown temperatures in the 90s with humidity in the same range. Spring and fall are quite agreeable, with high temperatures in the 60s and 70s during the day and the 40s and 50s at night. In winter, daytime highs often reach into the 40s, with nighttime mercury readings below freezing. Though mild by New England and Midwest standards, winters bring a good possibility of snow and freezing rain; the yearly precipitation is about 40 inches.

In winter, be sure to pack winter clothes, parkas, and footwear to repel the wet. In spring and fall, medium-weight jackets and sweaters are in order. And, despite the fact that light jackets and sweaters may never leave your suitcase in summer, take them anyway: You never know when a cold front will drop in from the north. It's a good idea to pack an umbrella at all times.

TOURIST INFORMATION

Contact the Philadelphia Convention and Visitors Bureau, 1515 Market Street, Suite 2020, Philadelphia, PA 19102, (215) 636–1666.

ATTRACTIONS

INDEPENDENCE NATIONAL HISTORICAL PARK ATTRACTIONS

On Independence Mall and at other locations around Philadelphia. (215) 597–8974.

Administered by the National Park Service, Independence National Historical Park is a group of attractions and museums that adorn the landscape of east Philadelphia. Most (but not all) of the buildings under the Park Service banner have significance in the United States' 18th-century struggle for independence from Great Britain. If you don't find a listing for a particular building in the Attractions section, look for it in the Museums section.

INDEPENDENCE NATIONAL HISTORICAL PARK VISITOR CENTER

3rd St. at Chestnut St., Independence Mall. (215) 597–8974. Use the Penn's Landing station on the Market-Frankford subway line. Limited metered street and pay lot parking.

Hours. Late June through Labor Day: daily, 9 A.M.–6 P.M. Rest of the year: daily, 9 A.M.–5 P.M.

Costs. Free.

An ultramodern building, the air-conditioned Visitor Center provides a dramatic look at the American Revolution with a movie shown in the upstairs theater. Directed by the late John Huston and featuring such luminaries as Pat Hingle, Ken Howard, William Atherton, Eli Wallach, and Anne Jackson, *Independence* provides perspective for the history you've come to Philadelphia to take in. On the main floor, *A Promise of Permanency* provides an interactive computer and video look at the first 200 years of the United States Constitution. The exhibit also features touch-activated video "time lines." Just touch the decade you wish to learn more about.

Kids' Facilities. No stroller rentals. No diaper-changing tables in restrooms (use benches). No bottle-warming facilities. No food services.

Ratings. Young children probably won't get much from the Visitor Center; however, those over age 7 with any kind of appreciation for computers are bound to learn from osmosis as they play with the interactive computers and video screens. At the very least, kids that age will be content to play with the computers while Mom and Dad enjoy the exhibit. 2–7, C; 8–11, B; 12–16, A.

INDEPENDENCE HALL

Chestnut at 5th St., Independence Mall. (215) 597–8974. Use the Independence station on the Market-Frankford subway line. Limited metered street and pay lot parking.

Hours. Late June through Labor Day: daily, 9 A.M.–8 P.M. Rest of the year: daily, 9 A.M.–5 P.M.

Costs. Free.

The 30-minute Independence Hall guided tour takes you through the building's three major attractions. The first is the British Colonial courtroom that was used for trials in the years before independence. Across the hall is the Assembly Room, where the Continental Congresses met in 1774 and 1775–1776, and where the Declaration of Independence and Constitution were signed. The final stop is the Governor's Reception Room, which has been restored and outfitted for state banquet. (*Note: Try to arrive at Independence Hall early in the day, especially in summer. Even though the National Park Service guides do a good job of moving people through, the lines are sometimes 4 hours long toward the middle of the day.)*

Kids' Facilities. No stroller rentals (there is one long stairway to negotiate). No diaper-changing tables. No bathroom facilities (use the bathrooms adjacent to the Liberty Bell Pavilion across the street). No food or bottle-warming facilities.

Ratings. You probably won't want to bring children under age 5, especially if there's any kind of line. It's simply too long a haul for young kids; besides, the tour information is probably over their heads. Also there are no bathrooms. 2–7, D; 8–11, C; 12–16, A.

CONGRESS HALL

6th and Chestnut Sts., Independence Mall. (215) 597–8974. Use the Independence station on the Market-Frankford subway line. Limited metered street and pay lot parking.

Hours. Late June through Labor Day: daily, 9 A.M.–6 P.M. Rest of the year: daily, 9 A.M.–5 P.M.

Costs. Free.

The red-brick Congress Hall served as the seat of the United States Congress from 1790 to 1800, and as the site of George Washington's second and John Adams' only inauguration. On view to the public are the original chambers of the House of Representatives and Senate. You're also welcome to take a peek (they're roped off to prevent foot traffic) at some committee rooms. All rooms in the building are furnished exactly as they were during the last decade of the 18th century.

Kids' Facilities. No stroller rentals. No diaper-changing tables. No bathrooms (use the facilities near the Liberty Bell Pavilion). No food or bottle-warming facilities.

Ratings. As long as you've endured the wait for the Independence Hall tour, you shouldn't miss a quick look inside: It's hardly ever very crowded. Since you can see it in less than 10 minutes, your younger children won't have time enough to get cranky. Beware, however, of the stairway leading upstairs to the Senate chamber: It's steep and not fit for strollers. 2–7, C; 8–11, B; 12–16, A.

OLD CITY HALL

5th and Chestnut Sts., Independence Mall. (215) 597–8974. Use the Independence station on the Market-Frankford subway line. Limited metered street and pay lot parking.

Hours. Daily, 9 A.M.–5 P.M.

Costs. Free.

In much worse repair than Independence and Congress Halls, Old City Hall served as the United States Supreme Court from 1791 to 1800. Until it's restored, there isn't much to see.

Kids' Facilities. No stroller rentals. No diaper-changing tables in restrooms. No food or bottle-warming facilities.

Ratings. The bad thing is that there's not much to see here. The good thing is that it takes no time in which to see it. The bathroom facilities on the lower level are enough to recommend a visit. 2–7, D; 8–11, C; 12–16, C.

LIBERTY BELL PAVILION

Market between 5th and 6th Sts., Independence Mall. (215) 597–8974. Use the Independence station on the Market-Frankford subway line. Limited metered street and pay lot parking.

Hours. Late June through Labor Day: daily, 9 A.M.–8 P.M. Rest of the year: daily, 9 A.M.–5 P.M.

Costs. Free.

When you consider the crush of folks lining up for the Independence Hall tour and the Liberty Bell Pavilion, its easy to see the kind of crowd-control problems the park rangers must have had before 1976. That was the year the massive bell (which was given the name Liberty in 1839 by a local abolitionist group and was cracked beyond repair when rung on George Washington's birthday in 1846) moved from Independence Square to its new home across the street. The modern steel-and-glass pavilion that holds it is staffed by park rangers who give interpretive talks on the bell and its significance. Visitors are permitted to touch the Liberty Bell during regular business hours. After closing, you can see it through the well-lighted pavilion's large glass windows.

Kids' Facilities. No stroller rentals. No diaper-changing tables in the adjacent restrooms. No food or bottle-warming facilities.

Ratings. The massive bell is certainly a kids' favorite in Philadelphia. All ages, A.

CARPENTER'S HALL

320 Chestnut St., Independence Mall. (215) 597–8974. Use the Independence station on the Market-Frankford subway line. Limited metered street and pay lot parking.

Hours. Tues.–Sun., 10 A.M.–4 P.M.

Costs. Free.

Operated by the Carpenter's Company of Philadelphia, Carpenter's Hall was the site of the First Continental Congress' 1774 debate on taxation without representation. It's still a meeting place for members of the exclusive carpentry guild. Handymen and old tool buffs will enjoy displays of Colonial building tools.

Kids' Facilities. No stroller rentals. No diaper-changing tables. No bathrooms. No food or bottle-warming facilities.

Ratings. Unless your kids have an interest in carpentry, you might want to skip it. 2–7, D; 8–11, D; 12–16, C.

BISHOP WHITE HOUSE

309 Walnut St. (215) 597–8974. Use the Independence station on the Market-Frankford subway line. Limited metered street and pay lot parking.

Hours. Daily tours, 9:30 A.M.–5 P.M.

Costs. Free, tickets required: Get them at the National Historical Park Visitor Center.

Conducted by park rangers and docents, the tour takes you through the home built by Pennsylvania's first Episcopal bishop. It gives a glimpse at the way upper-class Philadelphians lived in the late 18th century. The home is decorated with the finest the period had to offer.

Kids' Facilities. No stroller rentals. No diaper-changing tables. No food or bottle-warming facilities.

Ratings. The tour takes the better part of 45 minutes and is quite revealing for kids growing up in late-20th-century America. Smaller children may tire before the end of the tour. Steep stairways make stroller navigation impossible. 2–7, C; 8–11, B; 12–16, A.

THE TODD HOUSE

4th and Walnut Sts., Independence Mall. (215) 597–8974. Use the Independence station on the Market-Frankford subway line. Limited metered street and pay lot parking.

Hours. Daily tours, 9:30 A.M.–5 P.M.

Costs. Free, tickets required: Get them at National Park Visitor Center.

The Todd House was the home of Dolley Payne Todd, who later married President James Madison. While most of the furnishings are less ornate than those found in wealthy households, they are still better than most early-18th-century working stiffs could afford: The Todds belonged to the upper-middle class.

Kids' Facilities. No stroller rentals. No diaper-changing tables. No food or bottle-warming facilities.

Ratings. Like the tour of Bishop White's home, the Todd tour takes the better part of 45 minutes, and smaller children may tend to tire before the end. Steep stairways make stroller navigation tough. 2–7, C; 8–11, B; 12–16, A.

FRANKLIN COURT

Between 3rd and 4th, Chestnut and Market Sts. (215) 597–8974. Use the Independence station on the Market-Frankford subway line. Limited metered street and pay lot parking.

Hours. Late June through Labor Day: daily, 10 A.M.–6 P.M. Rest of the year: daily, 9 A.M.–5 P.M. (Post Office open daily, 9 A.M.–5 P.M. throughout the year.)

Costs. Free.

Franklin Court consists of four attractions located on property once owned by Benjamin Franklin; he lived there while attending the Continental Congresses and the Constitutional Convention. The **Franklin Post Office** is furnished and refurbished to look as post offices looked in 1775, when Franklin was appointed the first postmaster general. A working United States post office, it's open seven days a week, and all the mail it handles receives the unique Franklin postal cancellation mark highly prized by stamp collectors. Upstairs the **Franklin Post Office Museum** displays rare stamps and postal service memorabilia, including early cancellation equipment and a Pony Express saddle pouch. **The Printing Office** is a refurbished newspaper print room from about 1785, with a working press and book bindery. A few yards south, the **Underground Museum** displays artifacts retrieved from archaeological excavations done on-site.

Kids' Facilities. No stroller rentals. No diaper-changing tables. Use restrooms at Liberty Bell Pavilion a block away. No food or bottle-warming facilities.

Ratings. From stamps to excavated bottles, there's plenty to keep the kids occupied. Have your younger ones send postcards from the most interesting post office in the country. All ages, A.

SECOND BANK OF THE UNITED STATES

420 Chestnut St., Independence Mall. (215) 597–8974. Use the Independence station on the Market-Frankford subway line. Limited metered street and pay lot parking.

Hours. Daily, 9 A.M.–5 P.M.

Costs. Free.

Portraits of the Capital City, an ongoing exhibition of portraits of notable Philadelphians, shows the faces of the men and women who shaped the city and the country during the last decade of the 18th century. All our national heroes are here: Franklin, Jefferson, Washington, and Adams, plus most of the other signers of the Declaration of Independence and the framers of the Constitution. The glorious Greek Revival building was originally the Second Bank of the United States.

Kids' Facilities. No stroller rentals. No diaper-changing tables in the restrooms (and few benches). No food or bottle-warming facilities.

Ratings. Perhaps a bit dry for younger children, the Second Bank and its paintings should nonetheless be viewed. The paintings are on one floor, so it's easy going: only about 45 minutes for a quick walk-through. 2–7, C; 8–11, A; 12–16, A.

PENNSYLVANIA HORTICULTURAL SOCIETY

325 Walnut St., Independence Mall. (215) 625–8250. Use the Independence station on the Market-Frankford subway line. Limited metered street and pay lot parking.

Hours. Mon.–Fri., 9 A.M.–5 P.M.

Costs. Free.

Wedged between the Todd and Bishop White Houses of the Independence National Historical Park, the Horticultural Society displays antique gardening and farming tools like plows, butter churns, and coffee grinders, as well as some rusted garden doohickeys that leave you scratching your head as to their intended purpose. The Society maintains a pretty 18th-century garden adjacent.

Kids' Facilities. No stroller rentals. No restrooms. No diaper-changing tables. No food or bottle-warming facilities.

Ratings. If you want gardening hints, this is the place. Dozens of planting brochures are available free of charge. For older kids and grownups only. 2–7, D; 8–11, C; 12–16, B.

EDGAR ALLAN POE NATIONAL HISTORICAL SITE

532 N. 7th St., at Spring Garden St. (215) 597–8780. Use the Spring Garden station on the Broad Street subway line; the Poe house is 6 blocks east through a tough neighborhood. Free street parking.

Hours. Daily, 9 A.M.–5 P.M.

Costs. Free.

Poe's house in Philadelphia is where, it's said, he spent the happiest period of his often-troubled life: from early 1843 to April 1844. Most rooms are devoid of furniture, but visitors are welcome to poke around. The eerie empty rooms with broken plaster and half-torn-down walls (part of an ongoing excavation) seem appropriate for a house once owned by the author of horrific works like "The Raven" and "The Murders in the Rue Morgue." There are photographic exhibits about Poe, a 10-minute film on his life, and park rangers on hand to answer questions.

Kids' Facilities. No stroller rentals. Countertop in ladies' room is large enough for diaper changing. No food or bottle-warming facilities.

Ratings. The house is definitely not for younger children: There aren't enough visual distractions to keep them occupied, and it's easy for them to get into trouble on the narrow stairways and exposed beams in the excavated rooms. Older children, especially those who have been introduced to Poe, will get a kick out of the place. If you happen to be in Philadelphia around Halloween, this is the place. 2–7, D; 8–11, B; 12–16, A.

THADDEUS KOSCIUSZKO NATIONAL MEMORIAL

3rd and Pine Sts. (215) 597–9618. ½ mile south of the Penn's Landing station on the Market-Frankford subway line. Limited street parking.

Hours. Daily, 9 A.M.–5P.M .

Costs. Free.

The boarding house at 3rd and Pine Streets is a shrine to General Thaddeus Kosciuszko, one of the Revolutionary War's most famous foreign heroes. In 1776, the Polish patriot had offered his services to the Continental Army and was given an engineer's commission. His fortification of the American redoubt at Saratoga in 1777 aided greatly in the victory over the British. The fortifications he designed at West Point the next year were so formidable that the British never attacked. The reconstructed upstairs rooms look much as they did in 1797. The memorial features a number of exhibits, and visitors may view a 6-minute multimedia slide show detailing the life and achievements of Kosciuszko.

Kids' Facilities. No stroller rentals. No diaper-changing tables in restrooms. No food or bottle-warming facilities.

Ratings. Too dry for all but die-hard history buffs, although you can whip through the place in about 20 minutes. Older kids familiar with the Revolutionary War may find it interesting. 2–7, D; 8–11, C; 12–16, B.

BETSY ROSS HOUSE

239 Arch St. (215) 627–5343. Use the Penn's Landing station on the Market-Frankford subway line. Limited metered street parking.

Hours. Daily, 9 A.M.–5P.M. (9 A.M.–6 P.M. during Daylight Savings Time)

Costs. Free.

This is the home of the woman who sewed "Old Glory," the first United States flag. A narrow—make that exceedingly narrow—home, the rooms are tiny and the stairways almost too slender to navigate. Many of the rooms are furnished in authentic Colonial style. Highlights include the children's bedroom (complete with toys), a downstairs upholstery shop, and a basement kitchen area where the children made musket balls for the Continental Army.

Kids' Facilities. No stroller rentals; strollers are *way* too bulky for the stairs. No diaper-changing tables in the restrooms; go to the gift-shop building adjacent to the Ross house. Drinks from soft-drink machines are available in the gift-shop area. No food or bottle-warming facilities.

Ratings. Even though most kids don't know beans about history in general, they all seem to know about Betsy Ross. The rooms are small and the stairways are narrow, kind of like a playhouse in the eyes of younger children. Young kids are fascinated to hear that people living 200 years ago were smaller than adults of today. 2–7, A; 8–11, A; 12 –16, B.

THE SHIPS AT PENN'S LANDING

Between Market and Lombard Sts. along the Delaware River. (215) 922–1898. Use the Penn's Landing station on the Market-Frankford subway line. Pay lot parking on site.

Hours. July 1 through Labor Day: Mon.–Fri., 10 A.M.–5 P.M.; Sat. and Sun., 10 A.M.–6 P.M. Rest of the year: daily, 10 A.M.–4:30 P.M.

Costs. Adults, $3; under age 12, $1.50.

Although a number of different historical vessels dock at Penn's Landing throughout the year, three ships, the U.S.S. *Olympia*, the U.S.S. *Becuna*, and the lightship *Barnegat* are open to the public year-round. The U.S.S. *Becuna* is a guppy-class World War II submarine that completed several missions in the Pacific during the last months of the war. Visitors are allowed to explore nearly every inch of the craft. While the cramped quarters and diesel fumes produce adult claustrophobia, kids love it—they're not in danger of bashing their heads as they pass through the tiny hatchways.

The shiny *Olympia*, Admiral Dewey's flagship during the 1898 Spanish-American War, is white steel on the outside and polished brass and gleaming oak on the inside. It displays war memorabilia and weapons and uniforms of the era.

The *Barnegat*, a lightship built in 1904, kept the navigation lanes of the Delaware River safe for marine travel for sixty-three years. Lightships were necessary in any waterway where fluctuations in water levels caused dangerous changes in channel depth.

Kids' Facilities. No stroller rentals: Don't bring a stroller onboard the submarine *Becuna*. No diaper-changing facilities on any of the ships. No restrooms on any of the ships. No bottle-warming available. The *Olympia* has a snack facility that serves soda, coffee, and hot dogs, and has candy vending machines.

Ratings. Kids like the ships—especially the submarine—but should be over age 6 to really get anything out of a visit. The hot dogs aboard the *Olympia* are a big draw. 2–7, C; 8–11, A; 12–16, A.

U.S. MINT

5th and Arch Sts. (215) 597–7350. Use the Independence station on the Market-Frankford subway line. Limited metered street and pay lot parking.

Hours. May through September: daily, 9 A.M.–4:30 P.M. April and October through December: Mon.–Sat., 9 A.M.–4:30 P.M. January through March: Mon.–Fri., 9 A.M.–4:30 P.M.

Costs. Free.

The self-guided tour starts with an escalator ride past exhibits of old and rare coins, medals, and scales. Then it's onto a gallery above the Mint floor where visitors can watch the entire minting process—from the beginning, when the coins are stamped out of flat sheets of metal, through the stamping, washing, inspection, and bagging processes. At each of many stations along the tour, visitors push buttons to hear a running oral history and descriptions of the various steps. The tour ends at a coin and gift shop where visitors can buy souvenirs and, for a dollar, stamp their own souvenir coin.

Kids' Facilities. No stroller rentals. No diaper-changing tables in the restrooms. No food or bottle-warming facilities.

Ratings. Since a child's first concept of money usually comes from coins, kids under age 5 are enthusiastic about the Mint. The tour takes about 45 minutes. All ages, A.

FAIRMOUNT PARK ZOO

34th St. and Girard Ave. (212) 243–1100. No subway service; from downtown Philadelphia, take the Spring Garden St. bridge over the Schuylkill River and turn right on 31st St.; right at 34th St. to the zoo entrance. Pay parking, $2.

Hours. Mon.–Fri., 9:30 A.M.–5 P.M.; Sat. and Sun., 9:30 A.M.–6 P.M.

Costs. Adults, $4.50; ages 2–11, $3.50; under 2, free.

A well-laid-out 64-acre facility, the Fairmount Park Zoo is home to more than 1,800 animals from all over the world. The zoo features above-average reptile, primate, and lion and tiger houses, and an African Plains exhibit with animals in natural-looking outdoor surroundings. The 30-year-old children's zoo ($1 separate admission) has a lot to offer smaller kids, including sea lion and live-animal shows, and cow-milking and sheep-herding demonstrations. Our favorite exhibit at the kid's zoo is a menagerie of exotic insects. There's even a camel ride: one hump or two, take your pick. The Zoo Safari Monorail operates between March and November ($3 separate admission).

Kids' Facilities. Strollers rented at main gate for $2.50 plus a $1 deposit. The very large and clean bathrooms have diaper-changing tables. Fast-food alternatives abound. No bottle-warming facilities. There's a picnic area, and you can bring in your own lunch. The zoo gift shop is well stocked.

Ratings. This exceedingly good zoo has something for everyone. All ages, A.

SESAME PLACE

U.S. Rte. 1 and Oxford Valley Rd., Langhorne. (215) 757–1100 or (215) 752–7070. Take Interstate 95 north to the Morrisville/Route 1N exit; turn right on Oxford Valley Rd. to traffic lights and turn right. Free lot parking.

Hours. Early May through early June: daily, 10 A.M.–5 P.M. Early June through early July: daily, 10 A.M.–8 P.M. Early July through early September: daily, 9 A.M.–8 P.M. Early September through mid-October: Sat. and Sun., 10 A.M.–5 P.M. Mid-October through early May: closed.

Costs. Adults, $11.95; ages 3–15, $13.95; ages 2 and under, free.

Sesame Place is a combination water slide/game arcade/sandbox/stage-show made in the likeness of the popular PBS television show *Sesame Street*. While that may sound educational, try to rein in your expectations since Sesame Place is really a very commercial amusement park. It does, however, differ from run-of-the-mill amusement parks in a couple of interesting ways: It has a science-oriented activities center, a gallery for hands-on computer use, a safe indoor tumbling area for toddlers, and a cafeteria that serves healthy snacks (along with the regular fast-food stuff). We were most impressed by the Sesame Place gift shop, where you can buy games, stuffed animals, toys, and puzzles licensed by *Sesame Street* for truly reasonable prices.

Kids' Facilities. No stroller rentals. Diaper-changing tables in all bathrooms (with paper towels for disposable cleaning). A fully equipped first-aid center with a nurse and an emergency medical technician. No bottle-warming facilities. Plenty of food.

Ratings. Sesame Place is recommended for kids from age 3 to 13, and we couldn't find an unhappy kid customer. 2–7, A; 8–11, A; 12–16, B.

MUSEUMS

FRANKLIN INSTITUTE SCIENCE MUSEUM AND PLANETARIUM

20th St. and Benjamin Franklin Pkwy. (215) 448–1200 or (215) 564–3375. Eight blocks north of the 19th St. station on the Market-Frankford subway line. Limited metered street and pay lot parking.

Hours. September through June: Mon.–Fri., 9:30 A.M.–4:30 P.M.; Sat. and Sun., 10 A.M.–5 P.M. July and August: daily, 10 A.M.–5 P.M.

Costs. Adults, $5; ages 4–11, $4; ages 3 and under, free.

As a tribute to Ben Franklin, Philadelphia not only named their best science museum after him, they sculpted him in marble and put the statue in the center of the whole 4-story operation. In a word, the Franklin Museum is wonderful. It's chock-full of hands-on science experiments —telegraphs, telephones, picture phones, fiber optics, bicycle wheel gyroscopes, and places where kids can make things as diverse as tornadoes and paper. There's a computer learning center, an educational science games arcade, and a place where kids can make their own musical instruments. There's a large railroad exhibit, a working weather station, and a place to get all the latest science news. The rotunda in which Franklin sits features an exhibit of some of his scientific personal effects. The **Fels Planetarium** on the first floor offers daily astronomical programming. A day here is a day well spent.

Kids' Facilities. No stroller rentals. Diaper-changing and nursing areas in two of the ladies' restrooms on the 1st and 2nd floors; men use benches. No bottle warming. A large cafeteria is located on the 1st floor. Large gift shop with lots of science-related books and experiments.

Ratings. Even though most activities are geared toward children over age 6, a number of activities—especially many of the demonstrations–

are dramatic enough to keep the attention of younger children. 2–7, B; 8–11, A; 12–16, A.

ACADEMY OF NATURAL SCIENCES MUSEUM

19th St. and Benjamin Franklin Pkwy. (215) 299–1000 or (215) 299–1020. Seven blocks north of the 19th St. station on the Market-Frankford subway line. Limited metered street and pay lot parking.

Hours. Mon.–Fri., 10 A.M.–4:30 P.M.; Sat. and Sun., 10 A.M.–5 P.M.

Costs. Adults, $4.50; ages 3–12, $3.50; ages 2 and under, free.

Accurately reading the tastes of today's youth, the Academy recently spent $2.5 million to construct a superb dinosaur exhibit. Each of more than a dozen new dinosaur models has a computerized interactive video display. The oldest institution of its kind in the United States it also features mummies, a gems and precious stones exhibit, action dioramas with animals from North America and Africa, and the Outside-In gallery, a hands-on children's nature center featuring live animals, fossils, rocks, and a reading area.

Kids' Facilities. No stroller rentals. No diaper-changing tables in the restrooms (plenty of benches, however). No bottle-warming facilities. Snack foods from machines in lunch room. Large gift shop with plenty of dinosaur toys, books, and games.

Ratings. Without the dinosaurs and Outside-In, the Academy would be just a ho-hum natural science museum. Their presence makes the place a worthwhile stop, especially for younger children. 2–7, A; 8–11, A; 12–16, B.

PLEASE TOUCH MUSEUM

210 N. 21st Street. (215) 963–0667. Seven blocks north of the 22nd St. station on the Market-Frankford subway line. Limited metered street and pay lot parking.

Hours. Tues.–Sun., 10 A.M.–4:30 P.M.

Costs. General admission, $4; under age 1, free.

The first museum in the nation designed for children under age 8, Please Touch is filled with the things younger kids love—giant wooden blocks; a puppet theater where kids give the shows; small, furry animals;

and musical instruments. It also features the "act and dress like grown-ups" exhibits that have caught on at children's museums everywhere: the doctor's office, the grocery store, the business office, the city bus, the television studio (the equipment really works), and the adult clothing dress-up area. Antique toys are strategically placed at kid's-eye level in glass cases along a ramp that connects the 1st and 2nd floors. Special exhibits change about every six months.

Kids' Facilities. No stroller rentals. Diaper-changing tables in men's and ladies' restrooms downstairs. No food or bottle-warming facilities. The gift shop has plenty of educational toys and games.

Ratings. The museum is, as advertised, really only for those under the age of 8. 2–7, A; 8–11, C; 12–16, D.

Independence National Historical Park Museums

On Independence Mall.

ARMY-NAVY MUSEUM

Chestnut between 3rd and 4th Sts. Independence Mall. (215) 597–8974. Use the Independence station on the Market-Frankford subway line. Limited metered street and pay lot parking.

Hours. Late June through Labor Day: daily, 9 A.M.–6 P.M. Rest of the year: daily, 9 A.M.–5 P.M.

Costs. Free.

Dioramas at this small military museum recount the heroic exploits of the army and navy between the Revolutionary War and the War of 1812. Along with weapons and equipment from the period, there are exhibits on the 1804–1805 Lewis and Clark Expedition to scout the Louisiana Purchase and the little-remembered war between the United States and the Barbary Coast pirates. It also has a re-creation of the cramped gun deck of a fighting ship.

Kids' Facilities. No stroller rentals. No diaper-changing tables. No bathrooms (use the restrooms at the Marine Museum next door). No food or bottle-warming facilities.

Ratings. Despite the dioramas and weapons, the Army-Navy Museum is not terribly memorable. Conveniently located between the National

Park Visitor Center and Independence Hall, it's worth a quick visit: It takes only about 20 minutes to see it all, 2–7, C; 8–11, C; 12–16, B.

MARINE CORPS MEMORIAL MUSEUM

Chestnut between 3rd and 4th Sts., Independence Mall. (215) 597–8974. Use the Independence station on the Market-Frankford subway line. Limited metered street and pay lot parking.

Hours. Late June through Labor Day: daily, 9 A.M.–6 P.M. Rest of the year: daily, 9 A.M.–5 P.M.

Costs. Free.

The Marine Museum has only a few Revolutionary War uniforms and a few rifles. The only items of note are some lively contemporary paintings depicting Marine Corps actions that took place during the Revolutionary War.

Kids' Facilities. No stroller rentals. No diaper-changing tables in restrooms. No food or bottle-warming facilities.

Ratings. For Marine Corps aficianados only. 2–7, D; 8–11, D; 12–16, C.

ROSENBACH MUSEUM AND LIBRARY

2010 DeLancey Pl., at 20th St. (215) 732–1600. Three-quarters of a mile south of the 19th St. station on the Market-Frankford subway line. Limited metered street and pay lot parking.

Hours. Tues.–Sun., 11 A.M.–4 P.M. Closed during August.

Costs. Adults, $2.50; age 17 and under, $1.50.

Among other rare and beautiful items, the collection includes documents like 150 of General U. S. Grant's Civil War letters, the document proposing the thirteenth Amendment to the Constitution (abolishing slavery), a first edition of Cervantes' *Don Quixote*, Tenniel's drawings for *Alice in Wonderland*, and drawings by Maurice Sendak. The art, books, and manuscripts fill 3 stories of the converted row house a few blocks south of Rittenhouse Square.

Kids' Facilities. No stroller rentals (the stairways are too narrow to accommodate strollers). No diaper-changing tables in restrooms. No food or bottle-warming facilities.

Ratings. Interesting, but don't bring the little ones. 2–7, F; 8–11, F; 12–16, B.

CIVIL WAR LIBRARY AND MUSEUM

1805 Pine St. at 18th St. (215) 735–8196. Three-quarters of a mile south of the 19th St. station on the Market-Frankford subway line. Limited metered street and pay lot parking.

Hours. Mon.–Fri. 10 A.M.–4 P.M.

Costs. Adults, $2; ages 11 and under, free.

The War Between the States looms large in this 4-story townhouse filled to the rafters with books, journals, uniforms, swords, guns, maps, flags, hospital kits, mess utensils, and daguerreotypes. A large corner of one room is devoted almost entirely to portraits and busts of Abraham Lincoln. Of special note are a life mask and plaster hand casts of the sixteenth President, as well as a lock of his hair.

Kids' Facilities. No stroller rentals, and the stairs are too steep to chance with your own stroller. Two unisex restrooms; the one on the 2nd floor has a counter large enough for diaper changing. No food or bottle-warming facilities.

Ratings. Civil War buffs and a large cross-section of male prepubescents will enjoy the sabers, guns, and uniforms. Children under 8 will miss the point. 2–7, D; 8–11, B; 12–16, A.

RODIN MUSEUM

22nd St. and Benjamin Franklin Pkwy. (215) 787–5481. Three-quarters of a mile north of the 22nd St. station on the Market-Frankford subway line. Limited metered street and pay lot parking.

Hours. Tues.–Sun., 10 A.M.–5 P.M.

Costs. Adults, $1; children, 50¢.

The small but fully packed Rodin Museum is filled exclusively with the artist's bronze and marble statuary. Standing guard at the entrance to the front garden is Rodin's most famous work, *The Thinker*. Inside the compact Greek Revival structure are his monumental masterpieces *The Burghers of Calais* and *The Gates of Hell*.

Kids' Facilities. No stroller rentals. No diaper-changing tables in the restrooms (plenty of benches, however). No food or bottle-warming facilities. A small gift shop does a land-office business in *Thinker* post cards.

Ratings. If you don't have a taste for Rodin, don't bother going inside. However, kids respond to larger-than-life sculptures like Rodin's. In 20 minutes, you can see them all. 2–7, C; 8–11, B; 12–16, B.

PHILADELPHIA MUSEUM OF ART

26th St. and Benjamin Franklin Pkwy. (215) 763–8100 or (215) 787–5450. One mile north of the 22nd St. station on the Market-Frankford subway line; 1¼ mile west of the Spring Garden station on the Broad St. subway line. Pay lot parking at base of museum hill and Ben Franklin Pkwy: $3 per day.

Hours. Tues.–Sun., 10 A.M.–5 P.M.

Costs. Adults, $4; ages 5–17, $2; ages 4 and under, free.

Located atop the highest hill in lovely Fairmount Park, the Museum of Art's steep stairway was made famous by Sylvester Stallone in the first *Rocky* movie. Inside you encounter a collection of even more heroic proportion. With more than 500,000 pieces, the Philadelphia Museum of Art is the third-largest art museum in the United States. The 3-story PMA runs the art gamut: biblically themed 15th-century Flemish oils, 18th- and 19th-century European and American masters, medieval armor and weapons, and European and American modern artists including Miro, Klee, Picasso, Pollack, Rauschenberg, and De Kooning. Painting highlights include Picasso's *Man with a Guitar*, Edward Hicks' *The Peaceable Kingdom*, and numerous paintings by Philadelphia native Thomas Eakins.

Kids' Facilities. No stroller rentals. No diaper-changing tables in restrooms; some ladies' restrooms have plenty of bench space. No bottle-warming facilities at either the fast-food cafeteria or at the museum's sit-down restaurant. Gift and book shop.

Ratings. As with most large art museums, there's something here for every taste. There's enough of a variety to make an hour zip by. All ages, A.

NATIONAL MUSEUM OF AMERICAN JEWISH HISTORY

55 N. 5th St. (215) 923–3811. Use the Independence station on the Market-Frankford subway line. Limited metered street and pay lot parking.

Hours. Mon.–Thurs., 10 A.M.–5 P.M.; Fri., by appointment; Sun., 12 noon–5 P.M. Closed on Sat.

Costs. Adults, $1.75; students, $1.50; ages 5–11, $1.25; ages 4 and under, free.

This is the only museum in the United States that chronicles the growth of the American Jewish community within the framework of the development of the nation as a whole. It has only one permanent exhibition: *The American Jewish Experience*, a chronological look at Jews in America over the last three centuries. Changing exhibits range from displays of Jewish texts and religious articles from the Colonial period to exhibits of posters, playbills, and costumes from the early-20th-century Yiddish theater. Half the museum building is occupied by a Sephardic synagogue.

Kids' Facilities. No stroller rental. No diaper-changing table in the restrooms. No food or bottle-warming facilities. Gift shop.

Ratings. While of particular interest to Jews, the museum also underscores the United States' heritage of religious tolerance. Also, some of the artifacts displayed are fascinating. 2–7, B; 8–11, B; 12–16, B.

AFRO-AMERICAN HISTORICAL AND CULTURAL MUSEUM

7th and Arch Sts. (215) 574–0380. Use the 8th and Market station on the Market-Frankford subway line. Limited metered street and pay lot parking.

Hours. Tues.–Sat., 10 A.M.–5 P.M.; Sun., 12 noon–6 P.M.

Costs. Adults, $3.50; ages 11 and under, $1.75.

A large, stunningly modern building, the Afro-American Museum is used primarily for changing and traveling exhibits of paintings, sculpture, and drawings by famous (or soon-to-be-famous) black American artists. The permanent collection of more than 300,000 items includes paintings, photographs, books, and manuscripts. Several exhibits are presented at the same time.

Kids' Facilities. No stroller rentals. No diaper-changing tables in the restrooms (use sofas outside the restrooms). No food or bottle-warming facilities. Gift shop.

Ratings. Exhibits are always interesting and often rendered in different media. That variety keeps younger children attentive. All ages, B.

MUMMER'S MUSEUM

2nd St. and Washington Ave. (215) 336–3050. One mile east of the Ellsworth-Federal station on the Broad St. subway line. Free street parking.

Hours. Tues.–Sat., 9:30 A.M.–5 P.M.; Sun., 12 noon–5 P.M.

Costs. Adults, $1.50; ages 11 and under, 75¢.

The January 1 Mummer's Parade in Philadelphia is a colorful tradition of long standing. Each year, different clubs within the Mummer's organization slave for months over costumes in order to compete for prizes in a procession down Broad Street, Philadelphia's busy north-south main drag. The Mummer's Museum is both headquarters for the group and a showplace for many of the award-winning costumes of past parades. Parade music accompanies many of the outlandish costume exhibits. The origins of Mummery are spelled out in one exhibit, and another shows how some of the elaborate costumes are made. Photos of parades dating all the way back to the 1880s are also on display. Along the way, the museum shows a unique slice of city history.

Kids' Facilities. No strollers. No diaper-changing tables, but countertops in bathrooms are big enough. No food or bottle-warming facilities. Gift shop.

Ratings. After looking at the muted red bricks of Independence Hall and nearly every other historical Philadelphia building, kids appreciate the bright splash of color the Mummer's Museum offers. 2–7, A; 8–11, A; 12–16; B.

PORT OF HISTORY MUSEUM

Delaware Ave. and Walnut St., Penn's Landing. (215) 925–8832. Use the Penn's Landing station on the Market-Frankford subway line. Pay lot parking.

Hours. Wed.–Sun., 10 A.M.–4:30 P.M.

Costs. Adults, $2; ages 5–12, $1; ages 4 and under, free.

Part of the modernized Delaware Riverfront, the large poured-concrete Port of History Museum hosts traveling regional, national, and international art and industrial shows. Your enjoyment depends entirely on what is currently on exhibit.

Kids' Facilities. No stroller rentals. Change diapers on tables in both men's and ladies' restroom lounges. No food or bottle-warming facilities.

Ratings. No ratings due to changing programs.

ELFRETH'S ALLEY MUSEUM

126 Elfreth's Alley at 2nd St. (215) 574–0560. Use the Penn's Landing station on the Market-Frankford subway line. Limited metered street and pay lot parking.

Hours. Daily, 10 A.M.–4 P.M.

Costs. Free, donations accepted.

Elfreth's Alley is one of Philadelphia's many quaint, narrow streets that date back to the 1680s. All the homes along this short block have been refurbished to look much as they did before the Revolutionary War. All the houses along the street are private residences except number 126, a tall, narrow house that serves as a neighborhood museum. The main floor is a gift shop. If you venture up the extremely slender staircase, you'll find refurbished rooms with late-17th-century furnishings. A photographic exhibit chronicles the restoration process. Some of the private residences are open to the public during the first week of June: call for more information.

Kids' Facilities. No stroller rentals; stairways are too narrow to accommodate strollers. No diaper changing. No restrooms. No food or bottle-warming facilities.

Ratings. A quick turn through this old house will give the kids a good idea of how people lived in the 17th and 18th centuries. You can see it all in about 10 minutes—a worthwhile side trip if you're in the neighborhood to see the Fireman's Hall Museum (next listing), a block away. 2–7, A; 8–11, A; 12–16, B.

FIREMAN'S HALL MUSEUM

2nd and Quarry Sts., (215) 923–1438. Use the Penn's Landing station on the Market-Frankford subway line. Limited metered street and pay lot parking.

Hours. Tues.–Sat., 9 A.M.–5 P.M.

Costs. Free.

Run by the city's fire department, the Firehouse Museum is housed in an 1876 station filled with historic firefighting apparatus. The collection includes an 1809 pump cart, early fire hoses, a ladder truck from 1896, a water cannon wagon built in 1903, a steamer car from 1907, and the department's pride and joy: a hand-pulled fire engine from the 1730s. There's a huge display of leather fire hats, a large collection of toy fire trucks and a Gamewell Joker (1850), one of the first electric fire-alarm systems.

Kids' Facilities. No stroller rentals. Counters for diaper-changing in both men's and ladies' restrooms. No food or bottle-warming facilities.

Ratings. Give yourselves at least an hour because there's so much to see. Terrific for everyone. All ages, A.

NORMAN ROCKWELL MUSEUM

Curtis Publishing Building, 6th and Walnut Sts. (215) 922–4345. Use the Independence station on the Market-Frankford subway line. Limited metered street and pay lot parking.

Hours. Daily, 10 A.M.–4 P.M.

Costs. Adults, $1.50; students with I.D., $1.25; ages 11 and under, free with parent.

Located in the basement of the Curtis Publishing Company (publishers of the Saturday Evening Post), the Rockwell Museum features reproductions of all 324 Post covers Rockwell painted over his long career at the magazine, plus reproductions of works he did for advertisers (from Coke to coffee to Budweiser Beer), and a few of the paintings he did for Boy's Life, the official Boy Scout publication. There's also a half-hour video on the life of one of America's most famous commercial artists.

Kids' Facilities. No stroller rentals. No diaper-changing tables. Restrooms are located down the hall from the museum entrance. No food or bottle-warming facilities.

Ratings. Since Rockwell died more than ten years ago, he means little to most children. But the museum is nostalgia for mothers, fathers, and grandparents, who can stop in for a peek after Independence Hall. All ages, C.

ATWATER KENT MUSEUM

15 S. 7th St. between Market and Chestnut sts. (215) 686–3630. Use the Independence station on the Market-Frankford subway line. Limited metered street and pay lot parking.

Hours. Tues.–Sat., 9:30 A.M.–4:45 P.M.

Costs. Free.

The Atwater Kent Museum is filled with memorabilia from Philadelphia's 300-year history. The first floor contains pictures, paintings, and artifacts from the city's early years, from Quaker relics and Colonial and Revolutionary weapons, to a lock of George Washington's hair. Other galleries display odds and ends like the history of the fire department and gasworks, old police department mug books, and a stellar collection of antique toys.

Kids' Facilities. No stroller rentals. No diaper-changing tables in restrooms (only a few benches). No food or bottle-warming facilities.

Ratings. Even the youngest children will find something to interest them in the busy-looking glass exhibition cases. It's a wonderful place in which to get lost for an hour. 2–7, B; 8–11, A; 12–16, A.

PHILADELPHIA MARITIME MUSEUM

321 Chestnut St., (215) 925–5439. Use the Independence station on the Market-Frankford subway line. Limited metered street and pay lot parking.

Hours. Mon.–Sat., 10 A.M.–5 P.M.; Sun., 1 P.M.–5 P.M.

Costs. Donation, $1.

The museum features an extensive collection of wooden ship models, ship memorabilia from the 18th and 19th centuries, and a large collection of shipboard equipment and personal effects from survivors of the sinking of the *Titanic*. For Civil War buffs, there's even an exhibit on the ironclads *Monitor* and *Merrimac* featuring cutaway models and shipboard artifacts recovered from the watery grave of the sunken *Monitor*.

Kids' Facilities. No stroller rentals. No diaper-changing tables in restrooms. No food or bottle warming facilities.

Ratings. Anyone with even a passing interest in boats will enjoy this large museum. Figure on spending an hour, minimum. 2–7, C; 8–11, A; 12–16, A.

HOTELS

GUEST QUARTERS SUITE HOTEL—AIRPORT

One Gateway Center, at the entrance of the Philadelphia International Airport, (located approximately 5 miles southwest of downtown at the junction of Interstate 95 and State Rte. 291). (215) 365–6600 or (800) 424–2900. 251 units. Free parking.

Rates. $125.

This large, atrium-styled hotel is made up almost exclusively of 1-bedroom suites. If you don't mind a little airport noise, the location is ideal. Price includes full breakfast. Children under age 18 stay free with parents.
Cribs: Yes, no charge.
Rollaways: Yes, no charge.
Babysitting: Yes, referrals need 24-hour notice.
Pool: Yes, indoors.
Restaurant: Yes.
Kitchen facilities: Refrigerator.
Room service: Yes.
Closest emergency hospital: Mercy Catholic Hospital, 10 minutes away, (215) 748–9400.

GUEST QUARTERS SUITE HOTEL—PENNSYLVANIA TURNPIKE

640 W. Germantown Pike, Plymouth Meeting, (located approximately 12 miles northwest of downtown). Use Pennsylvania Turnpike exit 25; proceed ½ mile north on Germantown Road. (215) 834–8300 or (800) 424–2900. 252 units. Free parking.

Rates. $125.

All but one of the 252 units are 1-bedroom suites. Though far from downtown, some families may prefer the suburban setting and proximity to the Pennsylvania Turnpike. Children under 18 stay free with parents.
Cribs: Yes, no charge.
Rollaways: Yes, no charge.
Babysitting: Yes, referrals need 24-hour notice.

Pool: Yes, indoors.
Restaurant: Yes.
Kitchen facilities: Refrigerator.
Room service: Yes.
Closest emergency hospital: Chestnut Hill Hospital, 10 minutes away, (215) 248–8200.

QUALITY INN CHINATOWN SUITES

1010 Race St. (215) 922–1730 or (800) 228–5151. Pay parking.

Rates. $99 to $115.
  Just 5 blocks west of Independence Mall, the Chinatown Suites hotel is for families who'd rather walk than drive and stay in town instead of the suburbs. The location makes it ideal for those who like Chinese food. Kids under 18 stay free with their parents.
Cribs: Yes, no charge.
Rollaways: Yes, $10.
Babysitting: No.
Pool: No.
Restaurant: Yes.
Kitchen facilities: Full kitchen, deposit on utensils required.
Room service: No.
Closest emergency hospital: Hahnemann Hospital, 5 minutes away, (215) 448–7963.

QUALITY INN CHINATOWN SUITES

1010 Race St. (215) 922–1730 or (800) 228–5151. Pay parking.

Rates. $70 to $84
  Quality Inn City Center offers no-frills rooms and a handful of suites that are clean and comfortable. It's only 4 blocks from the Philadelphia Museum of Art and the Franklin Institute Science Museum. Kids under 18 stay free with parents.
Cribs: Yes, no charge.
Rollaways: Yes, $10.
Babysitting: No.
Pool: Yes.
Restaurant: Yes.
Kitchen facilities: No.
Room service: Yes.
Closest emergency hospital: Hahnemann Hospital, 10 minutes away, (215) 448–7963.

RESTAURANTS

Philadelphia has its share of fast-food franchises like McDonald's, Wendy's, and Arby's. Eastern and Midwestern families will also be familiar with chains like Roy Rogers (roast beef sandwiches, burgers, chicken), and International House of Pancakes. Philadelphia's greatest fast-food treasure is the Philly cheesesteak sandwich: a long hoagie-like bun filled with wafer-thin grilled beef and topped with melted cheese and fried onions. At literally hundreds of cheesesteak joints throughout the city and suburbs, the sandwich makes for a great break from the monotony of burgers.

Around Independence Mall, a full stomach is only as far away as the nearest hot dog/Italian sausage vendor. If hot dogs aren't your style, there are plenty of venders selling donuts or fresh fruit (during summer only). You could actually survive months without ever setting foot inside a restaurant.

GRANDE OLDE CHEESESTEAK

The Bourse Building on 5th St. between Chestnut and Market Sts. (215) 925–5579. Limited metered street and pay lot parking.

Hours. Mon.–Sat., 10 A.M.–6 P.M.; Wed. until 8 P.M.; Sun., 12 noon–5 P.M.

Located on the 2nd-floor balcony of the Bourse, a historic 19th-century office building that was converted into an indoor shopping mall, Grande Olde Cheesesteak shares the floor with a dozen or so other restaurants and a large grouping of common tables overlooking the shopping area. The cheesesteaks are wonderful, as are the rest of their deli sandwiches: All the ingredients are fresh and tasty. Only a block from the Liberty Bell pavilion, Grande Olde Cheesesteak makes a great lunchtime pit stop. Cash only. Most sandwiches are under $4. Beer available.

Kids' Facilities. No high chairs or booster seats. No diaper-changing tables in the Bourse restrooms. No children's menus; however, you can order smaller portions.

THE SPAGHETTI FACTORY

530 South St. (215) 627–5595. Limited metered street and pay lot parking.

Hours. Mon.–Thurs., 5:30 P.M.–10 P.M.; Fri. and Sat., 5:30 P.M.–11 P.M.; Sun., 5 P.M.–10 P.M.

South Street—Philadelphia's wild, wacky, off-center street—is home to an assortment of futuristic gadget shops, hip clothing stores, and bohemian restaurants. It's a place where shopping is an adventure and people-watching is at its best. Here resides the Spaghetti Factory (no relation to the Spaghetti Factory chain found elsewhere in the United States), an inexpensive purveyor of the pasta dishes kids like the best. Their spaghetti is less than $6, with more complicated Italian entrees no higher than $16. Alcohol is served. Credit cards.

Kids' Facilities. No high chairs. Plenty of booster seats. No diaper-changing tables in the restrooms. No children's menus. Children's portions available.

PIZZERIA UNO

511 S. 2nd St. (215) 592–0400. Limited metered street and pay lot parking.

Hours. Sun.–Wed., 11:30 A.M.–11:30 P.M.; Thurs., 11:30 A.M.–12 midnight; Fri. and Sat., 11:30 A.M.–1:30 A.M.

Just north of the South Street strip, Pizzeria Uno (Philadelphians pronounce it "Ooo-noauw") presents a full-range Italian menu that includes kids' favorites like pizza and pasta, plus parent-pleasing entrees like veal and seafood. It's a good place for lunch prior to a South Street shopping expedition. Full dinners run between $7 and $12, with lunches slightly less. Full bar. Credit cards.

Kids' Facilities. Booster seats and high chairs are available. No diaper-changing tables in restrooms. No children's menus.

MARABELLA'S

1420 Locust St., (215) 545–1845. Limited metered street and pay lot parking.

Hours. Sun.–Thurs., 11 A.M.–11:30 P.M.; Fri. and Sat., 11 A.M.–12:30 A.M.

Boisterous is the best way to describe Marabella's, an Italian-American restaurant in the city's theater district. Younger children love the high decibel level, and the de facto license to talk loudly makes lunch here a great release, especially after a subdued morning of museum hopping. From their homemade pastas to their delicious crab cakes, the food is very good. The fresh-baked Italian bread and sauted red and green pepper appetizers are out of this world. Most entrees are between $6 and $8. Full bar. Reservations accepted for lunch only. Credit cards.

Kids' Facilities. No high chairs. Plenty of booster seats. No diaper-changing tables in restrooms. Children's menu consists of burgers and fries.

Big Splurges

DILULLO CENTRAL

1407 Locust St., (215) 546–2000. Limited metered street and pay lot parking.

Hours. Mon.–Thurs., 11:45 A.M.–1:45 P.M. and 5:30 P.M.–10 P.M.; Fri., until 10:30 P.M.; Sat., 5 P.M.–10:30 only; open theater nights, 10 P.M.–11 P.M. Closed on Sun.

If you love Northern Italian cuisine (veal, seafood, and pasta with white, creamy sauces), DiLullo is your kind of place. The atmosphere is urbane, with an understated elegance. The food is so good that it's difficult recommend any particular dish. There is, however, a price to pay for DiLullos: It is one of the city's more expensive restaurants. Lunchtime entrees cost from about $17 to $20; dinners are in the $35 to $50 range. Full bar. Men should wear a coat and tie. Reservations strongly suggested. Credit cards.

RAYMOND HALDEMAN'S

110–112 S. Front St. (215) 925–9888. Limited metered street and pay lot parking.

Hours. Daily, 12 noon–12 midnight.

Philadelphia has nouvelle cuisine (strange and exotic food combinations served in an eye-pleasing fashion) and Raymond Haldeman was the first guy on the block to serve it. Located in a part of town now undergoing a face lift, Haldeman's is considered one of the "in" places by the region's restaurant writers. The menu includes odd-sounding dishes like mussels and melon-seed pasta and curried seafood: It's all delicious. A la carte is a way of life here. At dinner time, salads run about $7, appetizers $9, and entrees $20. Mom and Dad can figure on spending about $80 to $100 (with wine) for dinner without the kids; lunch is $20 less. Full bar. Men should wear a coat and tie. Reservations a must. Credit cards.

SHOPPING

For a city with as many tourist attractions, Philadelphia has few shops designed to separate visitors from their money. At present, there are two "historic" shopping malls: **Mellon Independence Center**, Market and 7th Streets, (215) 923–4571, and **The Bourse**, Chestnut and 5th Streets, (215) 625–0300. Both occupy a turn-of-the-century office building and have boutiques and fast-food restaurants. Both are located a block away from the Liberty Bell Pavilion. Neither offers much in the way of toys or gadgets for kids. However, they do offer something more important to a family tiring of a strict diet of historical sites: a break in the action and a place to get something to eat or drink (the Bourse has Grande Olde Cheesesteak: see Restaurants).

PHILADELPHIA GIFT SHOP

The Philadelphia Visitor Center, 16th St. and John F. Kennedy Blvd. (215) 569–4934. Limited metered street and pay lot parking.

Hours. Daily, 9 A.M.–5 P.M.

The Convention and Visitors Bureau sells all the Philadelphia ashtrays, Philadelphia pencil holders, and other sold-in-Philadelphia products your kids could ever want. The selection is vast, and the trinkets aren't overpriced. Credit cards.

ZIPPERHEAD

407 South St. (215) 928–1123. Limited metered street and pay lot parking.

Hours. Sun.–Thurs., 12 noon–11 P.M.; Fri. and Sat., 11 A.M.–12 midnight.

The best place in Philadelphia to see men and women with pastel-colored hair is on South Street, "the hippest street in town" according to the 1960s song named for the thoroughfare. And the place on South Street to view the wackiest bohemians is in and around Zipperhead, a crazy New-Wave shop that specializes in goofy gifts, outrageous jewelry, and kitschy housewares that serve no discernible purpose. Where else in Philadelphia could you find both Taiwanese plastic jumping frogs *and* pinhead greeting cards? The music is loud, the visuals are strange, and your kids will love the place.

NEWMAN'S TOYS

316 South St. (215) 925–5510. Limited metered street and pay lot parking.

Hours. Mon., 11 A.M.–6 P.M.; Wed. and Thurs., 11 A.M.–7:30 P.M.; Fri., 11 A.M.–8 P.M.; Sat., 11 A.M.–9 P.M.; Sun., 12 noon–5 P.M. Closed on Tues.

A full-service toy store, Newman's doesn't discriminate against any toys. That means that, along with the educational playthings, shelf space is also devoted to the commercial toys advertised on Saturday morning television shows. They have a large selection of Disney characters, puppets and marionettes, as well as officially licensed toys from major motion pictures.

THE LAST WOUND-UP OF PHILADELPHIA

617 South St. (215) 238–9440. Limited metered street and pay lot parking.

Hours. Tues.–Fri., 12 noon–11 P.M.; Sat., 11 A.M.–11 P.M.; Sun. and Mon., 12 noon–9 P.M.

Another outpost of the delightful, nationwide Last Wound-Up chain, shops that specialize in wind-up toys of all sizes and shapes.

TRANSPORTATION

PUBLIC TRANSIT

Philadelphia has an adequate public transit system that includes buses, subways, streetcars, and elevated railways (els). The integrated transit system that operates in the city of Philadelphia and the surrounding suburbs comes under the aegis of the Southeastern Pennsylvania Transportation Authority (SEPTA). Four main rail lines serve the city: the Broad Street subway line, which runs north and south; the Market-Frankford subway line, which runs east and west; the PATCO line, which connects downtown and suburban New Jersey across the Delaware River; and the Amtrak line, which serves the northern and southern suburbs. While the rails serve the city's core well (including downtown and Independence Mall), they leave something to be desired as far as more remote museums and attractions are concerned.

Buses and streetcars fill the gaps between the rail and subway lines. The charge for all vehicles is $1.25 per ride plus 25¢ for transfers. The system's main hours of operation are between the morning rush hour and midnight, and there is limited service thereafter. You must use exact change on any SEPTA vehicle. SEPTA's mid-city bus loop, between 17th and 5th Streets along Market and Chestnut Streets, operates every day between the morning and evening rush hours; it costs only 60¢. For schedules and information on any of SEPTA's vehicles, call (215) 574–7800.

TAXIS

While it is possible to hail taxis in Philadelphia, it's better to either phone for one or go to a large hotel or one of the designated taxi stations around the city. Cab travel is expensive, with companies charging anywhere from $2.10 to $2.32 for the first mile and $1.32 for each additional mile. The two principal taxi companies are Yellow Cab, (215) 922–7186, and United Cab Association, (215) 625–9170.

TOURS

BUS

Gray Line. (215) 569–3666. Conducts three daily tours throughout the year. The 3-hour Historic Philadelphia tour covers most of the sites on Independence Mall, as well as the Betsy Ross house and Elfreth's Alley (adults, $13.50; children, $8.25). The 2½-hour Cultural Tour hits the Academy of Science, the Philadelphia Museum of Art, and the Franklin Institute (adults, $15; children, $10.75). The third tour is a 5 ½-hour combination of the first two (adults, $24.50; children, $16).

Fairmount Park Trolley Tours. (215) 879–4044. Guided tours of picturesque Fairmount Park, operate between April and November. The motorized trolley cars depart the Philadelphia Visitor Center (16th Street and John F. Kennedy Blvd.) at 20-minute intervals throughout the day. The Fairmount Park tour lasts 90 minutes, but passengers are allowed to get off at any stop (including the Museum of Art, the Academy of Natural Science, and the Franklin Institute) and reboard at any time. The trolleys run daily between 10 A.M. and 4:20 P.M., and cost $3.

WALKING TOURS

Centipede Tours, Inc. (215) 735–3123. Conducts 90-minute walking tours of Society Hill and Historic Philadelphia from late May through the middle of October. Tour guides dress in Colonial costumes, and both tours depart City Tavern (2nd and Walnut Streets) at 6:30 P.M. Society Hill tours are given Wednesdays and Saturdays; Historic Philadelphia tours are scheduled for Fridays. (Adults, $4; children under 12, $3.50.)

Audio Walk and Tour. (215) 925–1234. Offers taped walking tours of the historic buildings at Independence National Historical Park. You rent the tape and a tape player that can be used by up to eight listeners (one person, $8; two people, $12; three to eight, $16). Included is a souvenir map and coupons for discounts at other Philadelphia attractions.

BOAT

R & S Harbor Tours. (215) 928–0972. Conducts 50-minute cruises along the Delaware River daily from mid-April through mid-October. Tours depart from Penn's Landing Marina (Delaware Avenue and Lombard Street) every hour on the hour between 10 A.M. and 5 P.M. Monday through Friday (adults, $4; children, $2), and from 12 noon to 6 P.M. Saturdays and Sundays (adults, $5; children, $3). There is also a 2-hour sunset cruise Thursday through Sunday at 7:30 P.M. (adults, $6; children, $4).

SEASONAL EVENTS

January

MUMMERS PARADE

Philadelphians wait all year for the January 1 parade that brings a splash of color, music, and fun to the winter-dulled streets of the city. Crowds of up to 30,000 line Broad Street to watch hundreds of clowns, string bands, and comics ham it up. For more information: (215) 336–3050.

May

JAMBALAYA JAM

This annual salute to all things New Orleans takes place every year around Memorial Day weekend at Penn's Landing. There's lots of New Orleans cooking and plenty of New Orleans–style jazz. Considering the price of New Orleans–style restaurants these days, the admission fee is a bargain (adults, $6; kids, $1—does not include food). For more information: (215) 636–1666.

July

FREEDOM FESTIVAL

Is there a better place to spend the July 4 weekend than in the city where independence was declared more than 200 years ago? Fireworks, free outdoor concerts, food festivals, and a big parade highlight the 4-day celebration. Make hotel reservations well ahead of time as the Fourth in Philly is a giant 96-hour party. For more information: (215) 636–1666.

September

ROCK 'A' RAMA

Ever since Dick Clark put Philadelphia on the musical map in the early 1950s with *American Bandstand*, the city has been proud of its contributions to rock 'n' roll. Every Labor Day weekend, Penn's Landing presents some of the top rock revival acts. The event usually lasts 3 days and nights, and tickets cost $6 ($1 for children). For more information: (215) 636–1666.

November

TINKERTOY EXTRAVAGANZA

During Thanksgiving weekend, the Franklin Institute of Science Museum holds its annual tribute to the 50-year-old Tinkertoy, the revered construction toy that's still going strong. Come and see what accomplished tinkerers build. For more information: (215) 448–1200.

CHILDREN'S THEATER

ANNENBERG CENTER

3680 Walnut St., University of Pennsylvania Campus. (215) 898–6791. Limited metered street and pay lot parking.

The Annenberg Center's Zellerbach Theater offers a yearly series of four children's plays between November and April. Each play has a 2-day run on a Friday and a Saturday, and there is often a mix of original plays and old favorites. In late May, the Annenberg Center hosts the annual International Theater Festival for Children featuring children's plays from all over the world. Call for information and current schedule.

THEATER CARAVAN

3680 Walnut St., University of Pennsylvania Campus (theater locations differ). (215) 898–6068.

A traveling Theater Caravan tours all over the Northeast. Their plays are a mixture of kids' favorites, with well-known characters in unfamiliar situations, plus the latest plays from the hottest children's playwrights in the English-speaking world. The season runs from October through May, and they try to do at least one Philadelphia-based run per year. Call ahead for their schedule.

PUBLICATIONS

Philadelphia Inquirer. Daily newspaper; a comprehensive calendar of weekly events, with an emphasis on the upcoming weekend, appears in the Friday edition.

Philadelphia Daily News. Daily newspaper; weekly entertainment calendar is published every Friday.

Philadelphia Magazine. Monthly magazine; a comprehensive calendar of events emphasizes adult activities (such as plays, concerts, celebrity appearances) but often has a few gems for children.

Skip Magazine. This free magazine-style monthly features four comprehensive calendars of events (entertainment and school activities calendars), articles on parenting, and ads for stores that cater to kids; available at stores and doctors' offices along the Main Line, a collection of well-to-do suburbs that stretches west from the city and includes Bryn Mawr, Haverford, and Radnor.

LOCAL TELEPHONE NUMBERS

Late-hours pharmacy: Andorra Pharmacy, Cathedral and Henry Aves., (215) 483–5152. Open daily, 9 A.M.–10 P.M.
Consumer complaints: (215) 560–2414.
Dental referral: (215) 925–6050.
Physician referral: (215) 563–5343.
Drug-abuse hotline: (215) 744–9796.
Poison-control hotline: (215) 386–2100 or (215) 386–2010.
Traveler's aid: (215) 546–0571.
Tourism office: (215) 636–3300 or (215) 636–1666 (hotline).
Police: 911.
Fire: 911.
Ambulance: 911.
Road conditions: (215) 686–4960.
Weather: (215) 936–1212.

SAN DIEGO

A few years back, while no one was looking, San Diego quietly slipped past San Francisco to become California's second-largest city. Currently ranked eighth in population in the United States, the bustling metropolis is one of the country's fastest growing. The vibrant expansion results from an influx of new residents, mainly from the Rust Belt and crowded Los Angeles, and to the growth of the aerospace industries. Thanks to its world-class zoo, Sea World, the San Diego Wild Animal Park, plus the friendliest climate on the Pacific Coast, San Diego approaches the 21st century as one of the best stops for traveling families in the western United States.

Because of its fine natural harbor, San Diego was the first California location claimed by Juan Cabrillo for Spain. Cabrillo National Monument on historic Point Loma marks the spot where the explorer stood in 1542. In 1602, the area was extensively charted by Sebastian Vizcaino, who officially named it San Diego.

Actual colonization waited another 160 years until, in response to a perceived threat to their toehold in North America from Great Britain and Russia, Spain's Gaspar de Portola established a small colony at San Diego in 1769. As was the custom in those days, a religious contingent accompanied any military venture. The head priest on this trip was Father Junipero Serra, who quickly established Mission Basilica San Diego de Alcala, the first of what would eventually grow to twenty-one Catholic missions stretching north from San Diego to Sonoma. The mission system pacified the native Indian tribes and helped California remain under Spanish control until the Mexican War in 1846, when California came under United States domination.

California was granted statehood in 1850. In 1867, a San Francisco merchant named Alonzo Horton came to San Diego and was amazed to find that the center of the city was located in Old Town, 2 miles from the bay. Quickly acquiring almost a thousand acres of waterfront property,

Horton tried to develop "New San Diego," going so far as to oversee in 1871 the removal of county records from Old Town to his new bayside enclave. The new town was slow to catch on and, unfortunately for the entrepreneur, it didn't happen fast enough to save him from bankruptcy. (As a posthumous consolation prize, Horton Plaza, a huge shopping mall, was named for him in 1985.)

Despite an occasional surge of business activity thanks to a wildly fluctuating economy and a local gold strike or two, San Diego's growth didn't really begin until the Japanese bombing of Pearl Harbor touched off World War II and forced the United States Navy to find a new location for the Pacific Fleet. Businesses grew up around the military bases, and, after the war, many sailors decided to stay.

With the Pacific fleet currently stationed in San Diego, the military still has a mighty profile. Along with the San Diego Naval Base, the city also has the North Island and Miramar naval air stations, a training station, a supply center, an amphibious base, and a command station. Besides active-duty military personnel, San Diego is also a haven for retirees, both military and nonmilitary, and civilian government workers. Employees of aerospace industries and people who work in the burgeoning tourist industries round out the population.

San Diego comes as a wonderful surprise to tourists who envision a trip to southern California as a test of stamina behind the wheel. Greater San Diego is relatively compact, stretching only about 20 miles from its downtown epicenter to the north, south, and east. Except for Tijuana, Mexico ("TJ" to locals)—for bullfights, leather goods stores, and auto repair shops—most tourist attractions are located near downtown or north only about as far as La Jolla.

If your frame of reference for driving in southern California is Los Angeles, you're in for a treat in San Diego. While there are slow-ups during rush hour periods, gridlock is rare. The freeways move smoothly, and most streets are wide enough to accommodate lots of traffic.

San Diego consists of five distinct areas: **downtown**, the center of the city, which includes the Embarcadero, the Maritime Museum, and the Firehouse Museum (see Museums); **Balboa Park**, just northeast of downtown, which features the San Diego Zoo (see Attractions) and eleven distinctive museums housed in eight buildings; **Old Town San Diego**, northwest of downtown, which boasts Mission Alcala (see Attractions), a number of historic old homes, and museums; **Mission Bay**, north of downtown on the coast, a marshland-turned-bay where Sea World (see Attractions) is located; and **La Jolla**, San Diego's well-to-do northern suburb, which is home to the La Jolla Museum of Contemporary Art, the San Diego Children's Museum, and the Scripps Aquarium and Museum (see Museums).

FREEBIES AND CHEAPIES
(Free or $3.50 and under for adults)

- ☐ Mission Alcala (see Attractions)
- ☐ Scripps Aquarium and Museum (see Museums)
- ☐ San Diego Union Museum (see Museums)
- ☐ Firehouse Museum (see Museums)
- ☐ Timken Art Gallery (see Museums)
- ☐ San Diego Light Rail Transit (see Transportation)
- ☐ Reuben Fleet Science Center (see Attractions)
- ☐ Cabrillo National Monument and Point Loma Lighthouse (see Attractions)
- ☐ San Diego Museum of Man (see Museums)
- ☐ Junipero Serra Museum (see Museums)
- ☐ Children's Museum of San Diego (see Museums)

THE LONG WEEKEND

Day One

- ☐ San Diego Zoo (see Attractions)

Day Two

- ☐ Balboa Park (see Museums)

Day Three

- ☐ Sea World (see Attractions)

CLIMATE

Except during Pacific rainstorms in winter and periods of low cloudiness mornings and evenings in May and June, the sun usually shines on the city. San Diego has the lowest rainfall on the Pacific Coast: about 9.5 inches per year (L.A. gets 14 inches). In winter, temperatures are often in the mid-60s and, at night, the mercury seldom dips below 40 degrees. Summer is characterized by sunny days in the mid-70s and nights in the mid-50s. The farther away you get from the ocean, the less moderate the temperatures. In El Cajon, about 12 miles east of San Diego, summertime thermometer readings are often 15 degrees higher during the day. In winter, look for lows at night that sometimes dip near freezing. Seldom, if ever, does San Diego proper dip as low as 32 degrees. In winter, pack a heavy sweater *and* a medium-weight jacket. In summer, a light sweater and light jacket are in order for the cool, dry evenings.

TOURIST INFORMATION

Contact the San Diego Convention and Visitors Bureau, 1200 Third Ave., Suite 824, San Diego, CA 92101, (619) 232–3101.

ATTRACTIONS

BALBOA PARK

6th Ave. and Interstate 5. (619) 239–0512. Free parking.

Hours. Dawn to dusk.

Costs. Park is free; the zoo and most museums charge admission.

A 1,158-acre oasis just outside downtown San Diego, Balboa Park is home to the world-renown **San Diego Zoo**, the **Reuben H. Fleet Space Theater and Science Center**, the **Spreckels Organ Pavilion** and many museums, plus loads of picnic grounds, playing fields, and golf courses. Set aside as a recreational facility in 1868, many of the Park's buildings were constructed for either the 1915–1916 Panama-California Exposition or the 1935–1936 California-Pacific International Exposition. *(Note: The House of Hospitality along El Prado has plenty of maps and information tidbits about Balboa Park.)*

SAN DIEGO ZOO

Zoo Dr. and Park Blvd., Balboa Park. (619) 234–3153 or (619) 231–1515. Free parking.

Hours. July 1 through Labor Day: daily, 9 A.M.–5 P.M. Rest of the year: daily, 9 A.M.–4 P.M.

Costs. *Zoo:* adults, $8.50; ages 3–15, $2.50; ages 2 and under, free. *Skyfari:* adults, $1.50, ages 3–15, $1; ages 2 and under, free. *Guided bus tour:* adults, $2.50; ages 3–15, $2; ages 2 and under, free. *Children's Zoo:* general admission, 50¢; ages 2 and under, free. *Deluxe tour package* (all of the above): adults, $13; ages 3–15, $6; ages 2 and under, free. *(Note: Go for the Deluxe Tour package. You'll save money.)*

With more than 3,200 animals spread over 100 lush acres, it's easy to see why people who know their zoos claim that it takes 3 days to see everything there is to see here. The facility has one of the largest reptile collections as well as some formidable numbers of rare animals of every family. It's also the only zoo we've seen with moving sidewalks. A bus tour and/or an aerial tram ride on the Skyfari will give you the lay of the land and help you decide where to concentrate your efforts. The new Tiger River section, a replica of a tropical rain forest, is a must. For small children, the kid's zoo can't be topped.

Kids' Facilities. Changing tables are found in a number of ladies' restrooms (in the men's restroom, too, at the Children's Zoo). Strollers ($5 per day) can be rented at the entrance. All manner of baby supplies (such as disposable bottles, diapers, and powder) are sold at the stroller-rental facility. Bottles can be warmed at a number of the many food stands and restaurants.

Ratings. Whether you have three days or just a portion of one, the San Diego Zoo is one of the finest (and most expensive) in the United States. All ages, A.

REUBEN FLEET SPACE THEATER AND SCIENCE CENTER

1875 El Prado, Balboa Park. (619) 238–1168. Free parking.

Hours. Sun.–Thurs., 9:45 A.M.–9:30 P.M.; Fri. and Sat., 9:45 A.M.–10:30 P.M.

Costs. *Science Center:* adults, $2; ages 5–15, $1; ages 4 and under, free. *Omnimax Theater:* adults, $5; ages 5–15, $3; ages 4 and under, free. Admission to Science Center free with Omnimax ticket purchase.

The tilted seats, domed 6-story screen, and 152 speakers of the Omnimax make a spectacular setting for a varying diet of science- and space-related movies. The Science Center's sixty exhibits include hands-on machines that guess your age, test your senses, and challenge your memory. A set of whisper disks lets kids converse quietly and privately in a noisy room—great fun!

Kids' Facilities. No stroller rentals. Diaper-changing tables in ladies' restrooms (men can use benches in the lobby). No bottle-warming facilities in the center's croissant shop.

Ratings. A wonderful attraction for school-aged kids on up. Kids below the preschool level are good only for an hour or less. 2–7, B; 8–11, A; 12–16, A.

SPRECKELS ORGAN PAVILION

El Prado and Presidents Way, Balboa Park. (619) 236–5717. Free parking.

Hours. Concerts Sun. and holidays, 2 P.M.

Costs. Free.

If you happen to be in the park on a Sunday afternoon anyway, the sound from the 3,500 pipes of the world's largest outdoor organ is something you and your family will never forget. Be advised that only in a climate free from drastic extremes of temperature and humidity can an instrument of this size remain in tune.

Kids' Facilities. Use facilities at nearby museums.

Ratings. The music's great, the organ's big . . . what's not to love? All ages, A.

SEA WORLD

Sea World Dr. and Ingraham St., Mission Bay. (619) 226–3901. Free parking.

Hours. Summer: daily, 9 A.M.–11 P.M. Rest of the year: daily, 9 A.M.–dusk; hours are often extended for special promotions and at holiday periods.

Costs. Adults, $17.95; ages 3–11, $11.95; ages 2 and under, free.

Highlights of the 135-acre facility, the smallest and oldest in the Sea World chain, include live-action human and aquatic mammal shows and plenty of hands-on educational exhibits.

For entertainment, there's the *Shamu Killer Whale Show*; the *City Streets Show*, where singers and dancers (human) cavort in an urban, dry-land setting; *Spooky Kooky Castle*, where a smart seal and a not-so-smart sheriff solve a crime; the *Muscle Beach Diving Show*, in which humans prove they too can be talented in the water; and the *New Friends Show*, for more interaction between marine mammals and human beings.

Educational attractions include exhibits of sea otters, the famed *Penguin Encounter* where penguins frolic on a man-made ice floe, walruses, sharks, and even a dolphin petting pool for little children. On a more recreational note, there's *Cap'n Kids World*, where little kids can romp in an acre of diversions like the Ball Crawl, pits filled with hollow plastic balls; the Swashbuckler's Swing; and dozens of arcade games. Sea World also features *Places of Learning*, where kids can walk from one end of the country to the other on a United States map that covers 1 square acre.

Kids' Facilities. Like the Disney facilities, Sea World takes every possible child-related need into consideration for their patrons. Strollers and wheelchairs ($3.50 per day) are available in huge numbers. Registered nurses are available to provide first aid: Simply alert any employee to an emergency and help will be on the way. Diapers can be changed on tables in the ladies' restrooms. For warmed bottles, ask the waiters or waitresses at PJ's, the park's sit-down restaurant.

Ratings. No matter how many times kids are given the opportunity to go to a place like Sea World or Disneyland, they jump at it. Fun for kids of all ages; tiring for adults. All ages, A.

VILLA MONTEZUMA

1925 K St., Downtown. (619) 239–2211. Limited street and pay lot parking.

Hours. Wed.–Sun., 1 P.M.–4:30 P.M.

Costs. Adults, $2; ages 12 and under, free

A Victorian home constructed in 1887 by noted early San Diegan Jesse Shepard, the Villa houses period curios and features some of the region's most beautiful residential stained glass windows.

Kids' Facilities. No stroller rentals. No diaper-changing tables in restrooms. No food or bottle warming.

Ratings. The Villa is not for younger children but older children with an interest in history might like it. 2–7, D; 8–11, C; 12–16, B.

WHALEY HOUSE

2482 San Diego Ave., Old Town. (619) 298–2482. Limited street and pay lot parking.

Hours. Wed.–Sun., 10 A.M.–4:30 P.M.

Costs. Adults, $2.50; ages 12–16, $1; ages 5–11, $.50; ages 4 and under, free.

In earthquake-prone southern California, it's unusual to find brick buildings of this vintage still standing. Built in 1856 by merchant Thomas Whaley, the city's oldest structure has served as a residence, a store, a theater, and, for a time, as the San Diego County Courthouse. It has a terrific collection of mid-19th-century furnishings. Don't miss the dolls in the furnished child's room upstairs.

Kids' Facilities. No stroller rentals. No diaper-changing tables. No bottle-warming facilities.

Ratings. Ask the docent on duty to spin a tale or two about the ghosts that are said to currently haunt the house. If Mom and Dad love old houses, the Whaley House is a winner. 2–7, C; 8–11, A; 12–18, A.

CABRILLO NATIONAL MONUMENT AND POINT LOMA LIGHTHOUSE

End of Cabrillo Memorial Dr. (State Rte. 209), Point Loma. (619) 557–5450. Free parking.

Hours. Daily, 9 A.M.–5:15 P.M.; extended hours in summer.

Costs. $3 per vehicle; $1 per person on tour buses.

The monument marks the spot where, in 1542, explorer Juan Cabrillo laid claim to California for Spain. Near the tip of gorgeous Point Loma, it offers a commanding view of the Pacific Ocean to the west and San Diego Bay and downtown San Diego to the east. The best vantage point for sightseeing is the high ground upon which the lighthouse (1855) is built. In winter, it's a terrific place to witness California gray whales on their annual migration between their summer home in the northern Pacific and their winter calving territory off the Baja California peninsula. The visitors center has exhibits of historic artifacts and a film on Cabrillo's historic voyage. There are plenty of tidal pools to explore near the shoreline and a 2-mile-long nature-trail hike.

Kids' Facilities. No stroller rentals. No diaper-changing tables (use benches outdoors or in the visitors center). No bottle-warming facilities.

Ratings. The view alone is worth the trip. Older kids will appreciate the history of the area. The younger ones will enjoy getting their hands and feet wet in the tidal pools. All ages, A.

MISSION ALCALA

10818 San Diego Mission Rd., Mission Valley. (619) 281–8449. Free parking.

Hours. Daily, 9 A.M.–5 P.M.

Costs. Adults, $1; ages 12 and under, free.

Founded in 1769 by Father Junipero Serra, Mission Basilica San Diego de Alcala was the first of what would eventually be a network of twenty-one missions extending from San Diego north to Sonoma County. Highlights include robes and records dating back to the Mission's founding. There is a small exhibit of weapons and assorted artifacts from the United States Army occupation of the mission between 1846 and 1862.

Kids' Facilities. No stroller rentals. No diaper-changing tables in restrooms (use benches). No food or bottle-warming facilities.

Ratings. Mainly for history and architecture buffs, the mission will probably leave younger children unimpressed. 2–7, C; 8–11, C; 12–16, B.

HOTEL DEL CORONADO

1500 Orange Ave., Coronado. (619) 435–6611. Free parking.

Hours. Open 24 hours.

Costs. Free; cassette taped tour of lobby, $3.

The Hotel del Coronado is one of San Diego's most popular attractions. Built in 1888 and refurbished for its centennial, the giant wooden structure has been the vacation retreat for 12 United States Presidents and an uncounted number of Hollywood luminaries. (The 1980 Peter O'Toole movie *The Stunt Man* was filmed on the premises.) The round turrets, many with rooftop observation decks and catwalks, are familiar sights to southern Californians. Lunch or drinks are fun ways to pass the time, or you can just sit in the lobby.

Kids' Facilities. No stroller rentals. No diaper-changing tables in restrooms (use couches in lobby). Bottles warmed in any of the hotel's three restaurants.

Ratings. The del Coronado is for older kids who can appreciate the architecture. 2–7, C; 8–11, B; 12–16, A.

SAN DIEGO WILD ANIMAL PARK

State Rte. 78, Escondido. (619) 747–8702. Parking, $1.

Hours. Mid-June through Labor Day: daily, 9 A.M.–9 P.M. March through mid-June and September through October: daily, 9 A.M.–5 P.M. November through February: daily, 9 A.M.–4 P.M.

Costs. Adults, $12.95; ages 3–15, $6.20; ages 2 and under, free.

Created by the people responsible for the famed San Diego Zoo, the 1,800-acre San Diego Wild Animal Park is the closest thing to an African safari this side of Kenya. Visitors take a 50-minute monorail ride through savannahlike territory inhabited by a roaming population of elephants, lions, tigers, giraffes, zebras, deer, and rhinos. After the monorail ride, you're encouraged to hike a 1¼-mile trail from which you can safely observe the animals and even stop for a picnic. The visit begins and ends at Nairobi Village, where the kids can pet animals and observe birds in the park's large aviary. Added attractions include elephant rides, animal shows, and even a nursery, where baby animals act cute and cuddly.

Kids' Facilities. Strollers can be rented for $2.50 per day. Diaper-changing tables located in the ladies' restrooms. Bottles can be warmed at any of the cafeteria-style restaurants. A nurse is always on duty.

Ratings. For a dusty (in summer and early autumn), delightfully exhausting day in the wilds of northern San Diego County, the Wild Animal Park is a tough act to top. All ages, A.

MUSEUMS

Balboa Park

Costs. The Balboa Park Passport admits adults to four of the nine Balboa Park museums that change admission for a single price of $8. Passports are available at participating museums.

AEROSPACE HISTORICAL CENTER [TWO MUSEUMS]

2001 Pan American Plaza, Balboa Park. (619) 234–8291. Free parking.

Hours. Daily, 10 A.M.–4:30 P.M.

Costs. Both museums for a single price. Adults, $4; ages 6–17, $1; ages 5 and under, free.

With two museums under one roof—the **San Diego Aerospace Museum** and the **International Aerospace Hall of Fame**—the center has something for every aviation taste. Most of the exhibits highlight the contribution of San Diego's two Navy air stations and countless aerospace companies. Exhibits include gliders from the Wright Brothers' era, a replica of Charles Lindbergh's *Spirit of St. Louis*, a mock-up of the U.S.S. *Yorktown* aircraft carrier with a Japanese Zero and its American counterpart, an F6F Hellcat, a Battle of Britain exhibit complete with a British Spitfire, and jets like a Russian MiG–15 and an American F–86. One exhibit pays tribute to female fliers.

Kids' Facilities. No stroller rentals. No diaper-changing tables (use benches). No bottle-warming facilities.

Ratings. Something comes over kids when they encounter planes sitting indoors at a museum: The Aerospace Center is a winner. All ages, A.

CASA DE BALBOA [FOUR MUSEUMS]

East end of El Prado, Balboa Park. Each museum has its own phone number. *Museum of San Diego History*, (619) 232–6203; *Museum of Photographic Arts*, (619) 239–5262; *San Diego Hall of Champions*, (619) 234–2544; and *San Diego Model Railroad Museum*, (619) 696–0199. Free parking.

Hours. *History:* Wed.–Sat., 10 A.M.–4 P.M. *Photography:* daily, 10 A.M.–5 P.M., Thurs. until 9 P.M. *Champions:* Mon.–Sat., 10 A.M.–4:30 P.M.; Sun., 12 noon–5 P.M. *Railroad:* Wed.–Fri., 11 A.M.–4 P.M.; Sat. and Sun., 11 A.M.–5 P.M.

Costs. *History:* adults, $2; under 12, free. *Photography:* adults, $2.50; under 12, free. *Champions:* adults, $2; ages 18–21, $1; ages 6–17, $.50; ages 5 and under, free. *Railroad:* adults, $1; under 18, free.

Four museums in one building!

The **Museum of San Diego History**, features artifacts and photos that date back to 1850, the early days of the American presence in the city. It also houses the city's research archives.

The **Museum of Photographic Arts** is devoted entirely to photography. Each year the facility presents six new exhibits, showcasing the best of contemporary and historical photographs, both in color and in black and white. There are also movie and video presentations.

The **San Diego Hall of Champions** displays memorabilia and photographs of some of the area's best-known local athletes: football's Marcus Allen, tennis player Maureen Connolly, and baseball players Ted Williams and Alan Trammel, to name but a few.

The **San Diego Model Railroad Museum** has four landscaped layouts depicting the history of rail transportation in southern California.

Kids' Facilities. The four museums share facilities. No stroller rentals. No diaper-changing tables in restrooms (two on each side of the building). Bottles can be warmed at the "Chocolate Lily," a quiche, salad, and sandwich restaurant shared by the museums.

Ratings. *History:* Not enough to enthrall the very young; a half hour, tops; 2–7, C; 8–11, B; 12–16, A. *Photography:* Since shows change regularly, its difficult to rate; some shows are geared to children, most are not. *Champions:* Kids (boys *and* girls) who like sports will enjoy themselves here; All ages, A. *Railroad:* There is still a childhood fascination with miniature scale machines that travel under their own power; all ages, A.

NATURAL HISTORY MUSEUM

El Prado and Park Blvd., Balboa Park. (619) 232–3821. Free parking.

Hours. Mid-June through mid-September: daily, 10 A.M.–5 P.M. Rest of the year: daily, 10 A.M.–4:30 P.M.

Costs. Adults, $4; ages 3–11, $1; ages 2 and under, free.

The new Hall of Desert Ecology includes a terrific California desert diorama and video learning center with buttons to push. In fact, there are plenty of opportunities for kids to reach out and touch things, including animal demonstrations and "please touch" exhibits of endangered animal species. With an emphasis on nature in southern California, Arizona, and northern Mexico, there are plenty of birds, animals, insects, and minerals. And how could it be a natural history museum without a dinosaur skeleton or two?

Kids' Facilities. No stroller rentals. Tables in basement restrooms for diaper changing (couch on main floor). No restaurant or bottle-warming facilities.

Ratings. The Hall of Desert Ecology and its "touch me" exhibits make the Natural History Museum a natural for kids. All ages, A.

SAN DIEGO MUSEUM OF ART

1450 El Prado, Balboa Park. (619) 232–7931. Free parking.

Hours. Tues.–Sun., 10 A.M.–4:30 P.M.

Costs. Adults, $4; ages 13–17, $2; ages 6–12, $1; ages 5 and under, free.

   Palm-tree-lined El Prado and the ornate, Spanish-styled museum build-ing make the ideal location for the city's premier art collection. With bits and pieces ranging from ancient Egypt to contemporary 20th-century art, the Museum's main areas of emphasis are Italian Renaissance painting and sculpture, American painting and sculpture, and French Impressionist painting. The Museum of Art also hosts many important touring exhibits.

Kids' Facilities. No stroller rentals. Diaper-changing tables in ladies' restroom. Bottles warmed at the Sculpture Garden Cafe.

Ratings. There's something here for every age and artistic sensibility. If younger children start to fidget, a quick run through the outdoor sculp-ture garden will pacify them. All ages, A.

SAN DIEGO MUSEUM OF MAN

1350 El Prado, Balboa Park. (619) 239–2001. Free parking.

Hours. Daily, 10 A.M.–4:30 P.M.

Costs. Adults, $3; ages 13–17, $1; ages 6–12, 25¢; ages 5 and under, free.

   A living tribute to the family of man, the museum has large collections of artifacts and folklore items from a cross-section of American Indian tribes, including a Plains Indian tepee and a Hopi Indian adobe house. An exhibit on the evolution of man features life-size mannequins showing the various stages of development of humans. Wednesdays through Sun-days, you can see live demonstrations of weaving and tortilla preparation done in the traditional manner. The *Wonder of Life* exhibit features a frank introduction to the development of the human being from conception to childbirth.

Kids' Facilities. No stroller rentals. Change diapers on bench in ladies' lounge. No restaurants and no bottle-warming facilities.

Ratings. There is something about human biological development that really seems to grab kids and hold their attention, whether it's models of Neanderthal men or modern fetuses. All ages, A.

TIMKEN ART GALLERY

Plaza de Panama and El Prado, Balboa Park. (619) 239–5548. Free parking.

Hours. Tues.–Sat., 10 A.M.–4:30 P.M.; Sun., 1:30 P.M.–4:30 P.M.

Costs. Free.

If the San Diego Museum of Art demands too big a commitment, pop into the Timken, one of the nation's great small art museums. The collection covers a wide range of mediums and styles, from early Renaissance through the 19th century, but their collection of rare Russian icon paintings and master works by Breughel, Copley, and Rembrandt are what make the trip worthwhile.

Kids' Facilities. No stroller rentals. No diaper-changing tables in restrooms (use benches inside or outdoors on El Prado). No bottle-warming facilities.

Ratings. Younger kids may not get the significance of the Russian icons, but most get a kick out of the little critters in Breughel's works. If your kids aren't art fans, you can finish your Timken visit before they realize they've been seeing art. All ages, A.

SAN DIEGO AUTOMOTIVE MUSEUM

Pan American Plaza, Balboa Park. (619) 231–2886. Free parking.

Hours. Daily, 10 A.M.–4 P.M.

Costs. Adults, $3.50; students, $2.50; ages 6–15, $1; ages 5 and under, free.

Opened in late 1988, the exhibits in this 16,000-square-foot museum range from collectible cars to hands-on displays on tires, fuel, and engines. Along with a permanent stable of fifteen historic automobiles (including a replica of an 1886 Benz and the seventeenth 1948 Tucker to roll off the manufacturer's short-lived assembly line), there are also temporary exhibitions of specialty vehicles like high-performance and sports cars. An extensive library contains rare books, catalogs, and repair manuals for cars manufactured between 1916 and 1960. The audio-visual center presents movies and slide shows.

Kids' Facilities. No stroller rentals. Diaper-changing table located in the ladies' restroom. No food or bottle-warming facilities.

Ratings. Americans love their cars, and children from about age 9 count the days until they can get behind the wheel. Leave toddlers at the hotel. 2–7, C; 8–11, A; 12–16, A.

FIREHOUSE MUSEUM

1572 Columbia St., Downtown. (619) 232–3473. Limited street and pay lot parking.

Hours. Thurs.–Sun., 10 A.M.–4 P.M.

Costs. Free (donations accepted).

The olden days of firefighting are highlighted in this refurbished station. On display are large pieces of equipment and turn-of-the-century firefighting artifacts like helmets, axes, hoses, and badges. Our favorite item is the large 1903 Metropolitan Steamer, a water-pumping wagon that used burning coal to activate the pump.

Kids' Facilities. No stroller rentals. No diaper-changing tables in the restrooms. No food or bottle-warming facilities.

Ratings. This old firehouse is small by today's firefighting standards and by today's museum standards. You can see everything in about a half hour. Younger kids tend to be fascinated by all the shiny equipment. All ages, A.

MARITIME MUSEUM

1306 N. Harbor Dr., Downtown. (619) 234–9153. Pay lot parking and limited street parking.

Hours. Daily, 9 A.M.–8 P.M.

Costs. Adults, $5; ages 13–17, $4; ages 6–12, $1.25; ages 5 and under, free. Family rate, $10.

The Maritime Museum consists of three restored vessels moored at two harborside locations 2 blocks apart. The *Star Of India*, a square-rigger of British manufacture, served as a merchant ship after its launching in 1863. Considered the oldest merchant vessel afloat, its laudable accomplishments include twenty trips around the world. It is tied up at the end of Ash Street. A tour of the *Star of India* accesses the captain's quarters and the staterooms used by first-class passengers, as well as the claustrophobic quarters utilized by the crew. The *Berkeley*, an 1898 ferryboat, carried passengers between San Francisco and Oakland, and helped with the evacuation of San Francisco after the 1906 earthquake. The *Medea*, a power yacht constructed in Scotland in 1904, served as a pleasure craft and a working ship during its years of service.

Kids' Facilities. No stroller rentals. No diaper-changing tables. No food or bottle-warming facilities.

Ratings. Older children will appreciate the cramped quarters aboard the *Star*. The younger ones might like the *Star*'s child's cabin, complete with toys and small rocking horse. For those children with short nautical attention spans, confine your visit to the *Star* alone: It's the best. 2–7, B, 8–11, A; 12–16, A.

OLD TOWN SAN DIEGO STATE HISTORICAL PARK

Between Congress, Juan, Wallace and Twiggs Sts., Old Town. (619) 237–6770. Limited street and pay lot parking.

Hours. Daily, 10 A.M.–5 P.M.

Costs. Each museum has its own admission price.

San Diego began in the 6 square blocks adjacent to the Presidio, the seat of the Spanish and Mexican government. Today, the narrow picturesque streets of Old Town are home to restaurants, art galleries, and places of historical interest, many dating back to the first half of the 19th century. Museums include **Cascade Estudillo**, the **Seeley Stables**, the **Historical Museum of California**, the **San Diego Union Museum**, and the **Junipero Serra Museum**.

CASA DE ESTUDILLO AND THE SEELEY STABLES

2656 San Diego Ave. and 2648 Calhoun St. (across the street from one another), Old Town. No phones.

Hours. Daily, 10 A.M.–5 P.M.

Costs. Adults, $1; ages 6–17, 50¢; ages 5 and under, free. Admission price good for both places.

Casa de Estudillo is the restored home of Jose Maria Estudillo, the Mexican commandant of the Presidio, who built it in 1827. It's filled with period furnishings and relics.

The **Seeley Stables** across the street, were built by A. L. Seeley, who owned the stage line that linked San Diego with Los Angeles. The 2-story barn is now a museum displaying antique horse-drawn wagons, stage coaches, and even covered wagons—modes of transport that fascinate most kids. Slide shows are given several times a day.

Kids' Facilities. No stroller rentals. No diaper-changing tables. No food or bottle warming (there are a number of restaurants nearby).

Ratings. Younger kids might like the dolls in Casa de Estudillo's children's room and the floor warmer in the living room that used hot rocks for heating. Most children find the Seeley Stables' carriages, wagons, and collection of 19th-century toys quite interesting. All ages, A.

HISTORICAL MUSEUM OF OLD CALIFORNIA AND SAN DIEGO UNION MUSEUM

2626 San Diego Ave. (next door to one another), Old Town. No phones.

Hours. Tues.–Sun. 10 A.M.–5 P.M.

Costs. Free.

For a glimpse of the city before the civic center shifted from Old Town to the downtown of today, the **Historical Museum** provides paintings and a scale model of 1870 San Diego.

The **San Diego Union Museum** was originally the Casa de Altamirano, the city's first (1851) wooden frame building. In 1868, it was acquired by the San Diego Union, which is still published today. A few years ago, the Union bought the building and restored it as an 1868 newspaper office, complete with period typewriters and an old lead-type printing press.

Kids' Facilities. No strollers. No diaper-changing tables. No food or bottle-warming facilities.

Ratings. They're free, small, and filled with information about early San Diego. All ages, B.

JUNIPERO SERRA MUSEUM

2727 Presidio Dr., Presidio Park, Old Town. (619) 297–3258. Free parking.

Hours. Tues.–Sat., 10 A.M.–4:30 P.M.; Sun., 12 noon–4:30 P.M.

Costs. Adults, $2; ages 12 and under, free.

Situated on a beautiful hill overlooking both Old Town and downtown San Diego, the museum marks the spot upon which Father Junipero founded the first of what would eventually become twenty-one missions throughout California. Construction began on July 16, 1769, and, while the mission itself was later moved (see Mission Alcala under Attractions) Serra's accomplishments are chronicled here in a charming mission-style museum.

Kids' Facilities. No stroller rentals. No diaper-changing tables in restrooms. No food or bottle-warming facilities.

Ratings. There isn't much here for kids any younger than school age; however, the grounds are beautiful. 2–7, C; 8–11, B; 12–16, A.

LA JOLLA MUSEUM OF CONTEMPORARY ART

700 Prospect St., La Jolla. (619) 454–3541. Limited metered street parking.

Hours. Tues.–Sun., 10 A.M.–5 P.M.; Wed. until 9 P.M.; closed the second week of August.

Costs. Adults, $3; students, $1; ages 5–12, 50¢.

Post-1955 American art here means big canvases, modern graphics, geometric abstraction, and pop art. This type of colorful, abstract stuff really catches the eye of younger kids. Combine it with a great view of the Pacific Ocean, La Jolla boutiques, and the fact that you're probably in La Jolla for the Children's Museum of San Diego anyway, and this could be a winner.

Kids' Facilities. No stroller rentals. No diaper-changing tables in restrooms. No food or bottle-warming facilities.

Ratings. Preschool kids really seem to take to abstract art. 2–7, A; 8–11, C; 12–16, A.

CHILDREN'S MUSEUM OF SAN DIEGO

8657 Villa La Jolla Drive, La Jolla. (619) 450–0767. Free parking.

Hours. Sun. and Wed.–Fri., 12 noon–5 P.M.; Sat., 10 A.M.–5 P.M. Closed on Mon. Open Tues. for groups only.

Costs. General admission, $2.75; ages 2 and under, free.

Everything within reach of a child is designed to be prodded, poked, and fingerprinted. Kids can build giant edifices with Lego blocks, get covered with a thin film of soap in the bubble room, and use a working vintage telephone switchboard. A health center contains a real dentist's chair, a hospital nursery, an examination table, and an X-ray machine. A self-images section has a shadow box with light-sensitive paper (when the light flashes, silhouettes remain on the paper), and a real television newsroom with a working video camera. There's a theatrical stage where kids can dress up in costumes, an art studio where children work on painting a mural, and a toddler area where the really small ones can run around. Most impressive is the Handicap Awareness Center: a braille machine, a wheelchair basketball setup, and a sensory wall where sighted children can feel their way along. There's also an exhibit on dyslexia.

Kids' Facilities. No stroller rentals. There are diaper-changing tables in the restrooms. No food or bottle-warming facilities.

Ratings. Even though many children's museums tend to lack activities for kids over the ages of 10 or 11, San Diego's museum rescues them with the mock television studio. Younger children will love it all. 2–7, A; 8–11, A; 12–16, C.

SCRIPPS AQUARIUM AND MUSEUM

8602 La Jolla Shores Dr., La Jolla. (619) 534–6933. Free and metered parking. *(Note: Parents of stroller-bound kids should use the metered aquarium parking lot as a last resort. Drive past the aquarium and try to get a metered space among the diagonal spots near the entrance or a free space on the street in front of the museum. If none are available, double back and hit the lot. Be prepared for a walk, however.)*

Hours. Daily, 9 A.M.–5 P.M.

Costs. Free (donations appreciated).

World famous for its oceanographic institute, Scripps (part of the University of California, San Diego) maintains an aquarium with more than

150 species of fish, lobsters, anemones, and other marine life. Kids prefer the sharks, starfish, and octopus. The outdoor tidal pool is a favorite among older kids. Try to time your visit for Sunday or Wednesday at 1:30 P.M. when the aquarium fish are fed. A new, larger aquarium is planned for 1990.

Kids' Facilities. No stroller rentals. No diaper-changing tables in restrooms. No food or bottle-warming facilities.

Ratings. We expected the biggest aquarium this side of the Pacific and were a bit disappointed to find one of medium size. We suggest a quick visit if you're already in the area for the Children's Museum. 2–7, B; 8–11, B; 12–16, A.

HOTELS

Mission Bay

HILTON BEACH AND TENNIS RESORT

1775 E. Mission Bay Dr., Mission Bay. (619) 276–4010. 354 units. Free parking.

Rates. $110 to $130, depending on the season.

The Hilton has a full-service beach and tennis club with plenty of activities for the kids (during summer), including movies, snacks, and arts and crafts classes. You can rent bicycles and sailboats, take water skiing lessons, learn windsurfing, and play video games. Most units have refrigerators. VCRs can be rented. Kids under 18 stay free in parent's room.
Cribs: Yes, no charge.
Rollaways: Yes, no charge.
Babysitting: Yes, see concierge.
Pool: Yes: large pool, kids' pool, and Jacuzzi.
Restaurant: Yes.
Kitchen facilities: No, but many rooms have refrigerators.
Room service: Yes.
Closest emergency hospital: Scripps Hospital, 10 minutes away, (619) 457–6150.

SAN DIEGO PRINCESS RESORT

1404 W. Vacation Rd., Mission Bay. (619) 274–4630 or (800) 542–6275. 449 units, 160 suites. Free parking.

Rates. $125 (room) to $280 (luxury suite); special package deals can lower rates to $98.

Owned by the "Love Boat" cruise lines, the Princess has special kids' activities during the summer, boats and bicycles for rent, and lots of tennis courts. Children 12 and under stay free in parents' room.
Cribs: Yes, no charge.
Rollaways: Yes, $10.
Babysitting: Yes, concierge referral.
Pool: Yes, five.
Restaurant: Yes, three.
Kitchen facilities: In 160 suites; all rooms have refrigerators.
Room service: Yes.
Closest emergency hospital: Mission Bay Hospital, 10 minutes away, (619) 274–7721.

BEST WESTERN BLUE SEA LODGE HOTEL

707 Pacific Beach Dr., Mission Bay. (619) 483–4700 or (800) 528–1234. 100 units. Free parking.

Rates. $120 to $140.

With the Pacific Ocean at your front door and Mission Bay at your back, the Blue Sea Lodge is a beautiful spot. The hotel offers free continental breakfast. Kids under 18 stay free in parents' room.
Cribs: Yes, no charge.
Rollaways: Yes, $15.
Babysitting: No.
Pool: Yes.
Restaurant: No, but there's one next door.
Kitchen facilities: Yes, in forty-eight of the 100 units.
Room service: No.
Closest emergency hospital: Mission Bay Hospital, 10 minutes away, (619) 274–7721.

Old Town

BEST WESTERN HACIENDA OLD TOWN ALL-SUITES

4041 Harney St., Old Town. (619) 298–4707 or (800) 528–1234. 152 units. Pay parking lot.

Rates. $90 to $110.

This all-suites hotel is within a few blocks of the Old Town historic

buildings and the Victorian houses of Heritage Park, and a short walk from Presidio Park. Kids under 16 stay free in parents' room.
Cribs: Yes, no charge.
Rollaways: Yes, $10.
Babysitting: No.
Pool: Yes, plus spa and gym.
Restaurant: Yes, two.
Kitchen facilities: Yes.
Room service: Yes.
Closest emergency hospital: Mercy Hospital, 10 minutes away, (619) 260–7000.

La Jolla

EMBASSY SUITES HOTEL—LA JOLLA

4550 La Jolla Village Dr., La Jolla. (619) 453–0400. 335 units Free parking.

Rates. $134 (with special weekend rates available).

Part of the excellent Embassy chain. All units are 1- and 2-bedroom suites. It's located about 3 miles east of the beach, and there's an ice rink in the shopping mall across the street. Kids under 12 stay free with parents.
Cribs: Yes, no charge.
Rollaways: No.
Babysitting: Yes, referrals.
Pool: Yes: large pool, kids' pool, and jacuzzi.
Restaurant: Yes (free breakfast plus evening happy hour)
Kitchen facilities: Yes.
Room service: Yes.
Closest emergency hospital: Scripps Hospital, 15 minutes away, (619) 457–6150.

RESTAURANTS

All the national and regional fast-food chain restaurants are represented here, including a number of Chuck E. Cheese Pizza Time Theaters where kids can eat pizza, listen to loud music played by Audio-Animatronic characters, and play video games. There are a few special restaurants for kids:

SAMPSON'S DELI

8861 Via La Jolla Dr., La Jolla. (619) 455–1461. Free parking.

Hours. Sun.–Thurs., 7 A.M.–11 P.M.; Fri. and Sat., 7 A.M.–12 midnight.

On Sunday nights half the restaurant is reserved especially for families. There's music, people dressed up as oversized cartoon characters like Big Bird and Cookie Monster, games, prizes, and even a clown or two. It's more fun than tongue on rye. Sampson's is reasonably priced: A family of four can get away for less than $25. Credit cards.

Kids' Facilities. They have high chairs and booster seats. No special children's menu but you can order a smaller portion (a half sandwich) at a lower price. No diaper-changing tables in restrooms.

HAMBURGUESA

4016 Wallace St., Old Town. (619) 295–0584. Lots of free parking.

Hours. Mon.–Thurs., 11 A.M.–10 P.M.; Fri. and Sat., 10 A.M.–10 P.M.; Sun., 9 A.M.–10 P.M.

Located in historic Old Town, Hispanic-flavored Hamburguesa serves indoors or on the Mexican patio. Since most southern Californians love the quesadilla (an exotic-sounding Mexican equivalent of the grilled cheese sandwich), it's no wonder that the restaurant's Hamburguesadilla is an all-time best seller. A separate kids' menu offers meals for around $2.75 and specially mixed children's fruit drinks. Meals for adults are in the $4 to $7 range. Credit cards.

Kids' Facilities. High chairs and booster seats are available. No diaper-changing tables in the restrooms.

RUEBEN E. LEE

880 E. Harbor Island Dr. (619) 291–1974. Free parking.

Hours. *Lunch:* Sun.–Fri., 11:30 A.M.–2 P.M.; Sat., 11:30 A.M.–3 P.M. *Dinner:* Sun.–Thurs., 4:30 P.M.–10 P.M.; Fri. and Sat., 4:30 P.M.–11 P.M. *Brunch:* Sun., 10 A.M.–2 P.M.

For dinner aboard a Mississippi River steamboat, Rueben's is the next best thing to New Orleans. Landlubbers rejoice: The boat is stationary. Along with authentic decor, there's a good children's menu, with entrees priced from $4.95 to $5.95. Reservations recommended. Most credit cards.

Kids' Facilities. High chairs and boosters seats are available. No diaper-changing tables in the restrooms.

BOBBIE MCGEE'S

5500 Grossmont Center Dr., La Mesa. (619) 589–0444. Free parking.

Hours. Mon.–Thurs., 5 P.M.–10 P.M.; Fri., 5 P.M.–10:30 P.M.; Sat., 4:30 P.M.–10:30 P.M.; Sun., 4:30 P.M.–9:30 P.M.

La Mesa is a good 10 miles east of downtown San Diego, but the costumed staff here makes it worth the drive. The costumes are as easily identifiable as Zorro or Snow White or as outrageous as an employee's own sartorial tastes. It all makes for a good, colorful time. The children's menu has kids' favorites that cost a maximum of $4.95. Reservations suggested. Credit cards.

Kids' Facilities. High chairs and booster seats are available. No diaper-changing tables in restrooms.

OLD SPAGHETTI FACTORY

275 Fifth Ave., Downtown. (619) 233-4323. Limited parking.

Hours. Mon.–Thurs., 5 P.M.–10 P.M.; Fri. and Sat., 5 P.M.–11 P.M.; Sun., 4 P.M.–10 P.M.

Part of a regional chain, the Spaghetti Factory is large, Victorian, and dirt cheap. Served quickly, the food is simple and much more wholesome than burgers and fries. The one-item children's menu offers spaghetti and red sauce for $2.95. No credit cards.

Kids' Facilities. Plenty of booster seats and high chairs. No diaper-changing facilities; however, there are plenty of sofas and benches.

Big Splurges

PEOHE'S

1201 First St., Coronado. (619) 437–4474. Free parking.

Hours. *Lunch:* Mon.–Sat., 11:30 A.M.–2:30 P.M. *Dinner:* Sun.–Thurs., 5 P.M.–10 P.M.; Fri. and Sat., 5 P.M.–11 P.M. *Brunch:* Sun., 10:30 A.M.–2 P.M.

Owned by the Chart House, a West Coast purveyor of the four S's—steak, seafood, salad, and sourdough bread—Peohe's hits the mark in both romance and cuisine. The decor is tastefully Hawaiian, with dim lighting and a cornucopia of real plants. There's even an outdoor dining area. The menu offers chicken and seafood, with specials from a changing menu of freshly caught Pacific fish. Dinner for two with wine runs costs about $70. Full bar. Credit cards.

THE MARINE ROOM

2000 Spindrift Dr., La Jolla. (619) 459–7222. Free parking.

Hours. *Lunch:* Mon.–Sat., 11:30 A.M.–2:30 P.M. *Dinner:* daily, 6 P.M.–10 P.M. *Brunch:* Sun., 10:30 A.M.–2:30 P.M.

The Marine Room offers a spectacular view of the Pacific Ocean: You're so close to the water that the waves actually break under the restaurant. The menu, while quite acceptable, is secondary to the setting. Fresh seafood is the mainstay, and the selection is comprehensive. Dinner for two with wine costs around $75 to $80. Full bar. Reservations are essential. Credit cards.

SHOPPING

SEAPORT VILLAGE

Harbor Dr. and Pacific Hwy., Downtown. (619) 235–4013. Free parking.

Hours. Daily, 10 A.M.–9 P.M.; restaurants have extended hours.

Seaport Village is made up of three separate but integrated villages: Spanish San Diego, an old New England fishing village, and Victorian England. Each is pleasing to the eye and provides respite from the hustle of downtown. There are fifteen restaurants and sixty-five specialty shops.

For kids, Seaport Village's most notable store is the **Seaport Kite Shop,** (619) 232–2268. If you can't wait to try out a new kite, the shopping area's harborside walkaway provides a perfect opportunity. Management also will be happy to provide a list of the best San Diego locales for kite flying. Video monitors demonstrate the various types of kites available, and free instructions come with every kite purchase.

HORTON PLAZA

Fourth Ave. and G St., Downtown. (619) 239–8180. Three hours free parking.

Hours. Mon.–Fri., 10 A.M.–9 P.M.; Sat., 10 A.M.–6 P.M.; Sun., 11 A.M.–6 P.M.; restaurants and movie theaters open longer.

The plaza is named for Alonzo Horton, the entrepreneur who conceived of moving San Diego's business and governmental core from Old Town to the waterfront in the 1860s. With four major department stores and more than 150 restaurants and specialty shops, this colorful hodgepodge of architectural styles is a favorite of both local and visiting shoppers.

The neatest shop in Horton Plaza is **Imaginarium**, (619) 237–0122, a great little toy store. It's not so much the merchandise (Brio and Lego building sets, puzzles, games, and expensive stuffed animals) as it is the presentation. Young kids enter through a separate, smaller door. There's a video screen showing children's movies, a long table with low stools for coloring and crafts, dress-up costumes, a computer area, an area for kids to give their own puppet shows, and a regular storytime when employees read books to young shoppers.

Brentanos, (619) 236–0849, and **Doubleday**, (619) 696–9616, are large bookstores that offer plenty of browsing space. **B. Dalton's Software, Etc.**, (619) 235–4327, is a great place to occupy school-age hackers. There are a number of computers up and running, some with game software. **FutureTronics**, (619) 238–0479, favors educational gizmos and gadgets. **The Price of His Toys**, (619) 696–0511, has more wild, wacky playthings and electronic toys.

GEPETTO'S—A CHILD'S FANTASY

Two locations: Bazaar del Mundo, 2754 Calhoun St., Old Town, (619) 291–4606, limited street parking. University Town Center Mall, 4545 La Jolla Village Dr., La Jolla, (619) 457–3401, free parking.

Hours. Old Town: daily, 10 A.M.–9 P.M. La Jolla: Mon.–Fri., 10 A.M.–9 P.M.; Sat., 10 A.M.–6 P.M.; Sun., 12 noon–5 P.M.

Gepetto's offers a great selection of imported toys. Most impressive is their collection of hand puppets. They also offer a good selection of imported cotton clothing for children from infancy through size 4-T. Their book department includes titles for kids from the toddler stage through junior high school. Like most good toy stores, the management isn't shy about letting kids play with floor samples.

THINKER THINGS

Two locations: Wall Street Plaza, 7863 Girard, La Jolla, (619) 454–0725, metered street parking. 2670 Via de la Valle, Del Mar, (619) 755–4488, free parking.

Hours. Mon.–Sat., 10 A.M.–6 P.M.; Sun., 11 A.M.–5 P.M.

The classic noncommercial toy store, Thinker Things has a good selection of old standbys like Lego and Brio building sets, imported dolls, science experiments, audio cassettes, puzzles, and arts and crafts supplies. They also have a good selection of books for all ages of juvenile readers.

TRANSPORTATION

BUSES AND TROLLEYS

San Diego Light Rail Transit (**LRT**)—the Tijuana Trolley—runs from the Amtrak depot on the west side of downtown to San Ysidro, 15 miles south, the gateway to Tijuana. Trolley cars operate daily between 5 A.M. and 1 A.M., making frequent stops along the way. A newer second line that takes passengers from the Amtrak station south and east to Euclid Avenue runs between 5 A.M. and 10 P.M. Fares range from 50¢ to $1.50 depending on the length of the trip. Kids love the old-fashioned red cars. For more information: (619) 231–1466.

San Diego Transit Corporation operates buses in the city and many of the outlying areas. The base fare is $1. For information and bus schedules, visit the Transit Store, Broadway and 5th Avenue, or call (619) 233–3004.

FERRY

The San Diego–Coronado Ferry runs 15-minute boat trips between the dock at Harbor Drive and Broadway in downtown San Diego to the Old Ferry Landing across San Diego Bay in Coronado at B Avenue and 1st Street. Boats leave every half hour between 10 A.M. and 10 P.M., Sunday through Thursday, and from 10 A.M. to 11 P.M. on Friday and Saturday. The fare each way is $1 with all-day passes priced at $4. For more information: (619) 233–6872.

TAXIS

Considering the vast distances between points of interest in San Diego, taxis can be expensive. Most companies charge about $2.40 for the first mile and between $1.20 and $1.40 for each additional mile. Hailing taxis is an exercise in futility. You should call them on the phone. Companies include USA, (619) 231–1144; Co-Op, (619) 280–5555; Checker, (619) 234–4477; and Yellow, (619) 234–6161.

TOURS

BUS

Gray Line. (619) 231–9922. Offers fifteen tour packages of San Diego, some including Los Angeles and Tijuana. The most popular is the half-day tour of San Diego that departs most major hotels at 9 A.M. and 2 P.M. (adults, $19; ages 3–11, $11; ages 2 and under, free). Their most popular full-day trip includes a harbor boat ride and a stop across the Mexican border in Tijuana; it departs daily at 9 A.M. (adults, $36; ages 3–11, $21).

El Paseo Tours. (619) 585–7495. Runs regular trips, with a Mexican flavor, to Tijuana and Ensenada, a seaport town about 75 miles to the south.

BOAT

San Diego Harbor Excursions. (619) 234–4111. Located at the downtown dock at Broadway and Harbor Drive, the company features two popular harbor excursions: a 1-hour, 12-mile trip (adults, $7.70; ages 3–11, $3.85; ages 2 and under, free), and a 2-hour, 25-mile ride (adults, $11; ages 3–11, $5.50; ages 2 and under, free). Call ahead for departure times, as they vary from season to season. They also have dinner cruises.

Invader Cruises. (619) 234–8687. Gives you a choice of a schooner, a motor yacht, or a sternwheeler for their 1- and 2-hour sightseeing excursions on San Diego Bay. The 1-hour trip costs $7 for adults and $3.50 for kids between 3 and 12; kids under 3 are free. The 2-hour trip is $10 for adults and $5 for children between the ages of 3 and 12; kids 2 and under are free. Call for excursion times.

DRIVING

The 52-mile Scenic Drive begins at the foot of Broadway at the downtown waterfront, but you can start anywhere along the route. Just follow the blue and yellow seagull signs, and you'll pass historic areas like the Embarcadero, Old Town, Point Loma, La Jolla, Balboa Park, and Mission Bay. The whole excursion takes about 4 hours, if you stop only for ice cream and bathroom breaks. Take the drive early in your visit to learn the city and plan out the rest of your vacation's itinerary.

SEASONAL EVENTS

January

WHALE WATCHING

One of the best activities for kids over 7 is keeping an eye out for California gray whales migrating from the Gulf of Alaska to their winter calving waters off Baja California between mid-December and February. Whale watching can be done from the land on the Point Loma high ground at Cabrillo National Monument, (619) 557–5450, or aboard ships a few miles off the coast. A number of excursion services offer whale watching, including the *Red Witch*, (619) 542–0646, a 72-foot-long sailing ship that makes 2 ½-hour trips from the Sheraton Harbor Hotel dock on Harbor Island.

March

OCEAN BEACH KITE FESTIVAL

Ocean Beach, just across the San Diego River from Mission Bay, is the location for this annual early-March event, which includes a parade, kite building, and kite flying competitions. For more information: (619) 223–1175.

ST. PATRICK'S DAY

San Diego celebrates the holiday in Balboa Park with dancing, music, a big parade, and an Irish Festival. For more information: (619) 299–7812.

April

DAY OF THE CHILD

Balboa Park is the site of this yearly event, usually on the first Saturday in April. Aimed at kids between ages 2 and 8, activities include face painting, storytelling, and art projects of every stripe.

May

CINCO DE MAYO

Cinco de Mayo (May 5), which commemorates the 1862 victory of Mexico over the French at the battle of Puebla, is a national holiday in Mexico and a big day in United States cities with sizable Mexican populations. San Diego's 2-day festival at Old Town State Park includes music, entertainment, arts and crafts demonstrations, and Mexican food. For more information: (619) 296–3161.

July

SOUTHERN CALIFORNIA EXPOSITION

The Del Mar Fairgrounds, site of the famed racetrack, hosts a terrific annual fair that begins July 4 and lasts two weeks. There is a carnival midway, hobby exhibits, fireworks, and concerts: something for everyone. For more information: (619) 755–1161.

U. S. OPEN SANDCASTLE COMPETITION

Exact dates vary, but the main activity remains the same: Imperial Beach, just south of the city, becomes the temporary site of some of the world's largest and most ornate sandcastles. For more information: (619) 423–8300.

September

THUNDERTUB REGATTA

This regatta is for customized sailing bathtubs, where the idea is to keep the water on the outside of the tub. Some succeed, others fail, but everyone has a good time. Viewing is free and great fun at beautiful Crown Point Shores on Mission Bay. For more information: (619) 232–1289.

October

OKTOBERFEST

There's old-fashioned *gemutlichkeit*, bratwurst, beer, and oompah band music at the annual event in downtown La Mesa. For more information: (619) 465–7000.

December

CHRISTMAS ON THE PRADO

Held on two successive nights in early December, Christmas on the Prado is Balboa Park's Christmas present to the kids of the city. The whole park is transformed into a winter wonderland (sans snow, of course). Museums and attractions offer lower-priced or free admissions, and there's all sorts of food, music, entertainment, and Santa and his elves. Arrive early to get a good parking space. For more information: (619) 239–2001.

CHILDREN'S THEATER

MARIE HITCHCOCK PUPPET THEATER

Palisades area of Pan-American Plaza in Balboa Park. (619) 466–7128. Free parking.

Marie Hitchcock and the San Diego Puppet Guild have been putting on puppet shows for the children of San Diego since 1948. Reasonably priced shows (adults, $1.50; children, $1) are presented Fridays at 10:30 A.M. and Saturdays and Sundays at 11 A.M., 1 P.M. and 2:30 P.M. The ever-changing programs are a delight for younger kids.

BABYSITTING SERVICES

SITTER SERVICE
(619) 281–7755

In business since 1946, Sitter Service can provide same-day sitters (though they'd like 24-hour's notice) at most major hotels in the greater San Diego area. Depending on location, there is a minimum 3-hour charge of between $18.50 and $20.50, plus $4 for each additional hour. This rate applies to one or two children; each additional child adds $1.50 to the minimum rate and 25¢ per hour. They do not charge a transportation fee. Sitters are licensed and bonded.

RELIABLE BABY SITTING AGENCY
(619) 296–0856

In business since 1965, Reliable hires only adult sitters (no teenagers). They charge a minimum rate of $18.50 for the first 3 hours for one or two children, plus $4 for each hour over the minimum. For three or four children from the same family, the 3-hour minimum is $20, plus $4 for each hour over the minimum. For children from two families, the rate is $24 for the first 3 hours, plus $4.50 for each additional hour.

PUBLICATIONS

San Diego Union and San Diego Tribune. Daily newspapers; both publish calendars of events on Friday; Wednesday *Tribune* has a kids' page.

Los Angeles Times San Diego Edition. Daily newspaper; activities calendar in Thursday "View" section; Friday "Calendar" lists entertainment options.

San Diego Family Press. Monthly calendars of events for parents and small children in the city; advertisers include the better toy and bookstores in San Diego; distributed free at children's book and clothing stores.

LOCAL TELEPHONE NUMBERS

Late-hours pharmacy: University City Pharmacy, 3338 Governor Dr., (619) 293–3397. Open Mon.–Fri., 9 A.M.–9 P.M.; Sat., 9 A.M.–8 P.M.; Sun., 10 A.M.–7 P.M.

Consumer complaints: General number (California lists complaint numbers by business), (213) 620–4360.

Dental referral: Dental Society of San Diego, (619) 223–5391.

Physician referral: (619) 696–9781.

Lawyer referral: County Bar Association, (619) 231–0781.

Drug-abuse hotline: (619) 236–3339 or (800) 351–0757.

Poison-control hotline: (619) 543–6000.

Traveler's aid: (619) 232–7991.

Tourism office: (619) 232–3101.

Police: 911.

Fire: 911.

Ambulance: 911.

Weather: (619) 289–1212.

Local car rentals: Courtesy, (619) 232–3191.

SAN FRANCISCO

If you ask a San Franciscan to name the most urbane, the most cultured, the most civilized, the greatest city on the West Coast (okay, the world!), chances are around 100 percent that the answer will be San Francisco. From the mayor to the man on the street, San Francisco isn't just the city, it's "The City." This attitude can be maddening enough to make you want to bludgeon an arrogant San Franciscan with a freshly baked loaf of sourdough bread. Of course, not only would that be a waste of great bread, but a gross injustice: San Francisco is easily one of the most beautiful cities in North America.

Home to steep, narrow streets, breathtaking hills, and more than 13,500 Victorian "painted ladies" (colorfully decorated turn-of-the-century homes) San Francisco provides intriguing photo opportunities at every turn. It's also a city of famous restaurants, user-friendly parks and green spaces, and some of the more interesting museums and historical attractions on the West Coast. A major part of any trip to San Francisco is an opportunity to take plenty of boat rides (San Francisco Bay consists of 435 square miles of water) and more than a few riding and walking trips across the four major bridges that connect San Francisco to the rest of California.

Looking a little like an unmanicured nail at the tip of an index finger, San Francisco occupies the peninsula that separates San Francisco Bay from the Pacific Ocean and is profoundly affected by the surrounding water. The cliffs on the west side were caused by the constant battering of Pacific waves, while the piers, landings, and harbors on the bay side were created by founding fathers who derived economic power from tapping into the vast resources of the sea.

For centuries the Bay Area, the local name for the land around San Francisco Bay, was home to the Modoc Indians. The beginning of the end of the Modoc's hold on the land dates back to September 17, 1776, when Spanish troops established a *presidio*, or fort, overlooking the entrance to San Francisco Bay. While both the Spanish and later the

277

Mexicans garrisoned troops in San Francisco, a real city with civilian rule, private enterprise, and local graft didn't emerge until the United States expelled the Mexican authorities in 1846 during the Mexican War.

After the discovery of gold in the hills east of Sacramento in 1848, the city began to grow. The Gold Rush made this small western outpost the fastest-growing city in the world, populated by treasure hunters from every corner of the planet. In March 1848, the population of San Francisco (still sometimes called by it's original name, Yerba Buena) was at a paltry 812; by 1850, it was 25,000.

While many of San Francisco's permanent residents dropped everything to go for the gold, crafty entrepreneurs found that the real money was to be made right in town outfitting would-be miners. That's how denim king Levi Strauss got started in a business that would later revolutionize fashion. The Gold Rush also established the port of San Francisco, one of the world's finest natural harbors.

San Francisco's boomtown image remained for decades as the city grew in both population and commercial promise. In the 1860s and 1870s, the railroads connected the West Coast with the rest of the country, providing outlets for Pacific seafood and produce from California's San Joaquin Valley. San Francisco's big businessmen imported culture, and with culture eventually came social acceptance. By the turn of the century, San Francisco had become the cultural center of the West Coast, with

---

FREEBIES AND CHEAPIES
(Free or $3.50 and under for adults)

- ❑ Fort Point National Historic Site (see Attractions)
- ❑ Presidio Army Museum (see Museums)
- ❑ Hyde Street Pier Ships (see Museums)
- ❑ National Maritime Museum (see Museums)
- ❑ Josephine D. Randall Junior Museum (see Museums)
- ❑ Old U.S. Mint (see Attractions)
- ❑ San Francisco Museum of Modern Art (see Museums)
- ❑ San Francisco Crafts and Folk Art Museum (see Museums)
- ❑ Cable Car Museum (see Museums)
- ❑ Museum of Modern Mythology (see Museums)
- ❑ San Francisco International Toy Museum (see Museums)
- ❑ Bay Area Discovery Museum (see Museums)
- ❑ Wells Fargo History Museum (see Museums)
- ❑ Golden Gate Park (see Attractions)
- ❑ San Francisco Experience Theatre (see Attractions)

opera, theater, and fine homes sprouting on the hills just above immigrant hovels, brothels, and bars.

Today, San Francisco has a cornucopia of museums, attractions, and diversions that meet the standards of even the most finicky kid. And in case you think that all this may sound too highbrow, rest assured that there are plenty of opportunities to buy fast food and a few attractions that are purely commercial and just plain fun.

CLIMATE

San Francisco has a reputation for inclement weather but that may depend on what you mean by inclement. If you like warm, sunny days in July and chilly, overcast skies in January, San Francisco may not be for you, since the weather takes its cue from the southern hemisphere. That's because San Francisco juts out farther into the cold Pacific than any other area on the West Coast. In the summer, when California's central valley

---

THE LONG WEEKEND

Day One

☐ San Francisco Experience Theatre (see Attractions)
☐ Alcatraz Island (see Attractions)
☐ The *Balclutha* (see Attractions)
☐ The U.S.S. *Pampanito* (see Attractions)
☐ Ripley's Believe It or Not Museum (see Museums)
☐ National Maritime Museum (see Museums)
☐ Hyde Street Pier Ships (see Museums)

Day Two

☐ Fort Point National Historic Site (see Attractions)
☐ Presidio Army Museum (see Museums)
☐ The *Jeremiah O'Brien* (see Attractions)
☐ Exploratorium (see Attractions)

Day Three

☐ Cliff House (see Restaurants)
☐ M. H. De Young Museum (see Museums)
☐ California Academy of Sciences (see Attractions)
☐ San Francisco Zoo (see Attractions)

---

regularly experiences temperatures in the 90s, San Francisco is cold and foggy. When the summer finally warms up the ocean by late September, the fog loosens its grip and temperatures rise. This phenomenon makes San Francisco warm and sunny from September through November and, except for brief winter rainstorms, makes November through May extremely tolerable, as well.

During the summer when Oakland and most of the territory to the east of San Francisco Bay are in the 80s and 90s, San Francisco is seldom much above a cloudy 65 degrees during the day, with lows in the 50s at night. In fall and spring, expect sunny daytime highs in the upper 60s and low 70s and lows in the 50s. In winter, expect sunny-to-partly-cloudy days in the high 50s or low 60s and nights in the 40s. However, since much of the city's 20 annual inches of rain fall in the winter, pack an umbrella between November and March. Take a jacket whenever you visit.

TOURIST INFORMATION

Contact the San Francisco Convention and Visitors Bureau, P.O. Box 6977, San Francisco CA 94101, (415) 974–6900. The Visitors Information Center is located on the lower level of Hallidie Plaza, 900 Market St., San Francisco, (415) 391–2000.

ATTRACTIONS

GOLDEN GATE PARK

Bordered by the Pacific Ocean on the west, Fulton St. on the north, Lincoln Way on the south, and Stanyan St. on the east. (415) 221–1311. Free parking.

Hours. Sunrise to sunset.

Costs. Free.

Golden Gate Park is one of America's great urban American green spaces. More than 1,000 square acres in size, Golden Gate contains the **De Young** and **Asian Art Museums** (see Museums), the **California Academy of Sciences**, two Dutch-style windmills, a myriad of playing fields, an arboretum, a garden conservatory, and even a fly-casting pool. Its proximity to the Haight-Ashbury district made the park a natural choice for love-ins and be-ins in the 1960s and it is still possible to spot an occasional fugitive from that era. On Sundays the main drag, John F. Kennedy Drive, is closed to automobile traffic.

THE CALIFORNIA ACADEMY OF SCIENCES

John F. Kennedy Dr. (415) 750–7145. Free parking.

Hours. July 4 through Labor Day: daily, 10 A.M.–7 P.M.; rest of the year: daily, 10 A.M.–5 P.M.

Costs. Adults, $4; ages 12–17, $2; ages 6–11, $1; ages 5 and under, free.

San Francisco's best-known science center has been in its present location since 1916. Not only is it home to natural science exhibits (such as dinosaurs, minerals, insects and interactive video offerings on California wildlife), the Academy also encompasses the Steinhart Aquarium (fish, a tidal pool, penguins, dolphins, and sea otters), the Morrison Planetarium (astronomy and Laserium shows), and the Junior Academy of Science Discovery Room (hands-on science demonstrations for younger kids).

Hours for planetarium shows vary and the Junior Academy has restricted hours: Tues.–Fri., 1 P.M.–4 P.M.; Sat.–Sun., 11 A.M.–3:30 P.M.

Kids' Facilities. No stroller rentals. No changing tables, but plenty of benches. Bottles can be warmed in the Jungle Cafe on the lower level; sandwiches, burgers, and hot dogs are served there.

Ratings. The Academy provides something for every member of the family. All ages, A.

EXPLORATORIUM

360 Lyon Street. (415) 563–7337. Limited free lot; metered and free street parking.

Hours. July 4 through Labor Day: Wed., 11 A.M.–9:30 P.M.; Thurs, and Fri., 11 A.M.–5 P.M.; Sat. and Sun., 10 A.M.–5 P.M. Labor Day through July 4: Wed., 1 P.M.–9:30 P.M.; Thurs. and Fri., 1 P.M.–5 P.M.; Sat. and Sun., 10 A.M.–5 P.M. Closed on Mon. and Tues.

Costs. Adults, $4.50; ages 6–17, $1; ages 5 and under, free. Free all day on the first Wed. of the month, and every Wed. from 6 P.M. to 9:30 P.M. Each ticket is good for unlimited free repeat visits over the following six months.

Seldom is science this much fun. Housed warehouse-style in the only remaining building from the 1915 Pan-Pacific Exposition, the Exploratorium offers more than 600 hands-on exhibits from nearly every segment of the science spectrum. You can play with lasers, experience optical illusions, move a 400-pound pendulum with a tiny magnet, boil water with friction, and create a tornado. You can also play musical instruments in a soundproof chamber or enter a pitch-black, crawl-through Tactile Dome where you're forced to rely only on your senses of smell and touch (additional fee and advance reservations needed for the Tactile Dome).

Kids' Facilities. No stroller rentals and no bottle-warming facilities (although you can get fast food at the refreshment area). Diaper-changing table located in the ladies' restroom. There are plenty of benches and sofas in the Exploratorium's first-aid center.

Ratings. If you do nothing else in San Francisco with your kids, this is the place. All ages, A.

LAWRENCE HALL OF SCIENCE

Centennial Dr. at Grizzly Peak Blvd., Berkeley. (415) 642–5133. Free parking.

Hours. Mon.–Sat., 10 A.M.–4:30 P.M.; Sun., 12 noon–4:30 P.M.

Costs. Weekdays: general admission, $1.25; under age 7, free. Weekends: adults, $2.50; ages 7–18, $1.50; under age 7, free.

Lawrence Hall, the University of California at Berkeley's public science center, has a large selection of hands-on experiments for kids, including computers, chemistry, and physics. Make your own kaleidoscope or view yourself on a video screen and change the on-screen colors by playing music on a keyboard. There are also two science labs where kids can perform static electricity experiments and handle animals. Toddlers love the Audio-Animatronic dinosaur just outside the gift shop. Lawrence Hall is also home to the Holt Planetarium, where three 1-hour shows are given on the weekends (extra admission fee of $1.50).

Kids' Facilities. Get bottles warmed at the cafeteria (fast food). No stroller rentals. Diaper-changing table in the ladies' restroom. Dads can use benches located throughout the museum.

Ratings. While the exhibits here are not as wide-ranging as those at the Exploratorium, it is well worth the drive from San Francisco—especially on Monday and Tuesday when the Exploratorium is closed. 2–7, B; 8–11, A; 12–16, A.

MARINE WORLD AFRICA USA

Interstate 80 and Marine World Pkwy. (State Hwy. 37), Vallejo. (707) 644–4000 or (707) 643–ORCA.

You can either drive to Vallejo or take a Red and White Ferry from San Francisco's Pier 41. The boat trip takes about an hour, during the week departing San Francisco at 8:45 A.M. and leaving Vallejo at 3:40 P.M. On weekends, boats leave San Francisco at 8:30 A.M. and 11:15 A.M., and Vallejo at 3:30 P.M. and 6:30 P.M. The package price for trip and admission: adults, $28.95; ages 4–12, $18.95; ages 3 and under, free.

Hours. Easter through Memorial Day: Wed.–Sun., 9:30 A.M.–5 P.M. Memorial Day to Labor Day: daily, 9:30 A.M.–7 P.M. Labor Day to November: Wed.–Sun., 9:30 A.M.–5 P.M. November to Easter: Sat. and Sun., 9:30 A.M.–5 P.M. Open some school holidays during off-peak seasons.

Costs. Adults, $14.95; ages 4–12, $9.95; ages 3 and under, free.

Sort of a combination African animal zoo/marine mammal research facility/theme fun park, Marine World's forte is live theater presentations involving the Noah's Ark of animals that reside at the facility. In a single jam-packed day, visitors can see animals in their native habitats and watch as cheetahs, elephants, primates, tigers, birds of prey, killer whales, dolphins, and barefoot water skiers are put through their paces. (*Note: Be careful where you sit at the water shows. There is a terrific amount of oversplash in the front rows.*)

Along with the shows, there's also a games arcade, plenty of animal training demonstrations, elephant and camel rides, a decent tropical aquarium, and a special play area for small children. There are plenty of gift shops and restaurants, or you can bring a picnic lunch. A first-class first-aid station is manned by paramedics and a concession rents video cassette cameras.

Kids' Facilities. Two types of strollers are rented at the main entrance: regular strollers for $3 per day and seal-shaped strollers for $4. There are diaper-changing tables in both men's and ladies' restrooms, and most food services have microwaves and would be glad to warm formula bottles for you.

Ratings. The only major theme park in the San Francisco area, it is therefore a *must* excursion that children really enjoy. 2–7, A; 8–11, A; 12–16, B.

SAN FRANCISCO ZOO

Sloat Blvd. and 45th Ave. at the Pacific Ocean. (415) 661–2023. Free parking.

Hours. Daily, 10 A.M.–5 P.M.

Costs. Adults, $4; ages 16 and under, free when accompanied by an adult paying full admission.

This attractive, well-designed zoo has more than 1,000 species of animals and innovative attractions like a state-of-the-art primate house and a koala bear exhibit complete with Australian eucalyptus trees. There is also a popular children's zoo (separate admission $1 for everyone over age 2), a carousel (75¢ per ride), a 20-minute zoo train ride (adults, $2; kids 2–17, $1; under age 2, free), and an insect zoo. Bundle up when visiting here. (Note: *If you plan to see the children's zoo, get there early. The kid's zoo has special hours: Winter: weekdays, 11 A.M.–4 P.M.; weekends, 10:30 A.m.–4:30 P.m. Summer: daily, 10:30 A.m.–4:30 P.m. The lines get long as the day progresses.*)

Kids' Facilities. Strollers are rented at a rate of $2 per day, with a $20 deposit. Diapers can be changed on benches outside the restrooms. There are a number of restaurants at which a bottle can be warmed.

Ratings. A good, all-around zoo. All ages, A.

ALCATRAZ ISLAND

San Francisco Bay. (415) 546–2896. Accessible only by Red and White Ferry, Pier 41, Fisherman's Wharf.

Hours. Summer: nine daily departures every hour from 8:15 A.M. Rest of the year: seven daily departures from 8:45 A.M.

Costs. Adults, $4.50 ($6.50 with audio tape tour rental); ages 5–11, $2.75 ($4.25 with tape); ages 4 and under, free.

The "Rock," as it was known between 1934 and 1963 when it served as a maximum security federal prison, began as a United States Army garrison in the 1870s and was commandeered by a group of protesting American Indians in the early 1970s. Today, it's possible to tour some of the island's prison facilities, from the cellblocks to the infirmary, and imagine what life was like for criminals like Al Capone, Machine Gun Kelly, or Robert Stroud, the Birdman of Alcatraz. There are park rangers to answer your questions, but you're left pretty much on your own to climb the steep hills and walk through the cold, damp cellblocks. (*Note: During the summer months, order your tickets a couple of weeks in advance. You can do so through Ticketron.*)

Kids' Facilities. The only restrooms are at the boat dock and on the boat itself. No diaper-changing facilities on the island, but the boats have tables in the ladies' restroom. No food service on the island, but the boats have snack bars and microwave ovens to warm bottles. No stroller rentals on the island. *(Note: Dress for chilly weather.)*

Ratings. Except for touring the facilities and taking in a lot of history, there is nothing to do on the island. Therefore, kids under the age of 7 could easily get bored. 2–7, D; 8–11, B; 12–16, A.

FORT POINT NATIONAL HISTORIC SITE

At the foot of Marine Dr. and San Francisco Bay. (415) 556–1693. Free parking.

Hours. Daily, 10 A.M.–5 P.M.

Costs. Free.

Built by United States Army engineers between 1853 and 1861, Fort Point was designed to prevent a hostile fleet from sailing into San Francisco Bay. With 5- to 12-foot-thick walls well able to withstand anything a 19th-century enemy could throw at it, the fort was engineered to hold 126 cannon and 600 men. Luckily, the fort's firepower was never tested—it never fired a shot in anger—and the real value of Fort Point today is as a repository of history. Docents dressed in Civil War Union uniforms happily guide tourists through the powder magazine, past the cannon, and into the barracks where soldiers awaited the war that never came. Kids will get a kick out of exploring all the nooks, crannies, and cubbyholes of the old building. *(Note: These old masonry buildings stay chilly even in warm weather, so take jackets.)*

Kids' Facilities. No strollers, no diaper-changing facilities, no bottle-warming available. The only restroom on the premises is a port-o-potty opposite the entrance. Flush-toilet restrooms can be found at the administration building a few hundred yards to the south on Marine Drive.

Ratings. Think twice about taking kids under 3 because of restroom deficiencies and lack of diversions for toddlers. You also may wish to pass if you have an infant; while there are benches upon which to change diapers, the air temperature is usually too chilly for a baby's behind. 2–7, B; 8–11, A; 12–16, A.

MISSION SAN FRANCISCO DE ASIS (MISSION DOLORES)

16th and Dolores Sts. (415) 621–8203. Limited free street parking.

Hours. Daily, 9 A.M.–4:30 P.M.

Costs. $1 donation requested.

Mission Dolores was the sixth of what would eventually be twenty-one California missions established by the Spanish Catholic church. Completed in 1791, the mission is the oldest building in San Francisco. It displays a number of early church documents and many of the gifts to Father Junipero Serra, the priest who established the California mission system. An adjacent cemetery contains the resting places of some of San Francisco's most important early residents.

Kids' Facilities. No stroller rentals. No bottle-warming facilities. Diapers can be changed on benches. No food service.

Ratings. Because a quick sweep can be made in about 15 minutes, younger children shouldn't get too antsy; however, the building, history, and contents are best appreciated by older kids with a sense of history. 2–7, D; 8–11, D; 12–16, B.

CHEVRON'S WORLD OF OIL

555 Market St. (415) 894–4895. Pay lot parking.

Hours. Mon.–Fri., 9 A.M.–4 P.M. Closed on major holidays.

Costs. Free.

Chevron's (Standard Oil of California's) prideful ode to fossil fuels is located in the lobby of the Chevron corporate headquarters in San Francisco's financial district. This compact museum explains the science and history of oil production. There are a few hands-on interactive computer exhibits along with some nifty old cars and old gasoline station memorabilia.

Kids' Facilities. No facilities whatsoever.

Ratings. It's easy to run through this museum in a few minutes—not including the multimedia presentation. But there's not a lot for kids under age 8. 2–7, D; 8–11, B; 12–16, B.

THE OLD U.S. MINT

5th and Mission Sts. (415) 974–0788. Pay lot parking nearby.

Hours. Mon.–Fri., 10 A.M.–4 P.M.

Costs. Free.

Once the financial center of the West Coast, this completely revamped 1874 building is home to some interesting financial exhibits, including more than $5 million in gold coins and bullion. A movie traces the history of the San Francisco Mint, and a guided tour explores the process by which coins were made during the years the mint was in operation (1874–1937). The Old Mint also has the Treasury Department's computer center and a numismatic shop where you can buy proof coins. A visit here is a must for kids who collect coins.

Kids' Facilities. No stroller rentals and no bottle-warming facilities. No diaper-changing facilities; however, there is hallway bench space. The restrooms are redone in Victorian style.

Ratings. Most kids above age 6 will get a kick out of seeing all that gold in the vault room. Tours are conducted every hour on the half hour. The movie runs every hour on the hour. 2–7, C; 8–11, A; 12–16, A.

SAN FRANCISCO EXPERIENCE THEATRE

Pier 39 at the foot of Stockton St. (415) 982–7394. Pay lot and metered street parking.

Hours. Daily, every half hour, 10 A.M.–9:30 P.M.

Costs. Adults, $3.50; ages 5–18, $2; ages 4 and under, free.

While this multimedia "experience" movie extolls the virtues of San Francisco to the edges of unashamed hoopla, it also imparts a terrific feel for the city's history. You come out of the theater after 30 minutes actually wanting to see more of the city.

Kids' Facilities. Restrooms have no changing tables, but there's plenty of bench space.

Ratings. The film has something for everyone. Younger kids will get a kick out of some of the multimedia tricks, such as "feeling" the 1906 earthquake. A half hour is just long enough. 2–7, B; 8–11, A; 12–16, A.

GOLDEN GATE BRIDGE

US 101 at the northern tip of the Presidio.

Hours. 24 hours a day.

Costs. (Autos) Northbound: free; southbound: Sun.–Thurs., $1.50; Fri. and Sat., $2.

Few bridges in the world compare to fifty-year-old Golden Gate, which connects the San Francisco peninsula to Marin County to the north. Nearly 2 miles in length, this massive orange-red (not golden: "Golden Gate" is the name of the strait it crosses) structure is one of the longest single-span suspension bridges in the world. The Golden Gate is also open to pedestrians, and weekends usually find joggers, hikers, and bicyclists making their way across to green, hilly Marin County.

Kids' Facilities. None.

Ratings. Younger kids may not fully appreciate what they're experiencing. 2–7, C; 8–11, A; 12–16, A.

MUSEUMS

CALIFORNIA PALACE OF THE LEGION OF HONOR

El Camino del Mar and Legion of Honor Dr., Lincoln Park. (415) 221–4811. Free lot parking.

Hours. Wed.–Sun., 10 A.M.–5 P.M. Closed on Mon. and Tues.

Costs. Adults, $4; under age 18, free.

Architecturally similar to the museum of the same name in Paris, the CPLH hosts many of the traveling exhibitions of San Francisco's fine arts museum (the CPLH, the De Young Museum, and the Asian Art Museum). Located on a hill overlooking the Pacific, its permanent collections feature an extensive assortment of French paintings, sculptures, and graphic arts.

Kids' Facilities. No stroller rentals. No diaper-changing facilities (plenty of bench space, however). Bottles can be warmed in museum restaurant's microwave.

Ratings. This small museum can easily be seen in about an hour, but has little to entertain young children. 2–7, D; 8–11, C; 12–16, A.

M. H. DE YOUNG MUSEUM

John F. Kennedy Dr., Golden Gate Park. (415) 221–4811. Free lot parking.

Hours. Wed.–Sun., 10 A.M.–5 P.M. Closed on Mon. and Tues.

Costs. Adults, $4; under age 18, free. (One charge admits you to this museum *and* the Asian Art Museum.)

Ancient Egyptian artworks along with primitive and traditional works of fine art from the Renaissance through the 19th century make up the De Young's collection. The museum also hosts regular traveling exhibitions.

Kids' Facilities. No stroller rentals. Diaper changing must be done on benches outside the restrooms. Warm bottles in the De Young Cafe's microwave.

Ratings. Again, this museum is not for the very young or the very antsy. There are occasional children's art programs (call ahead). 2–7, C; 8–11, B; 12–16, A.

THE ASIAN ART MUSEUM

John F. Kennedy Dr., Golden Gate Park (Located in the same building as the De Young). (415) 668–8922. Free lot parking.

Hours. Wed.–Sun., 10 A.M.–5 P.M. Closed on Mon. and Tues.

Costs. Adults, $4; under age 18, free (one charge admits you to this museum *and* the De Young).

The Asian Art Museum displays the distinguished Avery Brundage collection of Asian art. From glass to pottery to paper screens, the museum has pieces from the entire Asian continent.

Kids' Facilities. No stroller rentals. Diaper changing on benches outside restrooms. Warm bottles in De Young Cafe's microwave.

Ratings. Young children could get bored. 2–7, C; 8–11, B; 12–16, A.

SAN FRANCISCO MUSEUM OF MODERN ART

401 N. Van Ness Ave. (415) 863–8800. Pay meter and lot parking nearby.

Hours. Tues.–Fri., 10 A.M.–5 P.M.; Thurs. until 9 P.M.; Sat. and Sun., 11 A.M.–5 P.M. Closed on Mon.

Costs. Adults, $3.50; ages 7–16, $1.50; ages 6 and under, free.

In a structure that looks for all the world like a 1930s federal courthouse, this museum's forte is 20th-century abstract art and photography. All the major artists of the century are represented here, along with those currently making a splash in the art world.

Kids' Facilities. No stroller rentals. Diaper-changing tables are located in the ladies' restroom only, but there are benches for Dads. There is a cafe (serving sandwiches and salads) equipped with a microwave for bottle warming.

Ratings. While there is no children's museum on the premises, there are often children's art programs (call ahead). On the whole, kids seem to do better with colorful modern art museums than with traditional paintings and sculptures. If you limit your stay to about an hour, the color seems to placate potentially fidgety children. 2–7, B; 8–11, A; 12–16, A.

FORT MASON MUSEUMS

Marina Blvd. and Laguna St. These museums are located in five former military warehouse buildings on three piers a few hundred feet from the parking lot on the west side of Fort Mason. Free parking on the Fort Mason lot.

Kids' Facilities. There are none at any of the museums themselves, but each of Fort Mason's buildings has restroom facilities with benches outside for diaper changing. There are also restaurants nearby to warm bottles. No stroller rentals at any of the museums.

SAN FRANCISCO CRAFTS AND FOLK ART MUSEUM

Landmark Building A, (415) 775–0990.

Hours. Tues.– Sun., 12 noon–5 P.M.; Sat., 10 A.M.–5 P.M.

Costs. Adults, $1; ages 12–17, 50¢; ages 11 and under, free. Saturdays, free for all.

This tiny, colorful museum draws nearly 25,000 people a year and is a favorite with kids, perhaps because primitive works and folk art often look like what kids make and draw themselves. Then again, it could be the ultra-steep curved wrought iron staircase that kids like to play on.

Ratings. It takes no time at all to see this museum, and kids seem to like it. All ages, A.

AFRO-AMERICAN MUSEUM

Landmark Building C, (415) 441–0640.

Hours. Tues.– Sat., 12 noon–5 P.M.

Costs. Free; donations appreciated.

The Afro-American Museum displays collections of art by black Americans, African art, and photographs. It also has a large selection of books on black history. The volunteer staff makes it an educational experience by cheerfully answering any and all questions. The place is small and easy to see in 15 minutes.

Ratings. Exhibits continually change, and they tend to offer two or three different presentations at one time. 2–7, B; 8–11, A; 12–16, A.

MUSEO ITALOAMERICANO

Landmark Building C, (415) 673–2200.

Hours. Wed.–Sun., 12 noon–5 P.M.

Costs. Free, donations appreciated.

Predominantly an art museum, the Museo offers traveling exhibitions of drawings, paintings, sculpture, and photographs. A good funding base allows this institution not only to display artwork but also to offer Italian language classes, lectures, and special movie events.

Ratings. Like all of the Fort Mason museums, this one can be seen quickly. 2–7, B; 8–11, A; 12–16, A.

MEXICAN HERITAGE MUSEUM

Landmark Building D, (415) 441–0445.

Hours. Wed.–Sun., 12 noon–5 P.M.; first Thurs. of month, 12 noon–8 P.M.

Costs. Adults, $2; ages 10–18, $1; ages 9 and under, free.

By far the most spacious of the Fort Mason museums, the Mexican Heritage Museum has been around since 1974 and at this location since 1984. There is plenty of pre-Columbian pottery, along with ancient basketry and modern paintings.

Ratings. It's easy to see this museum in about 20 minutes; however, fidgety kids might get too antsy to allow you the full amount of time. 2–7, C; 8–11, B; 12–16, A.

AMERICAN CAROUSEL MUSEUM

633 Beach St. (415) 928–0550. Metered street and pay lot parking.

Hours. Summer: daily, 10 A.M.–6 P.M.; Winter: daily, 10 A.M.–5 P.M.

Costs. Adults, $2; ages 12–17, $1; under age 12, free.

With fewer than 250 merry-go-rounds in operation today, this is one of the few places in the United States where you're able to marvel at these aging, intricately carved and painted carousels while expert artists renovate them. Vintage band organs play continuously.

Kids' Facilities. No changing tables, no stroller rentals, and no provisions for getting a bottle warmed. There are restrooms across the street at the Cannery (see Shopping).

Ratings. On color and sound alone, this place rates an A for all ages.

CABLE CAR MUSEUM

Washington and Mason Sts. (415) 474–1887. Limited metered street parking.

Hours. November through March: daily, 10 A.M.–5 P.M. April through October: daily, 10 A.M.–6 P.M.

Costs. Free.

Because San Francisco holds the franchise on cable cars, this is the only museum of its kind in the world. There are antique cable cars, as well as the underground cable workings of the whole system, and a 16-minute movie on the 100-year-old-plus transportation phenomenon. The only drawback is the constant drone of the electric motors powering the cables.

Kids' Facilities. No stroller rentals. No diaper-changing tables (plenty of benches, however). No bottle-warming facilities.

Ratings. Kids really enjoy this place, especially when it's offered in conjunction with a cable car ride. All ages, A.

MUSEUM OF MODERN MYTHOLOGY

693 Mission St. at 3rd St., 9th Floor. (415) 546–0202. Lot and metered street parking.

Hours. Thurs.–Sat., 12 noon–5 P.M.

Costs. Adults, $2; ages 5–17, 50¢; ages 4 and under, free.

Here you'll find many of the dolls, toys, print advertisements, and point-of-purchase store displays of the products you told your mother you couldn't live without: Speedy Alka-Seltzer, the Pillsbury Doughboy, the Jolly Green Giant, and Mr. Peanut, to name but a few. Due to space restrictions (only 1,200 square feet of exhibit space) and the sheer number of artifacts available, exhibits rotate regularly.

Kids' Facilities. No changing tables, no bottle-warming capability, and no stroller rentals. The restrooms are located next door to the Museum.

Ratings. Despite its small size, this is a great trip down memory lane for the whole family. All ages, A.

NATIONAL MARITIME MUSEUM

At the foot of Polk St. at Beach St. (415) 556–2904. Metered street or pay lot parking.

Hours. Winter: Wed.–Sun., 10 A.M.–5 P.M. Summer: Wed.–Sun., 10 A.M.–6 P.M.

Costs. Free, donations accepted.

This building is actually only one quarter of the whole museum, which also includes a separate pier (two ships) and three ships at other locations on the San Francisco waterfront. (See the listings that follow.) The Art Deco building (1930) contains an assortment of ship models, figureheads, and hardware from every type of boat that has sailed in and around San Francisco Bay during the last 100 years. There's a terrific exhibit of photographs and hardware on the ships and men that sailed the Sacramento River delta from San Francisco to the state capital.

Kids' Facilities. No bottle-warming facility, no diaper-changing tables (although there's plenty of bench space), and no stroller rentals.

Ratings. If you have small children, make short work of the museum building and spend the lion's share of your time aboard the five ships docked nearby. 2–7, C; 8–11, B; 12–16, A.

The museum exhibits provide a good frame of reference for ships that you can board around the San Francisco waterfront:

THE HYDE STREET PIER SHIPS

The foot of Hyde St. at Jefferson St. (415) 556–6435. Pay lot and metered street parking.

Hours. Same as museum building.

Costs. Free; donations accepted.

The Hyde Street Pier is home to the *C. A. Thayer* (1895), a lumber schooner, and the *Eureka*, at one time the largest sidewheel auto ferry boat in the world. You're invited to come aboard.

Kids' Facilities. No strollers, no bottle warming, and no changing tables. The pier itself has only port-o-potties. More civilized restroom facilities can be found on the *Eureka*.

Ratings. Most kids get a big kick out of the Hyde Street Pier. 2–7, B; 8–11, A; 12–16, A.

THE *JEREMIAH O'BRIEN*

Pier 3, Fort Mason, Marina Blvd. and Laguna St. (415) 441–3101. Free parking at Fort Mason lot.

Hours. Daily, 9 A.M.–3 P.M.

Costs. Adults, $2; under age 13, $1; family of two adults and three kids, $5.

This is the last of more than 2,700 World War II Liberty Ships designed to ferry food and medical supplies to the Allies in both the European and Pacific theaters of the war. Meticulously cared for by volunteers, each section of the ship, from the engine room to the captain's quarters to the 50-caliber machine gun, is open for inspection. Once or twice a year, the *O'Brien* leaves its slip and steams off on a trip around San Francisco Bay.

Kids' Facilities. No stroller rentals, no changing tables, and no bottle-warming facility. There are, however, a number of restrooms on board.

Ratings. Kids under 6 could have a difficult time navigating the narrow, steep stairways between decks. 2–7, C; 8–11, B; 12–16, A.

THE BALCLUTHA

Pier 43 at the foot of Powell St. (415) 929–0202. Pay lot and metered parking.

Hours. Daily, 10 A.M.–6 P.M.

Costs. Adults, $2; ages 12–18, $1; ages 6–11, 25¢; ages 5 and under, free.

The *Balclutha*, a square-rigged Cape Horn sailing ship, is the oldest in the Maritime Museum collection. Launched in 1886, it carried California grain to Europe in exchange for manufactured goods. Its close proximity to Pier 41 and the Red and White Ferry line (see Tours) makes the three-masted ship great fun to visit. It's a natural, either before or after an excursion to Alcatraz.

Kids' Facilities. There are no facilities at all aboard the ship. Restrooms can be found on Pier 41.

Ratings. Except for the submarine U.S.S. *Pampanito*, this is the most popular ship with the younger set. 2–7, B; 8–11, A; 12–16, A.

U.S.S. PAMPANITO

Pier 45 at the foot of Taylor St. (415) 929–0202. Pay lot and metered parking.

Hours. Summer: daily, 9 A.M.–9 P.M. Winter: Mon.–Thurs., 9 A.M.–6 P.M.; Fri.–Sun., 9A.M.–9 P.M.

Costs. Adults, $3; ages 12–18, $2; ages 6–11, $1; ages 5 and under, free.

The *Pampanito* offers a self-guided tour with a tape deck and a set of earphones. Kids and adults marvel at how World War II sailors lived during month-long patrols in search of Japanese targets.

Kid's Facilities. No facilities at all. Use restrooms at Pier 41 or one of the many restaurants in the area (don't tell them we sent you).

Ratings. By far the most popular of all the Maritime Museum boats, but if you're claustrophobic, you may want to pass on this one. You might also want to skip it if your children are younger than 6, because of narrow passageways and shaky footing. 2–7, C; 8–11, A; 12–16, A.

THE WAX MUSEUM

145 Jefferson St., (415) 885–4975. Pay lot and street parking.

Hours. Sun.–Thurs., 9 A.M.–10:30 P.M.; Fri. and Sat., 9 A.M.–11:30 P.M.

Costs. Adults, $6.95; ages 4–12, $2.75; ages 3 and under, free.

Here you'll find more than 270 wax celebrities in seventy scenes. Included are movie stars like Chuck Norris, nonagenarians like George Burns, and all sorts of infamous historical types. With exhibits like the Chamber of Horrors and Fairyland, the Wax Museum tries hard to have something for everyone.

Kids' Facilities. No stroller rentals, no bottle-warming capability, and no place to change dirty diapers.

Ratings. The unashamed commercial appeal of this museum makes it an almost instant hit with everyone. Fairyland wins the day for the little ones. All ages, A.

GUINNESS MUSEUM OF WORLD RECORDS

235 Jefferson St. (415) 771–9890. Pay lot and metered parking.

Hours. Mon.–Thurs. and Sun., 10 A.M.–10 P.M.; Fri. and Sat., 10 A.M.–11 P.M.

Costs. Adults, $5.95; ages 5–11, $2.75; ages 4 and under, free.

Among the curiosities are statues of the world's tallest and fattest men, the smallest bicycle, the tiniest book, and the biggest electric guitar.

Kids' Facilities. No stroller rentals, no changing facilities, and no places to warm bottles.

Ratings. Kids love this stuff, though some of the information may be a bit beyond the really small ones. 2–7, B; 8–11, A; 12–16, A.

RIPLEY'S BELIEVE IT OR NOT MUSEUM

175 Jefferson St. (415) 771–6188. Pay lot and metered street parking.

Hours. Summer: Sun.–Thurs., 9 A.M.–11 P.M.; Fri. and Sat., 9 A.M.– 12 midnight. Winter: Sun.–Thurs., 10 A.M.–10 P.M.; Fri. and Sat., 10 A.M.–11 P.M.

Costs. Adults, $5.95; ages 13–17, $4.75; ages 5–12, $2.75; ages 4 and under, free.

A drum made from a human skull, a human skin mask, the world's smallest violin, an entire gold tea service the size of the nail of your little finger. You get the picture. This 8,000-square-foot museum is one of seven "odditoriums" (their word, not ours) located in the United States and Canada. The late Robert Ripley sanitized the image of the freak show and made it possible to view some of the world's more bizarre oddities in air-conditioned comfort.

Kids' Facilities. No strollers rentals. No diaper-changing tables (although there are benches). There's no food service at which to warm a bottle.

Ratings. The collections here are eclectic enough to interest any kid. All ages, A.

JOSEPHINE D. RANDALL JUNIOR MUSEUM

199 Museum Way at Roosevelt Rd. (415) 863–1339. Free parking.

Hours. Winter: Tues.–Sat., 10 A.M.–5 P.M. Summer: Mon.–Fri., 10 A.M.–5 P.M.

Costs. Free, donations accepted.

Actually a nature center and home to a number of animals and birds cared for by local kids and the museum staff, the Josephine D. Randall Junior Museum is housed in an old elementary school. There are a number of natural science exhibits and dioramas, classes, and field trips for local kids and members of the museum society. The basement is home to the Golden Gate Model Railroad Club. On weekends, you're invited to drop in and watch the members play with their elaborately landscaped train set.

Kids' Facilities. No stroller rental, no food (and therefore no bottle-warming) service, and no diaper-changing tables, although there are benches in the lobby.

Ratings. With animals to view (and touch, if you get an attendant to supervise), the younger kids will fare better here than the older ones. 2–7, A; 8–11, A; 12–16, C.

SAN FRANCISCO INTERNATIONAL TOY MUSEUM

2801 Leavenworth St., 3rd Floor. (415) 441–8697. Pay lot and metered street parking.

Hours. Daily, 10 A.M.–6 P.M.

Costs. General admission, $3; under age 5, free.

This museum lets kids play with a wide range of probably indestructible toys: Legos, Quadros, and toys to ride on. There are also "hands-off" exhibits of antique toys, toy trains, and toys from valuable, well-known collections.

Kids' Facilities. No stroller rentals, no bottle-warming facilities, and no restaurants. Restrooms with changing tables are located a few doors away on the same floor.

Ratings. This place caters to young children, even though older kids might get a kick out of some of the toy exhibits. 2–7, A; 8–11, C; 12–16, C.

BAY AREA DISCOVERY MUSEUM

428 Corte Madera Town Shopping Center, Corte Madera. (415) 927–4722. Free parking.

Hours. Wed.–Sun., 11 A.M.–5 P.M.

Costs. $1 per person; kids under age 2, free.

A new 2,300-square-foot facility that offers plenty of hands-on, creative play opportunities, the Museum provides play areas like the Space Maze, an interpretive play space, and a kid-sized boat complete with two decks and a captain's bridge. A large stage and plenty of costumes encourage kids to playact. For organized activities, there's face painting, storytelling, and even paper weaving. The Discovery Museum also features changing exhibits. It is slated to move sometime in the next year or two to a restored former army building at Fort Baker, beneath the northern terminus of the Golden Gate Bridge.

Kids' Facilities. No stroller rentals, no bottle warming, and no changing tables; there is, however, plenty of bench space.

Ratings. This place is geared for toddlers and kids up to the age of about 10. 2–7, A; 8–11, A; 12–16, D.

WELLS FARGO HISTORY MUSEUM

420 Montgomery St. (415) 396–2619. Pay lot parking.

Hours. Mon.–Fri., 9 A.M.–5 P.M.

Costs. Free.

Located at the Main branch of the Wells Fargo Bank in the San Francisco financial district, the museum contains an authentic Wells Fargo stagecoach, real gold mined from various California diggings, rare coins, stamps, and early bank certificates. Upstairs, kids can climb into a stagecoach replica in which they'll hear a recording about what it was like back when a coach was the only means of overland travel. There's also a telegraph office complete with a hands-on working telegraph. A run-through takes only about 20 minutes.

Kids' Facilities. No stroller rentals, diaper changing, bottle warming, or restrooms.

Ratings. This small museum is well worth a quick visit if you happen to be in the neighborhood. The younger kids get a real kick out of the stagecoach replica and the telegraph. The older ones will like the gold and money exhibits. All ages, A.

PRESIDIO ARMY MUSEUM

Lincoln Blvd. and Funston Ave., The Presidio. (415) 561–4115. Free parking.

Hours. Tues.–Sun., 10 A.M.–4 P.M.

Costs. Free.

Housed in what during the Civil War was the post hospital, this museum is packed floor to ceiling with memorabilia dating from the time of the Spanish rule 200 years ago through the Vietnam War. The place is a treasure trove of old uniforms, weapons, original maps, and photographs from the Presidio's long history. Special exhibits are dedicated to the 1906 earthquake, the coastal defense at the turn of the century, and the beginnings of the O.S.S., the forerunner of the C.I.A.

Kids' Facilities. No bottle warming or stroller rentals. Diaper-changing table in ladies' restroom.

Ratings. While really young children may not be interested, kids from 8 on should find something to catch their interest. 2–7, C; 8–11, A; 12–16, A.

HOTELS

With hotels of nearly every conceivable size and stripe, from intimate bed and breakfasts to full-service chain hotels, San Francisco offers something for every taste and pocketbook. Hotels in the city tend to be more expensive than their suburban counterparts, especially if you're planning to make use of a car during your stay. Garage space will add at least $10 per day to the price. Most suburban hotels have free parking.

San Francisco

THE ARGYLE SUITES HOTEL

146 McAllister St. (415) 552–7076 or (415) 864–1714. 95 suites. Pay parking in nearby public garages.

Rates. $65.
  Located just across the street from the San Francisco Civic Center, which includes the main branch of the public library, City Hall, the opera house, and the Museum of Modern Art, the Argyle services visiting opera and theater companies, as well as the tourist trade. Even though they don't offer much in the way of children's activities, you can't beat the price inside the city limits. Kids 12 and under stay free with parents.
Cribs: Yes, no charge.
Rollaways: Yes, $10.
Babysitting: No.
Pool: No.
Restaurants: No, but there is one right next door.
Kitchen facilities: Yes.
Room service: No.
Closest emergency hospital: St. Francis Hospital, 9 blocks away, (415) 775–4321.

KING GEORGE HOTEL

334 Mason St. (415) 781–5050 or (800) 556–4545 (in California) or (800) 227–4240. 137 units. Pay garage parking.

Rates. Rooms: $79. Suites: $158.

A British-flavored "small hotel," this narrow 10-story establishment is one of the most comfortable bargains in the Union Square district. It's only one block from the Powell Street cable car line, and only a few blocks more from downtown San Francisco's most prestigious department stores: Macy's, Gump's, and Neiman-Marcus. The Bread & Honey Tea Room serves traditional English high tea Mondays through Saturdays, a real kick for older kids. Kids 10 and under stay free with parents.

Cribs: Yes, no charge.
Rollaways: Yes, $10.
Babysitting: Yes, referrals.
Pool: No.
Restaurants: 2; Japanese restaurant and tea room.
Kitchen facilities: None in rooms; suites have full kitchens.
Room service: No.
Closest emergency hospital: St. Francis Hospital, 7 blocks away, (415) 775–4321.

South San Francisco

COMFORT SUITES

121 E. Grand Ave. (415) 589–7766. 165 units. Free parking.

Rates. $63 to $69.

Each suite has a king-size bed and a queen-size sofa bed. The hotel is only a few miles north of the San Francisco airport, but far enough away to avoid the jet noise. Downtown San Francisco is only 20 minutes away by freeway. Kids 16 and under stay free with parents.

Cribs: Yes, no charge.
Rollaways: No.
Babysitting: Yes, referrals with 24-hour notice.
Pool: No.
Restaurants: No, but a free shuttle to local eateries.
Kitchen facilities: Just refrigerators; also, free continental breakfast.
Room service: Yes, local deli.
Closest emergency hospital: Kaiser-Permanente Medical Center, 10 minutes away, (415) 742–2511.

Millbrae

MILLWOOD MOTEL

1375 El Camino Real. (415) 583–3935. 34 units. Free parking.

Rates. $48, plus $2 for each extra person.

This small motel is one of the best values in the Bay Area if you don't mind being near the airport, about a mile to the east. Recently renovated, each suite has a good refrigerator and a new microwave oven. Full kitchens are available to guests who stay for seven days or more (and pay a $49 charge). Those who stay fewer than seven days still get use of the refrigerators. No special children's rate: $2 additional is charged for each extra child or adult.

Cribs: Yes, no charge.
Rollaways: Yes, $2.
Babysitting: No.
Pool: No.
Restaurants: No, but there's one next door.
Kitchen facilities: Yes, but only for guests staying more than a week ($49 charge).
Room service: No, but continental breakfast served.
Closest emergency hospital: Peninsula Hospital, Burlingame, 1 mile away, (415) 872–5500.

Burlingame

EMBASSY SUITES

150 Anza Blvd., Burlingame. (415) 342–4600 or (800) 362–2779. 344 units. Free parking.

Rates. $89 to $129.

The Embassy Suites has all the deluxe features parents are often thankful for: pools, whirlpools, saunas, and a restaurant if the folks get tired of preparing meals in the suite. Seventeen miles south of the city, it's only a 25-minute drive to San Francisco. Kids 12 and under stay free with parents.

Cribs: Yes, no charge.
Rollaways: No.
Babysitting: No.
Pool: Yes, plus a sauna and two Jacuzzis.
Restaurants: Yes.
Kitchen facilities: Yes.
Room service: Yes.
Closest emergency hospital: Peninsula Hospital in Burlingame, 5 minutes away, (415) 872–5500.

San Mateo

RESIDENCE INN-SAN MATEO

2000 Windward Way. (415) 574–4700. 160 units. Free parking.

Rates. $104–$129.

Residence Inns nationwide go all out in support of guests with children. That fact is evidenced here with an on-premises sitting service, a sport court for all sorts of racquet diversions, and a terrific playground. Kids under 18 stay free with their parents.

Cribs: Yes, no charge.
Rollaways: Yes, $10.
Babysitting: Yes, referrals.
Pool: Yes, plus two Jacuzzis.
Restaurants: No, but free daily continental breakfast.
Kitchen facilities: Yes.
Room service: Yes, from local restaurant.
Closest emergency hospital: Mills Hospital, San Mateo, 6 minutes away, (415) 597–2000.

RESTAURANTS

San Francisco offers the typical array of fast-food alternatives, including McDonald's, Burger King, Carl's Jr., Wendy's and others too numerous (and familiar) to mention. Fisherman's Wharf, however, has its own brand of fast food which is a wonderful alternative to burgers and fries. The Wharf's outdoor seafood stalls serve freshly steamed crabs, coleslaw, sodas and beer, and terrific sourdough bread. The prices are only slightly higher than the burger joints.

THE CLIFF HOUSE

1090 Point Lobos Ave. (415) 386–3330. Free street parking.

Hours. Daily, 9 A.M.–10:30 P.M.; Fri. and Sat. until 11 P.M.

Located in a Victorian building, the Cliff House has been serving meals since 1850 and still offers one of the most spectacular dining views in the city. Seal Rocks, just outside the restaurant's large picture windows, are where dozens of seals cavort playfully in and out of the water. While lunch and dinner are served (seafood is recommended), the best family meal is breakfast, where you have a choice of forty-five omelets, all served with potatoes and an unlimited supply of whole-wheat English muffins.

Kids' Facilities. Plenty of high chairs and booster seats. While there are no changing tables in the restrooms, there's plenty of bench space throughout the restaurant.

REAL GOOD KARMA RESTAURANT

501 Dolores St. (415) 621–4112. Street parking.

Hours. Daily, 11:30 A.M.–2:30 P.M. and 5 P.M.–9:30 P.M.

Opened in 1967, the year of San Francisco's famed Summer of Love, this is one of the city's best-known vegetarian restaurants. While younger kids tend to turn their noses up at vegetarian menus, even the fussiest will savagely devour a batter-fried tempura dinner. The salads are good and so are the tofu dishes. Dinners and lunches start at about $5. No credit cards.

Kids' Facilities. Good Karma deserves just that for the high chairs they stock, but they have no booster seats. No diaper-changing tables in the the restrooms and no kids' menus.

HOG HEAVEN

770 Stanyan Street. (415) 668–2038. Inexpensive municipal parking lot across the street and limited street parking.

Hours. Mon. and Tues., 5 P.M.–9 P.M.; Wed.–Sat., 11 A.M.–10 P.M.; Sun., 11 A.M.–9 P.M.

Home of the city's only Memphis-style barbeque, the place serves up both pork and beef ribs as well as chicken. The walls are adorned with pig caricatures and cartoons. Besides main courses with a southern touch, the dessert menu includes Dixie favorites like key lime and black bottom pie. Sandwiches start at about $6, and rib platters run from the $10 to $12 range. You can eat in, take out, or have the food delivered.

Kids' Facilities. Booster seats and high chairs available. Changing table in ladies' restroom. Children's portions available.

CASTAGNOLA'S RESTAURANT AND CAFETERIA

286 Jefferson St. (415) 776–5015. Pay lot and metered street parking.

Hours. Cafeteria: daily, 11 A.M.–5 P.M. Restaurant: daily, 9 A.M.–11 P.M.

Castagnola's is one of the old-line seafood restaurants on pricey Fisherman's Wharf. While the downstairs restaurant neither overexcites nor disappoints, the real gem here is the inexpensive upstairs cafeteria. Open to the lunch and late-afternoon snack crowd, the cafeteria offers as good a wharfside view as the restaurant, but with a sandwich and soup menu that lets a family of four skid by for less than $20 (compared with downstairs where a la carte items cost from $5.95 to $25). The clam chowder is really good, and Mom and Dad can get a reasonably priced glass of wine or bottle of beer.

Kids' Facilities. Booster seats and high chairs available. No changing tables in the restrooms; however, there's plenty of bench space. Kids' menus available.

BRANDY HO'S HUNAN FOOD

217 Columbus Ave. (415) 788–7527. Pay lot and metered street parking. *(Beware. Chinatown street parking at night is scarce and lot parking is outrageously expensive: $7 to $10 just for dinnertime.)*

Hours. Daily, 11:30A.M.–11 P.M.

There are many restaurants in San Francisco's Chinatown and most of them are quite good. Brandy's differs in two important respects: They use no MSG, but they more than make up for it with liberal use of chili peppers. If you order your food medium-spiced, be prepared for a five-alarm experience; if you order it hot, you may need a skin graft on your mouth. For young, sensitive palates, most dishes can be ordered without any chili. Chicken, seafood, and pork dishes are terrific, and the average entree costs about $6.

Kids' Facilities. Booster seats and high chairs are plentiful. No changing tables in the restrooms. No special children's menu.

Big Splurges

CHEZ PANISSE

1517 Shattuck Ave. Berkeley. (415) 548–5525. Street parking.

Hours. Two dining areas: The Dining Room: dinner only; four seatings per night between 6 P.M. and 9:15 P.M. The Cafe: lunch: Mon.–Fri.,

11:30 A.M.–3 P.M.; Sat., 11:30 A.M.–4 P.M.; dinner: Mon.–Sat., 5 P.M.–11:30 P.M.

Renowned chef Alice Waters has converted this old Berkeley residence into one of California's most popular eating spots. The award-winning restaurant features two separate dining areas: The Dining Room, which offers a prix fixe dinner that boasts fresh ingredients culled daily from local meat, fish, and vegetable markets; and the Cafe, which offers a la carte selections from an ever-changing menu of pizzas, pasta, and salads. Reservations for the Dining Room must be made about a month in advance. The Cafe takes lunch reservations only. The Dining Room's prix fixe price is $50 per person, exluding wine and tip. A meal at the Cafe will set you back about $25 per person. Wine and beer only. Credit cards.

STAR'S

150 Redwood Alley. (415) 861–7827. Pay lot on the corner of Polk and McAllister.

Hours. Nightly, 5:30 P.M.–11 P.M.

One of the trendy San Francisco restaurants owned by Chef Jeremiah Tower, Star's is to San Francisco what Spago is to Los Angeles. The grilled fish entrees are all excellent. Desserts are irresistible—we loved the homemade custards and tortes. Don't expect a romantic low-keyed evening; Star's is on the noisy side. A dinner will run from $40 and up per person. They have a full bar and a terrific wine list featuring local Napa Valley wines. Reservations recommended. Credit cards.

SHOPPING

THE CANNERY

Columbus Ave. and Leavenworth St. (415) 771–3112. Pay lot and limited metered street parking.

Hours. Mon.–Fri., 10 A.M.–6 P.M.; Sat., 9:30 A.M.–7 P.M.; Sun., 10:30 A.M.–6 P.M.

Once the proud home of the Del Monte fruit and vegetable canning factory, the Cannery now houses expensive shops and boutiques and three notable establishments.

Play, (415) 775–5483, is a neat little toy emporium specializing in kites (that can be flown at nearby Fort Mason), paper and balsa wood planes, dinosaurs, and other novelty toys.

All Dolled Up, (415) 441–3256, sells very old and highly collectable dolls. Some are worth hundreds of dollars, but don't worry because the really expensive ones are locked away from curious but careless fingers.

The International Toy Museum, (415) 441–8697, (see Museums) is a must-see, especially for small kids who are ready for some hands-on fun.

PIER 39

Foot of Stockton St. and the Embarcadero. (415) 981–7437. Pay lot and limited meter parking.

Hours. Daily, 10:30 A.M.–8:30 P.M.

This shopping/dining complex is geared especially to tourists.

Music Tracks, (415) 981–1777, is a recording studio where, for a small fee, you can sing along with prerecorded musical tracks and create a souvenir to send to your relatives.

Magnet P.I., (415) 989–2361, sounds like a bad pun (and it is), but it's also a store that sells nothing but refrigerator magnets. From fake burgers and fries to relief maps of San Francisco, there's a magnet here for everyone's refrigerator. Be aware that young kids often think food magnets are edible.

S. Claus, (415) 392–2222. Although they may be confused by the appearance of Christmas trees in July, kids love shopping at this year-round Christmas store.

Left Hand World, (415) 433–3547, is a shop devoted to folks who insist upon doing things the hard way (that is, left-handed). From left-handed pens to scissors to cookware, this store has as much merchandise as there are tasks to vex southpaws.

F. A. O. SCHWARZ FIFTH AVENUE

180 Post St. (415) 391–0100. Pay lot parking.

Hours. Mon.–Sat., 9:30 A.M.–6 P.M. (Thurs. until 7 P.M.); Sun., 12 noon–5 P.M.

From hobbies to games to models to toys, this San Francisco version of the New York original is the city's biggest toy store.

PLAY WITH IT, LTD.

1660 Haight St. (415) 621–8787. Limited free street parking.

Hours. Mon.–Fri., 10 A.M.–7 P.M.; Sat., 10 A.M.–6 P.M.; Sun., 12 noon–5 P.M.

In business for a dozen years or so in the midst of the fabled Haight-Ashbury hippie area of the 1960s, this store is one of the more progressive toy establishments in the city. It sells a vast array of European toys, as well as some of the more educational American brands like Fisher Price. Parents and kids alike love this place for its great play area.

TRANSPORTATION

BUSES AND TROLLEYS

The bus and electric trolley system run by the San Francisco Municipal Railway offers extensive coverage throughout the city's 47 square miles. Bus and trolley rates are 75¢ (exact change), and some lines operate 24 hours a day. Transfers are free and are good for two vehicle changes within a 90-minute period. For more information: (415) 673–6864.

CABLE CARS

Administered by the San Francisco Municipal Railway, the historic cable cars run at 9 ½ miles per hour on three hilly routes in the northeastern section of town: between Fisherman's Wharf and the financial district and through Chinatown. Fares are $1.50 for adults and 75¢ for kids ages 5 to 17 (with free transfers), and the cars operate between 6 A.M. and 1 A.M. Tickets can be purchased from the conductor/brakeman at the rear of the vehicle or from self-service ticket machines at major stops. For more information: (415) 673–6864.

RAIL

Bay Area Rapid Transit (BART) is a 71-mile-long ultramodern rail system that connects San Francisco with Daly City (south of San Francisco) and Oakland, Berkeley, and other municipalities east of San Francisco Bay. BART travels above and below ground and under the Bay. There are more than twenty-five stations along the route, and rates vary according to distance traveled. For $2.60, you can purchase an excursion ticket that entitles you to ride the entire length of the system, stopping wherever you wish, as long as you don't leave any of the terminals. Daily service hours are 6 A.M. to 12 midnight (Sunday, 9 A.M. to 12 midnight). For more information: (415) 788–2278.

Caltrain is a railway that moves passengers between San Francisco and San Jose 45 miles to the south. Trains run from about 5:30 in the morning until nearly midnight. Rates vary depending on length of trip. For more information: (415) 557–8661 or (800) 558–8661 (within northern California).

BOAT

The Red and White Fleet (Pier 41, Fisherman's Wharf) offers daily service across San Francisco Bay to Tiburon and Sausalito in Marin County. Both Tiburon and Sausalito ferries depart every hour and a half starting at 11:20 A.M. weekdays and 10:50 A.M. on weekends. The half hour one-way trips cost $4 for adults, $2 for ages 5–11, and are free for ages 4 and under. Red and White also offers daily trips to Angel Island and Alcatraz (see Attractions). For more information: (415) 546–2896 or (800) 445–8880 (in California).

Golden Gate Ferries (Ferry Bldg. at the foot of Market St.) offers daily crossings to Sausalito and Larkspur in Marin County. The Sausalito ferry runs frequently and costs $3.50 one way. The Larkspur ferry also runs frequently at a weekday cost of $2.20 for adults and $1.65 for ages 6 to 12; it's free for ages 5 and under. Weekend trips to Larkspur are $3 for adults; $2.25 for kids under 12; and free for kids under age 12 traveling with an adult. For more information: (415) 332–6600.

TAXIS

Taxi rates are high! In the city, cabs charge $1.40 for the first mile and $1.50 for each mile thereafter. Cabs can be called or hailed. Taxi companies include Yellow, (415) 626–2345; Allied, (415) 826–9494; DeSoto, (415) 673–0333; and Veteran's, (415) 552–1300.

TOURS

BUS

Gray Line Tours. (415) 896–1515. Offers all sorts of northern California tours. Their main stocks in trade, however, are their half-day (3 ½ hours) city tours, which take in most of the popular tourist attractions: Fisherman's Wharf, Golden Gate Park, the financial district, and Chinatown. Their half-day Deluxe City Tour is the best value, at $19.50 for adults and $9.75 for kids between 5 and 11 (ages 4 and under, free when sharing a seat with Mom or Dad).

Dolphin Tours. (415) 441–6810 or (800) 843–5960 (nationwide) or (800) 247–9998 (in California). Offers a terrific, comprehensive 6-hour tour of the city, including portions of Marin County aboard mini vans. The tour also includes a complementary San Francisco Bay cruise, all for $34 for adults and $23 for kids to age 12 (ages 11 and under, free if they share a seat with parents). Call for reservations no later than the night before.

SELF-DRIVING

The 49-mile Scenic Drive. Passes every attraction San Francisco has to offer. Initiated in the 1930s, and marked by signs featuring a seagull, the route begins and ends at the Civic Center and passes through Chinatown, past Telgraph Hill, Fisherman's Wharf, the Presidio, Golden Gate Park, the Zoo, Mission Dolores, the waterfront, and the financial district. (Note: You can start and stop at any point, and you're best off traveling on a weekend to escape commercial traffic. Pick up a free *Drive* map at the San Francisco Visitors Information Center, lower level, Hallidie Plaza, Powell and Market Streets.)

WATER

Red and White Fleet. (415) 546–2896 or (800) 445–8880 (in California). Offers San Francisco Bay tours and tours to Alacatraz (see Attractions), as well as excursions to Tiburon and Sausalito (see Transportation), Marine World (see Attractions), and Angel Island, an uninhabited island in San Francisco Bay that caters to picnickers and hikers. The 45-minute Bay tour is $9.95 for adults; $6.95 for ages 12 to 18; and $4.95 for ages 5 to 11 (ages 4 and under, free). The Angel Island excursion is $7.10 for adults; $4.05 for ages 5 to 11 (ages 4 and under, free). Most tours and excursions begin at about 10 A.M. and run throughout the day. Call ahead for specific times. Buy tickets at the Red and White dock (Pier 41) or from Ticketron. During the summer, order your tickets weeks in advance for the Alcatraz tour and Marine World excursion.

Blue and Gold Fleet. (415) 781–7877. The 1¼-hour tour of San Francisco Bay makes a circuitous route that covers much of the territory from the Oakland Bay Bridge to the Golden Gate Bridge. Boats depart several times a day from Pier 39, beginning at about 10 A.M. Prices range from $11 for adults to $6 for ages 5 to 18 (ages 4 and under are free). Call ahead for specific times. During the summer months, get to the Pier early to assure a space on the boat of your choice.

AIR

Commodore Helicopters. (415) 332–4482. Offers spectacular views of San Francisco and the Bay. Three tours to choose from: a 5-minute flight over Alcatraz and Angel Island ($20; $10 for kids), a 10-minute ride over the Bay and Golden Gate Bridge ($40; $20), and a 15-minute flight over the Bay and the Pacific Ocean ($60; $30). The ride is silky smooth and even those with the most sensitive stomachs are unaffected by motion sickness. Choppers fly daily from 9 A.M. to dusk and depart from Pier 43½.

SEASONAL EVENTS

For more information about San Francisco events, call the Convention and Visitors Bureau, (415) 974–6900.

February

CHINESE NEW YEAR

The compact Chinatown area is ablaze with red firecrackers, dragon costumes, and general merriment. There is the crowning of Miss Chinatown USA, the Golden Dragon Parade and a carnival in a Chinatown park. Dates for this vary according to the Chinese calendar (sometimes it's in January).

March

ST. PATRICK'S DAY

Along with flag-raising ceremonies, festivities at the United Irish Cultural Center, and religious services at St. Patrick's Church, there's green beer in the taverns and a snake race in the financial district.

April

CHERRY BLOSSOM FESTIVAL

San Francisco's Japanese community goes all out for this yearly late-April celebration. There's lots of food and festivities at the Japanese Cultural and Trade Center at Post and Buchannan Streets and a big parade on the last day of the festival.

May

CINCO DE MAYO

San Francisco was part of Mexico until 1846. This celebration (usually the weekend after May 5) comes complete with a parade in the Mission District, the crowning of a queen, food, cultural festivities, and live entertainment. It celebrates the 1862 victory of the Mexican government of Juarez over the French troops of Napoleon III.

June

CARNIVAL

This mid-June celebration is like the Mardis Gras of New Orleans but on a much smaller scale. The mainstays of this Mission District celebration are a parade, a costume contest, and a street festival.

Summer

THE STREET FESTIVALS

June through September, a number of neighborhood street festivals celebrate the diversity of the city. June brings the *Union Street Spring Festival* (Union Street from Gough to Fillmore), the *Haight Street Fair* (on Haight from Masonic to Stanyan), and the *New North Beach Fair* (upper Grant Avenue). September marks the *Folsom Street Fair* and the *24th Street Fair* (Mission District). Food, crafts, and music abound at all.

July

FOURTH OF JULY

Criss Field, a wide, multipurpose playing field between the Presidio and Fort Mason on the Bay, is the site of the city's best fireworks display. All-day family festivities get going at around 3 P.M. with the fireworks show commencing at 9 P.M. Bring jackets and sweaters as summer nights get downright chilly.

September

FESTA ITALIANA

The restaurants of Fisherman's Wharf, with its overwhelming Italian presence, host this annual late-September cultural fest. (See the Street Festivals under Summer.)

October

FLEET WEEK

During the second week of October, all naval vessels are open to the public, and the precision flight team, the Blue Angels, performs above the city.

COLUMBUS DAY

The Italian community steps to the foreground to commemorate Columbus' discovery of the New World. Early-October activities in North Beach and at Fisherman's Wharf include a "Queen Isabella" coronation, a blessing of the fishing fleet, food, and a parade on the last day of the festival.

November

RUN TO THE FAR SIDE

Golden Gate Park is the place for the annual running event featuring syndicated cartoonist Gary Larson, of "Far Side" cartoon fame.

CHILDREN'S THEATER

THE NEW CONSERVATORY THEATRE

Performs at the Zephyr Theatre Complex, 25 Van Ness Ave. (415) 861–4914. Pay lot and limited metered street parking.

San Francisco has a dearth of live stage productions for kids. The New Conservatory fills the void with issue-oriented plays. Their productions address world problems like racism, ecology, and politics. (In 1987 they produced a play on the impact of AIDS.) They cull their many youthful performers from their own theater school. Performance times and prices vary; call ahead.

BABYSITTING SERVICES

BAY AREA BABYSITTERS
(415) 991–7474.

Licensed and bonded, Bay Area covers all of San Francisco and the peninsula as far south as Foster City. For one to three children they charge

$4.50 per hour with a 4-hour minimum, plus a transportation cost of $3 to $5 in the daytime and $8 at night. Second families can be added for a charge of time-and-a-half.

PUBLICATIONS

San Francisco Chronicle. Daily newspaper (morning); Friday entertainment calendar.

San Francisco Examiner. Daily newspaper (afternoon); Friday entertainment calendar.

Penninsula Parent. Monthly magazine; focuses on San Francisco south to Palo Alto. Calendar of events lists museum exhibits, movies, and parents' seminars. Available free in toy stores, kids clothing stores, etc.

Parents' Press. Free monthly magazine; focuses on East Bay (Oakland, Berkeley); calendar of children-oriented events.

LOCAL TELEPHONE NUMBERS

Late-hours pharmacy: Convention Center Pharmacy, 351 3rd St. (415) 543–7471. Open Mon.–Fri., 6:30 A.M.–9 P.M.; Sat., 9 A.M.–8 P.M.; Sun., 9 A.M.–5 P.M.
Consumer complaints: Consumer Action Line, (415) 777–9635.
Lawyer referral: San Francisco Bar Association, (415) 391–6102.
Dental emergency: San Francisco Dental Society, (415) 421–1435.
Physician referral: San Francisco Medical Society, (415) 567–6230.
Drug-abuse hotline: (415) 752–3400; (415) 431–1714.
Poison control: (415) 476–6600.
Traveler's aid: (415) 781–6738.
Tourism office: (415) 974–6900.
Police: 911.
Fire: 911.
Ambulance: 911.
Road conditions: (415) 557–3755.
Weather: (415) 936–1212.
Local car rentals: Reliable, (415) 928–4414; RPM, (415) 589–4444.

SEATTLE

Though the temptation is mighty to bone up on "rain" song lyrics in preparation for your visit to the Pacific Northwest you will be pleasantly surprised to find that it doesn't rain nearly as much as you've probably heard. According to United States Government statistics, only a shade less than 39 inches of rain fall each year on Seattle, a figure that compares favorably with New York (41), Boston (52), and Washington, D. C. (42).

Rain or shine, Seattle is one of the most naturally beautiful sites on the North American continent. Blessed with verdant foliage and blue-gray water, saline Puget Sound is at Seattle's front door, and the Olympic Mountains glitter in the distance. Fresh-water Lake Washington stands at the city's rear gate, with the Cascade Mountains farther to the east. When the sky clears, just after a winter rainstorm, the city is so pretty it hurts to look at it. It's easy to see why Seattle was nicknamed "the Emerald City."

Discovered by British Explorer George Vancouver in 1792, the Seattle area was settled in the early 1850s by Americans who made a hard right turn at the Oregon Trail. Almost immediately, the lumber industry began to grow, pioneered by entrepreneurs like George Yesler, who turned the hilly terrain into a lumber skid to get his logs down to his harborside sawmill. For years the thoroughfare that became the present Yesler Way was known as Skid Road. Later, when the area became a gathering place for the out-of-luck and the out-of-work, the nickname evolved into "Skid Row." Pioneer Park, the original city center (1852), is still home to many of the city's luckless. In the Park and the nearby Pioneer Square historical district, an interesting mix of transients and chic shopkeepers coexist.

Seattle really didn't attract much attention until 1962, when the world's fair bequeathed the skyline its distinctive Space Needle. These days, Seattle has a large aerospace industry (the Boeing Company) and is a growing computer software center. Since it is the closest United States

---

FREEBIES AND CHEAPIES
(Free or $3.50 and under for adults)

❑ Alweg Monorail (see Attractions)
❑ Space Needle (see Attractions)
❑ Seattle Children's Museum (see Museums)
❑ Coast Guard Museum (see Museums)
❑ Frye Art Museum (see Museums)
❑ Museum of History and Industry (see Museums)
❑ Seattle Art Museum (see Museums)
❑ Thomas Burke Memorial Washington State Museum (see Museums)
❑ Pacific Arts Center (see Attractions)
❑ Seattle Aquarium (see Attractions)
❑ Klondike Goldrush National Historical Park (see Attractions)
❑ Hiram M. Chittenden Locks (see Attractions)
❑ University of Washington Arboretum (see Attractions)
❑ Woodland Park Zoo (see Attractions)
❑ Gas Works Park (see Attractions)

---

port to the Orient, the harbor on Puget Sound's Elliott Bay handles a booming import-export business. This metro area of 1.5 million is home to major league sports franchises (football's Seahawks, baseball's Mariners, and basketball's SuperSonics), opera, ballet, and a first-rate symphony orchestra. And new high-rise buildings dwarf the quarter-century-old Space Needle.

CLIMATE

Prepare yourselves for precipitation with an umbrella, a raincoat, and water-resistant footwear. Regarding temperature, Seattle is quite mild all year. In winter, fall, and spring, the daytime high temperatures usually reach the 50s, with nighttime lows dropping into the 40s and sometimes the upper 30s—rarely freezing. In summer, highs can range into the 70s during the day, dipping into the 50s at night. Fall, winter, and spring are generally more rainy than summer.

TOURIST INFORMATION

Contact the Seattle-King County Convention and Visitors Bureau, 666 Stewart, Seattle, WA 98101, (206) 447–4241.

```
┌─────────────────────────────────────────────────┐
│                                                   │
│              THE LONG WEEKEND                     │
│                                                   │
│                  Day One                          │
│                                                   │
│   ❏ Seattle Center (see Attractions)              │
│                                                   │
│                  Day Two                          │
│                                                   │
│   ❏ Seattle Aquarium (see Attractions)            │
│   ❏ Omnidome Theater (see Attractions)            │
│   ❏ Washington State Ferries (see Transportation) │
│   ❏ Olde Curiosity Shop (see Attractions)         │
│   ❏ Bill Spiedel's Underground Seattle (see Tours)│
│                                                   │
│                 Day Three                         │
│                                                   │
│   ❏ Hiram M. Chittenden Locks (see Attractions)   │
│   ❏ Woodland Park Zoo (see Attractions)           │
│   ❏ University of Washington Arboretum (see Attractions) │
│                                                   │
└─────────────────────────────────────────────────┘
```

ATTRACTIONS

SEATTLE CENTER

5th Ave. N. and Broad St. (206) 625–4234. Pay parking lots ring the perimeter of the Center.

This 89-acre plot was the site of the 1962 Seattle World's Fair and its early-1960s architectural version of the 21st century is accented by lush landscaping and frothing fountains. It is the terminus for the **Alweg Monorail**, which runs a little over a mile from the new Westlake Mall at 4th Avenue and Pine Street. The Seattle Center also encompasses some of the city's best-known attractions: the **Space Needle**, the **Seattle Children's Museum** (see Museums), the **Pacific Science Center**, the **Fun Forest Amusement Park**, the **Center House Theater** (see Children's Theater) and the **Pacific Arts Center**. The Center is also home to the Seattle Opera House and the Coliseum, site of rock concerts and Seattle SuperSonics basketball games.

SPACE NEEDLE

Phone. (206) 443–2100

Hours. June 15 through Labor Day: daily, 7:30 A.M.–1:30 A.M. Rest of the year: daily, 9 A.M.–12 midnight.

Costs. Adults, $3.50; ages 5–12, $1.75. Free when dining at either of the Needle's two revolving restaurants (see Restaurants).

The 605-foot Space Needle's wraparound observation deck (518 feet) affords one of the most breathtaking views in the Pacific Northwest. It also has a number of machines that, for 25¢, flattens out pennies and reimprints them with an image of the Space Needle. It's a perfect diversion for kids who tire of the geographical grandeur of Puget Sound, Mount Rainier, the Olympic Mountains, and the hills of Seattle. There are observation decks both indoors and outdoors, with the outdoor deck surrounded a by cage that only minimally detracts from the view.

Kids' Facilities. No changing tables, but plenty of benches in the indoor observation area. No stroller rentals. Should an emergency bottle need warming, the restaurant staff will be happy to do so, even if you're not dining there.

Ratings. There is plenty to amuse even kids who don't want to observe the landscape. You can prepare for the trip by renting video tapes of the two movies filmed there: Elvis Presley's *It Happened at the World's Fair* (1962) and Warren Beatty's *The Parallax View* (1974). All ages, A.

FUN FOREST AMUSEMENT PARK

Phone. (206) 624–1585.

Hours. Memorial Day to Labor Day: daily, 12 noon–12 midnight. April 1 to Memorial Day *and* Labor Day to September 30: Fri., 7 P.M.–12 midnight; Sat. and Sun., 12 noon–12 midnight.

Costs. Ride prices vary (from less than a dollar), but discounts are offered on ticket books.

Although smaller than the average amusement park, the Fun Forest nevertheless has kid-pleasing rides, including the rattling Wild Mouse and the infamous Zipper. This is not a world-class facility but you can take in all the rides and still have enough daylight for other activities.

Kids' Facilities. No changing tables in restrooms; however, there are benches aplenty. No stroller rentals. No bottle-warming facilities, but these can be found at the nearby Center House. Fast-food stands.

Ratings. Most rides cater to kids above the age of 6; however, there are a few diversions for the younger kids. 2–7, B; 8–11, A; 12–16, A.

PACIFIC ARTS CENTER

Phone. (206) 443–5437

Hours. Wed.–Sat., 10 A.M.–3 P.M.

Costs. Free.

Tucked between the Center House and the Pacific Science Center is this small art gallery designed with kids in mind. The multimedia installations of modern art change from time to time, but there's always something to touch and often something to crawl through.

Kids' Facilities. No changing tables. No strollers (the place is too small). No food or bottle-warming facilities.

Ratings. En route to the Science Center, the gallery takes only 10 minutes to see. All ages, A.

PACIFIC SCIENCE CENTER

Phone. (206) 443–2001.

Hours. July 1 to Labor Day: daily, 10 A.M.–6 P.M. Rest of the year: Mon.–Fri., 10 A.M.–5 P.M.; Sat. and Sun., 10 A.M.–6 P.M. Closed on Thanksgiving and Christmas.

Costs. Adults, $3.50; ages 6–17, $2.50; ages 2–5, $1.50; under age 2, free. IMAX Theater: adults and ages 6–17, $1 extra; ages 5 and under, free.

All that kids (and adults) would want to know about science is contained in the PSC's six connected buildings. There's a starlab, a planetarium, an environmental monitoring center, salt water tidal pools, a big screen IMAX theater, and a Laserium theater. There are three new hands-on areas: Kids Works, where kids can make bubbles, hold small animals, and have water pistol shootouts; Body Works, where they can test their senses in a sensory maze, find out how much blood is in their bodies, and gauge their lung capacities; and Water Works, where they can see interactive displays of the properties of water. There's also a special area for kids under age 6 and a restaurant, the Fountains Cafe.

Kids' Facilities. Changing tables in both the men's and ladies' restrooms. No stroller rentals; however, there are free wheelchairs for really tired kids. Bottles can be warmed by the restaurant staff.

Ratings. There's something here for everyone. All ages, A.

ALWEG MONORAIL

Hours. Summer: daily, 10 A.M.–12 midnight. Rest of the year: Mon.–Fri., 10 A.M.–9 P.M.; Sat. and Sun., 10 A.M.–12 midnight.

Costs. One way: adults and children 5 and over, 60¢; children under 5, free.

When the World's Fair first opened in the spring of 1962, it was envisioned that monorail travel was the wave of the future. A quarter of a century later, the future has not yet arrived: too bad, because this mode of travel is quick (about 45 miles per hour), comfortable, quiet both inside and out, and efficient—not to mention fun. The run between downtown and the Seattle Center takes only about 90 seconds.

Kids' Facilities. None.

Ratings. All ages, A.

SEATTLE AQUARIUM

Pier 59 at Alaskan Way, Waterfront Park. (206) 625–4358. Pay parking meters across Alaskan Way from the pier.

Hours. Memorial Day to Labor Day: daily, 10 A.M.–7 P.M. Rest of the year: daily 10 A.M.–5 P.M.

Costs. Adults, $3.25; ages 13–18, $1.50; ages 6–12, $.75; under age 6, free.

Most aquariums settle for indoor fish tanks. Some even feature outdoor displays. Few have both, and Seattle Aquarium's unique underwater habitat exhibit actually takes you beneath the surface of Puget Sound for a fish-eye view of the annual salmon and trout ritual that propels these fish upstream from salt to fresh water to spawn. Along with tanks filled with fresh and salt-water tropical fish, there's a great display of electric eels and an outdoor area inhabited by frisky seals and comical otters. There are also tanks where kids can touch samples of marine life.

Kids' Facilities. Diaper-changing facilities only in the ladies' restroom; however, there are lots of indoor and outdoor benches. No bottle-warming capabilities, and no stroller rentals. There are a number of restaurants on nearby piers.

Ratings. All ages, A.

OMNIDOME THEATER

Pier 59 at Alaskan Way, Waterfront Park. (206) 622–1868. Meter parking across Alaskan Way.

Hours. Daily, 10 A.M.–9 P.M. Two 30-minute movies are usually shown every 30 minutes throughout the day.

Costs. Adults, $4.50; ages 13–18, $3.50; ages 6–12, $2.75; children under 6, free.

Seattle's second big theater does IMAX (at the Pacific Science Center) one better. The giant screen is curved to give the viewer a 180-degree fish-eye view of the image projected onto the screen. A favorite of Washingtonians is *The Eruption of Mt. St. Helens*, which takes the viewer by helicopter into the volcano's steaming crater just after the May 1980 eruption and before, during, and after subsequent blasts.

Kids' Facilities. No changing tables (use benches in the lobby). There's regular movie fare (popcorn, soda, etc.) in the lobby, but the employees have no way of warming a baby's bottle.

Ratings. The younger ones tend to squirm, 2–7, C; 8–11, A; 12–16, A.

YE OLDE CURIOSITY SHOP

Pier 51 at Alaskan Way. (206) 682–5844. Meter parking across Alaskan Way.

Hours. Summer: daily, 9 A.M.–9 P.M. Rest of the year: daily, 9:30 A.M.–6 P.M. Closed on New Year's Day, Thanksgiving, and Christmas.

Costs. Free.

Imagine a circus freak show housed in a cluttered religious gift shop, and you begin to get an idea about the 90-year-old Olde Curiosity Shop.

Along with the usual tourist post cards and trinkets are an amazingly large collection of shrunken heads (including the world's smallest adult head), two bona fide 19th-century mummies, the Lord's Prayer written on the head of a pin, a two-headed pig in a jar, and much, much more.

Kids' Facilities. No washrooms, no restaurant, no strollers.

Ratings. You'll probably have to restrain the younger ones. The temptation to touch the colorful, kid-level merchandise will be overwhelming. All ages, A.

KLONDIKE GOLDRUSH NATIONAL HISTORICAL PARK

117 S. Main St. (206) 442–7220. Metered street and pay lot parking nearby.

Hours. Summer: daily, 9 A.M.–6 P.M. Rest of the year: 9 A.M.–5 P.M. Closed on New Year's Day, Thanksgiving, and Christmas.

Costs. Free.

In 1897 and 1898, Seattle was the most active jumping-off point for the Alaskan Gold Rush. This small museum is a repository for old murals and photos of the people and the city of Seattle at the turn of the century. It also has a hefty amount of mining memorabilia. Feature-length movies are shown, along with regular free Saturday and Sunday showings (3 P.M.) of Charlie Chaplin's silent movie *The Gold Rush.*

Kids' Facilities. No changing tables, bottle-warming facilities, or stroller rentals.

Ratings. Younger kids are easily bored, but historic-minded older children will get a kick out of it. 2–7, D; 8–11, C; 12–16, A.

HIRAM M. CHITTENDEN LOCKS AND LAKE WASHINGTON SHIP CANAL FISH LADDER

3015 N.W. 54th St. (206) 783–7059. Free parking in lot.

Hours. Visitors Center: June 15 through September 15: daily, 11 A.M.–8 P.M. Rest of the year: Thurs.–Mon., 11 A.M.–5 P.M. Locks: daily, 7 A.M.–9 P.M.

Costs. Free.

Built in 1916, the locks are a popular place to watch both sports craft and small commercial vessels make the transition between the fresh water of the Ship Canal, Lake Union, and Lake Washington and the salt water of Puget Sound. The locks are necessary because the difference between the level of the lakes and Puget Sound varies (depending on the season) between 6 and 26 feet. The new fish ladder, which opened in 1976, replacing the antiquated 1917 ladder, has an underwater viewing area where you can observe three varieties of salmon and two varieties of trout migrate upstream into fresh water to spawn. Except for the second half of April and the month of May, there are almost always fish to observe. The Visitors Center has exhibits on the locks and the fish ladder; it's surrounded by the Carl S. English gardens, a perfect place for a picnic.

Kids' Facilities. The restrooms are immaculate. No diaper-changing tables; however, there are plenty of benches. No stroller rentals. The restrooms at the fish ladder are almost as clean, but no changing tables.

Ratings. The younger ones may get bored watching the boats, but they will definitely enjoy seeing the fish. All ages, A.

UNIVERSITY OF WASHINGTON ARBORETUM (WASHINGTON PARK)

Lake Washington Blvd. E. and E. Madison St. (206) 543–8800. Free parking.

Hours. Daily, 8 A.M.–sunset.

Costs. Free.

This beautiful 200-acre park is crisscrossed with nature trails and has plenty of places for a picnic. A greenhouse is open to the public on weekdays from 8 A.M. to 4 P.M.

Kids' Facilities. No changing tables. No stroller rentals. No bottle-warming facilities.

Ratings. A great place to tire the kids out. All ages, A.

JAPANESE GARDEN AND TEAHOUSE

Lake Washington Blvd. E. and E. Madison St. (206) 625–2635. Free parking.

Hours. Open daily March 1 through November 30. Closed December 1 through February 28. June 1 through August 31: 10 A.M.–8 P.M. May

1 through May 31: 10 A.M.–7 P.M. March 1 through April 30 and September 1 through October 31: 10 A.M.–6 P.M. November 1 through November 30: 10 A.M.–4 P.M. Tea ceremonies every third Sunday of the month at 2 P.M. and 3 P.M.

Costs. Adults, $1; ages 6–18, 50¢; under age 6, free.

The 3½-acre garden in the Arboretum is meticulously designed: There is a purpose for the placement of each rock, tree, and shrub. As a testimony to the skill of the Japanese designer, the copper-roofed tea house was constructed without the use of bolts, screws, or nails. The whole place is a work of art.

Kids' Facilities. No stroller rentals. No diaper changing facilities (although there are plenty of park benches). No restaurant. In fact, no food or drinks are allowed into the Japanese Garden.

Ratings. Not terribly interesting for younger children. 2–7, D; 8–11, C; 12–16, A.

ENCHANTED VILLAGE/ WILD WAVES WATER PARK

36201 Kit Corner Rd., Federal Way. Located 17 miles south of Seattle; take the first left off Interstate 5, exit 142B, and follow signs). Enchanted Village: (206) 838–1700 or (206) 927–4100. Wild Waves: (206) 838–8828 or (206) 927–4223. Lot parking.

Hours. *Enchanted Village:* Mid-May through Labor Day: daily, 10 A.M.–9 P.M. April 1 through mid-May and Labor Day through September 30: Sat. and Sun., 10 A.M.–9 P.M. *Wild Waves:* Memorial Day through Labor Day: Sun.–Thurs., 10:30 A.M.–7:30 P.M.; Fri. and Sat., 10:30 A.M.–9 P.M.

Costs. *Enchanted Village:* adults and children, $7.95; after 4 P.M., $5; kids 2 and under, free. *Wild Waves:* adults and children, $12.95; after 4 P.M., $7.95; kids 2 and under, free.

Enchanted Village is a scaled-down Disneyland, with rides, live entertainment, picnic areas, video games, and a children's zoo. Wild Waves features water slides, the only wave pool in the Pacific Northwest, and kiddie pools for the little ones. Both places offer a plethora of junk food and both forbid you to bring in your own food and beverages.

Kids' Facilities. No stroller rentals. Change diapers on one of many benches. Most restaurants and food stands have microwaves and will be glad to warm bottles.

Ratings. Enchanted Village is geared for younger kids. 2–7, A; 8–11, B; 12–16, D. Wild Waves is tailor made for teens and preteens. 2–7, C; 8–11, A; 12–16, A.

WOODLAND PARK ZOO

5500 Phinney Ave. N. (206) 789–7919. Pay lot parking.

Hours. Opens daily at 8:30 A.M. April through September: closes at 6 P.M. October and March: closes at 5 P.M. November through February: closes at 4 P.M.

Costs. Adults, $2.50; ages 13–17, $1; ages 6–12, 50¢; under age 6, free.

Unlike most zoos, this 90-acre facility on the shores of Green Lake does not display animals in phylogenetic groups (monkey house, reptile house, etc.) but rather by natural, geographic habitat: African Savanna, Asian Forest, Marshland, and Desert and Tropic houses. Their Family Farm has an animal nursery and a place for kids to pet some of the residents. The Zoo also houses the Seattle Children's Theater (see Theaters).

Kids' Facilities. Changing tables in both men's and ladies' restrooms. There's a first-aid center as well as three fast-food concession areas where it is possible to get a bottle warmed. Large-wheeled, heavy-duty strollers can be rented for $1.62 per day. We recommend them over your regular umbrella stroller because they're built for the zoo's varying terrain.

Ratings. All ages, A.

GAS WORKS PARK

N. Northlake Way and Meridian Ave. N.

Hours. Dawn to dusk.

Costs. Free.

What can you do with an old industrial site? Instead of razing the pipes and boilers and other gizmos from an old gas plant, keep them, paint them, and build a park around them. While most of the structures are posted off-limits to climbing kids, legitimate playground apparatus is built into others. There's a covered area for picnics and the often-wind-swept 21-acre park is a great place for kite flying. It also offers an unobstructed view of the high-rise buildings downtown.

Kids' Facilities. There are restrooms, but no diaper-changing facilities. No bottle warming. No stroller rentals.

Ratings. With playground fun for the younger kids already in place, all you need are a couple of kites for the older kids and everybody's happy. 2–7, A; 8–11, (with kites) A; 12–16, (with kites), B.

SEATTLE TIMES

Fairview Ave. N. and John St. (206) 464–2285. Metered street and pay lot and garage parking nearby.

Hours. September through May only. Mon., Tues., and Thurs., 11 A.M. and 12:45 P.M. *You must call ahead for reservations.*

Costs. Free.

This all-inclusive 1-tour takes you through the pressroom, composing room, editorial department, classified ad department, and mail room of Seattle's afternoon paper. It's great fun, especially when kids realize how many processes and people it takes to put out a daily newspaper.

Kids' Facilities. No stroller rentals. No diaper-changing tables. No bottle-warming facilities.

Ratings. Kids under 9 not admitted. 9–11, A; 12–16, A.

MUSEUMS

SEATTLE CHILDREN'S MUSEUM

At Center House in **Seattle Center**, 305 Harrison St. (206) 441–1768. Plenty of pay parking in Seattle Center lots.

Hours. Tues.–Thurs. and Sat., 10 A.M.–5 P.M.; Fri., 10 A.M.–8 P.M.; Sun., 12 noon–5 P.M. Closed on Mondays, Thanksgiving, Christmas, and New Year's Day. Open on Mondays only during Seattle school holidays. Museum closes for repairs in early September, so call ahead.

Costs. Adults and children, $2.50; kids under age 1, free.

In operation since 1981, the SCM has already moved to larger quarters once and is contemplating yet another move. Role playing is the name of the game at this little city within a city. There are a number of shops and offices (doctor, dentist, school, restaurant, grocery store, etc.) where kids are encouraged to take part in the activities they've seen adults do. Many of the facilities have authentic working machinery, like cash registers, books, and telephones. There is a space for little kids to climb around and even a birthday room that can be reserved for parties. The best attraction is the bubble room, where a 2-by-3-foot wire frame is dipped into a soapy mixture, creating a wall of bubble that bends and curves when kids blow on it.

Kids' Facilities. Changing tables are located in the ladies' restroom. There is no food facility; however, there are restaurants nearby. Strollers aren't rented but aren't needed because of the museum's compact size and the fact that kids are encouraged to walk around and touch things.

Ratings. Except for the bubble room, appreciated by all ages, this is for younger kids only, 2–7, A; 8–11, C; 12–16, F.

COAST GUARD MUSEUM

Pier 36 and Alaskan Way. (206) 442–5019. Limited free parking on grounds.

Hours. Mon., Wed., and Fri., 10 A.M.–4 P.M.; weekends and holidays, 1 P.M.–5 P.M.

Costs. Free.

This small museum provides a glimpse at Coast Guard history through photographs, drawings, uniforms, ship models, and shipboard memorabilia. This museum, which can be seen in less than 20 minutes, is worth the trip. Also on Pier 36 is the Coast Guard Vessel Traffic Center (open daily from 8 A.M. to 4 P.M.), where you can watch the personnel monitor ship traffic on Puget Sound. It also has a 20-minute film. Call in advance for a tour: (206) 442–5896.

Kids' Facilities. No changing facilities. No restaurant. No stroller rental.

Ratings. This one's for the older kids. 2–7, C; 8–11, B; 12–16, A.

FRYE ART MUSEUM

704 Terry Ave. at Cherry. (206) 622–9250. Free parking at 705 and 707 Terry.

Hours. Mon.–Sat., 10 A.M.–5 P.M.; Sun. and holidays, 12 noon–5 P.M. Closed on Christmas and Thanksgiving.

Costs. Free; donations are appreciated.

This seven-gallery museum has a large collection of 19th- and 20th-century paintings, with traveling shows of contemporary art that change about once a month.

Kids' Facilities. No changing facilities. No restaurant. No stroller rental.

Ratings. Older artistically inclined kids will enjoy the Frye—smaller ones probably won't. 2–7, D; 8–11, C; 12–14, A.

HENRY GALLERY

15th Ave. N.E., and N.E. Campus Parkway on the University of Washington campus. (206) 543–2280. Pay parking garage next to museum.

Hours. Tues., Wed., and Fri., 10 A.M.–5 P.M.; Thurs., 10 A.M.–7 P.M.; Sat. and Sun., 11 A.M.–5 P.M. Closed on Mon.

Costs. Free; donations accepted.

This relatively small former private gallery has more than 1,500 pieces, mostly 19th- and 20th-century paintings, prints, and ceramics. It also has some modern art. Visiting exhibits change about once a month. (*Note: Since it is located on the busy university campus, traffic is terrible on Friday afternoons when school is in session and on Saturdays when there are major university sporting events.*)

Kids' Facilities. No diaper-changing facilities, restaurant, or stroller rentals.

Ratings. Not for little kids, 2–7, D; 8–11, C; 12–16, A.

MUSEUM OF FLIGHT

9404 E. Marginal Way S. (206) 764–5700. Free parking.

Hours. Daily, 10 A.M.–5 P.M.

Costs. Adults, $4; ages 13–18, $3; ages 6–12, $2; ages 5 and under, free.

The new 142,000-square-foot, glass-and-steel gallery displays a mind-boggling collection of beautifully restored historic aircraft: old biplanes, World War II aircraft, helicopters, and a recently decommissioned Navy F-4 jet flown by the Blue Angels. The Museum's Red Barn annex, the original Boeing Factory, still has a number of old flying artifacts and flight uniforms. Films and button-activated slide and audio presentations detail early balloon and fixed-wing flight. Parents beware: The gift shop has scores of books and trinkets you will be badgered to buy.

Kids' Facilities. No changing tables; however, there are ample benches. No restaurant and no stroller rentals. However, the museum does have two wheelchairs you may be able to use.

Ratings. Not enough buttons to push for the younger kids, 2–7, C; 8–11, A; 12–16, A.

MUSEUM OF HISTORY AND INDUSTRY

2700 24th Ave. E., at McCurdy Park. (206) 324–1125. Free parking.

Hours. Mon.–Sat., 10 A.M.–5 P.M.; Sun., 12 noon–5 P.M. Closed on New Year's Day, Thanksgiving, and Christmas.

Costs. Adults, $1.50; ages 6–12, 50¢; ages 5 and under, free. Free admission on Tues.

Located just south of the Lake Washington Ship Canal in the shadow of University of Washington's Husky Stadium, the Museum details the early history of commerce in Seattle, principally the lumber industry and the steamships in Puget Sound. It takes only about a half hour to see everything here en route to a picnic in the University of Washington Arboretum a few blocks away.

Kids' Facilities. A changing table in the ladies' restroom only. No restaurant and no stroller rentals, although there are a few wheelchairs you can use.

Rating. Not for younger kids. 2–7, D; 8–11, C; 12–16, B.

NORDIC HERITAGE MUSEUM

3014 N.W. 67th St. (206) 789–5707. Street parking.

Hours. Tues.–Thurs., 11 A.M.–3 P.M.; Sat. and Sun., 1 P.M.–5 P.M. Closed on holidays.

Costs. Adults, $2.50; ages 6–16, $1. Free on Wed.

This museum chronicles the epic journey of Scandinavian immigrants across the Atlantic Ocean to Ellis Island, and then west across the United States to the Pacific Northwest. It traces the development of the fishing and lumber industries in the area, and displays native handicrafts. It also has a replica of an Atlantic passenger ship.

Kids' Facilities. Changing area in ladies' restroom only. Strollers allowed, but no elevators. No food facilities.

Ratings. The heavy historical slant will probably bore the young ones. 2–7, D: 8–11, B: 12–14, B.

SEATTLE ART MUSEUM

14th Street E. and E. Prospect Ave. (206) 625–8900. Free parking in lot.

Hours. Tues.–Sat., 10 A.M.–5 P.M., Thurs. until 9 P.M.; Sun., 12 noon–5 P.M.

Costs. Adults, $2; students (age 6 and up), $1; ages 5 and under, free.

If you do nothing but look at the outside of this wonderful Art Deco building and gaze at the grounds of beautiful Volunteer Park, you've done well. The museum itself has a large collection of Asian and European paintings and sculptures, plus traveling exhibits several times a year.

Kids' Facilities. Changing table is located in ladies' restroom. No changing, however, in men's restroom. No restaurants. No stroller rentals.

Ratings. Since there is no area designed specifically for young kids, their interest may wane. However, it's small enough to get through quickly if you're determined to take a toddler along. 2–7, D; 8–11, C; 12–16, A.

WING LUKE ASIAN MUSEUM

407 7th Ave. S. (206) 623–5124. Pay street parking.

Hours. Tues.–Fri., 11 A.M.–4:30 P.M.; Sat., 12 noon–4 P.M.; Sun. (June through August only), 12 noon–4 P.M.

Costs. Adults, donations accepted; children (taking tour), $1; children (not taking tour), 50¢.

Named for a city councilman killed in a 1965 plane crash, the museum focuses on Seattle's Asian community, from their first appearance in 1860 to the present day. Exhibits change, but there are always hands-on activities for kids. Call ahead for information about upcoming exhibits.

Kids' Facilities. No changing tables. No strollers. Lots of local Chinese restaurants nearby. Try dim sum (a kid favorite) at the Silver Dragon, 421 7th Ave. S.

Ratings. For a rare glimpse at Oriental culture, this place offers a real change of pace. All ages, B.

THOMAS BURKE MEMORIAL WASHINGTON STATE MUSEUM

N.E. 45th St. and 17th Ave. N.E. (206) 543–5590. Inexpensive campus parking next door.

Hours. Mon.–Fri., 10 A.M.–5:30 P.M.; Sat. and Sun., 9 A.M.–4:30 P.M.

Costs. Free; donations accepted.

If your kids like dinosaurs (and what kids don't?), this is the place to go in Seattle. Along with a dinosaur and a fossilized dinosaur footprint, it has much in the way of local Northwest Indian tribal culture and a great bird exhibit with buttons to activate taped bird calls.

Kids' Facilities. No changing tables; however, bench space is available. No stroller rental. The coffee shop, the Boiserie, on the lower level will warm bottles.

Ratings. Despite the dinosaurs and push-button bird calls, this museum still doesn't have much to interest the little ones. 2–7, C; 8–11, B; 12–16, A.

HOTELS

Seattle offers an eclectic collection of hotels; however, the area's best bets are suite hotels. Unfortunately, none are in the city's center.

South

ALL SUITES INN—BIRCHWOOD

3445 S. 160th St. (located 1 mile east of Sea-Tac Airport). (206) 246–8550. 48 units. Free parking.

Rates. Suites from $28 to $50.

This amazingly inexpensive hotel is located amid the jungle of hotels that surrounds Sea-Tac airport. Despite aesthetic shortcomings, it has all the amenities. All units are either 1- or 2-bedroom suites with sofa sleepers for extra family members. Kids under 10 stay free with parents.

Cribs: Free.
Rollaways: No.
Babysitting: Yes, referrals.
Pool: Yes, outdoor, for summer use only.
Restaurants: No.
Kitchen facilities: Yes, with limited utensils.
Room service: Yes, from local restaurant.
Closest emergency hospital: Riverton Hospital, 10 minutes away, (206) 244–0180.

ALL SUITES INN—INNSBRUCK

3223 S. 160th St. (located 1 mile northeast of Sea-Tac Airport). (206) 241–2022. 29 units. Free parking.

Rates. Suites range from $28 to $50.

This hotel is owned by the same outfit that runs the Birchwood. They are 2 blocks apart and offer all the same services.

CONTINENTAL COURT APARTMENT MOTEL

17223 32nd Ave. S. (located 2 blocks east of Sea-Tac Airport). (206) 241–1500. 330 units. Free parking.

Rates. $30 to $105.

This attractive 1- and 2-bedroom suite motel is situated on spacious grounds, and there are a number of buildings which make it look more like an apartment complex than a motel. The Continental is located near busy and somewhat noisy Sea-Tac Airport. Kids under 6 stay free with parents.
Cribs: They offer deluxe playpens that easily double as cribs, $5.
Rollaways: Yes, $5.
Babysitting: No.
Pool: Yes, outdoor; also a sauna.
Restaurant: No, but there are plenty nearby.
Kitchen facilities: Yes, including a dishwasher.
Room Service: No.
Closest emergency hospital: Riverton Hospital, 12 minutes away, (206) 244–0180.

RESIDENCE INN—SEATTLE SOUTH

16201 West Valley Hwy.; (located 4 miles east of Sea-Tac Airport). (206) 226–5500. Free parking.

Rates. $85 to $105.

As with many Residence Inns, this hotel offers a number of extras, including barbecue and picnic facilities and a grocery shopping service, free Christmas gift wrapping, tree decorating, caroling during the season, and Halloween parties for the kids. Free breakfasts and evening snacks are served in a living-roomlike lobby that is also stocked with board games and tables and a fireplace for roasting marshmallows. The staff is receptive to the special needs and desires of guests with children. Kids under 18 stay free with parents.

Cribs: Yes, $5.
Rollaways: Yes, $10.
Babysitting: Yes, referrals.
Pool: Yes, outdoor, plus three spas.
Restaurants: No, but free continental breakfast and evening snack served. Signing privileges at local restaurants.
Kitchen facilities: Yes.
Room service: No.
Closest emergency hospital: Valley Medical Center, 5–8 minutes away, (206) 228–3450.

East

RESIDENCE INN—SEATTLE EAST

14455 N.E. 29th Place, Bellevue (located off Hwy. 520 between Lake Washington and Lake Sammamish; approximately 17 miles northeast of Sea-Tac Airport off Interstate 405). (206) 882–1222. Free parking.

Rates. $84 to $120.

See Residence Inn—Seattle South.
Cribs: Yes, free.
Room service: Yes, set up with local restaurant.
Closest emergency hospital: Overlake Hospital, 10 minutes away, (206) 454–4011.

North

RESIDENCE INN—SEATTLE NORTH

18200 Alderwood Mall Blvd., Lynwood. Located approximately 14 miles north of Pioneer Square off Interstate 5, 28 miles north of Sea-Tac Airport. (206) 771–1100. Free parking.

Rates. $68 to $98.

This Residence Inn has many of the same features as Residence Inn —Seattle South and East, except for the following.
Cribs: Yes, $5.
Pool: Yes, outdoor pool only.
Closest emergency hospital: Steven's Hospital, 6–7 minutes away, (206) 774–0555.

RESTAURANTS

Fast food abounds in Seattle and all the standard national chains are represented (McDonald's, Burger King, Dairy Queen, Denny's, Kentucky Fried Chicken, Shakey's, Chuck E. Cheese,), along with some regional chains, including Ivar's for clams and fish fries, the Arctic Circle for burgers, and the Frankfurter for grilled hot dogs. Most places are open for long periods of the day and night, and have high chairs and booster seats. Other restaurants provide kids and parents with more than just food:

LIONS, TIGERS AND BEARS

352 Roy St. (206) 285–7221. Limited free lot parking. Metered street parking or pay lot parking at Seattle Center.

Hours. Lunch: daily, 10 A.M.–5 P.M. Dinner: Sun.–Thurs., 5–11:30 P.M.; Fri. and Sat., 5 P.M.–12:30 A.M.

It's not so much the food here as it is the ambiance for younger kids. As the name implies, there are lions, tigers, and bears (in picture form) on the walls, with stuffed Teddies and a large stuffed lion surveying the whole place. The old Victorian house contains a number of dining rooms. Food consists of burgers, sandwiches, and salads. Prices are inexpensive. Credit cards.

Kids' Facilities. High chairs, but no special diaper changing facilities.

THE OLD SPAGHETTI FACTORY

2801 Elliot Ave. (206) 623–3526. A good supply of parking spaces.

Hours. Lunch: daily, 11:30 A.M.–2 P.M. Dinner: Mon.–Thurs., 5P.M. –10 P.M.; Fri. and Sat., 5 P.M.–11:30 P.M.; Sun., 4 P.M.–10 P.M.

Old Spaghetti Factories are located in most major cities, and they seldom disappoint. Along with Victorian decor, this one features a vintage 1917 Bellingham trolley car. Speaking of trollies, while you eat you can watch the waterfront trolley travel along Alaskan Way and the waterfront. Food is downright cheap, and kids love it. No credit cards.

Kids' Facilities. High chairs and booster seats. No special changing facilities for infants, but plenty of benches.

PIZZA 'N PIPES

100 N. 85th St. (206) 782–0360. Ample parking.

Hours. Sun.–Thurs., 11 A.M.–10 P.M.; Fri. and Sat., 11 A.M.–12 midnight.

We have pizza and Animatronic robots (Chuck E. Cheese) and pizza and banjo music (Shakey's), so why not pizza and pipe organs, silent movies, and soap bubbles. It's all good, clean, noisy high-cholesterol fun. The pizza's cheap and there's usually a birthday party going on. No credit cards.

Kids' Facilities. They have booster seats and will gladly warm a baby's bottle. No special diaper changing facilities.

IRON HORSE RESTAURANT

311 3rd Ave. S. (206) 223–9506. Metered street parking nearby.

Hours. Summer: Mon.–Sat., 11 A.M.–9 P.M.; Sun., 12 noon–7 P.M. Winter: Mon.–Thurs., 11 A.M.–8 P.M.; Fri. and Sat., 11 A.M.–9 P.M.; Sun., 12 noon–7 P.M.

A restaurant that's also a model train museum? Pretty interesting stuff, but it gets better. Four sets of large-scale model trains actually chug up to your table carrying your order. There's railroad memorabilia on the walls and an HO-gauge train runs overhead. The fare includes hamburgers, soups, salads, fish and chips, and sandwiches, with full meals for between $3 and $6. Credit cards.

Kids' Facilities. Men's and ladies' restrooms have diaper-changing facilities. High chairs and booster seats available.

IVAN'S INDIAN SALMON HOUSE

401 N.E. Northlake Way. (206) 632–0767. Free street and lot parking.

Hours. Lunch: Mon.–Fri., 11:30 A.M.–2 P.M. Dinner: Mon.–Thurs., 5 P.M.–10 P.M.; Fri., 5 P.M.–11 P.M.; Sat., 4 P.M.–11 P.M.; Sun., 4 P.M.–10 P.M. Brunch: Sun., 10 A.M.–2 P.M.

If you can't make it to Tillicum Village on Blake Island (see Tours) for a traditional salmon dinner in an authentic Northwest Indian longhouse, Ivan's replica is the next best thing. Prices are moderate: salmon dinner is about $13. The children's salmon dinner costs about $5, and there are other items to tempt young palates. Credit cards.

Kids' Facilities. Diaper-changing facilities along with high chairs and booster seats. Children's dinner.

SPACE NEEDLE RESTAURANTS

Space Needle, Seattle Center. (206) 443–2100. Metered street and pay lot parking.

Hours. Summer: 7:30 A.M.–1:30 A.M. Winter: Sun.–Thurs., 11 A.M.–12 midnight; Fri.–Sat., 11 A.M.–1:30 A.M.; Sun. brunch, 10 A.M.–3 P.M.

The Space Needle's two restaurants revolve 360 degrees an hour to give diners a terrific view of the city and the surrounding countryside. The 180-seat Space Needle Restaurant is slightly less expensive; the 50-seat Emerald Suite is more intimate, and menu items are slightly pricier. The Space Needle Restaurant offers a kids' menu with burgers, chicken, and peanut butter and jelly sandwiches. Prices range from moderate to expensive, but the view is worth it, and you get a free trip to the observation deck. Credit cards.

Kids' Facilities. No diaper-changing areas in restrooms, but there are plenty of benches. Both high chairs and booster seats are available.

Big Splurges

ADRIATICA

1107 Dexter N., Seattle. (206) 285–5000. Free lot parking after 5 P.M.

Hours. Mon.–Fri., 5 P.M.–10 P.M.; Sat. and Sun., 5 P.M.–11 P.M.

Located in a converted old house, Adriatica is a cozy, romantic restaurant where food is served in many different rooms. The cuisine is Greek and Italian, specializing in local seafood. Try their great desserts. Dinners run around $30 per person. Full bar. Reservations required. Credit cards.

THE HUNT CLUB

900 Madison St. (in the Sorrento Hotel). (206) 622–6400. Validated valet parking.

Hours. Dinner: Sun.–Thurs., 5:30 P.M.–10 P.M.; Fri. and Sat., 5:30 P.M.–11 P.M.

The Hunt Club is appropriately named for its emphasis on locally caught game and seafood. Venison, quail, lamb, and rabbit dishes figure heavily on their menu. We recommend their terrific salmon entrees. For dessert, loosen your belt and order the triple chocolate cheesecake. Dinners are $35 and up per person. Full bar. Reservations recommended. Credit cards.

SHOPPING

GREAT WINDS KITE SHOP

402 Occidental Ave. S. (206) 624–6886. Metered street and pay lot parking.

Hours. Mon.–Sat., 10 A.M.–5:30 P.M.; Sun., 12 noon–5:30 P.M.

Great Winds' 400 different kites appeal to every ability level and every pocketbook. Store personnel will match you with the perfect kite and give pointers for the novice flyer.

MAGIC MOUSE TOYS

603 1st Ave. (206) 682–8097. Metered street and pay lot parking.

Hours. Daily, 10 A.M.–6 P.M.

Every stuffed animal, every game, and every European toy known to kids can be found here. Even a vast array of learning toys. There's a second level downstairs.

THE WOOD SHOP

320 1st Ave. S. (206) 624–1763. Metered street and pay lot parking.

Hours. Mon.–Sat., 10 A.M.–5:30 P.M.; Sun., (during November and December only), 12 noon–5 P.M.

Fabulous handmade wooden toys and a large selection of animal puppets are the hallmarks of this terrific store.

THE PUZZLE SHOP

309 Occidental Ave. S. (206) 682–6173. Metered street and pay lot parking.

Hours. Mon.–Sat., 10:30 A.M.–5:30 P.M.; Sun., 12 noon–5 P.M.; extended hours during Christmas season.

Along with puzzles, this store handles mind teasers, books, and wind-up toys. The shop caters to kids as young as 2, all the way up to experts able to conquer puzzles with as many as 75,000 pieces.

PIKE PLACE MARKET

Pike St. and 1st Ave. (206) 682–7453. Metered street and pay lot parking.

Hours. Mon.–Sat., 9 A.M.–6 P.M.

This indoor-outdoor market began as a place where farmers and fishermen could sell their wares. It hasn't changed in more than 80 years: It's just gotten a bit more sophisticated and bigger. Along with open-air and indoor stalls of fish, meat, vegetables, and flowers, there are toys, restaurants, bookshops, and stalls selling crafts by local artisans. It's a terrific place to roam in quest of souvenirs or just lunch. The market is on a number of levels and now incorporates the Pike Hillclimb: shops built along the stairway on the hill, which connects the market with Pier 59 and Alaskan Way. There are several highlights for kids.

The Great Wind-Up, (206) 621–9370, boasts the largest selection of wind-up toys in the Northwest and offers everything from a simple hopping frog ($3) to a King Kong bank ($20). The Wind-Up also sells nostalgia toys and notions, not the least of which is Pez candy and dispensers and Clark's Teaberry gum (yes, it's fresh!).

City Kites, (206) 622–5349, located on the Pike Hillclimb, will match you with the perfect kite. Watch a television that continuously plays a video demonstrating the many kinds of kites they sell.

Let's Play, (206) 340–0209, located at 1503 Post Alley, across from the main Market building, is Pike Place's only full-service toy store, featuring everything from stuffed animals to books and puzzles. They also have a good selection of baby toys and puppets.

SECRET GARDEN CHILDREN'S BOOKSTORE

7900 Green Lake Dr. N. (206) 524–4556. Street parking.

Hours. Mon.–Sat., 10 A.M.–6 P.M.; Thurs., 10 A.M.–8 P.M.

The Secret Garden (named for the 1911 children's book by Frances Hodgson Burnett) stocks titles for the very young reader all the way up to the junior-high level. Occasionally, the Secret Garden's ad in Seattle's Child (see Publications) offers a 10-percent discount on all purchases.

ISLAND BOOKS

3014 78th Ave. S.E., Mercer Island. (206) 232–6920. Take Interstate 90 and the Lacy Murrow Bridge east over Lake Washington to Mercer Island; get off at exit #7. Street parking.

Hours. Mon.–Sat., 10 A.M.–6 P.M.; Thurs. until 5 P.M.
This wonderful bookstore encourages you to bring the kids while you shop or browse. Deposit the kids in the playhouse right in the store and browse in peace.

IMAGINATION TOYS

Wallingford Center, N. 45th St. and Wallingford Ave. N. (206) 547–2356. Street parking.

Hours. Mon.–Wed., 10 A.M.–7 P.M.; Thurs. and Fri., 10 A.M.–9 P.M.; Sat., 10 A.M.–6 P.M.; Sun., 10 A.M.–5 P.M.
Wallingford Center is a former schoolhouse in which all the classrooms have been turned into shops. Imagination Toys specializes in wooden and European toys, books, and educational games. A bathtub filled with water displays bath toys.

ACADEMY SUPPLIES

18034 72nd Ave. S., Kent. (206) 251-0574 or (800) 543-7707. Located approximately 2½ miles east of Sea-Tac Airport. Take Interstate 5 to Interstate 405; get off at West Valley Hwy., exit #1; proceed south about 2 miles. Street parking.

Hours. Mon.–Fri., 9 A.M.–5 P.M.; Sat., 9 A.M.–3 P.M.
Academy Supplies carries one of the largest selections of educational supplies and children's records and tapes in the Pacific Northwest. There's a kids' play area where you can plant the little ones while you shop.

TRANSPORTATION

The way Seattle streets and avenues come by their north-south-east-west designations can be tricky for the unindoctrinated. Therefore, even if you're planning to get around by cab or public transportation, it's a good idea to purchase a detailed city map (or get one free from the American Automobile Club, if you're a member).

BUSES

The Seattle Metro covers the city as well as all of King County. It's a well-run system with buses on busy routes arriving every few minutes. The basic fare is 65¢ during rush hours and 55¢ the rest of the day. On weekends and holidays, an all-day pass costs only $1. The best deal in town is Metro's Magic Carpet Service—free bus transportation at all times in the 120-square block downtown area. The free zone extends from the waterfront west to 6th Avenue, and from Battery Street south to S. Jackson Street, encompassing attractions like Pioneer Square and Pike Place Market. The free zone stops 5 blocks from Seattle Center: Walk the rest of the way or take the monorail. For Metro information: (206) 447–4800.

TROLLEY

A vintage 1927 trolley car from Melbourne, Australia, runs on a 1½ mile stretch of abandoned railroad track along the waterfront on Alaskan Way between Broad Street (Pier 70) and S. Main Street (Pier 48), an area that includes nearly all waterfront attractions. Spaces are limited (52 seats, standing room for 40 more), so be prepared for a wait on summer weekends. The fare is 60¢, and you can get off at any time and reboard without additional charge. The ticket is free with a Metro transfer. Tickets can be purchased from automatic machines at each station. The trolley shuts down at sunset. For information: (206) 447–4800.

FERRIES

While tourists tend to look at the Washington State Ferries as tourist attractions (see Tours), they're transportation for natives who commute from Bainbridge Island and Bremerton. Thus, be prepared for crowded conditions during rush hours. For information: (206) 464–6400 or (800) 542–7052 (within Washington).

TAXIS

Cabs are pricey in Seattle. The base rate is $2 for the first mile plus $1 for each additional mile within the city limits. There's a 50¢ charge for sharing a cab. Outside the city limits (and this means the airport), each additional mile costs $1.40. The fare from the airport to downtown runs about $15.

Hail cabs on the street or call Yellow Cab, (206) 622–6500; Graytop, (206) 782–TAXI; or Far West, (206) 622–1717.

ALWEG MONORAIL

The monorail is great, quick fun for 60¢ (see Attractions).

TOURS

ON FOOT

On Broadway Tours. (206) 328–1221. Offers a 2-hour participatory tour of Broadway Avenue E., the city's music, theater, and dance district. Tours leave from 112 Broadway Avenue E. on Thursdays and Fridays at 8 P.M. from mid-May through the end of September. This one is for adults and older kids. (Price, $4.)

Chinatown Discovery. (206) 447–9230. Offers a 3-hour tour of Seattle's 12-square-block Chinatown/International District. Included are a stop at an herb dispensary, a Chinese printing press, a Chinese pavilion, a typical Chinese market, and a dim sum restaurant for lunch. Tours are given Tuesday through Saturday at 10:30 A.M. and 1:30 P.M. (adults, $18; children ages 5–11, $12). There are also nighttime tours for groups of ten or more.

Bill Speidel's Underground Tour. (206) 682–4646 or (206) 682–1511. One of the best tours in any city. It takes you underneath historic Pioneer Square, where the original sidewalks and ground-level building entrances once stood, before late-19th-century floods and outbreaks of bubonic plague. The tour guide's primer on Seattle history is delivered with tongue placed firmly in cheek. It begins and ends at Doc Maynard's Public House (610 First Avenue), a restaurant where you eat after the tour. Ninety-minute tours are offered between three and seven times a day, depending on the season. Parents of small children should be prepared to carry both child and umbrella stroller down a flight or two of steps. (Adults, $3.75; ages 13–17, $3.25; ages 6–12, $2; kids under 6, free.) *Reservations are a must.*

BUS TOURS

Grayline Tours. (206) 624–5813. Grayline conducts a number of tours in and around Seattle and the Olympic and Cascade Mountains. Their most popular city tour lasts 2½ hours and covers most important sights.

Between June and September, tours run daily at 9 A.M., 10 A.M., 12 noon, 2 P.M., 3 P.M., and 7 P.M. From September to June, tours are daily at 12 noon and 3 P.M. Tours depart from various locations. (Adults, $14; ages 5–12, $9; under age 5, free.)

BOAT TOURS

Washington State Ferries. (206) 464–6400 or (800) 542–7052 (within Washington). One of the best ways to see Seattle, western Washington, and Puget Sound is a trip on one of twenty-two state ferry boats. Kids go absolutely wild for them. The main routes from Seattle's Pier 52 go to Winslow on Bainbridge Island (35 minutes away) and Bremerton (1 hour away). Boats leave about once an hour from around 6 A.M. until 2 A.M. and cost about $3.30 per round trip (more if you take a car, a bicycle, or travel to one of the far-flung islands).

The ferries on the Seattle runs are large, have plenty of places to sit, cafeteria-style restaurants, and outdoor decks. There are a total of eight routes between Anacortes and Tacoma with crossings as short as 10 minutes and as long as 4 hours. You can even go to Vancouver Island, British Columbia.

Anchor Excursions. (206) 282–8368. Offers 4-hour educational Puget Sound tours aboard the 49-foot research vessel *Snow Goose*. The trip comes complete with an ecology lecture and an explanation of navigation. Tours leave from Fisherman's Terminal on the Lake Washington Ship Canal. Schedules vary, so call ahead. (Adults, $15; ages 13–18, $12.50; 12 and under, $10.)

Grayline Water Sightseeing Tours. (206) 441–1887. Offers a waterside tour of the Port of Seattle, Elliott Bay, and the Lake Washington Ship Canal. Departs daily from Pier 57: mid-June through August, at 9 A.M., 12 noon, and 3 P.M.; May 1 through mid-June and September 1 through mid-October, 12 noon and 3 P.M. (Adults, $12; ages 5–12, $7; 4 and under, free.)

Major Marine Tours. (206) 783–8873. Offers an hour-long sternwheeler tour of Seattle harbor. Boats leave hourly between 12 noon and 4 P.M. every day between June 1 and late September. There's also a dinner cruise nightly between 5 P.M. and 7 P.M. (Day cruises only: adults, $5; ages 6–11, $2.50. Call for prices of dinner cruises.) They also offer fishing excursions.

Seattle Harbor Tours. (206) 623–1445. Docks at Pier 56 and conducts 1-hour tours of the Seattle waterfront. June 1 through September 30:

daily, 11 A.M., 12:15 P.M., 1:45 P.M., 3:15 P.M., 4:30 P.M. May 1–31 and October 1–31: daily, 12:15 P.M., 1:45 P.M., and 3:15 P.M. (Adults, $4.50; ages 5–11, $2.)

Tillicum Village–Blake Island Tour. (206) 329–5700. This 4-hour excursion includes a visit to a Northwest Indian village, a baked salmon dinner prepared in the native way, carving demonstrations, and native dances. You can even stay an extra 2 hours and hike Blake Island's nature trails. These tours run year-round (January through April and mid-October through December on weekends only) two or three times a day. Call for the current schedule. (Adults, $24; ages 6–13, $10; ages 3–5, $3; 2 and under, free.)

Princess Marguerite. (206) 441–5560 or (206) 441–8200. A luxurious steamship that makes a daily trip between Seattle and Victoria, British Columbia. This Old-World ship has a huge dining room, a nursery, a children's playroom, and a game room—welcome facilities because the trip takes more than 4 hours each way. Leave Seattle at 8 A.M. and arrive in Victoria at 12:15 P.M. for an afternoon of shopping and sightseeing, and return to the boat for a 5:30 P.M. departure. You arrive in Seattle again at 9:45 P.M. The ship leaves from Pier 69 daily from early May through mid-October. (Adults, $29, [round trip]; ages 5–11, $18; ages 4 and under, free.)

The Victoria Clipper. (206) 448–5000. This jet catamaran cuts the travel time between Seattle and Victoria, British Columbia, to about 2½ hours. There is less to do on the *Clipper* than on the *Marguerite*, so the kids might slide into boredom. The restaurant serves a continental breakfast and light snack-style fare for reasonable prices. Between mid-May and early September, there are two sailings a day from Seattle (approximately 8 A.M. and 3 P.M.) and two from Victoria (11:30 A.M. and 6:15 P.M.); from September to May, there's one per day (from Seattle, 8 A.M.; from Victoria, 4:30 P.M.) (Adults, $49 [round trip]; ages 5–15, $39.)

(Note: You're crossing an international border, so remember to take proof of citizenship.)

TRAIN TOUR

Puget Sound and Snoqualmie Valley Railroad. (206) 746–4025 or (206) 888–3030. This old-fashioned steam train takes passengers on a 1-hour, 10-mile round trip between North Bend and Snoqualmie Falls, Washington, 30 miles east of Seattle (take Interstate 90 east to exit 31 and follow the signs). It's truly a step backward to the turn of the century, when steam trains were the only mechanized way to travel. The train runs weekends, 11 A.M. to 5 P.M., from April through October and for two weekends in early December. (Adults, $5; ages 5–15, $3; under age 5, free.)

SEASONAL EVENTS

February

CHINESE NEW YEAR

Since Seattle has a large Oriental population and a good-size Chinatown (also known as the International District), New Year's is special. There are parades with dragons and fireworks, and it's a good excuse to eat dim sum, a Seattle favorite. The 12-block International District is located just northeast of the Kingdome Stadium in an area bordered by Yesler Way, Interstate 5, S. Dearborn Street, and 4th Avenue. For information: (206) 447–7273.

May

FOLKLIFE FESTIVAL

The Seattle Center (see Attractions), home of the Space Needle, brings together area ethnic groups to celebrate their heritage. For more information: (206) 684–7165 or (206) 684–7200.

PIKE PLACE MARKET FAIR

A terrific attraction any time of the year (see Shopping), the shops and food and craft stands really put on the dog for this special annual fair. For a list of the special activities and times, call the Visitors Bureau or Pike Place Market, (206) 682–7453.

July

BITE OF SEATTLE

Many of the famous restaurants offer small portions of their house specialties for your sampling enjoyment. It all takes place at Seattle Center (see Attractions). For more information: (206) 684–7165 or (206) 684–7200.

July/August/September

SEAFAIR

In celebration of the city's water and waterfronts, both salt- and fresh-water, the city holds more than twenty "Seafair" events in July and August. In July, there's the Hispanic Seafair Festival in Seward Park across from Mercer Island on the shore of Lake Washington. Also in July, there are Seafair Grand and Torchlight parades through downtown and the International District. The Seafair Unlimited Hydroplane races in August on Lake Washington often set marine speed records. Watch anglers (or be one) take huge salmon out of Puget Sound during the Salmon Derby.

BUMBERSHOOT

Bumbershoot is the city's yearly, early-September art festival. Seattle Center (see Attractions) is home to all the kids' events, including theater presentations, clowns, art demonstrations, hands-on activities, free photographs, and storytelling. For information: (206) 447–7273.

October

OKTOBERFEST

The German decendents in Seattle stage a fairly good Oktoberfest, complete with German bands, food, beer for the grownups, and root beer for the kids. It all happens at the Seattle Center. For information: (206) 684–7165 or (206) 684–7200.

December

CHRISTMAS AROUND THE WORLD

The Museum of History and Industry (see Museums) offers a glimpse of yuletide activities from the far reaches of the planet. For more information: (206) 324–1125.

SANTA CLAUS TRAIN

During the first two weekends in December, the Puget Sound and Snoqualmie Valley Railroad (see Tours) fires up its ancient steam train for a winter ride through the valley. You might even see Santa Claus. For more information: (206) 746–4025.

CHILDREN'S THEATER

PICCOLI BIG THEATRE FOR LITTLE FOLK

1932 2nd Ave. (performances at the Seattle Center House Theater in Seattle Center). (206) 441–5080. Pay meter and lot parking at Seattle Center.

The Piccoli has presented children's stage plays since 1961. Presentations consist of original workings of age-old themes: Raggedy Ann and Andy, Pooh Bear, Mother Goose, and Peter Pan. Productions are often multimedia combinations of live actors and puppets. Singing and dancing abound. Most shows are scheduled for the daylight hours. The theater is next door to the Seattle Children's Museum. Call for schedule and ticket prices.

WORLD MOTHER GOOSE THEATER

P.O. Box 9170 (performances at Seattle Center House Theater in Seattle Center). (206) 441–7569. Pay meter and lot parking near Seattle Center.

Mary Poppins, the Wizard of Oz, and Puss in Boots, are just some of the characters that come to life on stage with this fine troupe. There are often seasonal shows, and most plays utilize original material. Most performances are in the daytime. The theater season consists of five productions staged between October and May. Call for schedule.

SEATTLE CHILDREN'S THEATER

305 Harrison St. (performances at the PONCHO Theater at the Woodland Park Zoo, Fremont Ave. N. and N. 50th St., entrance next to Children's Zoo). (206) 633–4591. Pay parking in the zoo lots.

With five productions each year, the Children's Theater season runs from October to June. They also offer theater workshops for kids. Call for schedule.

SEATTLE MIME THEATER

915 E. Pine St., #419, (locations vary for this traveling troupe). (206) 324–8788.

This talented mime troupe performs at schools and gives workshops all over the Seattle area. Call for their current schedule.

TICKLE TUNE TYPHOON

P.O. Box 15153, Seattle, 98115 (performances change locations). (206) 524–9767.

This musical theater performs original revues with messages concerning such topics as relationships, respect, and postitive self-worth. Every October, they stage a Musicfest at the Museum of History and Industry (see Museums).

BABYSITTING SERVICES

BEST SITTERS
(206) 682–2556

Al Matulich has been running this outfit since 1969. His sitters are reliable, drive their own cars, and are over age 25. Best charges $22 for a 4-hour minimum and $4 per hour after that for one to three children. For each additional child over 3, it costs an extra $1 per hour. If you're staying at a local hotel, you'll have to pay the parking fee. Best covers the greater Seattle area.

PUBLICATIONS

Seattle Post-Intelligencer. Daily newspaper (morning); calendar of events on Fridays.

Seattle Times. Daily newspaper (afternoon); calendar of events on Fridays.

The Weekly. Free weekly newspaper; calendar section lists current movies, concerts, and other artistic endeavors; good restaurant guide. Pick it up in shops and restaurants.

Seattle's Child. Free monthly newspaper; calendar section lists all the kid-related theater, concerts, workshops, and films in the Seattle area. Pick it up at kids' stores.

LOCAL TELEPHONE NUMBERS

Late-hours pharmacy: Jordan Drug, 2518 E. Cherry St. (206) 322–3050 or (206) 322–3835. Open 7 A.M.–2 A.M.
Consumer complaints: City, (206) 625–2482; state, (206) 464–6684.
Dental emergency: Joe Whiting Memorial Clinic, (206) 938–1314.
Laywer referral service: (206) 623-2988.
Medical referral: Visiting Nurse Association, (206) 545–9330. Home Health Services, (206) 382-9700.
Drug-abuse hotline: (206) 722–3700.

Poison control: (206) 526–2121.

Traveler's aid: (206) 447–3888.

Tourism: Seattle-King County Convention and Visitors Bureau, (206) 447–4241.

Police: 911.

Fire: 911.

Ambulance: 911.

Road conditions: Highway Department Information, (206) 764–4097.

Weather: (206) 382–7246.

Local car rental: Rent-a-Dent, (206) 824–7878; Xtracar, (206) 365–7422; Lake City Auto Rentals, (206) 363–3665.

WASHINGTON, D.C.

After earlier attempts in New York City (1789–1790) and Philadelphia (1790–1800), the fledgling United States finally established a permanent national capital on 10 square miles of Maryland swampland along the Potomac River in 1800. The newly created federal district quickly came under fire for its breathless summer heat, its legions of mosquitoes, and its distance from anything that resembled 18th-century civilization.

Today, Washington is one of the most awe-inspiring and educational cities in the United States: a place every American should see. It's a treasure trove of giant, monumental structures and museums filled with the nation's most important artifacts. And nearly everything open to visitors is absolutely free.

Most Washington, D.C., activities are centered around the National Mall, West Potomac Park, and the Ellipse, three connected chunks of National Parkland running more than 2 miles from the United States Capitol building on the east to the Lincoln Memorial on the west. About midway along this broad expanse of lawn, the park widens to include the land surrounding the White House on the north and the Jefferson Memorial on the south.

To say that French-born architect Pierre-Charles L'Enfant was thinking big when he began to lay out the future capital in 1791 is to put it mildly. He designed these wide streets and gargantuan buildings not for a country with thirteen states and a population of 3 million, but rather for a country with fifty states and *500 million* inhabitants. In L'Enfant's vision, the city of Washington would one day hold 800,000 inhabitants. He was quite a soothsayer.

Today, Washington, D.C., is a city of about 623,000 people with 3.5 million in the metro area. It has the dizzyingly large buildings of the federal government and the nongovernmental agencies that need to be close to the seat of government. Washington is also home to the diplomats who staff the many foreign embassies as well as the ballooning number of employees of incumbent Presidential administrations.

The population of the city remains about 70 percent black: a legacy from the Civil War when 40,000 freed slaves from Virginia and Maryland arrived to work for the war effort. Slum neighborhoods and housing projects stand only a few blocks from lavish embassies and expensive neighborhoods like Georgetown and Adams-Morgan; troubled, under-funded public schools are near some of the most prestigious private educational institutions. In few other places do such contrasts coexist in such close quarters.

While its uniqueness is its charm, Washington gives its visitors (especially those with children) some pitfalls unmatched in other parts of the country. However, if you know about them in advance, it's very easy to plan around them.

DISTANCES

As most innocent first-time visitors glance at their maps, they're often relieved to see so many of the important sites crowded within blocks of the National Mall. But while it's true that the United States Capitol Building (see Attractions) is a mere 4 blocks from the Smithsonian's National Air and Space Museum (see Museums), a closer investigation reveals that 1 city block in the territory near the National Mall is equal to 3 or 4 city blocks elsewhere in the city.

Even with the wonderful, tourist-friendly Washington Metro subway (see Transportation), be prepared to walk great distances. For example, the Smithsonian Metro station, the closest to the Washington Monument, is nearly a half mile away. Consequently, it's imperative that parents of small children bring their own strollers—preferably umbrella strollers that can be folded and carried with ease on the Metro and on escalators.

FOOD

Choices in the tourist areas are pretty much limited to the restaurants of the Smithsonian museums and streetside vendors selling hot dogs, pretzels, and potato chips. About the only other alternatives are the indoor shopping malls located in L'Enfant Plaza on 12th Street and Independence Avenue, SW, and the Old Post Office Pavilion on 12th Street and Pennsylvania Avenue, NW, where you can get pizza, submarine sandwiches, and culinary alternatives other than the uninspiring Smithsonian fare. No matter how you slice it, dining near the popular Washington sites leaves a lot to be desired.

PARKING

Parking is troublesome on two levels: It's hard to find space, and it's expensive. While there are lots of metered parking spaces along the major tourist thoroughfares, unless you arrive long before the museums and attractions open and are prepared to keep feeding the meters all day, you're out of luck. Indoor lots in office buildings, many a mile from the National Mall attractions, charge up to $3 per hour to park, with a maximum of about $12 per day. The best alternatives are to take the Metro (see Transportation), be prepared to do a lot of walking, and take the reasonably priced taxi cabs (see Transportation).

CLIMATE

The summers are often stifling, with temperatures and humidity readings into the 90s during the day and the mid-70s at night. Air-conditioning is essential in your hotel *and* car. Periodic summer rainstorms occasionally drop daytime temperatures into the low 80s. Winters can be cold and

---

FREEBIES AND CHEAPIES
(Free or $3.50 and under for adults)

- ❑ Washington Monument (see Attractions)
- ❑ White House (see Attractions)
- ❑ United States Capitol Building (see Attractions)
- ❑ Bureau of Engraving and Printing (see Attractions)
- ❑ J. Edgar Hoover F.B.I. Building (see Attractions)
- ❑ National Zoological Park (see Attractions)
- ❑ National Aquarium (see Attractions)
- ❑ Arlington National Cemetery (see Attractions)
- ❑ Lincoln Memorial (see Attractions)
- ❑ Jefferson Memorial (see Attractions)
- ❑ Vietnam Veterans Memorial (see Attractions)
- ❑ Smithsonian Institution—14 museums (see Museums)
- ❑ National Archives (see Museums)
- ❑ Marine Corps Museum (see Museums)
- ❑ Navy Museum (see Museums)
- ❑ National Geographic Society's Explorer's Hall (see Museums)
- ❑ Washington Dolls' House and Toy Museum (see Museums)

damp, with rain, sleet, and measurable snowfalls a couple of times during the season. Winter temperatures usually hover in the 30s and 40s, with nighttime lows dropping into the 20s. Spring and fall are glorious, with high temperatures in the 70s and lows at night in the mid-40s.

With an average annual rainfall of about 42 inches, precipitation can occur just about any time. In the warm months, pack an umbrella (or buy a cheap one from a street vendor for about $5). In the winter, pack a warm parka. In summer, take a light jacket, even though it may languish in the suitcase for the entire trip.

TOURIST INFORMATION

Contact the Greater Washington, D.C., Convention and Visitors Association, 1212 New York Avenue, NW, Washington, D.C. 20005, (202) 789–7000.

Note on locations and directions. Washington, D.C., is divided into four sections: Northwest (NW), Southwest (SW), Southeast (SE) and

---

THE LONG WEEKEND

Day One

- ❑ Old Town Trolley Tour (see Tours)
- ❑ The Shops of the Pavilion of the Old Post Office (see Shopping)
- ❑ The Smithsonian's National Museum of American History (see Museums)
- ❑ United States Capitol Building (see Attractions)

Day Two

- ❑ Washington Monument (see Attractions)
- ❑ The Smithsonian's National Museum of Natural History (see Museums)
- ❑ Wright Place (see Restaurants)
- ❑ The Smithsonian's National Air and Space Museum (see Museums)
- ❑ The Smithsonian's National Portrait Gallery (see Museums)

Day Three

- ❑ Kings Dominion (see Attractions), or
- ❑ C & O Canal Boat Tour (see Tours)

Northeast (NE). The boundary lines run through the United States Capitol Building along E. Capitol, N. Capitol, and S. Capitol Streets (the only streets with a single directional notation in front of the name), and through the middle of the Mall. When someone mentions the corner of 7th and I Streets, remember that there could be four such corners—one in each section of town. You'll need to know whether it's SE, SW, NE, or NW to complete the address.

ATTRACTIONS

THE WASHINGTON MONUMENT

The National Mall, 14th St. and Madison Dr., NW. (202) 426–6841. Use the Smithsonian station on the Orange or Blue Metro line. Limited metered parking.

Hours. April 1 through Labor Day: daily, 8 A.M.–12 midnight. Labor Day through March 31: daily, 9 A.M.–5 P.M.

Costs. Free.

The Washington Monument shares with the White House the distinction of being the city's most popular attractions. Visitors used to be able to walk the stairs to the top of the 555-foot stone obelisk, the tallest free-standing masonry edifice in the world. These days you have to take the elevator. Once on top, you're able to peer out the small windows for the most famous views of the city. Be prepared for a wait—especially in summer when it's not unusual to wait for an hour or more (sometimes as long as 4 hours!), with the monument itself providing the only shade. In summer, we suggest you go early in the day or wait until dusk; at least you'll be cooler.

Kids' Facilities. No stroller rentals. No diaper-changing tables. Restrooms, snack bar, and gift shop located in building about 50 yards east of the monument. No bottles warmed.

Ratings. Except for the wait, the time spent in the monument itself is short: about 20 minutes or so. Therefore, if you can somehow amuse your smaller kids while they wait, your Washington Monument experience can be a good one. 2–7, B; 8–11, A; 12–16, A.

THE WHITE HOUSE

1600 Pennsylvania Avenue, NW. (202) 456–2200. Use the McPherson Sq. station on the Orange or Blue Metro line. Limited metered parking.

Hours. Labor Day through Memorial Day: Tues.–Sat., 10 A.M.–12 noon. During this period, simply line up at the east entrance on Executive Ave. at 10 A.M. Visitors are admitted in large groups.

Memorial Day through Labor Day: Tues.–Sat., 10 A.M.–12 noon. During this heavy tourist season, visitors must first get a ticket at the booth located on the southern edge of the Ellipse at Constitution Ave., NW, about a quarter of a mile from the tour entrance. Tickets can be obtained *only* between 8 A.M. and 12 noon, and are *good only for the specific time listed on the ticket*. If you are not there by 8 A.M. or 9 A.M. at the very latest, chances are you won't be able to tour the White House that day. To see from a distance if there are any tickets remaining, look for the flag flying above the ticket booth. A red flag signifies that there are no more tickets for that day. A yellow flag means there are only a few left, and you'd better hurry. A green flag means there are plenty of tickets still available. Visitors are asked to assemble under the portable covered bleachers on the Ellipse to wait for their tour to line up. Each tour time is issued a number; on a sign near the assembly area, your number will be posted when it's time for your group to line up. *During the summer months, there can be a long, hot wait for this tour! Also, White House tours can be stopped without notice for special or last-minute functions.*

Costs. Free.

Your enjoyment of the White House tour depends a great deal on the time of year you choose. In the summer, with average daily visitors running upward of 4,500, the White House tour may not be worth the time and trouble. Counting the time it takes to get your tickets, wait for your group's number to be posted, wait outside the White House for your group to pass through the X-ray machine, and finally get inside, you lose a half day of valuable sightseeing time.

This is not a guided tour. Once inside the White House, you're on your own and can browse at your leisure—but always under the watchful gaze of the Secret Service. Limited to the State Dining Room, the Red, Blue, Green, and East Rooms (only five of 132 rooms), you can look at furnishings, china, and paintings purchased by a succession of Presidential administrations. You aren't allowed anywhere near the living quarters or the Presidential offices.

Kids' Facilities. No stroller rentals. No diaper-changing tables. No bottle-warming facilities. No restrooms; use public bathrooms on the Ellipse.

Ratings. Small children stay a lot happier during the off season, when you can get in and out of the White House quickly. You'll find the long wait in summer intolerable for children under 10, and only slightly better for older children and adults. 2–7, F; 8–11, D; 12–16, C.

THE UNITED STATES CAPITOL BUILDING

Capitol Hill, National Mall (east end). (202) 224–3121. Use the Capitol South station on the Orange or Blue Metro line. Limited metered parking.

Hours. Easter through Labor Day: daily, 9 A.M.–10 P.M. (tours 9 A.M.–3:45). Labor Day through Easter: daily, 9 A.M.–4:30 (tours 9 A.M.–3:45).

Costs. Free.

You begin as you do with most Washington governmental buildings —by going through the X-ray machine. Then it's into the massive rotunda, where a guide fills you in on all the wonderful trivia that makes the white marble building with the 180-foot dome come to life (for example, you could fit the Statue of Liberty inside the rotunda and her torch wouldn't come close to the ceiling). The 20-minute tour takes you to the crypt below the rotunda for a look at some exhibits on the construction of the building. Then you're turned loose and can roam the hallways, though certain areas and most offices and conference rooms are off-limits. When Congress is not in session, you can sit in the House and Senate galleries; when it's in session, you must obtain a pass from a House or Senate member, usually a few weeks in advance. The marble corridors are filled with interesting statues, two from every state in the union. If you happen to be touring near mealtime, you can pop into either the House or Senate restaurants for a quick sandwich. Take time to walk to the steps on the west side of the building: You'll get one of the more spectacular views of the National Mall, the buildings of the Smithsonian, and, in the distance, the Lincoln Memorial.

Kids' Facilities. No stroller rentals. No diaper-changing tables, but plenty of restrooms. No bottle-warming facilities.

Ratings. As with the White House, children under 10 may tend to get bored. But with the tour taking only 20 minutes and a quick elevator ride to the galleries taking only 15 minutes more, you can be out of the Capitol before they get too cranky. 2–7, B; 8–11, A; 12–16, A.

BUREAU OF ENGRAVING AND PRINTING

14th and C Sts. SW. (202) 447–9709. Use the Smithsonian station on the Blue or Orange Metro line. Limited metered parking.

Hours. Mon.–Fri., 9 A.M.–2 P.M.

Costs. Free.

Money and some stamps thrown in for good measure make this an extremely popular tour. You enter on the east side of the building and line up in an indoor walkway filled with displays of old bills, photographs, and descriptions of various printing processes. A film on bureau history is shown before you enter a corridor that takes you through the entire tour. Along the way, there are lots of photo exhibits. Windows along the tour corridor allow you to watch the printing of $1 bills and the stacking, cutting, and bundling of $10 notes. The tour ends at the Visitor Center, where there are video and print displays on the engraving and printing process. You can also purchase stamps, commemorative notes, and— the favorite of every kid—a small bag containing $150 in shredded money that sells for 50¢.

Kids' Facilities. No stroller rentals. No diaper-changing tables in the restrooms. (The only restrooms are those you can use before beginning the tour; there are none during the tour or after.) No restaurant or bottle-warming facilities. *There are times during the tour when parents must fold and carry strollers.*

Ratings. At about 25 minutes, the tour is short enough even for kids with limited attention spans. However, since the windows through which you view the printing of money are about 4 feet off the ground, be prepared to lift smaller children to see the action. If your kids are under 8, you may want to pass on the Bureau of Engraving and Printing if the line extends to the sidewalk outside the entrance. With the inside walkway/ waiting area full, the wait is usually about a half hour. 2–7, C; 8–11, A; 12–16, A.

J. EDGAR HOOVER F.B.I. BUILDING

E Street between 9th and 10th Sts. NW. (202) 324–3447. Use the Federal Triangle station on the Orange or Blue Metro line. Limited metered and pay lot parking.

Hours. Mon.–Fri., 8:45 A.M.–4:15 P.M.; tours begin at 15-minute intervals

Costs. Free.

The 1-hour guided tour gives visitors a behind-the-scenes look at the use of modern technology in crime fighting. Prior to viewing the crime labs, you see exhibits on the history of the scientific battle against crime, including the use of fingerprints and microfilm. Exhibits highlight some of the Bureau's successes, such as the crusade against gangsters in the 1930s, the capture of members of the ten-most-wanted list, and the arrests of spies. The most fascinating part of the tour explores scientific techniques like serology (identifying suspects through bodily fluids), firearm reference and identification (5,000 different guns used for comparisons and test firings), and microscopic analysis (through which experts can determine a person's identity through a single strand of hair). The tour ends with a demonstration of firearms.

Kids' Facilities. No stroller rentals. No diaper-changing tables in restrooms (plenty of benches, however). No food or bottle-warming facilities. *Note: Parents with strollers must fold and carry them when the tour changes floors via a series of escalators.*

Ratings. Since the tour is a full hour with quite a bit of talking and instruction from the guide, think twice about taking kids under age 8. 2–7, D; 8–11, A; 12–16, A.

NATIONAL ZOOLOGICAL PARK

3000 Block of Connecticut Ave. NW. (202) 673–4800 or (202) 673–4717. Use the Woodley Park-Zoo station or the Cleveland Park station on the Red Metro line; if driving, use the Harvard St. or Beach Drive entrance, and follow signs to parking lot. Lot parking is $3.

Hours. May 1 through September 15: buildings open daily, 9 A.M.–6 P.M.; grounds open daily, 8 A.M.–8 P.M. September 16 through April 30: buildings open daily, 9 A.M.–4:30 P.M.; grounds open daily, 8 A.M.–6 P.M.

Costs. Free.

The National Zoo occupies 163 hilly acres and has more than 2,800 animals. Despite wonderful indoor and outdoor exhibits that include some of the finest specimens of primates, pachyderms, reptiles, and invertebrates, most visitors flock to the zoo for Hsing-Hsing and Ling-Ling, the country's only permanent panda residents. The zoo is a walker's paradise with six distinctive trails, each with animals from specific groups or world regions. All are connected to the zoo's main drag, the Olmstead Walk. The zoo also has three distinct hands-on learning centers for children—BIRDlab, HERPlab, and ZOOlab—where kids can get up close and personal with birds, snakes, and animals in general.

Kids' Facilities. Strollers can be rented for $3 per day (plus a $35 deposit or a driver's license) and are obtained from booths near the Panda exhibit and the Lion House. The Main Building (near the Connecticut Ave. entrance) has diaper-changing tables in the ladies' restroom. The Zoo has plenty of fast-food stands and one sit-down restaurant (the Mane Restaurant) not far from the lion and tiger exhibits. No bottle-warming facilities. *(Note: Families arriving via the Metro should bring their own strollers. The walk from both Metro stations is nearly a quarter mile, all uphill. Drivers should be aware that parking is limited. Try to arrive early in the day to get a $3 space.)*

Ratings. Even if the zoo didn't have pandas, it would be a must attraction for families, especially for younger children. All ages, A.

NATIONAL AQUARIUM

14th St. and Constitution Ave. NW (entrance mid-block on 14th St.). (202) 377–2825. Use the Federal Triangle station on the Orange or Blue Metro line. Limited metered parking.

Hours. Daily, 9 A.M.–5 P.M.

Costs. Adults, $1.50; ages 12 and under, 75¢ (good for an entire week's admission).

With the I. M. Pei-designed National Aquarium in Baltimore attracting most of the attention, Washington's National Aquarium is often overlooked. That's too bad because, aside from being the country's oldest aquarium (1873), it's one of Washington's most informative and least-crowded attractions. The aquarium has more than 1,000 specimens of fish, invertebrates, reptiles, and amphibians from almost every corner of the world. The staff cheerfully answers every question and, upon request, provides lots of printed information. There are shark and piranha feedings, a student-staffed touch tank, and the Crab Cove Discovery Room where younger kids can participate in special programs and hands-on out-of-the-water exhibits on shells, coral, and hardened star fish.

Kids' Facilities. No stroller rentals. Change diapers on sofas in the Crab Cove Discovery Room. Free access to the Department of Commerce cafeteria on the lower level next door. No bottle-warming facilities.

Ratings. Unlike many Washington attractions that overwhelm you with their size, the aquarium is intimate and friendly. In this relaxed atmosphere parents are more apt to encourage their kids to touch and learn. All ages, A.

ARLINGTON NATIONAL CEMETERY

Across the Potomac River via the Arlington Memorial Bridge, Arlington, VA. (703) 692–0931. Use the Arlington Cemetery station on the Blue Metro line. Free parking.

Hours. Cemetery: April through September: daily, 8 A.M.–7 P.M. October through March: daily, 8 A.M.–5 P.M. Arlington House: April through September: daily, 9:30 A.M.–6 P.M. October through March: daily, 9:30 A.M.–4:30 P.M.

Costs. Free.

The most famous national cemetery, Arlington is the final resting place of American luminaries such as astronaut Virgil Grissom, President William Howard Taft, General John J. Pershing, George C. Marshall, and boxer Joe Louis. The cemetery's most magnetic attractions are the John F. and Robert F. Kennedy grave sites, the Tomb of the Unknown Soldiers, and Arlington House, ancestral home of General Robert E. Lee. Each of the Arlington Big Three are impressive: the Kennedy sites for their simple dignity; the Tomb of the Unknown Soldiers for the changing of the guard every half hour; and Arlington House for its interesting history and antebellum architecture. *(Note: Driving through the cemetery is not permitted. You are welcome to walk the grounds and stop at the various grave sites and attractions. We recommend the Tourmobile Tour, which sets out from the Visitors Center [see Tours]. It stops at the three major cemetery sites, provides informative narration, and saves shoe leather.)*

Kids' Facilities. No stroller rentals. No diaper-changing tables. Restrooms are located at the Visitors Center, the Tomb of the Unknowns, and Arlington House (which also has a gift shop and bookstore). No food or bottle-warming facilities.

Ratings. Most children under 8 will probably be bored with the long stops at the Tomb of the Unknowns and the Kennedy grave sites. They might be mildly amused with the museumlike Arlington House, but by and large, Arlington is better suited to older kids and adults. The Tourmobile Tour takes about an hour and a half. 2–7, D; 8–11, C; 12–16, A.

LINCOLN MEMORIAL

In West Potomac Park at 23rd St. and Henry Bacon Dr. NW. (202) 426–6841. Use the Foggy Bottom-G.W.U. station on the Orange or Blue Metro line. Limited metered parking.

Hours. Daily, 24 hours. Tours, upon request: daily, 8 A.M.–12 midnight.

Costs. Free.

During daylight hours, the steps to the Lincoln Memorial are usually filled with tourists. Some are resting on the strenuous climb to the seated marble figure of our sixteenth President. Others are turned around to take in the spectacular view of the Reflecting Pool, the Washington Monument, and the Capitol. Modeled after a Greek temple, the Memorial building is supported by thirty-six marble columns—one for every state in the Union during Lincoln's presidency. Along with the famed 19-foot-high statue, the interior also has the Emancipation Proclamation and Lincoln's Second Inaugural Address chiseled into the walls on either side of the statue. Day or night, the statue and the view are magnificent.

Kids' Facilities. No stroller rentals. No diaper-changing tables in restrooms (located behind the monument). No food or bottle-warming facilities. Gift shop and bookstore located in room off statue area.

Ratings. If your children can climb the stairs (carry the little ones), they'll probably enjoy both the view and the statue, especially since you can see it all within 20 minutes. All ages, A.

JEFFERSON MEMORIAL

In East Potomac Park, Ohio Drive at the Tidal Basin SW. (202) 426–6841. Use the Smithsonian station on the Orange or Blue Metro line. Free parking.

Hours. Daily, 24 hours. Tours, upon request: daily, 8 A.M.–12 midnight.

Costs. Free.

The Jefferson Memorial is located in one of the most beautiful spots in all of Washington. In early April, the Tidal Basin comes magically alive with the blooming of 650 cherry trees. The Memorial itself is a giant rotunda with a 19-foot bronze statue of the third President at its center. The rotunda wall is covered with quotes from the Declaration of Independence and other of his writings. The base of the rotunda houses a gift and bookshop and a half dozen displays listing some of Jefferson's lesser-known accomplishments, including the invention of the swivel chair and a revolutionary redesigning of the plow.

Kids' Facilities. No stroller rentals. No diaper-changing tables in the restrooms. No food or bottle-warming facilities (there is a snack bar near the parking lot).

Ratings. With fewer steps than the Lincoln Memorial, a 20-minute stop-over is well worth the effort, even with small children. Watch out that they don't head for the Tidal Basin, which is too close to the Memorial for you to let your guard down. All ages, A.

VIETNAM VETERANS MEMORIAL

Constitution Ave. and Henry Bacon Dr. NW. (202) 426–6841. Use the Foggy Bottom-G.W.U. station on the Orange or Blue Metro line. Limited metered parking.

Hours. Daily, 24 hours.

Costs. Free.

One of the most moving monuments in the city, the black granite memorial in the northwest corner of the National Mall contains the names of all 58,156 Americans who died in or are still missing in action from the United States' most divisive war. As you walk along the wall, the real cost of the Vietnam War comes home.

Kids' Facilities. No stroller rentals. No diaper-changing tables (bathrooms at nearby snack area a few hundred feet south of the Memorial). No bottle-warming facilities.

Ratings. While younger children have no comprehension of the meaning of the Memorial, kids seem to react intuitively to the demeanor of their parents. For older kids, it can be educational; a way to open a dialogue about a time that tore at the fabric of American society. It's a quick visit, about 20 minutes, that no family should miss. 2–7, C; 8–11, B; 12–16, A.

KINGS DOMINION

State Rte. 30 and Interstate 95, Doswell, VA. (804) 876–5000. Located about 75 miles south of Washington. Parking, $2.

Hours. Late March through late May and early September through mid-October: Sat. and Sun., 9:30 A.M.–8 P.M. June through August: daily, 9:30 A.M.–10 P.M.

Costs. General admission, $16.95; under age 2, free.

Kings Dominion is where kids from all over the mid-Atlantic states come to ride rides, eat junk food, and pose for pictures with people in oversized cartoon character costumes. The 400-acre park has forty-two rides, including white-water rafts, stomach-defying roller coasters, and a 50-foot log flume ride. Along with wandering cartoon characters like Yogi Bear and the Smurfs, there are live stage shows featuring actors, singers, dancers, and trained animals. On summer weekends, the park features a nightly fireworks display—a great drawing card for kids over three.

Kids' Facilities. Strollers rented for $3 per day. Diaper-changing, bottle-warming, and private nursing rooms at the Pampers Baby Care Center. Lots of fast-food stands and a sit-down Mexican restaurant.

Ratings. No question about it, most kids would rather be here than at the National Archives. All ages, A.

WILD WORLD

State Rte. 214 (Central Ave.), Largo, MD. (301) 249–1500. Located about 12 miles east of Washington. Parking $2.

Hours. May and September: Sat. and Sun., 10 A.M.–8 P.M. June through August: daily, 10 A.M.–9 P.M.

Costs. Adults, $13.25; ages 3–10, $11.25; 2 and under, free.

Wild World has reduced amusement park fun to the bare essentials: wave pools, water slides, and roller coasters. Along with a very good wooden roller coaster, the park has a pool capable of foot-high waves and some fast slides. In addition to the big kid fun, there are some gentle pools and slides, and rides for the little ones. There's also a high-dive show and a musical puppet show.

Kids' Facilities. Strollers rented for $2 per day. Counters for diaper-changing in both ladies' and men's locker rooms. No bottle-warming facilities. Fast food only; no sit-down restaurant.

Ratings. While parents may be repulsed, for kids this place means hours of water-logged poolside fun. All ages, A.

MUSEUMS

SMITHSONIAN INSTITUTION

Comprised of fourteen museums (eleven of which are described here) and the National Zoo, the Smithsonian Institution is the biggest museum complex in the world. Founded in 1846, the Smithsonian and its incredible holdings of art, scientific objects, and artifacts might never have been if not for the generous endowment of English scientist James Smithson. A gifted scientist, he spent most of his life in Europe studying with learned men of the time. A bachelor, he left his entire estate to a nephew. When his nephew died without an heir, the estate went to the United States government to build "an establishment for the increase of knowledge."

Here is a museum-by-museum breakdown of the Smithsonian:

THE SMITHSONIAN INSTITUTION BUILDING

1000 Jefferson Dr. SW, the National Mall. (202) 357–2700. Use the Smithsonian station on the Orange or Blue Metro line. Limited metered street parking.

Hours. Daily, 10 A.M.–5 P.M.

Costs. Free.

Dubbed the "Castle," the distinctive red-brick Victorian building was constructed in 1855 to house the Institution's first acquisitions. Closed to the public since late in 1987, the building is scheduled to reopen in late 1989 with a new Smithsonian Information Center.

Kids' Facilities. Not known at press time.

Ratings. Not available at press time.

THE SMITHSONIAN'S NATIONAL MUSEUM OF AMERICAN HISTORY

14th St. and Constitution Ave. NW, the National Mall. (202) 357–2700. Use the Smithsonian station on the Orange or Blue Metro line. Limited metered street parking.

Hours. Daily, 10 A.M.–5:30 P.M; extended summer hours, determined annually, are often 10 A.M.–9 P.M.

Costs. Free.

Nearly every aspect of United States cultural, technological, and scientific history is on display—from Eli Whitney's patent model cotton gin to Mary Pickersgill's original Star Spangled Banner flag to a collection of the oldest and biggest railroad locomotives. About half the floor space is occupied by long-running but temporary exhibitions. The other half features much-loved permanent exhibits like the world's largest stamp collection, the inaugural gowns of the nation's First Ladies, rare firearms, and some of the most barbaric-looking medical instruments you've ever seen. The museum store has books, kids' publications, stuffed animals, and science experiments.

Kids' Facilities. No stroller rentals. No diaper-changing tables (use benches outside restrooms and throughout the museum). No bottle warming. The cafeteria on the lower level has fast food, salads, and drinks of all sorts. The Victorian ice cream parlor on the first floor is a real winner.

Ratings. There is something for every taste and every age group. Younger kids get a kick out of the trains and some of the early automobiles on the first floor. All ages, A.

THE SMITHSONIAN'S NATIONAL MUSEUM OF NATURAL HISTORY

10th St. and Constitution Ave. NW, the National Mall. (202) 357–2700. Use the Smithsonian station on the Orange or Blue Metro line. Limited metered street parking.

Hours. Daily, 10 A.M.–5:30 P.M.; extended summer hours, determined annually, are often 10 A.M.–9 P.M.

Costs. Free.

One of Washington's most familiar sights is the huge stuffed African bush elephant in the rotunda just inside the Mall entrance to the museum. And that's just one item of 80 million plus in the Museum's collection of natural science objects. Every aspect of the natural sciences is covered here: the world's native cultures, the origin of mankind, every manner of animal life, and all kinds of fossils. Tops on kids' wish lists are the stellar collection of dinosaur bones, the insect zoo, and the first floor Discovery Center: a hands-on museum where young children can wrap their fingers around rocks, shells, bones, and other objects parents usually yell at them for picking up in the yard. The Natural History Museum has a great shrunken head display and three mummified corpses. There are gold nuggets as big as your head, along with the crowd-pleasing Hope Diamond.

Kids' Facilities. No stroller rentals. The ladies' restroom on the ground floor has a diaper-changing table. No bottle warming at the first floor cafeteria.

Ratings. There's something to amuse all children here. All ages, A.

THE SMITHSONIAN'S ARTS AND INDUSTRIES BUILDING

900 Jefferson Dr. SW, the National Mall. (202) 357–2700. Use the Smithsonian station on the Orange or Blue Metro line. Limited metered street parking.

Hours. Daily, 10 A.M.–5:30 P.M.; extended summer hours, determined annually, are often 10 A.M.–9 P.M.

Costs. Free.

The beautiful Victorian Arts and Industries Building was first used in 1881 for President James Garfield's inaugural. These days it re-creates an 1876 industrial exposition, with train locomotives, huge ship models, early patent prototype models, and lots of late-19th-century weaponry. The building also houses the Smithsonian's Discovery Theater, which presents children's performances from October through June (see Children's Theater).

Kids' Facilities. No stroller rentals. No diaper-changing tables in the bathrooms. No food or bottle-warming facilities.

Ratings. While most of the Arts and Industries exhibits are geared for adults and older children, a quick detour through the building won't hurt, especially if the reward at the end of the line (in summer) is a ride on the Mall's nearby carousel. 2–7, C; 8–11, B; 12–16, A.

THE SMITHSONIAN'S HIRSHHORN MUSEUM

7th St. and Independence Ave. SW, the National Mall. (202) 357–2700. Use the L'Enfant Plaza station on the Orange, Blue, or Yellow Metro line. Limited metered street and pay lot parking.

Hours. Daily, 10 A.M.–5:30 P.M.; extended summer hours, determined annually, are often 10 A.M.–9 P.M.

Costs. Free.

Opened in 1974, the round Hirshhorn displays the works of renowned modern American artists like Roy Lichtenstein, Andy Warhol, Robert Indiana, Robert Raushenberg, Jackson Pollock, and George Segal. It also hosts interesting temporary exhibitions. The outdoor sculpture garden contains large installations of works by Rodin, Calder, Moore, and Matisse.

Kids' Facilities. No stroller rentals (in fact, you must leave your stroller at the checkroom and, if you wish, pick up a free infant backpack). No diaper-changing tables (sofas throughout the museum will do). No food or bottle-warming facilities. Along with checking your stroller, you must also surrender any large bags.

Ratings. Because of the paranoia about strollers and large tote bags (strollers can damage low-lying artworks and it's possible to hide stolen art in a diaper bag), the Hirshhorn may not be worth the trouble if you have kids between 2 and 5. 2–7, D; 8–11, A; 12–16, A.

THE SMITHSONIAN'S NATIONAL GALLERIES OF ART (EAST AND WEST BUILDINGS AND CONCOURSE)

Constitution Ave. between 6th and 3rd Sts., NW, the National Mall. (202) 737–4215. Use the Archives station on the Yellow Metro line. Limited metered street and pay lot parking.

Hours. Daily, 10 A.M.–5:30 P.M.; extended summer hours, determined annually, are often 10 A.M.–9 P.M.

Costs. Free.

The nation's largest art repository consists of two buildings connected by an underground passageway. The *West Building* is filled with 13th- through 19th-century European paintings and sculptures and 17th- through 19th-century American art. With a large rotunda and two massive floors (100,000 square feet), it's filled to the brim with works by Picasso, Da Vinci, Peale, Monet, and Rembrandt. Most noteworthy to Americans are Gilbert Stuart's famous portraits of Presidents Washington, Adams, Monroe, and Madison. The *East Building*, which focuses on 20th-century American art, houses changing exhibitions. The *Concourse*, the gleaming below-ground connector, has a large book and gift shop and two of the complex's four restaurants. The Concourse has a terrific waterfall that is of great fascination to children.

Kids' Facilities. Strollers available for free at many entrances. No diaper-changing tables (use sofas near most ladies' restrooms). Bottles warmed at the three restaurants that are staffed with waiters and waitresses (one in the West Building, one in the East Building, one in the Concourse). Fast food available at cafeteria in Concourse.

Ratings. With eight centuries and a potpourri of national origins to choose from, the Galleries have something to entertain every member of the family. Be warned, however, that the monumental West Building is a maze, and you may spend more time than younger kids can tolerate trying to find your way out. Most of the more brightly colored works of art that seem to appeal to young tastes are to be found in the East Building. All ages, A.

THE SMITHSONIAN'S ARTHUR M. SACKLER GALLERY

1050 Independence Ave. SW, the National Mall. (202) 357–2700. Use the Smithsonian station on the Orange or Blue Metro line. Limited metered and pay lot parking.

Hours. Daily, 10 A.M.–5:30 P.M.; extended summer hours, determined annually, are often 10 A.M.–9 P.M.

Costs. Free.

Both the Sackler Museum and its twin, the National Museum of African Art (next listing), were completed in 1987, making them the newest additions to the National Mall. The ultramodern Sackler is built like a bunker with one level above ground and three below. Named for its benefactor, the museum has more than 1,000 pieces of Oriental art, mostly from China, southeast Asia, and the ancient Near East. If you like Buddahs or fertility sculptures from the Fertile Crescent, this is the place for you. If none of that seems particularly exciting, pop in for a few minutes to check out the building's design and the interesting twists and turns of its intimate patchwork of galleries. An underground gallery connects the Sackler with the African Museum.

Kids' Facilities. No stroller rentals. No diaper-changing tables in the restrooms (use benches throughout the building). No food or bottle-warming facilities.

Ratings. Most of the significance of fine Oriental art is lost on younger kids, although they may approve of some of the grotesque images of lions, tigers, and dragons. At any rate, you can breeze through in 20 minutes. 2–7, C; 8–11, B; 12–16, A.

THE SMITHSONIAN'S NATIONAL MUSEUM OF AFRICAN ART

950 Independence Ave. SW, the National Mall. (202) 357–2700. Use the Smithsonian station on the Orange or Blue Metro line. Limited metered and pay lot parking.

Hours. Daily, 10 A.M.–5:30 P.M.; extended summer hours, determined annually, are often 10 A.M.–9 P.M.

Costs. Free.

The Museum of African Art is a beautiful modern building with the bulk of its exhibit space on three floors below ground level. Most of its works are sculptures and everyday vessels from sub-Saharan Africa that are made from clay, metal, wood, and ivory. There are also examples of many of the tools used by native craftsmen.

Kids' Facilities. No stroller rentals. No diaper-changing tables in restrooms (use nearby benches). No food or bottle-warming facilities.

Ratings. While younger children like the primitive-looking dolls and wonderful ceramic and wooden masks, the museum is best appreciated by kids over 10. However, a 20-minute run-through shouldn't ruffle too many young feathers. 2–7, C; 8–11, B; 12–16, A.

THE SMITHSONIAN'S FREER GALLERY OF ART

12th St. and Jefferson Dr. SW, the National Mall. (202) 357–2700. Use the Smithsonian station on the Orange or Blue Metro line. Limited metered and pay lot parking.

Hours. Daily, 10 A.M.–5:30 P.M.; extended summer hours, determined annually, are often 10 A.M.–9 P.M.

Costs. Free.

The Freer opened in 1923 as an archive for benefactor Charles Lang Freer's huge collection of Asian and Near Eastern art objects. Still predominantly an Oriental museum, the Freer also has one of the foremost collections of works by 19th-century American painter James McNeill Whistler and other 19th- and 20th-century artists whose work Freer thought greatly complemented Eastern art. The collection of Japanese paper and silk screens is exceptional.

Kids' Facilities. No stroller rentals. No diaper-changing tables in restrooms (use nearby benches). No food or bottle-warming facilities.

Ratings. Not likely to appeal to younger kids. 2–7, D; 8–11, C; 12–16, B.

THE SMITHSONIAN'S NATIONAL PORTRAIT GALLERY AND NATIONAL MUSEUM OF AMERICAN ART

8th and F Sts. NW. (202) 357–2700. Use the Gallery Place station on the Yellow or Red Metro line. Limited metered and pay lot parking.

Hours. Daily, 10 A.M.–5:30 P.M.

Costs. Free.

While historical figures from the arts, sciences, and letters are all represented in the Portrait Gallery, the favorites here are portraits of the Presidents and the gallery devoted entirely to Abraham Lincoln. The National Museum of American Art, which shares floor space with the Portrait Gallery, has more than 33,000 paintings, sculptures, folk art objects, and photographs by important American artists. The two museums occupy a beautiful 150-year-old building that once served as the United States Patent Office and, during the Civil War, as a hospital where poet Walt Whitman nursed the wounded. It was also the site of Abraham Lincoln's 1865 inaugural ball.

Kids' Facilities. No stroller rentals. No diaper-changing tables in restrooms; use benches nearby. No bottle-warming facilities in the gallery's cafeteria.

Ratings. Kids under the age of about 10 are too young to spend too long here. Give them a quick tour through the Hall of Presidents on the second floor and a stop at the collection of primitive folk art, which has some neat-looking toys. 2–7, B; 8–11, A; 12–16, A.

THE SMITHSONIAN'S NATIONAL AIR AND SPACE MUSEUM

6th St. and Independence Ave. SW, the National Mall. (202) 357–2700. Use the L'Enfant Plaza station on the Orange, Blue, or Yellow Metro line. Limited metered street and pay lot parking.

Hours. Daily, 10 A.M.–5:30 P.M.; extended summer hours, determined annually, are often 10 A.M.–9 P.M.

Costs. Free; fees charged for IMAX movies and planetarium shows.

More than 9 million people a year make the Air and Space Museum not only the Smithsonian's most popular museum, but one of the most popular tourist attractions in the world. Exhibit areas on two levels display nearly every airplane and NASA space capsule that has made a major contribution to the advancement of air and space technology. Among the historic aircraft hanging from the rafters are the Wright Brother's 1903 flyer, Charles Lindbergh's *Spirit of St. Louis*, General Chuck Yeager's *X-1* (the jet that broke the sound barrier), the *Apollo 11* command module, the *Viking* Lander, Astronaut John Glenn's *Friendship 7* capsule, and the *Voyager*, the ultralight plane that in 1987 circled the world in nine days without refueling. There are lots of planes from the two world wars and a smattering of experimental jet aircraft. The museum also has loads of special exhibits on technological advances in nearly every form of flight, from hot-air balloons to deep space probes of the future. Add to that a terrific planetarium, two IMAX theaters, hands-on computer exhibits, and the best of all the Smithsonian restaurants, and you can easily make a whole day of it.

Kids' Facilities. No stroller rentals. Diaper-changing tables, nursing rooms, and bottle-warming facilities at the baby service station (on the first floor near the Early Flight exhibit). From sandwiches to full restaurant meals, the Wright Place, the Museum's new cafeteria (see Restaurants), answers every gastronomic need and does so with plenty of high chairs and booster seats.

Ratings. We defy your kids to be bored. With every buzzer, bell, and colorful visual diversion, there is something here to capture the attention of every child. All ages, A.

THE NATIONAL ARCHIVES

8th St. and Constitution Ave. NW. (202) 523–3183 or (202) 523–3000 (recorded message). Use the Archives station on the Yellow Metro line. Limited metered street and pay lot parking.

Hours. April 1 through Labor Day: daily, 10 A.M.–9 P.M. Rest of the year: daily, 10 A.M.–5:30 P.M.

Costs. Free.

Armed security guards search your purses, briefcases, and backpacks, admonish you not to take flash photographs, and force you to spit out your chewing gum before entering the building. Once inside, you understand why. On an altar at the far end of the rotunda, bathed in helium under thick glass to prevent further deterioration, are the nation's most important documents: the Constitution, the Bill of Rights, and the Declaration of Independence. Visitors file by slowly and solemnly. At the near end of the rotunda, also under gas-filled glass, is a ratified copy of England's Magna Carta (the original was signed by King John in 1215; this copy is dated 1297). A semicircular gallery that loops around behind the Constitution and Declaration houses special exhibits that change every two years or so. These temporary exhibits are usually multimedia productions from the nearly 9 billion textual documents, 91 million feet of motion picture film, and 122,000 video and sound recordings stored at the Archives. While tackling heady constitutional issues like voting rights, searches and seizures, and public education, these exhibits are easy to understand. Kids enjoy them because they can activate films and videos by pushing the buttons. The Archives Central Research Rooms are open to the public, Monday through Saturday.

Kids' Facilities. No stroller rentals. No diaper-changing tables in the restrooms (only a few benches available for changing). No food or bottle-warming facilities.

Ratings. Kids under 10 probably won't fathom the importance of the documents stored here. If young kids are a consideration, try to get there early in the day when the lines aren't too long. 2–7, D; 8–11, B; 12–16, A.

THE MARINE CORPS MUSEUM

9th and M Sts. SE, Building 58, the Washington Navy Yard. (202) 433–3534. Use the Eastern Market Station on the Orange and Blue Metro lines. The museum is located approximately 8 blocks south of the station. *It's wise to take a cab in this part of town.* Free parking in Marine Museum parking lot; you must pass the guard station at the Navy Yard entrance.

Hours. Mon.–Sat., 10 A.M.–4 P.M.; Sun., 12 noon–5 P.M.

Costs. Free.

Documents, paintings, weapons, and uniforms positioned chronologically form a time tunnel of the 200 years of leatherneck history. With loads of colorful memorabilia on the big wars (Revolutionary, Civil, the world wars, Korea, and Vietnam), there are displays on some of our history's lesser-known, more controversial military adventures: against the Barbary Pirates in 1804, the Mexican War in 1846, the Boxer Rebellion in China in 1900, and the many Marine campaigns in Central America in the 20th century. The exhibits might be presented with emotion, but they are lacking in political bias. The presentation of fact without proselytization allows parents free range to interpret history as they see fit.

Kids' Facilities. No stroller rentals. No diaper-changing tables in restrooms (use bench near main entrance). No food or bottle-warming facilities. Gift shop.

Ratings. Kids under 8 couldn't probably care less about the Marine Corps. Older ones, especially boys, enjoy themselves. In either case, you can run through the museum in less than a half hour. 2–7, D; 8–11, B; 12– 16, A.

THE NAVY MUSEUM

9th and M Sts. SE, Building 76, the Washington Navy Yard. (202) 433–2651. Use the Eastern Market Station on the Orange and Blue Metro line. The museum is located approximately 8 blocks south of the station. *It's wise to take a cab in this part of town.* Free parking in Navy Museum parking lot; you must pass the guard station at the Navy Yard entrance.

Hours. June through August: Mon.–Fri., 9 A.M.–5 P.M.; Sat. and Sun., 10 A.M.–5 P.M. September through May: Mon.–Fri., 9 A.M.–4 P.M.; Sat. and Sun., 10 A.M.–5 P.M.

Costs. Free.

The cavernous warehouse is home port to all sorts of ship's guns, from cannons from ships that fought the Revolutionary War, to anti-aircraft guns from World War II aircraft carriers. Kids are free to climb aboard and take aim. Hanging from the ceiling are a Navy *Corsair* from World War II, as well as a Japanese kamikaze. There's also astronaut Allan Shepard's *Mercury* space capsule, as well as John Young's space suit and an authentic undersea exploration bathysphere. The museum has a reconstructed life-size Revolutionary War ship's fighting top and a cannon deck, low ceiling and all. Kids flock to the realistic interior of a World War II submarine equipped with two periscopes that are in constant use. Add to that all manner of ship models and memorabilia from famous sailing vessels and you have one of the most comprehensive naval museums anywhere.

Kids' Facilities. No stroller rentals. No diaper-changing tables in restrooms. No food or bottle-warming facilities. There's a civilian cafeteria on the other side of Building 76.

Ratings. Even though the Navy Museum has memorabilia pertaining to the history of naval warfare, the emphasis is on the technological advances of ocean-going vessels and aircraft. Younger children really get a kick out of playing in the submarine room. It's a large museum, but you can see the major exhibits in about an hour. 2–7, B; 8–11, A; 12–16, A.

NATIONAL GEOGRAPHIC SOCIETY'S EXPLORER'S HALL

17th and M Sts. NW. (202) 857-7588 or (202) 857–7000. Use the Farragut North station on the Red Metro line. Limited metered and pay lot parking.

Hours. Mon.–Sat., 9 A.M.–5 P.M.; Sun., 10 A.M.–5 P.M.

Costs. Free.

With 11 million copies per month, National Geographic magazine has the third-largest circulation of any magazine in the United States. No wonder then, that Explorer's Hall, the society's museum, is a popular tourist stop. Along with changing exhibits of artifacts collected by Society explorers and many hands-on and hand-activated video presentations, Explorer's Hall has permanent exhibits that include a theater presentation tracing 4 million years of human history, the bones and skulls of some of the planet's earliest inhabitants, souvenirs from Byrd's and Peary's polar explorations and, in the lobby, the world's largest free-standing globe. Finish your tour at the bookstore, where nearly all the National Geographic Society's publications are on sale.

Kids' Facilities. No stroller rentals. No diaper-changing tables in the restrooms. No food or bottle-warming facilities.

Ratings. It takes only about a half hour to walk through the museum. Even the youngest children will find something to relate to. All ages, A.

NATIONAL FIREARMS MUSEUM

1600 Rhode Island Ave. NW, Scott Circle. (202) 828–6253. Use the Farragut North station on the Red Metro line. Limited metered and pay lot parking.

Hours. Daily, 10 A.M.–4 P.M.

Costs. Free.

The National Firearms Museum has one of the world's largest gun collections: at least one of nearly every weapon ever manufactured in significant numbers. Tucked away in a corner of National Rifle Association headquarters, the museum's fine examples of weapons making dating back to the 1400s are tempered with polemics against any form of gun control.

Kids' Facilities. No stroller rentals. No diaper-changing tables in restrooms. No food or bottle-warming facilities. No ammo sales.

Ratings. You can whip through the museum in about a half hour. Younger kids won't have much to look at, but the older ones will be intrigued. 2–7, D; 8–11, A; 12–16, A.

CAPITAL CHILDREN'S MUSEUM

800 3rd St. NE. (202) 543–8600. Use the Union Station stop on the Red Metro line; walk 3 blocks north to H Street and head east; take the bridge over the train tracks and turn left at 3rd Street. Limited metered street parking, plus reduced-rate validated parking in lot at 3rd and I Sts.

Hours. Daily, 10 A.M.–5 P.M.

Costs. Ages 2–59, $4; ages 60 and older, $1; under age 2, free.

Located in a former convent and nursing home, the Capital Children's Museum is one of the largest and most user-friendly kids' museums. The exhibits encourage kids to roll up their sleeves and figure things out for themselves. There's a Mexican village where, under supervision, they can make tortillas or dabble in Mexican crafts, try on clothing, dance to native music, and visit a tourist agency; in "Changing Environments," they can work simple machines, drive a bus, visit a doctor's office, watch manufacturing at an automated factory, run through a maze, and learn the metric system; in a communication area, they can learn about old-time radio, visit a television studio, learn Morse code, work at a printer's shop, and type on a Braille typewriter; and in "Future Center," they can learn how to use computers. One of the nicest features is that children can take home any craft item they make.

Kids' Facilities. No stroller rentals. Diaper-changing tables and nursing room located on the first floor. No bottle-warming facilities. The lunchroom has soda and ice cream vending machines.

Ratings. The Capital is designed for a wide range of ages: 2 through 12. While it's possible to fly through in about an hour and a half, your kids will probably want twice that much time. However, interest drops off quickly after age 12. 2–7, A; 8–11, A; 12–16, C.

WASHINGTON DOLLS' HOUSE AND TOY MUSEUM

5236 44th St. NW. (202) 244–0024. Use the Friendship Heights station on the Red Metro line. Limited metered street parking.

Hours. Tues.–Sat., 10 A.M.–5 P.M.; Sun., 12 noon–5 P.M.

Costs. Adults, $2; ages 14 and under, $1; infants, free.

The Dolls' House and Toy Museum has plenty of old-fashioned playthings, many dating back to Victorian times. Their inventory includes rare dolls and even rarer dollhouses that exult workmanship and an eye for detail. The painted backdrops for some of the doll groupings are fantastic: there's a zoo, a circus, and a diorama showing President Teddy Roosevelt on safari.

Kids' Facilities. No stroller rentals. No diaper-changing tables in restrooms. No food or bottle-warming facilities.

Ratings. If your kids can handle the frustration of looking but not touching, they ought to enjoy this blast into the past. 2–7, B; 8–11, A; 12–16, A.

HOTELS

Downtown

QUALITY INN DOWNTOWN

1315 16th St. NW. (800) 368–5689 or (202) 232–8000. 135 units. Pay parking.

Rates. $75 to $118; also a limited number of rooms at special rate for families of four.

This mostly suites hotel is located on Scott Circle, not far from National Geographic's Explorer's Hall and the National Rifle Association's Firearms Museum. The neighborhood is filled with office buildings and embassy residences. Children under 16 stay free in their parents' room.
Cribs: Yes, free.
Rollaways: Yes, $12.
Babysitting: No.
Pool: No.
Restaurant: Yes.
Kitchen facilities: Yes.
Room service: Yes.
Closest emergency hospital: George Washington Medical Center, 10 minutes away, (202) 328–6677.

QUALITY INN EMBASSY SQUARE SUITES

2000 N St. NW. (800) 228–5151 or (202) 659–9000. 242 units. Pay parking.

Rates. $99 to $129.
This all-suites Quality Inn located in the embassy section of the city

is less than a mile north of the White House and just over a mile north
of the National Mall. Children under 16 stay free with parents.
Cribs: Yes, free.
Rollaways: Yes, $15.
Babysitting: No.
Pool: Yes.
Restaurant: Yes.
Kitchen facilities: Yes.
Room service: Yes.
Closest emergency hospital: George Washington Medical Center, 5 min-
utes away, (202) 328–6677.

RAMADA INN CENTRAL

1430 Rhode Island Ave. NW. 186 units. (800) 368–5690 or (202) 462–
7777. Pay parking.

Rates. $99 to $129; also a limited number of rooms with special rates
for families of four.

Suites and efficiencies make up the lion's share of the hotel's rooms.
Like its neighbor, the Quality Inn Downtown, the Ramada is close to
National Geographic's Explorer's Hall and a number of international
embassies. Kids 18 and under stay free in a room with their parents.
Cribs: Yes, free.
Rollaways: Yes, $10.
Babysitting: No.
Pool: Yes, rooftop pool.
Restaurant: Yes.
Kitchen facilities: Yes.
Room service: Yes.
Closest emergency hospital: George Washington Medical Center, 10 min-
utes away, (202) 328–6677.

Arlington, Virginia

BEST WESTERN ROSSLYN WESTPARK HOTEL

1900 N. Fort Myers Dr., Arlington, VA. 308 units. (800) 368–3408 or
(703) 527–4814. Pay parking.

Rates. $89.

While buildings in Washington cannot be taller than the Washington
Monument, numerous tall buildings have gone up in the Rosslyn section
of Arlington. The Westpark is in the heart of that concrete and steel

forest, right across the Potomac River from the Georgetown section of Washington. Near the Rosslyn station on the Orange and Blue Metro lines. Children under 18 stay free in their parents' room.

Cribs: Yes, free.
Rollaways: Yes, $6.
Babysitting: Yes, referrals.
Pool: Yes, indoor.
Restaurant: Yes.
Kitchen facilities: No.
Room service: Yes.
Closest emergency hospital: Georgetown University Hospital, 10 minutes away across the Key Bridge, (202) 784–2118.

Bethesda, Maryland

GUEST QUARTERS SUITE HOTEL—BETHESDA

7335 Wisconsin Ave., Bethesda, MD. (800) 424–2900 or (301) 961–6400. Pay parking.

Rates. $175 is the standard rate, but a number of suites are available for $89.

One of the prettiest and newest all-suites chains, Guest Quarters offers free buffet breakfasts (not just donuts and coffee) and an afternoon hors d'oeuvre reception. While this hotel is on the outskirts of town, it's close to the Bethesda station on the Red Metro line. Children under 18 stay free in their parents' suite.

Cribs: Yes, $10.
Rollaways: Yes, $10.
Babysitting: Yes, referrals, with 24-hour notice.
Pool: Yes, rooftop outdoor pool.
Restaurant: Yes.
Kitchen facilities: Yes.
Room service: Yes.
Closest emergency hospital: Suburban Hospital, 10 minutes away, (301) 530–3880.

RESTAURANTS

Home to numerous five-star restaurants charging five-star prices, Washington, D.C., leaves much to be desired when it comes to feeding kids. Except for the many curbside hot dog vendors and the restaurants at the Smithsonian museums, the National Mall offers few fast-food alternatives. If you shop for restaurants by walking or riding by and making a decision based on looks or premonition, cruise over to Georgetown or the Adams-Morgan district, areas of town where restaurants, including some very expensive ones, abound.

THE WRIGHT PLACE

In the Smithsonian's Air and Space Museum, 6th St. and Independence Ave. SW, the National Mall. (202) 371–0754. Limited metered street and pay lot parking.

Hours. Daily, 11 A.M.–5 P.M.; open later in summer.

The food is pretty good, the prices are reasonable, the decor is clean and ultramodern (lots of glass and light), and the kids seem to love eating only a few yards from those wonderful old airplanes and space capsules. The restaurant serves the typical Smithsonian fare of burgers, hot dogs, salads, and sandwiches, plus hot entrees and lots of desserts. It's not nouvelle cuisine, but it'll do on a day filled with sightseeing. Lunch for a family of four runs about $15. No credit cards.

Kids' Facilities. Plenty of high chairs and booster seats. Diaper-changing tables nearby in museum.

ICE CREAM PARLOR

In the Smithsonian's National Museum of American History, 14th St. and Constitution Ave., the National Mall. (202) 357–1832. Limited metered street and pay lot parking.

Hours. Daily, 11 A.M.–5 P.M.; open later in summer.

With all sorts of turn-of-the-century accents—oak and cast iron, marble countertops, and staff in period dress—the Ice Cream Parlor is like stepping back in time. The ice cream is good, the sundaes are large and imposing, and there's nothing quite like the feel of cool marble on a hot Washington afternoon. The restaurant also serves salads and sandwiches. The food is inexpensive, about $20 for lunch for a family of four—with dessert, of course. No credit cards.

Kids' Facilities. Plenty of booster seats and high chairs. No diaper-changing tables in restrooms.

THE RESTAURANTS OF THE OLD POST OFFICE PAVILION

12th St. and Pennsylvania Ave. NW. (202) 289–4224. Limited metered street and pay lot parking.

Hours. Mon.–Sat., 10 A.M.–9:30 P.M.; Sun., 12 noon–8 P.M.

The restaurants of the Old Post Office Pavilion (built in 1899 and once the headquarters of the Post Office Department) purvey all manner of fast foods at take-out establishments. You grab your food and sit at one of hundreds of tables. The Old Post Office also has souvenir shops and a stage where an assortment of acts, from clowns to concert pianists, perform throughout the day. The glass-and-steel-covered atrium gives the late-Victorian architecture a modern touch. Most of the eateries are inexpensive. The sit-down places accept credit cards. *(One of the best-kept secrets is the Pavilion's clock tower. Tourists can take a free elevator ride to a 350-foot-high observation deck for a view topped only by the Washington Monument.)*

Kids' Facilities. High chairs and booster seats available. No diaper-changing tables in the restrooms.

Big Splurges

CITIES

2424 18th St. NW., Adams-Morgan District. (202) 328–7194. Limited metered street and valet parking.

Hours. Nightly, 5 P.M.–11:30 P.M.

As the branches of a deciduous tree denote the changing of the seasons, trendy nouvelle-cuisine Cities switches its menu and geographic accent every calendar quarter. While we were in Washington, the flavor of the quarter was Bangkok, and their version of Thai cooking was terrific. The restaurant also has a changing menu with a more American accent. The decor is wildly avant garde and unlike many other night-on-the-town restaurants, Cities doesn't require men to dress up. Dinners run in the neighborhood of $16. Full bar. Reservations a must. Major credit cards.

THE RED SEA

2463 18th St., Adams-Morgan District. (202) 483–5000. Limited metered street parking.

Hours. Daily, 11:30 A.M.–2 A.M.

On the inexpensive side but as good as restaurants costing much more, The Red Sea has been named one of the city's top-rated restaurants every year since 1982. This Ethiopian eatery makes abundant use of poultry, beef, lamb, and seafood, and also offers up tasty vegetarian dishes—25 different entrees at last count. The spicing is ample (order to taste, if you're cautious) and the food is first-rate. Injera, Ethiopian flat bread, is a great alternative to dinner rolls. After dinner, take a stroll on 18th Street, the Adams-Morgan district's main drag and witness the neighborhood that rivals Georgetown for nightclubs and trendy bars. Spend the money you save at The Red Sea on drinks and music elsewhere on 18th Street. Dinner for two will run about $25. Full bar. Reservations suggested. Major credit cards.

SHOPPING

THE SHOPS OF THE OLD POST OFFICE PAVILION

1100 Pennsylvania Ave. NW. (202) 289–4224. Limited metered street and pay lot parking.

Hours. Mon.–Sat., 10 A.M.–9:30 P.M.; Sun., 12 noon–8 P.M.

Built in 1899 and long ago abandoned by the Post Office Department, the Old Post Office is now a restaurant and shopping complex that provides a bastion of free enterprise close to the National Mall. Souvenirs, jewelry, and knickknacks abound, as well as special interest shops, including **The Last Wound-Up**, (202) 842–0635, where all manner of inexpensive wind-up toys can be found; and the **Make-a-Book** pushcart with personalized storybooks for your kids.

GIFT SHOP AT THE SMITHSONIAN'S NATIONAL MUSEUM OF NATURAL HISTORY

10th St. and Constitution Ave. NW, the National Mall. (202) 357–1535. Limited metered street parking.

Hours. Daily, 10 A.M.–5 P.M.; open later in summer.

Easily the best of the Smithsonian museum stores, the huge Natural History gift shop offers books for kids and adults, both Smithsonian publications and general-interest books, stuffed animals, science toys and experiments, T-shirts, and knickknacks.

GIFT SHOP AT THE SMITHSONIAN'S NATIONAL AIR AND SPACE MUSEUM

6th St. and Independence Ave. SW, the National Mall. (202) 357–1387. Limited metered street and pay lot parking.

Hours. Daily, 10 A.M.–5 P.M.; open later in summer.

Your children's eyes are bound to light up when confronted with the planes and space-related toys and books at this gift shop.

GIFT SHOP OF THE WASHINGTON DOLLS' HOUSE AND TOY MUSEUM

5236 44th St. NW. (202) 244-0024.

Hours. Tues.– Sat., 10 A.M.–5 P.M.; Sun., 12 noon–5 P.M.

To placate young kids frustrated by the fact that they can't touch the antique dolls in the museum, buy them a similar (but less expensive) one at the gift shop. All kinds of dolls, miniature furnishings, and books to choose from.

TRANSPORTATION

BUSES AND SUBWAY

Thanks to the subways of the Metro Regional Transit Service, public transportation in Washington is a pleasure. The clean, safe, efficient Metro subway system's four color-designated lines—Blue, Red, Yellow, and Orange—link the District of Columbia and Virginia suburbs to the west and south and Maryland suburbs to the north and east. The system runs weekdays from 5:30 A.M. to 12 midnight; Saturdays from 8 A.M. to 12 midnight; and Sundays from 10 A.M. to 12 midnight. It's easy to spot Metro stations by the brown column with a large letter M at the top. Beneath the letter, colored stripes indicate the Metro lines served by the station. The column also indicates the name of the station.

The fare depends on the distance traveled and the time of day. During the morning and evening rush hours (6–9:30 A.M. and 3–6:30 P.M.), fares are higher than at other times of the day. The average fare is $1.10 during rush hour and 80¢ at all other times. Long trips, however, can cost as much as $2.40 during rush hour. Payment is made through automated farecard machines at each station: select the amount you need, insert bills or coins, and a farecard for that amount will be delivered. Every time you enter and exit a station, you must place your farecard in a turnstile slot. At the end of each ride, the cost is deducted from your card and, if it still retains credits, the card is returned. Children under 5 ride free (maximum two kids per adult at that rate). If you plan to use the Metro a lot during your stay in Washington, buy a farecard worth $5 or so: It will save you the trouble of having to use the farecard machines for each trip.

(Note: despite the terrific service, Metro stations are not as convenient as you'd like them to be. In some downtown areas, stations are as many as 10 long blocks apart. Even if your children think they're old enough to get around by themselves on foot, you should probably take an umbrella stroller if they're under age 5.)

The bus system is also operated by the Metro Regional Transit Service. The buses, which run throughout the District of Columbia, Maryland, and Virginia, link up with the subway system. Transfers can be used when going from subway to bus, but not from bus to subway. On a zone system, Metro buses cost about as much as a subway ride of equal length. The base rate is 80¢ with fares going up to $2.50. For more information about the bus and subway system: (202) 962–1234.

TAXIS

Because of the distance between Metro subway stops in Washington, most tourists sooner or later end up hailing a cab. The pleasant surprise is that Washington taxis are cheap, working on a zone system without meters. It's possible to go long distances inexpensively: The basic zone fare is $2.10, with a surcharge of $1.25 for each additional person, and the maximum fare for one person within the entire District of Columbia is only $8.05. You can hail cabs on the street or telephone for them (65¢ surcharge for calling). Companies include Yellow Cab, (202) 544–1212; Liberty, (202) 544–4411; and Capitol, (202) 546–2400.

TOURS

BUS TOURS

Gray Line. (301) 386–8300. Offers eight Washington sightseeing tours, including half-day excursions past many of the city's most important landmarks, half-day treks inside many of the more famous buildings, full-day combination tours, and a deluxe two-day tour on which you see everything. Prices run from $15 (children, $7) for the interiors tour, to $18 (children, $9) for the half-day motorized trips, to $50 (children, $25) for the 2-day grand tour.

TROLLEY AND TRAM TOURS

Tourmobile. (202) 554–7950. An open tram that winds its way along a route past most of the sites on the National Mall, the Ellipse, West Potomac Park, and Arlington National Cemetery. The tram makes eighteen stops at strategic locations where you can get off and explore on your own. Afterward, catch the next tram and continue on to the next attraction. Tourmobiles come by every 20 minutes or so. En route, guides deliver running anecdote-filled travelogues. It's a great way to see Washington without the hassle of parking. Rates for the Washington-Arlington route: adults, $7.50; kids ages 3–11, $3.75; ages 2 and under, free. One fee is good for a whole day, and you can begin at any well-marked stop. Pay the driver or buy a ticket at one of several ticket booths located at various tour stops.

Old Town Trolley Tours.   (202) 269–3020. Covers some of the same turf as Tourmobile plus downtown Washington and some of the farther-flung museums. Each vehicle is a motorized replica of a 1920s electric trolley car. You can take the full 2-hour motorized tour or get off at any one of sixteen stops and explore on your own. Reboard another trolley —they travel at 30-minute intervals—at your leisure. One fee is good for a whole day's travel. (Adults, $11; students, $9; ages 12 and under, free.) Begin at any well-marked stop.

BOAT

C & O Canal Boat.   (202) 472–4376. One of the great touring treats in Washington is a mule-drawn boat trip on the old C & O Canal, the main commercial route between Harper's Ferry and Washington before the railroads appeared in the 1830s. C & O offers a 1½-hour trip along the Georgetown leg of the canal from mid-April through mid-October. Trips depart three times a day, Wednesday through Sunday. (Adults, $4.50; ages 2–13, $3.) It's a great trip for kids.

SEASONAL EVENTS

February

REVOLUTIONARY WAR ENCAMPMENT

The first of many of the year's Revolutionary and Civil War reenactments takes place in the middle of the month at Fort Ward Park in Alexandria, VA. Hobbyists reenact both an encampment and a battle skirmish in full period military dress. For information: (703) 838–4848.

CHINESE NEW YEAR

Washington's Chinatown (H and I Streets between 6th and 11th Streets NW) pulls out all the stops for this annual late-January to mid-February festival complete with food, fireworks, and parades. For more information: (202) 638–1041.

March

ST. PATRICK'S DAY

In Washington on March 17 (or a convenient date near the 17th), bands, dancers, bagpipers, and floats head down Constitution Avenue. For more information: (301) 424–2200.

SMITHSONIAN KITE FESTIVAL

The Washington Monument grounds are where hundreds of kite fliers vie for trophies and prizes on the last Saturday of the month. For more information: (202) 357–3030.

April

NATIONAL CHERRY BLOSSOM FESTIVAL

Usually held the first week in April, the festival celebrates the blooming of some of the world's most beautiful trees and is the occasion for lots of sightseeing and picture taking (especially around the Tidal Basin and the 650 trees that surround it), a huge parade, fireworks, concerts, a marathon run, and the annual Japanese Lantern Lighting ceremony. For more information: Contact the Jaycees at (202) 296–8675 or the National Park Service at (202) 485–9651.

June

MILITARY BAND SUMMER CONCERT SERIES

Scheduled throughout the city and throughout the summer is a series of outdoor concerts performed by the Army, Navy, Air Force, and Marine bands. The locations vary but usually include bandstands on the west side of the Capitol Building and the Sylvan Theater on the grounds of the Washington Monument. For more information, call the bands: Army, (202) 696–3647; Marines, (202) 694–3502; Navy, (202) 433–6090; and Air Force, (202) 767–9253. Concerts are usually scheduled for 8 P.M. Often there is no charge.

POTOMAC RIVERFEST

On the first two weekends in June there's fun stuff for the whole family on the Potomac. Activities include fireworks, arts and crafts, boat rides, water events, ethnic foods, and entertainment, plus an occasional a few majestic tall ships. For more information: (202) 387–8292.

CIVIL WAR LIVING HISTORY WEEKEND

Fort Ward Park in Alexandria, Virginia, is the location for hobbyists to don replica uniforms, make camp, parade, and do battle. The reenactment usually takes place the second weekend of the month. For more information: (703) 838–4848.

July

INDEPENDENCE DAY CELEBRATION

Festivities include a big parade, fireworks at the Washington Monument, and a free concert by the National Symphony Orchestra given on the steps of the Capitol Building. For more information: (202) 485–9666.

September

NATIONAL FRISBEE FESTIVAL

The National Mall hosts the world's biggest noncompetitive frisbee toss in the world, often held the day before Labor Day. Lots of champion throwers and catchers, including a legion of frisbee-retrieving canines. For more information: (202) 843–1800.

INTERNATIONAL CHILDREN'S FESTIVAL

Wolf Trap Farm Park in suburban Virginia is the place for concerts, workshops, and arts and crafts exhibits throughout the Labor Day weekend. Kids from all over the world take part. For more information: (703) 941–1527.

November

WASHINGTON'S REVIEW OF TROOPS

This annual early-November event commemorates George Washington's final review of his Virginia troops in 1798, thirteen months before his death. Hobbyists dress in period soldier's uniforms and stand for review outside Gadsby's Tavern in Alexandria, Virginia. For more information: (703) 549–0205.

STORYTELLING FESTIVAL

In mid-November, Elva VanWinkle, a children's librarian at the District of Columbia Public Library since 1950, is mistress of ceremonies for a storytelling marathon at the Martin Luther King Library. For more information: (202) 727–1151.

December

PAGEANT OF PEACE/ LIGHTING OF THE NATIONAL CHRISTMAS TREE

In mid-December, the President throws the switch lighting the National Christmas Tree, located on the Ellipse across from the White House. That kicks off two weeks of Christmas festivities, including music and caroling. The National Mall is the nightly scene of choral performances by a number of talented singing groups. There's also a yule log burning and a Nativity scene. For more information: (202) 485–9651.

CHILDREN'S THEATER

ADVENTURE THEATER IN GLEN ECHO PARK

7300 MacArthur Blvd., Glen Echo Park, Glen Echo, MD. (202) 320–5331. Free parking.

Throughout the summer, the Adventure Theater (and other theater groups) take to the Glen Echo stage, usually on weekends. Plays run the theatrical gamut from standbys like *Peter and the Wolf* and *The Wizard of Oz* to original works. Tickets cost around $4. Call ahead for the schedule and list of productions.

DISCOVERY THEATER

Smithsonian's Arts and Industries Building, 900 Jefferson Dr. SW, the National Mall. (202) 357–1500. Limited metered street and pay lot parking.

The recently renovated Discovery Theater in the gorgeous Victorian Arts and Industries Building presents an assortment of children's theater presentations (puppets, dancers, musicians, actors, singers, and even movies) throughout the school year, when the tourist trade isn't quite as heavy as in the summer. The season runs from September through June; call ahead for the schedule.

THE NATIONAL THEATER

1321 Pennsylvania Ave. NW. (202) 783–3370. Limited metered street and pay lot parking.

The newly restored National Theater is the site of *Saturday Morning at the National*, a continuing series of free programs that at times feature puppets, singers, dancers, and children's plays. Call ahead for a schedule of events and reservations (a must).

BABYSITTING SERVICES

SITTERS UNLIMITED, D.C./NORTHERN VIRGINIA (703) 250–5250

Franchise owners Barbara Parkerson and Nancy Richards run the Washington branch of Sitters Unlimited, a national company started in 1979. The standard rate charged is $7 per hour for one child with a 4-hour minimum, and 50¢ per hour for each additional child. For overnight care, Sitters Unlimited charges a flat rate of $75 per child, with a $10 surcharge for each additional child. There's a $4 transportation fee for hourly sitting and a $10 charge for overnight stays.

PUBLICATIONS

Washington Post. Daily newspaper; Friday "Weekend" section includes calendar of events in Washington and Baltimore for adults and children.

City Paper. Free weekly; calendar of events; pick it up at boutiques and restaurants.

Washingtonian Magazine. Monthly magazine; excellent entertainment listings.

LOCAL TELEPHONE NUMBERS

Late-hours pharmacy: Northwest Pharmacy, 930 Kennedy St. NW (Kennedy and Illinois), (202) 723–7250. Open Mon.–Fri., 9:30 A.M.–9 P.M.; Sat., 9:30 A.M.–6 P.M.

Pharmacy with 24-hour answering service: Paramount Pharmacy, 1109 7th St. NW, (202) 898–0907.

Consumer complaints: (202) 272–7000.

Dental referral: (202) 686–0803.

Physician referral: (202) 872–0003 or (202) 331–3888.

Drug-abuse hotline: (202) 783–1300.

Poison-control hotline: (202) 625–3333.

Travelers' aid: (202) 347–0101.

Tourism office: (202) 789–7000.

Police: 911.

Fire: 911.

Ambulance: 911.

Weather: (202) 936–1212.

Local car rental: Arcoa's Drive-a-Bargain, (703) 522–2500; Northeast Ford Rental Cars, (202) 526–5632.

◆ Authors' Note

If you're interested in learning more about family travel or sharing with us your own favorite, kid-tested destinations and activities, please write to the Wilsons, c/o P.O. Box 1594, Studio City, California, 91604.